UNTIL HE COMES

Daily Inspirations for Those Who Await the Savior

UNTIL HE COMES

Calvin Miller

BROADMAN
&HOLMAN
PUBLISHERS

Nashville, Tenessee

Printed in the United States of America

0–8054–1654–4

Published by Broadman & Holman Publishers, Nashville, Tennessee
Page Design: Anderson Thomas Design
Editorial Team: Vicki Crumpton, Janis Whipple, Kim Overcash
Page Composition: Desktop Miracles

Published in association with the literary agency of Alive Communications, Inc.,
1465 Kelly Johnson Blvd., Suite 320, Colorado Springs, CO 80920

Dewey Decimal Classification: 242

Subject Heading: JESUS CHRIST—MEDITATIONS/
BIBLE. N.T. GOSPELS—MEDITATIONS

Library of Congress Card Catalog Number: 98–24500

Library of Congress Cataloging-in-Publication Data

Miller, Calvin.
    Until He Comes : daily inspirations for those who await the Savior / Calvin A. Miller
        p. cm.
    ISBN 0–8054–1654–4 (hb)
      1. Jesus Christ—Meditations.   2. Bible. N.T. Gospels—Meditations.   3. Devotional calendars.   I. Title.
    BT306.4.M55   1998
    242'.2—dc21   98–24500
                                                        CIP

1 2 3 4 5 02 01 00 99 98

Peter therefore
seeing him said to Jesus,
"Lord, and what about this man?"
Jesus said to him,
"If I want him to remain
UNTIL I COME,
what is *that* to you?
You follow Me!"

John 21:21–22

(emphasis added)

To Barbara,
whose companionship and
counsel over four decades have
liberated everything of value
in my once-locked life

TO THE READER

I have often read through the life of Christ asking myself *What would Jesus like to say directly to me?* This book became a kind of reckoning with him about the specifics of his will. His instructions came as I used a harmony of the Gospels to listen to the events of his life as they unfolded throughout his ministry. This devotional guide records my pilgrimage, made over several years, but written in its final form over only a few months. This book is an outing—a listening walk with the Master. If my journey is notable, it is only because it focuses on *his* journey just as it occurred between his birth and ascension.

As is true of all that I have written, I have sought a lot of help in preparing this manuscript. Barbara's endless typing and editing have made this work possible. Once again I have relied on my great friend and counselor in prayer, Deron Spoo. Vicki Crumpton and others have been generous with their insights. To all who have worked to make this book a possibility, I am most grateful.

If you choose to walk with Christ through the unfolding years of his ministry, simply read these devotions day by day. After all, day by day is how he lived his life too. May I suggest that you note in the margin of this guide the specific things he may be saying to you that vary from all I felt him saying to me. You may even want to create your own daily journal of interaction with the Bible. I find that as I journal in his presence, I remember longer the exact words of those instructions he means for me alone.

I realize it may be somewhat risky to put words in the mouth of Christ that are not biblically his. However, every time I sat to write, I strove to be sure that I did not record him as saying things that would contradict what is in the Bible. This was most important to me. Perhaps Thomas à Kempis, writing of Christ in the same way, has influenced me by way of precedent. Besides the Scripture, no work has influenced me like his. I know I have not done it as well as he did, but I intended to borrow from his lofty example.

This further counsel: If you want to keep the church calendar in mind as you read through the book, days 265–328 cover the Crucifixion and Resurrection. You might want to read these entries out of sequence to coincide with your devotional life during Lent. Days 329–365 end the book with the birth of Christ. This was done to bring this bloc of Scriptures into parallel with the birth of Christ and the Advent season.

I do hope our mutual examination of the life and teachings of Christ will make us friends as yet unmet. As friends of Jesus, we ought to strengthen each other by virtue of our common worship and concern for each other. Perhaps the real theme of this volume is "O come let us adore him . . . together."

1-1-02

Jesus, Lord of All Time

Luke 3:1–2

Now in the fifteenth year of the reign of Tiberius Caesar, when Pontius Pilate was governor of Judea, and Herod was tetrarch of Galilee, and his brother Philip was tetrarch of the region of Ituraea and Trachonitis, and Lysanias was tetrarch of Abilene, in the high priesthood of Annas and Caiaphas, the word of God came to John, the son of Zacharias, in the wilderness.

I began my life in the fifteenth year of Tiberius.

Luke begins his account of my life with what seems to be historical tedium. Does he seem too interested in who ruled what? The point is that God always acts to save in the ordinary moments of somebody's history. Every act of God occurred when someone was governor of something. More often than not these rulers were people of swaggering vanity. Their political sway, like their importance, was rarely as great as they imagined it to be. Still, they were each judged to be significant in their own time. I came at a definite moment in history to save human beings, and my coming was as real as the calendar itself. The dates of my life can be given the same kind of notations as the Punic Wars or the League of Nations.

I began my own preaching ministry when Herod was tetrarch of Galilee. Herod did the world little good. He was a tyrant whose father, Herod the Great, attempted to take my infant life by slaughtering all the babies in Bethlehem. Does it seem odd to you that Luke dated my own years in terms of such power-driven monsters? Should they not rather have dated their own tyrannical regimes in terms of my life? Of course, in time that would be the case.

The point to be made from all this is that I am just as historical as Herod Antipas ever was. Beware those errant scholars who teach that Tiberius was a real man, but I was not. Tiberius was neither great nor noble. He was not even a particularly good man. But do you not find it odd that no one ever says, "Tell me, do you believe in Tiberius?" Everyone believes in Tiberius—at least they believe there was a Tiberius.

But I didn't come merely to challenge Tiberius or Herod historically. I came to save all those who felt the crushing heel of their evil politics. I also came for people like you— the ageless millions throughout time whose mini-histories never made the books. I came so all who live unmarked lives and die in unmarked graves will be able to say, "I believed in Jesus in my own particular era of history and like him, 'behold I am alive for ever and ever'" (Rev. 1:18). The life I came to give is yours to cherish. Receive and cherish this life, for if you do not it will be as though I never came at all. Come therefore and enjoy my time with you during your time on earth. I will make your life rich with my presence. Come daily and taste my everlasting love.

Prayer
> Lord Jesus,
> In these brief hurried days of my life, I recognize that
>   you are sovereign over all time. I received you in my own seemingly
>   unimportant time that I may be received into life eternal.
> You came to us as Lord of history.
> To wrap us in your saving mystery.
> Amen.

The Get-Ready Man

Matthew 3:3–5

For this is the one referred to by Isaiah the prophet, saying, "THE VOICE OF ONE CRYING IN THE WILDERNESS, MAKE READY THE WAY OF THE LORD." . . . Now John himself had a garment of camel's hair, and a leather belt about his waist; and his food was locusts and wild honey. Then Jerusalem was going out to him, and all Judea, and all the district around the Jordan.

John the Baptist came as the emcee of a new age. Time was turning the A.D. corner. Grace was supplanting law. I was about to step into human significance. In the act of my birth, the remote Jehovah became touchable. Temporal empires would soon be rendered superfluous by the eternal importance of my kingdom. In me, the Almighty was on earth like a king awaiting a fanfare.

But who was to play this fanfare? John. John was perfect for the job. He knew how to keep a low profile in the presence of dignity. He was humble, not shy. He had a strong voice and the courage to tell the world to "get ready." Best of all, he was a man whose integrity could not be bought off by his own popularity. He had learned how to step down from the theater of human applause to achieve the applause of God.

John Bar Zacharias was his whole name. He rarely ever used it. He wasn't ashamed of it. It just seemed irrelevant to him. He was content to be a "voice crying in the wilderness." He was God's hermit, a herald in camel's hair.

Let John point out this truth in your own life: God will not declare himself in your world without your consent. Like John, seek simplicity in your life and you will be used of God. Then dress your heart for the affair. Learn to wear the camel's hair of spiritual inwardness. Embrace me in the sweet wilderness of your own devotion.

All Jerusalem went out to see John and to hear his cry. Why? The world has always sought the truly selfless. Point to yourself and say, "Here I am!" and the world will soon ignore you. But point to me and say, "There is Jesus, the Lamb of God!" and the world will stand in the joyous whirlwind of your pronouncement. Have courage! Go past the narrow gates of your own small self-importance and you will find the immensity of God. There in your loving solitude where God is large, I will wait for you and our love will be for both of us a crown of life.

Prayer
  Lord Jesus,
  I have such a stranglehold on my poor self-concern
    that I cannot let it go.
  Teach me the wilderness simplicity.
  Help me to point to you, honestly and joyously,
    as the threshold of all that really matters.
  Ego is a god too small for me—
    a little baal of small idolatry.
  Amen.

What May Be Seen

Luke 3:5–6

"Every ravine shall be filled up, and every mountain and hill shall be brought low; and the crooked shall become straight, and the rough roads smooth; and all flesh shall see the salvation of God."

My Father is love. He never judges anyone who cannot see because the light is poor. But the light holds a loving obligation. God's plan for redeeming the world has been declared in the open. Neither my coming nor my cross was hidden. John the Baptist declared this open truth from the poetry of Isaiah: The way has been prepared—made smooth like a highway laid in open desert. The mountains were hauled down. The ravines were filled up. The curves were taken out of the road. Human vision was unobstructed! As Isaiah said, "all mankind together will see" (Isa. 40:5) the salvation of God.

Light always declares itself. Stand early some morning upon a country hilltop and watch the sun rise. Its splendor, like my love for you, is self-declaring.

If you want to know your place in relation to the light, look at John the Baptist. He did not want to be the sun, only its declaration. As you watch the birth of morning, the lesser stars will fade. These lesser lights will flee as the sky gives up its velvet blackness to the paling east.

But notice the one light that defies the coming sun. It is the morning star. It dares to linger till sun has forced its way into the morning. Only when it must will this bold star yield and fade and disappear. But the fading star has served. It has announced the sun, that greater light that ripens grain, matures the fruit, and creates harvest.

I am the light that makes life possible.

John was that final star of promise who announced the dawn of human hope.

Let your life announce to all our daylight love.

Tell all you meet that God has prepared a highway in the desert; the ravines have been filled in. Tell the grieving and the disconsolate that the curves have all been taken from the road. Tell every weary traveler that the mountains have been leveled. Nothing now can obstruct the vision of those who will see. Be like John, my forerunner. Point to me and say, "See, God is at the gates of your life. Cast off your despair. Christ is at hand. Cleanse your hearts. Get ready for his presence. Look and see the salvation of God. Hope."

Prayer
Lord Jesus,
I know that if people do not see your salvation,
it is because they are oblivious to light.
I cannot make them see if they choose to live in willful darkness,
but I will not stand by without letting my little light, like the morning star,
remind all those I meet that they may see
your light revealed in bright resplendency.
Amen.

Children from Stones

Matthew 3:7–9

But when he saw many of the Pharisees and Sadducees coming for baptism, he said to them, "You brood of vipers, who warned you to flee from the wrath to come? Therefore . . . do not suppose that you can say to yourselves, 'We have Abraham for our father'; for I say to you, that God is able from these stones to raise up children to Abraham."

Did John seem overly harsh to the religious leaders of his day? He was not. He was only using strong rhetoric to keep them from walking backward into the future. Religious people are so fascinated with what God *has* done that they seem to exhibit little interest in what he is about to do. Tradition should constantly remind us of all the great things that God has achieved. But God is ever out ahead of you; beware too great a focus on the past. The future is where God is leading us.

Why are we so intrigued by the God of tradition? Could it be because tradition is safe? Celebrating the "was" is never as risky as facing the "could be." Old doctrines are as charming as they are settled. The uncomfortable horror of everything new is only celebrated when it is so far in the past that it actually looks beautiful. It comes without danger. You can't mess up yesterday. But dust the old truths off, and you will find they were once new and fiercely contested. Peel back the mold from old liturgies, and you will find at their heart raging storms of protest.

The Pharisees loved honoring Abraham. After all, he had been dead for 1,700 years. It was John the Baptist's fiery new messianism they suspected.

The Pharisees and Saducees had lots of doctrinal disagreements, but they were united on this: The old ways are best. They found the God who beckoned them toward the edges of tomorrow to be nerve-racking. They loved the God who had been their help in ages past. They loved building monuments to all God used to be.

John may have lacked tact, but not honesty. He thundered against these keepers of yesterday, "You snakes! Get out of the way of the all-consuming fire of the new. The new is coming . . . the kingdom of God. Don't tell us you are Abraham's children. God can make from these desert stones such children." God is not static, nor is he content to be praised for what he used to do. God is now. He forbids all who claim to love him to sit and play with their heritage in the center of his highway to the future.

I am the Christ. I beckon you toward tomorrow. You and I have great things to accomplish there.

Prayer
Lord Jesus,
I would remember each day
which allegiances are prior and
which are not.
I want to live on that thin strip of time where
the past and future meet.
I want to examine the past only long enough to thank you
for the heritage that produced me.
Then I'll turn and follow you as one—
to claim "the yet" where life is lost or won.
Amen.

Baptizing Tax-Gatherers

Luke 3:10

And the multitudes were questioning him, saying, "Then what shall we do?"

John's baptism was a "scrub-up" for the new kingdom. The religious leaders doubted that the sometimes wealthy tax-gatherers were the best place to start that kingdom. It was like trying to build a sacrificial world with tycoons. It seemed to people of that day that new religions should start with notable philanthropists or religious scholars. But John could see that tax-gatherers really were the best starting place. It was generally agreed that tax-gatherers were pretty bad people, so they were less defensive about their morality. Tax-gatherers themselves knew they cheated people. Everybody knew it. When your sins are this obvious, you don't really need to confess them. Other people will do it for you.

By contrast, religious people have such a hard time owning up to their sins in front of each other. Besides, crying over sin makes church look hyperemotional. That's why the religious often print their confessional psalms in the worship bulletin. It's easier not to reveal your real needs if you're reading from the liturgy. This purely formal repentance gets you out of church earlier than taking the time to get really serious with God.

Here and there, some really needy sinners might actually get interested in God. And if you let them, before you can say, "Gloria in excelsis!" they'll ask you how to be saved. They will sometimes weep much too loudly for their sins and rarely at those places where the liturgy calls for it.

What do you do with those whose repentance inconveniences religion?

Well, John baptized them.

I think it was because they kept asking, "Lord, what shall we do?" Now that's a question that rarely comes from formal repentance! John knew that the truly needy cannot afford this protective formality. They need a God who answers their questions with his sufficiency. "Yes," they weep, "I am a sinner who has disappointed God. What shall I do?"

Then they were baptized; they left their brokenness beneath the Jordan as all of their self-sufficiency swirled away in the brown river water. And these happy new tax-gatherers felt great. They knew that across town there were Pharisees whose confessions were more literary. But no matter. It is good to know who you are—to live without pretense. Then you can leave the river a new person. Then you are ready for the Kingdom. The Kingdom of God is born at exactly the place where the need for religious respectability is less than the hunger to be clean.

Prayer
Lord Jesus,
How long has it been since my sins were so obvious
I had to confess them?
I'm such a discreet sinner that I need to ask you to shine
the light of your grace fully on my need.
Teach me those tears that are the distillation of utter honesty.
I'll know my penance real when I have cried,
and given up my sweet religious pride.
Amen.

Baptized by Fire

Matthew 3:11

"As for me, I baptize you with water for repentance, but He who is coming after me is mightier than I, and I am not fit to remove His sandals; He will baptize you with the Holy Spirit and fire."

The passions of our heart declare our identity. We must feel a thing to know that *it* is real. We must feel to know that *we* are real. The rage that shakes our frame, the love that wraps our hearts, the unhallowed fear that raises the hair on the nape of the neck, the empathy that feels the forehead of a feverish child—these passions tell us we're alive. They tell us what matters to us.

The stronger we feel about anything, the more we know we are alive. What we really feel we cannot hide. There is something so exhibitionist in honest passions that it dances in the daylight.

I want joy to be such a passion in your life. Pray, therefore, to be filled with the pure fire of the Holy Spirit. See again the disciples on the day of Pentecost. Joy came in tongues of fire and rushing wind. A tempest of love had settled on the church. They spoke with tongues ecstatically and all at once. The mystery confounded them.

"They have had too much wine" (Acts 2:13), said their critics.

"Hardly," said Peter, "This is the prophecy of Joel fulfilled before your very eyes. 'In the last days, God says, I will pour out my Spirit on all people. Your sons and daughters will prophesy, your young men will see visions, your old men will dream dreams'" (Acts 2:17). Why this disruptive, delirious exhibitionism? Was there no sensible liturgy of quiet rehearsal available to them? Was there nothing from the Psalter that they could intone?

Please hear John's own prophecy of me. "After me will come one more powerful than I, the thongs of whose sandals I am not worthy to stoop down and untie. I baptize you with water, but he will baptize you with the Holy Spirit" (Mark 1:7–8). How gloriously my Father chops into mundane living with exotic joy.

It is a cold formality that says, "Please. I want a religious experience I can feel comfortable with. Let me worship God in my own inner way! I like tasting God one bite at a time, from my demitasse and doily. I keep my Jehovah in a jar—a silver jar, of course."

Come. Take me on my terms. Welcome those passions that are too large to hide in your timid psyche. Let your love declare itself. Joy comes as fire!

Prayer
Lord Jesus,
Forgive me for making you a discussion
    and forgetting that you would prefer to be a consuming fire.
Forgive me for wanting my faith to be so tidy and liturgical
    that I keep my passions zipped in my prayer book.
Give me more than I think I want.
Baptize me in the ardor of desire.
Not water, Lord. I beg you for the fire!
Amen.

The Separating Work of God

Matthew 3:12

"And His winnowing fork is in His hand, and He will thoroughly clear His threshing floor; and He will gather His wheat into the barn, but He will burn up the chaff with unquenchable fire."

A grain of wheat is a remarkable thing. It is really a small plant in embryo. It is impatient life willing to sleep only until the temperature and water are just right. It has studied only one lesson: the miracle of natural law. Give it a tiny drink and keep it warm, and you will speak to its inwardness. Its thin containing shell will split. The plant will send its silky head toward sunlight and its silver roots into the dark earth.

But chaff! It holds no embryo. You can water it forever. Nothing will burst inside it. No life will come. No sprout will shoot up. No roots will go down. Chaff is a dead thing that will not reproduce itself, ever. Here is my Father's most insistent command: That which can reproduce itself must do so. That which cannot is chaff. Its sterility demands it must be burned.

It is no hostile act by which my Father destroys the chaff. He does not hate chaff. He is God. He knows no grudge; nor can he hold any lingering resentment. But the chaff is in the way. It mires and threatens honest life. It collects above the wheat to steal its sun. It soaks the moisture that might cause the grain to live and grow. God grieves all things dead if they be content to remain so.

Consider the lesson of the winnowing fork. The fork throws both grain and chaff into the wind. But the grain is heavy and has substance enough to settle back to the threshing floor. The chaff, little of weight, is caught by the wind and carried away.

Sadly, chaff is often possessed of such flighty arrogance that it supposes itself to be more than it is. The ungodly, said the psalmist, are like that chaff which the wind drives away (Ps. 1:6). While presuming themselves to be people of real content, they prove at last that there's nothing of substantial value in their lives.

God is looking for that good seed that produces fruit. Strive to contain the life principle. Strive to pass the test of the winnowing fork.

Prayer

Lord Jesus,
When the winnowing comes and the Lord of the Harvest
    seeks those whose lives reproduced themselves.
Help me to be numbered among those in whose heart
    the principle of eternal life is always multiplying itself
    in the hearts of those who wanted life,
    and could freely admit that they needed it.
Blow wind through me till I hear heaven laugh,
    and in the laughter separate the chaff.
Amen.

Identity with the Community

Matthew 3:13–15

Then Jesus arrived from Galilee at the Jordan coming to John, to be baptized by him. But John tried to prevent Him, saying, "I have need to be baptized by You and do You come to me?" But Jesus answering said to him, "Permit it at this time; for in this way it is fitting for us to fulfill all righteousness." Then he permitted Him.

John was baffled the day I asked him to baptize me. John's baptism symbolized the washing away of sin. I had never sinned, and John knew it. But I knew the definition of baptism would be growing. I knew that the church would someday define it as more than the mere washing away of sin. In time it would come to stand for identity with the people of God. So I said to John, "It is proper!"

How true that was.

There was no finer way to endorse what John was teaching than to allow him to baptize me. I said clearly, "All that John has been teaching is right. I take my stand with John. See, I submit to him. John and I are both in this world pursuing one thing: the kingdom of God." All who saw that baptism knew that John and I were not each vying to start our own separate religions. We were one in the purpose of forming the new community of God. So I met my kinsman, John, in the river Jordan. It was not a muddy river, but it was always colored brown by the flux of desert silt. Yet when the sun fell full upon the Jordan, it was gold.

We met there within the heart of God. We threw our faces to the sky and praised the new order that was on the way. The kingdom of God was here and now! I fell full backward into the joy of the world's glorious new beginning. The water closed over me. The old was gone. And when I rose back through the eddies of the golden Jordan, the new order had been born.

Now I stood with John in the shallows of a brown river. I knew that river's bold metallic flow would color all earth's oceans with its joy. And in the washing shoals of centuries, thousands of thousands and millions of millions would come through the waters of this simple ritual of beginnings.

Yet they would not come by thousands or millions. They would come one at a time. I would not spoil the uniqueness of anyone's personal salvation by saving even two people at once. Each one would have the fullness of my love and the glorious focus of my singular attention. This is the way of the river. This is the way of God's kingdom.

Prayer
Lord Jesus,
Here am I in utter need of your particularity.
I am yours singularly as you are my singular Lord.
If I was the only one who had needed it, you would have died for me.
If I was the only one who felt lonely, you would walk with me.
I met you first with vows where water flowed,
*   to walk as friend to friend one quiet road.*
Amen.

The Affirmation of the Almighty

Matthew 3:16–17

And after being baptized, Jesus went up immediately from the water; and behold, the heavens were opened, and he saw the Spirit of God descending as a dove, and coming upon him, and behold, a voice out of the heavens, saying, "This is My beloved Son, in whom I am well-pleased."

After I was baptized I heard the voice that ricocheted across the waters.

This *bath qol,* this "loud voice," was the confession of God. "This is my beloved! I am pleased with him."

God announced our relationship in the thunder that sounded over the river. "This is my Son!" Think of those times when you and your parents were welded into oneness. Was it not those times that your parents were so spontaneously proud of you that their pride erupted before some gathering of family or friends? True pride will burst propriety to bits. If there is no one to hear the compliment of love, pride will speak it to the wind. If there are none to applaud, the rocks will cry out.

Such times of special affirmation can never be diminished. For on that day the *voice* called out, I realized it was my Father's oneness with me that was the fount of all my joy. I also realized that his affirmation and praise meant more to me than anyone else's ever could.

What is it that fuels your spirit and makes you hungry to please God? If you are truly my brother, honestly my sister, you must certainly care about what God thinks. And if you really care what God thinks, you will relish his compliment and deplore his censure.

Someday, of course, his great compliment will be "well done . . . you have been faithful over a few things; I am about to make you a ruler over many." Every life well lived loved me and waited for that compliment. When that day comes and when at last you begin to thrill at the affirmation of God, you will know the joy I felt that day at the Jordan River. For in those finishing moments of time you will hear my Father say to you, "Behold, all the angels of heaven! This is my child, faithful and beloved, and in this child I am well pleased!" Spend your entire soul and every waking moment of your life to purchase such a compliment. Desire it. Live in such anticipation.

Prayer
Lord Jesus,
It is clear that Heaven held no shame
in your incarnation.
Help me to be as forthright
in announcing that you are my Lord
as God was in announcing
you were his Beloved.
There is but one magnificent obsession:
And that's a firm magnificent confession.
Amen.

The Days of Our Lives

Luke 3:23

And when He began His ministry, Jesus Himself was about thirty years of age.

From the vantage point of your walk with God, do you see mostly question marks? It was true for me as well. In becoming a man, I gave up my right to many of the attributes of my Godhood. One was explicit foreknowledge. I knew I was God's Son, and I knew I would die for human sin. But the exact incidentals of when I should pass certain points on the clock and calendar were hidden from me.

I knew, too, that my life would not be long. And yet I also knew that my years would be the most significant to pass across the globe. There was but one question that occupied my days. Morning by morning I rose and asked, "What is it you have for me to do today, Father?" All that he had for me to do on that day, I did.

There really are only two rules for the disciple. First, number your days. This will make you a good steward of your years. Did not the psalmist say, "Teach us to number our days aright, that we may gain a heart of wisdom" (Ps. 90:12)?

The second rule is that your life is not your own. You gave it away when you claimed me as your Lord. Since your life belongs to me, your desire with each sunrise should be, "Lord, what do you want me to do today?" Such love for me will fill your years with meaning. Such love will cause you to see the needs of your world. You will minister to those in need, and your entire life will gain significance.

Learn to see the various seasons of your life in two ways. First, do not begrudge those waiting times when you struggle to know what God wants with you and how you are to accomplish it. This part of my own life took thirty years. The second part of your life must consist in faithfully pursuing what you know to be God's will. This second part of my life took only three years. Which part is more important? They are equally important. My first thirty years were lived with that consistency that knew no sin. My final three years yielded to God's plan which drove me to please my Father by completing all he asked.

Let us not talk of life's hardness but of its sweetness. For once I knew the obligation of the cross, I knew that my union with my Father would be all-important. Would you make your life sweet? You have only to obey all my Father asks. Nothing that he asks will be easy. But it will be glorious. Glorious because the rigors of his requirement will cause you to need him. Then God will become for you not a luxury but a sweet necessity. Pray for such a necessity. Live in such a communion.

Prayer
Lord Jesus,
It is not the number of years you have given me,
but the calling,
that will mark my life as significant.
It is neither when I start nor when I finish
that is important,
But how I completed what you gave me to do.
It's not enough to number our short days.
Obedience alone elicits praise.
Amen.

The First Temptation

Matthew 4:1–4

Then Jesus was led up by the Spirit into the wilderness to be tempted by the devil. And after He had fasted forty days and forty nights, He then became hungry. And the tempter came and said to Him, "If You are the Son of God, command that these stones become bread." But He answered and said, "It is written, 'MAN SHALL NOT LIVE ON BREAD ALONE, BUT ON EVERY WORD THAT PROCEEDS OUT OF THE MOUTH OF GOD.'"

After I had endured almost six weeks of hunger, the Tempter came to me. Doesn't he always come at such times? He knows those moments when our defenses are weakest. I well remember our meeting in the wilderness. I had ended a forty-day fast with ravenous hunger. He was lurking in the shadows. With a curl in his lip he simply asked, "Hungry?"

He knew I was. His question caused my eyes to fall on some rounded stones. They looked as round and brown as those loaves my mother once baked in Nazareth. They needed only my command to become what I really would have liked them to be.

Oh, I was hungry!

As I studied the stones I thought of all my power. I knew I could do it. I could turn stones to bread. Then the voice of the Tempter came once again from the shadows: "Why not?"

I did not yield. I understood that using the power of God to indulge my appetites was set against every principle of the Kingdom. In fact, to use God's power to meet any of my own needs was set against all I would later teach about self-denial.

Appetites can tempt us to become totally self-serving. They can lure us to have *what* we want, *when* we want it. They can deceive us into believing that we no longer have to wait on anything. Finally we will begin to see life only in terms of ourselves. Soon we will become only the sum of all our cravings.

Are there stones in your life that are right now begging you to change them into loaves of what might seem a sweet indulgence? Are you jealous because someone in the corporation was promoted above you? Are you envious of someone else's pay? Are you toying with sexual infidelity? At every juncture, the Enemy is in the shadows saying to you, "Why not?" and "Why not right now?" Beware that you do not covet things to which you have no right. Your yielding at any moment will make Satan's work all the easier the next time. All too soon you will be manacled in the steel of your own indulgence. Drunkenness, gluttony, and infidelity, which may seem lovely at first, in the end bring only captivity. Be careful. Addictions can begin in the act of changing one little stone into one little loaf. Do not yield. Deny yourself. Live free.

Prayer
Lord Jesus,
My appetites tell others who I am;
Let them keep me informed as well.
It does no good to claim publicly that I belong to you,
while I pursue my private lusts.
Help me to put my passions underneath
those promises committed to your keep.
Amen.

The Second Temptation

Matthew 4:5–7

Then the devil took Him into the holy city; and he had Him stand on the pinnacle of the temple, and said to Him, "If You are the Son of God throw Yourself down; for it is written, 'HE WILL GIVE HIS ANGELS CHARGE CONCERNING YOU'; and 'ON THEIR HANDS THEY WILL BEAR YOU UP, LEST YOU STRIKE YOUR FOOT AGAINST A STONE.'" Jesus said to him, "On the other hand, it is written, 'YOU SHALL NOT PUT THE LORD YOUR GOD TO THE TEST.'"

Fame! What an allurement for the ego. We can never get enough of it, and yet it does us so little good. It is never wholesome and ever demanding. It is a powerful and all-consuming fire. Fame turns the church into a theater. It uses the hands for applause when it should lift them in prayer. It treasures trifles and scorns humility. Fame would have cheap messiahs leaping from the temple battlements rather than serving their God in suffering fields of human contagion. The urge to perform is not easily shouted down.

My second temptation came largely as a vaudeville stunt. If I could throw myself down from the pinnacle of the temple and land unhurt, a crowd would gather around. It would be easy to go from anonymity to fame. You can always gather a crowd by skipping rope on the high battlements.

My Enemy was really suggesting that I might avoid dying on Good Friday by becoming a one-man circus. I could get elected Messiah without the ugly necessity of the cross. I could have the glory without the gore. I could eliminate the jeers of my trial and move directly to the applause of the masses.

But the whole point of my Incarnation was to live life as ordinary people have to live it. No one has the option of leaping off a spire to become a local hero. No one. If I was going to endure existence for people, I had to do it the way they had to do it. Fame is the province of a few, but pain is sooner or later the province of all. Dying is harder than a publicity stunt. But dying is universal. So I died.

Serve me. There are no theatrical shortcuts. So you must learn the art of dying daily. There are those who are willing to serve me as long as it puts them in some arena of applause. I call you to the difficult way of the cross. Are we together on this? Then take my cross as yours. Turn from applause. Embrace integrity. Victory over your weaknesses will make you ever stronger. The chains of temptation, once resisted, become the silver cords that bind my soul to yours.

Prayer
Lord Jesus,
What is the lure in fame?
What is the lure in wanting everyone to know who I am?
Why cannot I be content to be anonymous?
Why am I not willing to be less,
*   that you may be more?*
Forgive my need to lead some grand parade—
*   to leap, unharmed, the temple balustrade.*
Amen.

The Third Temptation

Matthew 4:8–10

Again, the devil took Him to a very high mountain, and showed Him all the kingdoms of the world, and their glory; and he said to Him, "All these things will I give You, if You fall down and worship me." Then Jesus said to him, "Begone, Satan! For it is written, 'YOU SHALL WORSHIP THE LORD YOUR GOD, AND SERVE HIM ONLY.'"

Power can be glorious. But when human beings crave it, it breeds within their souls a narcotic addiction. A few are content at first to want power only for the good it does others. But most long for it, for the leverage it gives them over all they want to control.

How easily we are drawn into its subtle web. The day the Tempter showed me all the kingdoms of the world, I reflected on how much good a world ruler might do. Surely every tyrant at first saw only the good that might be done. But the current history of the planet is the bloody tale of many civilizations whose leaders killed and pillaged their way to control. Every tyrant in turn believed that he would use power only to make the world better. But corrupted by this lust to control, he used his power at last only for blood and death.

Corporations are often led by those who ascended some ladder to claim a noble throne. Satan knows that there is something dark in each of us that would like to control others.

The way of the Kingdom is not the way of instant monarchy. Observe a child who is trying to tell her distracted father something very important. Finally the child will take her father's broad chin in her chubby little hands and pull his face toward her own. When their eyes are looking into each other's, she will tell her father all she wants him to know.

This is a picture of all that God wants for us in claiming his kingdom. He wants no distraction between his children and himself. You, too, are mine. I would have you for my subject if no one else ever called me King. Rejoice! You are loved.

> *Prayer*
> *Lord Jesus,*
> *Give me that God-given joy*
> *of enjoying people without controlling them.*
> *I want to walk among people serving them,*
> *not using them.*
> *I want no power residual in myself.*
> *I want only that power of yours—*
> *that flow-through power—*
> *that enables me to minister in your name*
> *but leaves others unable to remember mine.*
> *May I become a channel whose one course*
> *is a conduit into a living force.*
> *Amen.*

The Celebration of the Angels

Matthew 4:11

Then the devil left Him; and behold, angels came and began to minister to Him.

A certain steward was asked by his master to take a business trip into a far country. The nature of his business was such that he would have much free time for sexual exploits when he arrived. The coming license of his trip began to dominate his thinking. He began to anticipate the revelries and indulgences he would grant himself. Finally he began to swim in his feelings of desire. He saw his own marriage as something trivial which he would sacrifice to his mental fancies. His children were of no consequence. His lust was all consuming.

He abandoned his inhibitions and began to stalk his desires. Finally he willfully contemplated it for all the joy it seemed to promise. The force of all his intentions at last camped night and day in his soul until the day of the trip came. It was the force of his faith in me that at last began to speak to him. He began, at long last, to quit asking what he owed himself and began asking what he owed God.

At the heart of all he owed God was the issue of righteousness. Righteousness is the great "I Ought to!" It is the moral salary for those who ask, "What is my part in the universal value system?" When we confront the great "I Ought to," God's answer does not come back in totally satisfying recompense. It is often more fun to do that which fulfills some appetite than that which does not. There is always pleasure in sin for a season.

But when you ask the great "I Ought to" questions in the presence of God, you get answers in terms of the ultimate satisfaction and not the immediate. Yes, there are seasons of life that are rather barren in terms of ego gratification. Raising children often comes without all the affirmation parents would like to get. There are times when spouses forget to tell their mates just how much they mean to them. But when life becomes harsh, the true children of God distinguish themselves by refusing to abandon the only morality that God can honor.

So this story ends well. The steward turned at last to righteousness for its own sake. He learned the only moral truth that matters: it is good to do good because only good really endures. Such morality is rooted in the hearts of all those whom my Father calls his friends. The angels came that night and ministered to a common steward because he had an uncommon love of right. The angels love to celebrate the victories of ordinary people with extraordinary character.

Prayer
Lord Jesus,
I know that I am much more shaped
by what I deny myself
than I am by my indulgences.
The evil things that I allow myself
become the bars
that soon imprison me for life.
The apples left in Satan's tempting bowl
are stored in heaven's vaults as fruit of gold.
Amen.

The Key to Who You Are

John 1:19–23
And this is the witness of John, when the Jews sent to him priests and Levites from Jerusalem to ask him, "Who are you?" And he confessed and did not deny, and he confessed, "I am not the Christ." And they asked him, "What then? Are you Elijah?" And he said, "I am not." "Are you the Prophet?" And he answered, "No." They said then to him, "Who are you, so that we may give an answer to those who sent us? What do you say about yourself?" He said, "I am A VOICE OF ONE CRYING IN THE WILDERNESS, 'MAKE STRAIGHT THE WAY OF THE LORD,' as Isaiah the prophet said."

Those who achieve the most in this life are those who gradually lose the distinction between what they do and who they are. John was one of these. More than all else he desired to please God. As a result, pleasing God became his reason for getting up each morning. Who he was was hidden in his desire to announce the new age. He was given the task of preaching the Kingdom so that when the Messiah appeared, everyone would clearly recognize him.

A similar task of identification belonged to John the Baptist. He furnished the photos for all who were looking for hope. He preached the King and his Kingdom, and when I at last appeared in the crowd, John's work reached its pinnacle of glory. It is no wonder that I would later say that of all those born of women, none was greater than John.

It would have been so easy for John to have taken for himself the glory he knew was mine. When they asked him if he was the Christ, he could have said, "How nice you are to notice," or "You may be sure of it." But to take advantage of such a claim never seemed to occur to him. He would not steal my title, nor even borrow from my glory.

I am sure that you have never been tempted to call yourself the Christ, but you may have profited by calling yourself Christian. Many politicians would never call themselves "Christ," but they have found it politically expedient to be a Christian.

Study John. He never gave the inquiring crowds his own name, for he felt his own name held no significance. This is the sign of true greatness. If you serve me well, you could become well known for your service. Your name might someday be listed beside my own. But let your love for me glorify me. Seek John's wisdom and always give me first place. Love me for my sake, as I have loved you for your sake.

Prayer
Lord Jesus,
Am I too central in my witness to your excellence?
Do I too quickly pass out my *card to those in need?*
Do I point to you and say, "Behold the King!"
Or rather to my ego-driven self?
Help me to point and cry, "The King! The King!
In Christ alone is hidden everything!"
Amen.

Ecce Agnus Dei

John 1:29

The next day he saw Jesus coming to him, and said, "Behold, the Lamb of God who takes away the sin of the world!"

Grand pronouncements seem quaint in little settings. One day I walked into the midst of a largely rural assemblage. Gathered there were farmers and shepherds and the ordinary poor of Israel. John called me the universal sacrifice that would deal forever with the problem of human sin.

The occasion seemed prosaic, but had you been there you would have known immediately that this was just the right place to make such an announcement. The Bible, throughout, is the tale of God doing glorious things in front of those who rarely experienced the acts of God. John's words should have been carried by official heralds and heard in official places.

It all happened at the river Jordan. Here in this common and very earthy place, a carpenter and a desert prophet met. The Spirit, dove-like, came down and marked the spot. And none of the world of that day knew how cosmic the event really was. None, of course, except for the shepherds, the farmers, and the poor.

So many times in the Gospels, the four evangelists say that I was moved with compassion for those who hurt or were in need. It is true. Yet when I met John at the river, the dove descended. God himself was unmistakably moved with compassion. There among these simple and needy people he proclaimed himself as a God who would not just offer gilt-edged salvation to the elite in high places.

My Father loves the poor. It is not for their sins only that I died. But he knows the rich often find their security in what they own. The poor, out of need, are far more prone to find their security in who owns them.

Therefore, seek that fellowship of neediness where the Spirit descends like a dove. Welcome the Spirit. Let us meet beneath the dove as I once met John. Our love for each other will grow from our brokenness. I was broken on the cross, and you have been broken by your sinfulness. Our double brokenness will delight my Father, for only the broken fall on their knees and cry the river words *Ecce Agnus Dei*—"Look, the Lamb!"

Prayer
  Lord Jesus,
    Have I accepted my church friends
      as though the having of such friends
      is the reason I go to church?
      Help me to make my church that kind of place
      which sees the needy crying for the warmth of God's favor.
    I want to be an evangel to any who are in need.
    I want to cry,
    "Look, the Lamb of God! He comes again
      to wash with grace your neediness and sin."
  Amen.

Surrendering Your Allegiances

John 1:35–42

Again the next day John was standing with two of his disciples, and he looked upon Jesus as He walked, and said, "Behold, the Lamb of God!" And the two disciples heard him speak, and they followed Jesus. And Jesus turned, and beheld them following, and said to them, "What do you seek?" And they said to Him, "Rabbi (which translated means Teacher), where are You staying?"

He said to them, "Come, and you will see." They came therefore and saw where He was staying; and they stayed with Him that day, for it was about the tenth hour. One of the two who heard John speak, and followed Him, was Andrew, Simon Peter's brother. He found first his own brother Simon, and said to him, "We have found the Messiah" (which translated means Christ). He brought him to Jesus. Jesus looked at him, and said, "You are Simon the son of John; you shall be called Cephas" (which is translated Peter).

How protective are you about your friends? Do you see how freely John gave his disciples to be my own? Now here is a rich example to the church. John must have loved his disciples. How much every teacher's students mean. How hurt teachers can get when someone else lures students away from them. None of us like seeing our friends give their allegiance to another person. How closely we prize the loyalty of our companions. We hang little invisible signs on our friends that say "mine." Some have been known to call their employees "my staff" or "my people." Churches can be particularly zealous over their members. They become edgy when they hear that one of their members has visited another church.

John had been waiting all his life to point people to the Messiah. When my ministry began, he proved his allegiance to me by openly allowing his disciples to become mine.

How could I receive those disciples who had meant so much to him and claim them as my own? It was because neither John nor I were in business for ourselves. John existed to serve me, and I existed to serve my Father. This simple truth holds the key to your own happiness: you are not your own, and you do not exist to serve yourself. Those friends in your circle of allegiances are not yours. They belong, like all people, to God. If you struggle to possess them, you are destined to feel loss when they move away from you. But if you can remember that every person belongs only to God, then you will free yourself from the desolation that comes with such possessiveness. You will begin to live for the God who owns both you and your friends.

"Will those friends whom I can so readily surrender really mean anything to me?" you may ask. Your friends will mean more once you see that both of you are part of God's family. Then you will quit having mere friends and start having brothers and sisters.

Prayer
  Lord Jesus,
  I must confess my insecurity to you.
  I don't feel good about life unless I know
      that I own a few friends who are going to be there for me
      at those desperate seasons of need.
  Help me give up my need to own my friends
      or use a single soul for my own ends.
  Amen.

A Somebody from Nowhere

John 1:45–46

Philip found Nathanael and said to him, "We have found Him of whom Moses in the Law and also the Prophets wrote, Jesus of Nazareth, the son of Joseph." And Nathanael said to him, "Can any good thing come out of Nazareth?" Philip said to him, "Come and see."

It is hard for us to believe that great people can come from small addresses. There are many little places about which we would have never known except for the ennobling touch of someone who made that small place famous.

It is fortunate for Nazareth that I came from there. Otherwise, no one would ever have heard of the place. Now my name is rarely spoken except that Nazareth is referred to as well. Jesus of Nazareth, they called me. "Jesus of what?" was Nathanael's question. "Can anything good come out of Nazareth?" Nathanael had committed the sin of sanctifying geography.

Be grateful that God once for all sanctified the globe and in so doing, every place became sacred. Every little place held some possibility of declaring God's immensity.

Where was that bit of nowhere where you found me? What was your Nazareth? How did God come to you to hallow your nothingness and consecrate your own small situation?

When God called Abraham to come up out of Ur of the Chaldees, he came into new and barren land, which was destined to become the Holy Land. It was really no holier than anywhere else. It was just that within its tiny, eastern Mediterranean boundaries, God would become involved with all the people of the world. It is people getting involved with God who sanctify any land and make it holy. Nonetheless, as Abraham came into the land, he piled up stones and built a little altar. He offered a sacrifice to God. He called the place *Bethel*—House of God. There was really no house there, only a crude little altar. But Abraham returned to that primitive pile of stones from time to time to remind himself that whatever God touched was holy.

Can anything good come out of Nazareth? Of course, I did. But you too came from your own Nazareth. And when I entered you, your Nazareth, like mine long ago, held the fullest possibility of God.

Prayer
Lord Jesus,
You made the names of Bethlehem and Nazareth
*   household words.*
It was because you were so submitted to your Father's will
*   that your perfect execution of all that he had called you to do*
*   redeemed the entire globe and left these two little pinpoints of geography*
*   with great significance.*
Help me with your supreme obedience,
*   to give each place I touch significance.*
Amen.

The Continuing Wonder of Discipleship

John 1:48–50

Nathanael said to Him, "How do you know me?" Jesus answered and said to him, "Before Philip called you, when you were under the fig tree, I saw you." Nathanael answered Him, "Rabbi, You are the Son of God; You are the King of Israel." Jesus answered and said to him, "Because I said to you that I saw you under the fig tree, do you believe? You shall see greater things than these."

When I first saw Nathanael, he was under the fig tree, lost in wondering about who the Messiah would be. Then suddenly he met me. Even as he did, I reminded him of all that he had been considering in his fig-tree reverie. He was amazed. I had been looking into his soul. When he grasped my unknown probings, he came alive with wonder.

I had to remind him that reading his mind was a simple wonder. I called him into discipleship. If anything about my disciples amazed me, it was that they were so easily amazed. In following the course of God, you ought to prepare yourself for an emerging life of wonder. You cannot get mixed up with God and expect things to be ordinary and predictable.

This is the beauty of the redeemed life. *New* becomes a common word. When you think you are beginning to grasp what might be expected, everything becomes unexpected. Just when you think the sun comes up in the east, it comes up in the south and you are left trying to explain the extraordinary in vain.

Follow me, but watch where you step! For your lowly path may suddenly become the footbridge over exhilarating heights.

A father who drank himself into abusiveness suddenly found Christ. The moment I came into his life he was able to quit drinking, and the money he had once squandered to support his habit became usable, spendable currency. Not long after his conversion, he fell in among a group of "scholars" arguing about whether I had really turned 120 gallons of water into wine. When the scholars each had taken their turn at the debate, the new convert chimed in. "I cannot say whether or not Jesus turned water into wine, but I can tell you that in my case he turned beer into furniture."

So Nathanael's amazement that I could do the extraordinary is the first musing of every childish Christian. If you have me in your life and still find your life ordinary, despise the inconsistency. Get ready for splendor, for my presence always leads to miracles. Get used to them. Expect them. Enjoy them. Desire them. I am your Lord. Your ordinary living was over the moment you received me into your life.

Prayer
Lord Jesus,
I have sinned
   for claiming to follow a Christ who can do anything,
   yet remaining content
   to do almost nothing.
There has often been so little wonder in my life,
   so I have caused people only to see an ordinary Christ.
Forgive me, therefore, for each humdrum hour
   I've lived content with weakness, shunning power.
Amen.

The People's Gospel

John 2:1–5

And on the third day there was a wedding in Cana of Galilee, and the mother of Jesus was there; and Jesus also was invited, and His disciples, to the wedding. And when the wine gave out, the mother of Jesus said to Him, "They have no wine." And Jesus said to her, "Woman, what do I have to do with you? My hour has not yet come." His mother said to the servants, "Whatever He says to you, do it."

The wedding feast went on long after the wine gave out. My disciples and I were part of the reason that the host ran short of wine in the first place. You cannot expand the guest list to include twelve hungry, thirsty men and not run the risk of a few social inconveniences. So, considering that we partly caused the wine shortage and that my mother told the hostess she could count on me to alleviate the situation, I did it. Theologians have long objected to this water-made wine. It always seems to them that my first miracle should have been something more related to human meaning, something more spiritually deep: an exorcism, a healing, or a storm-calming.

The first of all my mighty works had simply to do with good sociology: my mother's friends were out of wine. By the host's own admission, they had drunk plenty already. Still, propriety owned the day. I made the wine—120 gallons or so, for it was a large wedding—and saved the host the embarrassment of appearing cheap.

This first miracle forever focused on the importance that people hold for God. People are the preoccupation of God. Why, then, does this first miracle befuddle so many Christians? Some who emphasize temperance would have much preferred that I change wine into water.

And to some extent I agreed with those critical theologians: this water-to-wine miracle does not hold the immense meaning of my later healing of a clubfooted child. It does not hold the natural splendor and power of my later calming of the Galilee storm. It also lacks the impressive theological grandeur of the Transfiguration.

But it does make a theological statement that cannot be denied. My Father loves people. So I made water—humble water—serve the moment in a better way than water can imagine. I made wine. I made good wine—all agreed.

As Rabbi Akiba would later say, "All that God does is done well." I've never gotten through changing water into better stuff. Are your own social ills ever unmanageable? Have you chewed all the goody out of life? I'm the master repairer of needy sociology. Bring me the watery weakness of all your interrelationships. Now dip into that insipid water. See, there is sweetness. Behold, there is life.

Prayer
Lord Jesus,
Help me to move through life seeing those circumstances
in which I might be of help.
What little things could I do?
Hold a door? Take a casserole to the sick?
Bake a loaf of bread for the hungry?
Where is that Cana my poor life might find?
Where is the water I might change to wine?
Amen.

To Hallow the Humdrum

John 2:11
This beginning of His signs Jesus did in Cana of Galilee, and manifested His glory, and His disciples believed in Him.

As a likeness of the Kingdom, this first miracle is significant. If water could become wine at my command, then the plain could be ornate. The humdrum could be festive.

I was often criticized by the Pharisees for being a "glutton and a drunkard" (Matt. 11:19). They criticized me because I went to parties. Their criticism was meant to be a put-down. But parties really represent the best opportunity of God. Lonely people come to parties looking for relationships. Despondent people come to parties looking for a good time. Hungry people come to parties looking for something to eat. People often meet their lifetime mates at parties. Wherever you find a party in progress, you may be sure my Father would like to be there. For in such needy functions, heaven answers emptiness with substance.

And as a metaphor for change, consider how much greater is the value of wine over water. Water may slake the thirst, but wine incites it. Water cannot excite the mind and make it heady with adventure, but wine can. Water cannot make the timid bold, but wine incites the courage. Wine has the power to elicit heady conversations from the most socially inept.

Considering all things, can you see why on the day of Pentecost, the crowd of foreigners thought that the disciples had all been up late with new wine? The Spirit and his exhilarating reality emboldened the timid church to go into the streets. Their wonderful exuberation was mistaken for party-going drunkenness. But they were only the first to see that the wonderful gift of the Spirit had brought the church out of her withdrawn solitude into the joyous marketplace.

How long has it been since your innate joy has caused any to accuse you of being full of new wine? Have you claimed to be filled with me and sometimes lived a humdrum existence? There is one other great attribute of wine. Water cannot addict you to its necessity. But wine is a delicious narcotic. Do you, in glorious inebriation, thirst more and more for my presence in your life? Please, the Kingdom of God is a party. Come to the excitement. Let the taste of new wine be a continuous miracle of joy in your life.

Prayer
Lord Jesus,
Here I am, so often weak and watery
in my witness.
I am so often so tasteless and so bland in my walk with you
that I make you appear bland as well.
Please touch and change my aqueous salvation
to heady, happy, bold intoxication.
Amen.

Marketplace Christians

John 2:13–17

And the Passover of the Jews was at hand, and Jesus went up to Jerusalem. And He found in the temple those who were selling oxen and sheep and doves, and the moneychangers seated. And He made a scourge of cords, and drove them all out of the temple, with the sheep and the oxen; and He poured out the coins of the moneychangers, and overturned their tables; and to those who were selling the doves He said, "Take these things away; stop making My Father's house a house of merchandise." His disciples remembered that it was written, "ZEAL FOR THY HOUSE WILL CONSUME ME" [Ps. 69:9].

God is often good for business. Those in the first century who bought and sold oxen appeared on the surface to be doing worshipers a favor. Those pilgrims who had come a long way—often from distant provinces—could not bring their altar sacrifices all that way. Those from closer locales were often merchants or lawyers and were too "citified" to raise their own sacrificial animals. These temple merchants served all Jews by selling oxen which the wealthy could buy for sacrifice. They also kept sheep for the moderately wealthy and doves for the very poor to buy.

While it appeared to be a thoughtful little business to help those who had no livestock of their own, the temple merchants were making extravagant livings by offering these animals for sale. Many of them wrangled to outsell the other vendors who were also hawking their bleating, mooing, and cooing wares. They had done it for so long that they had gotten used to making money in the house of the Lord. Candidly they joked among themselves that they were getting rich off the sins of the people.

Woe to all those who join the church merely to profiteer off their brothers and sisters. Woe to those who bring their wares into the house of God to make the church their own private marketplace instead of a temple. Has your church ever been a courtyard where you hawk self-interest? Or is church for you a quiet altar where God may find an easy place to enter your needy heart? I have no whip of small cords to drive self-interest from the greedy hearts of modern-day worship centers. Therefore, purge your own motives. Bring me the sacrifice of your heart each week. You will find me when you seek me with all your heart.

Prayer
Lord Jesus,
Help me not to pursue self-interest
*   in the guise of worshiping you.*
Help me, rather, to come to the altar
*   not with something to sell but eager to spend all I am*
*   to gain your complete Lordship in my life.*
Your altar is the place I spend my soul,
*   lay down caprice, and surrender control.*
Amen.

The Process of Learning the Truth

John 2:18–22

The Jews therefore answered and said to Him, "What sign do You show to us, seeing that You do these things?" Jesus answered and said to them, "Destroy this temple, and in three days I will raise it up." The Jews therefore said, "It took forty-six years to build this temple, and will You raise up in three days?" But He was speaking of the temple of His body. When therefore He was raised from the dead, His disciples remembered that He said this; and they believed the Scripture, and the word which Jesus had spoken.

Not all truth comes to us in rote, like the memorization of mathematical tables. Some truth is born in us in stages. The leaders of the Jews were naturally outraged that I drove them from the temple for merchandising animals. They wanted to know by whose authority I had taken so audacious a step. They were literally asking, "Who do you think you are?" I knew who I was, but I knew they would never believe me if I came right out and said it. So I decided to speak to them with a kind of truth that would only reveal itself in the process of time.

"Destroy *this* temple," I said, pointing to my own body, "and I will raise it in three days." My words eluded them. Even as I said it, they looked not at me; they looked outward upon the magnificent temple that they had profaned in the merchandising of their animals. They reminded me that it had taken nearly a half-century to build that temple. I smiled. The sheer glory of this double meaning would gradually emerge as a greater truth than they could imagine. The disciples, while puzzled themselves over exactly what I meant, marked the statement and stored it away for later examination.

Perhaps even before you received me as your Lord, someone told you, "Oh, if you could only know how wonderful Jesus is! Oh, if you could only trust, then indeed you would know. But receiving Christ is like a rare delicacy, delicious, but unknowable except by taste. Someone else, having tasted it, cannot make you understand its deliciousness. You must taste for yourself."

There was little good that day in trying to make the Jewish leaders understand the marvelous truth on the way. And the disciples themselves were so new at all my teachings that the glory of the Resurrection still lay beyond them. But afterward, they remembered the savory glory of the yet untasted. Delightfully, then, they relived the taste of all my promises.

The day is already coming when all you thought you knew of me will be heightened by my Second Coming. You will arrive in heaven. Then you will taste what you have only imagined. The full reality of heaven will be so much more than you contemplated. Hold such things in your temporal conscience, so that after you are home with me you may remember and exult.

Prayer
Lord Jesus,
I come to you celebrating only my braggadocio.
I know that what is on the way is much more than I have imagined.
I trust that when I see it all I'll sing
*   and not have wrongly clung to anything.*
Amen.

Preparing Yourself to Deal with Fickle Commitment

John 2:23–25

Now when He was in Jerusalem at the Passover, during the feast, many believed in His name, beholding His signs which He was doing. But Jesus, on His part, was not entrusting Himself to them, for He knew all men, and because He did not need anyone to bear witness concerning man for He Himself knew what was in man.

Disappointment comes when we trust those who prove treacherous.

Human nature at its best is a mixture of reliability and treachery. If you doubt this, think of those times when you have disappointed someone else because you found yourself breaking oaths you had fully intended to keep.

In everyone's life there come times of high elation. At the outset of my ministry I experienced such a time in Jerusalem. Because of all the miracles I had done, there was a rich harvest of disciples. Reports of my teaching ministry were glowing and positive. My followers were basking in the warm glow of my early success. They promised me a kind of loyalty, and those promises were as yet untarnished.

So when they came up to pat me on the back and say, "Good show, Jesus!" I smiled warmly at them. I breathed a prayer to my Father, that he would see them through their giddy and flighty loyalty when the real showdown came. You must trust your brothers and sisters and sustain them with the kind of prayer and ministry that befits your calling. But remember, even your finest Christian friends are only one sin away from betrayal and abandonment. Therefore, be wise. Never attach your faith to the church, only to me. Then when believers disappoint you, you will not be disappointed with God.

Love me supremely. Trust me completely. Never give this same wholehearted trust to anyone else. I will never leave you nor forsake you (Heb. 13:5). Others may. All things are possible through me (Mark 10:27), not through others. My God will supply all your needs according to his riches in glory (Phil. 4:19); there is no such promise living even in the very finest people in the church.

When you experience killing hurt, it is often because you accorded mere Christians the steadfast faithfulness you should have given to me alone. Never serve me while giving your trust to others. Rather, give me all your trust so you can serve others wholeheartedly.

Prayer
Lord Jesus,
  I want to shield myself from that dissolution
    of soul that comes from giving
    more trust to my fellow believers
    than their fallen natures could ever permit them to keep.
  Help me not to shield myself from hurt that others will
    give me from time to time.
  I'll give myself to all and not in part,
    yet help me not forget what's in their hearts.
  Amen.

On Being Born

John 3:1–7

Now there was a man of the Pharisees, named Nicodemus, a ruler of the Jews; this man came to Him by night, and said to Him, "Rabbi, we know that You have come from God as a teacher; for no one can do these signs that You do unless God is with him." Jesus answered and said to him, "Truly, truly, I say to you, unless one is born again, he cannot see the kingdom of God." Nicodemus said to Him, "How can a man be born when he is old? He cannot enter a second time into his mother's womb and be born, can he?" Jesus answered, "Truly, truly, I say to you, unless one is born of water and the Spirit, he cannot enter into the Kingdom of God. That which is born of the flesh is flesh, and that which is born of the Spirit is spirit. Do not marvel that I said to you, 'You must be born again.'"

It is not uncommon for severely distraught people to say, "I wish I were dead." Such statements often come from those who really are dead in trespasses and sin. They are dead to every possibility of all that my Father would like to make of them. They are often dead to hope. They are dead to honest dreams of living a meaningful life.

But no despair need be terminal. All life can begin again. Anyone can start over.

The ugly crush of life can lash people to the skeletons of their own despair. But consider birth for a moment. A little human form issues from the birth canal. The birth fluids are cleaned away. The umbilical cord is cut, and there is independent life.

At such a moment, no one talks about how poorly this newborn child may someday turn out. Rather, all is hope. All is glory. Hope is the stuff of birthing rooms and new lives.

But with maturity comes harsh reality.

Enter life!

Enter suicide!

Enter pain!

Can you see the glory of what I said to Nicodemus? He could start over. You can too. You literally can be *born again*. You can abandon dreary existence and find a place of glorious beginning. I can live my life through you, touching all your failure with consequence and enduring hope.

You were once born physically.

What an odd insecurity is physical life. Such a birth is all of the flesh. Flesh is woundable, temporary, and outworn by time. But to be born of the Spirit is life everlasting. It is not life after death. It is life instead of death. It will bear you to the Father, to live in his presence forever. It is simple logic to choose life. So choose it. Be born again. Embrace the Spirit. Start over.

Prayer
Lord Jesus,
I choose to live forever.
I choose to reject my sole love for that physical life
*   which may sometimes be noble*
*   but is never eternal.*
I choose that life begotten from above.
I'm born again in everlasting love.
Amen.

Honor the Wind

John 3:8

"The wind blows where it wishes and you hear the sound of it, but do not know where it comes from and where it is going; so is everyone who is born of the Spirit."

Here I give you a saving image. It is the wind. Wind is the emblem of the Spirit, who is my indwelling presence. In some ways, wind is the best symbol for God himself. In the Old Testament God first committed himself to the heroes of the faith under the name *Yahweh*. This 'breathy' word for God was likely at first also a form of the word for 'Being.' To say the word *Yahweh* calls to remembrance the wind. Was it not this Yahweh wind that Israel felt in the stinging sands of Sinai? Was it not in the wind of howling desert gales that Israel felt God as he moved all about them? Was not God the God of power, the Storm God, who blew as Israel lived out her frail and needy existence in the desert?

The wind blew and God was there. He could be felt! He could be seen when the proud banners of Israel's legions floated on his breath. The wind was evidence of his providence, for it blew and there was manna and quail. The wind was evidence of his power, for it flattened their frail tents, made them cower among the splitting rocks. Wind came, and God came and ordered nature. He blew and the clouds scattered and the sun came. The lambs were born.

Consider the power of this joyous moving symbol. Stand upon a sea-cliff with the wind in your face. And as sure as you know there is wind in this high and lofty exhilaration, know that I am that moving, invisible force, empowering and unceasing.

This is the force I have shut up in your soul.

This is the force of the Holy Spirit in which you have been born again.

I do not need to tell you of his power. He blew, and your addictions confessed themselves and flew. He blew, and your doubt died and you openly cried out that you belonged to God. The neverending stirring of this wind is my gift to you. It is myself, enthroned and glorious. It is my earthly, indwelling self. I am the wind, heart-sized and powerful, as fierce and glorious and real as the storms of Sinai.

This wind can set you free to witness with such power that the world around you will celebrate me. You have but to fall on your knees and bow your head. Then you will know the full force of that inner stirring that I have given to you. It will never be taken from you. Celebrate the wind.

Prayer
Lord Jesus,
I am in awe of your invisible stronghold.
I know you are there as I know the wind exists.
Blow on me, Spirit of God.
Fill me with your Holy Breath divine,
 and whisper in the wind that you are mine.
Amen.

The Folly of Unyielding Arrogance

John 3:13–15

"And no one has ascended into heaven, but He who descended from heaven, even the Son of Man. And as Moses lifted up the serpent in the wilderness, even so must the Son of Man be lifted up; that whoever believes may in Him have eternal life."

Killing pride destroys humility. In Sinai during the Exodus, the fiery serpents came. They stung the people for their arrogant complaints against my Father. But after they were bitten, God told Moses to make a brass serpent and put it on a pole. With God's judgment came a simple requirement: those who were bitten had only to look at the brass snake to live. It was hard for many of them to admit that they had sinned against God. Some were hard of heart, and died rather than confess. Pride always wants to do things on its own. Pride is the garment of ego. Pride is the naked self-pretending to be dressed. Pride is the great unthinkable wall between God's redemption and all those who would rather manage their own salvation.

Repentance is the grand word of those who have learned humility. Repentance is that state of heart that readily confesses the serpents in our lives. Repentance unstops the ears of our rebellion. Then we can hear God shout down his saving promise, "Look and live!"

Yet, it was my Father's will that my cross be lifted up. It carried a joyous and bitter requirement. Anyone may look and live. But most will die holding their hard faces away from my compassion. Here is history's great deciding point. Peasants have clamped their eyes shut, refusing to look, and have died. But kings have come to the brass serpent and dropped their foolish cankered crowns and lived.

The serpent on the pole is the milepost of grace, for all of those willing to taste its sweet refreshing. Now I ask you, is not my Father wonderful? Will you taste his everlasting forgiveness? Will you not come to him yielded and in love? Will you not seek him while your own need is great? Behold his love! The dying sunlight is falling upon the golden snake. Your entire life can be born as golden light on a brazen serpent. Bow your head. Turn and look. See! You're alive forevermore! Do not be surprised. Living always begins with looking.

Prayer
Lord Jesus,
Teach me the vanity of looking on the serpent.
I was not weaned from pride by just one look.
It comes to me again and again.
My heart is made haughty by a single compliment.
I am made to celebrate my own pitiful reputation
*   at every passing accolade.*
Please bid me daily look and be made whole.
Please! Never take the serpent from the pole.
Amen.

There Is Only One Lord

John 3:25–30

There arose therefore a discussion on the part of John's disciples with a Jew about purification. And they came to John and said to him, "Rabbi, He who was with you beyond the Jordan, to whom you have borne witness, behold, He is baptizing, and all are coming to Him." John answered and said, "A man can receive nothing, unless it has been given him from heaven. You yourselves bear me witness, that I said, 'I am not the Christ,' but, 'I have been sent before Him.' He who has the bride is the bridegroom: but the friend of the bridegroom, who stands and hears him, rejoices greatly because of the bridegroom's voice. And so this joy of mine has been made full. He must increase, but I must decrease."

John's disciples were not able to make a smooth transition from exalting their master to exalting me. Thus they had languished in the sloughs of bruised egos. It is difficult to give up the limelight. They had known the wonderful exhilaration of center stage. Now my disciples were taking that enviable center of reputation that John's disciples had once enjoyed.

John reminded them of what they had known all along. Their ministry had only existed to exalt me. Now they were unable to allow me my rightful place as Lord of all. John made it clear to his followers that when I began my public ministry, his was over.

John was the first to preach God's new order of things. He knew too that the church could only have one Lord. I am Lord of the church. She is my bride and I am her bridegroom. Let us not introduce any bigamy into the church. I alone am her Sovereign Groom. Humility is easily defined under such a one-sovereign system. None may swagger or boast about their personal accomplishments within my church. I provided the last drop of my blood for her redemption. I bought her. I love her as love has never since been measured.

Here is the most glorious testament of my kinsman, John: "He must increase, but I must decrease." Learn this marvelous phrase. It purges the Kingdom of any possibility of arrogance. Think of the power that would come instantly upon my church if every cleric and layman would begin and end each day addressing me with these words: "He must increase, but I must decrease." In such a continuing confession, Pentecost would come with every sunrise.

Prayer
Lord Jesus,
I am in need of that generosity of spirit
that frees everyone—all my friends—
to have their own affair
with you.
I want to let them relate to you their way with their priorities
always there to give them leave, at least,
that I decline and you alone increase.
Amen.

The Ministry Compulsion

John 4:1–4

When therefore the Lord knew that the Pharisees had heard that Jesus was making and baptizing more disciples than John (although Jesus Himself was not baptizing, but His disciples were), He left Judea, and departed again into Galilee. And He had to pass through Samaria.

Galilee lies directly north of Jerusalem. The distance between these two places is not great, but between the two lies Samaria. Jews and Samaritans didn't care much for each other. They would walk for miles to avoid speaking to each other.

Further, Jews and Samaritans had distinct and separate worship facilities as well. They both worshiped the same God, equally convinced that God liked them best. They rarely spoke to God or about God in each other's presence.

John wrote of me that I had to go through Samaria. A strange compulsion was on me. What was this compulsion? My Father's love.

At the well in Sychar I met a Samaritan woman and asked her for a drink of water. In a world where there were separate drinking places for Jews and Samaritans, she was surprised I even talked to her. She entered into a conversation with me, which was highly self-protective. This did not surprise me. People always protect their prejudices. Their prejudices give them a powerful identity with all those people who agree with them. But prejudices are rarely honest. That day honesty won out.

The woman at the well had been married in succession to several men, and the man with whom she was currently living was not her husband. As she examined the water of life I gave her, she drank unto life eternal. Then she made her way quickly back to her village. We stayed there several days evangelizing among her friends. In fact, a revival broke out around her open acknowledgment of her sins.

Revivals are always born with such confessions. Are you in bondage to some confining prejudice? I know that outwardly you would say no, for it is fashionable among Christians to deny their inner biases. But I beg you to remember that God is in love with all people. He loves those people beyond your favorite color or race or socioeconomic group. What you need is to find yourself in a gathering of people who need me. You must go where they are. Since Samaritans never came to Jewish wells for water, I went to their well. I asked for a drink because I saw them as God saw them. I loved them as God loved them. If you want to bring life to a dead world, go and perch yourself on the edge of some needy well and wait. The lost will come to you. Then ask them for a drink, and get ready to love them. The water will flow with the life you offer.

Prayer
Lord Jesus,
I want to feel the great "have to's" of Christian compulsion.
You "had to" go through Samaria,
   for there was a needy woman from a needy community.
Give me Samarias I must pass through.
Show me the saving work that I must do.
Amen.

The Price of Truth

Luke 3:19–20

But when Herod the tetrarch was reproved by him on account of Herodias, his brother's wife, and on account of all the wicked things which Herod had done, he added this also to them all, that he locked John up in prison.

Telling the truth can be costly. But truth is a trait among the real messengers of God. Their truth is given courage because they identify so completely with God. They are blessed by all that God blesses. They become repulsed by all that repulses God. Their value system is rooted in the holiness of God. They cannot change the subject, and they will not change their minds. It was this fervent commitment to righteousness that got John in trouble with the crown.

Adultery is wrong. Everyone in any age has known that. But high-level adultery is often winked at. Adulterers with enough civil power are rarely criticized at all. Still John, like the God he adored, acted out of only one motive: he denounced sin as sin. To tell the truth is always hazardous. To tell it to powerful people is the stuff of crucifixions.

Civil law has pressurized believers in every age. In the first century, it was labeled civil disobedience for Christians *not* to burn incense to the deified Caesar. In other ages, it was called disobedience to read from English Bibles, or even to translate them. Law has often acted in ways that try to silence conscience.

The church in this age, as in every age, has tried to convert the state which in many parts of the world is committed to her destruction. There are as many people dying for my name now as at any time in Christian history. John's lesson to all is this: never yield your convictions to civil pressure. You are citizens of two kingdoms. Live and enjoy both of them. But if ever the civil kingdom makes laws that force you to live outside your Christian principles, remember the example of John the Baptizer. He stood for God and thus lost both his status and life.

When they led John the Baptist to the block and took his head, he did not die in panic or fear. He died in confident joy that he had clearly fulfilled his mandate from God. In such a state he stepped from Herod's executioners into the presence of angels. Eternal life is the final confident step of all whose faith kept courage with confidence.

> *Prayer*
> *Lord Jesus,*
> *Righteousness extracts a price*
>   *in places where collegiality determines values.*
> *When human congresses decide what's sin*
>   *and what is not,*
> *The ancient law of God becomes too stern a mandate*
>   *for the world to honor.*
> *And those who stand for godly righteousness*
>   *become fodder for the consuming fires of secular morality.*
> *Help me to stand for what I know is right,*
>   *to define your day in this dark moral night.*
> *Amen.*

1–31–01

Your Work Is Interrupting

John 4:7–9

There came a woman of Samaria to draw water. Jesus said to her, "Give Me a drink." For His disciples had gone away into the city to buy food. The Samaritan woman therefore said to Him, "How is it that You, being a Jew, ask me for a drink since I am a Samaritan woman?" (For Jews have no dealings with Samaritans.)

I shocked the woman at the Sychar well. I was a foreigner, a Jew, and spoke directly to a Samaritan. The prejudice between our groups was old.

Prejudice is the black art of hating those our community agrees to call "outsiders." It may seem that my asking for a drink was a very small thing. But my simple request for water was an abridgement of all convention. The very idea that I would ask a Samaritan woman for a drink "from her dipper" was repulsive and inappropriate. But an even worse taboo was violated. I had presumed upon her personal and private agenda. I had interrupted her and required something of her. What right did I have to do such a thing? My right lay in my office as the Savior of the world. To bring salvation to anyone presumes the right to interrupt their work-a-day habits. You, too, have this right to interrupt those outside of my love by reminding them of the agenda of God.

You have the right to rescue the perishing. Do not, therefore, be intimidated by those who curse you or ask you, "What business do you have prying into my private affairs?"

How glorious is grace! For those who are committed to ignore cross-love, God weepingly agrees with their right to go to hell if they will have none of heaven.

But to those who reject my sacrifice, God can guarantee no happiness. He is their Creator, and he agonizes over their determination to perish outside his saving love. That is why he gives you the permission to interrupt them. This interruption is a saving interruption. It is not a sin to cry "fire" in a burning theater. It is a sin not to. You have the right, even the obligation, to presume upon their private enjoyment of the play to call them to their own salvation.

This is the desperate and joyous work of all who took my calling when they took my cross.

Prayer
   Lord Jesus,
   There is but one worthy reason
      we who love you can presume upon private schedules:
      the divine imposition.
   We do have the right to cry "fire" in any theater—
      in the midst of the most engrossing films.
   We are called to deliver the message entrusted to us.
   To interrupt the world requires a kind of courage.
   It is a courage that invades the trivia of life
      to supply the imperative word of life.
   We must feel free to argue the sublime,
      "Please, sir, God wants a minute of your time."
   Amen.

2-07-01

The Unquenchable Thirst

John 4:11–15

She said to Him, "Sir, You have nothing to draw with and the well is deep; where then do You get that living water? You are not greater than our father Jacob, are You, who gave us this well, and drank of it himself, and his sons, and his cattle?" Jesus answered and said to her, "Everyone who drinks of this water shall thirst again; but whoever drinks of the water that I shall give him shall never thirst; but the water that I shall give him shall become in him a well of water springing up to eternal life." The woman said to Him, "Sir, give me this water, so I will not be thirsty, nor come all this way here to draw."

Pascal well said that within every heart there is a God-shaped vacuum that only God can fill. Only once does the Bible bring up the subject of atheism: "The fool says in his heart, 'There is no God'" (Ps. 53:1). The Bible is silent on the subject because the very notion of atheism is too absurd to waste time on. But for all its absurdity, atheists seem to talk incessantly about the God "they don't believe in." Why can they not stop talking about the God they can't accept? Because human beings are innate believers.

We fear the argument of atheists. We are also afraid of those who are "overly open" about God. We back away from those who bring up the issue of God too suddenly and fiercely. Fanaticism frightens us. We like the dedicated but casual lovers of God. We want even the most ardent disciples to start out gently when they talk about God. Let them bring up the matter of the weather first. Is it unseasonably warm? Is the humidity high? Will it continue dry on the morrow? But please, not too much of God too soon after your casual "hello." This Samaritan woman proves the point. She had to be goaded into a conversation about God. Once into it, however, she hurried eagerly to the issue.

Do you want to tell others about me? How can you get into the conversation with enough finesse to open people up rather than close them down? The issue is to start gently. I asked the Samaritan, "Could I have a drink?" This is, of course, a better place to start than, "Aha, sweet lady, I perceive that you are a multiple divorcee with a huge self-image problem. Get right with God before he strikes you dead and you perish in this well. After that there's fire forever, you know."

Such harsh tactics have been used too often as it is. It is true that everybody is thirsty for living water. But it is best to let them have it one dipper at a time rather than to throw them in the well.

My kingdom is blessed by these two truths. First, everybody's thirsty. Second, it is best to pass on the water of life in such attractive ways that people long to drink it and are saved forever.

Prayer
Lord Jesus,
There is in every heart
an empty cup,
longing to be filled with the clean, pure,
drinkable grace.
I, therefore, bring my cup to your high shelf
and beg you fill it daily with yourself.
Amen.

The Temple of the Heart

John 4:19–21

The woman said to Him, "Sir, I perceive that You are a prophet. Our fathers worshiped in this mountain, and you people say that in Jerusalem is the place where men ought to worship." Jesus said to her, "Woman, believe Me, an hour is coming when neither in this mountain, nor in Jerusalem, shall you worship the Father."

The God of the local shrine ended on the day of Pentecost. That day the Holy Spirit made God global. Now there are no holy lands. There are no special places where God is to be found above all other places. Do not sanctify any feature of geography or architecture as though one place is the sole dwelling place of God. The only temple in which God lives is the temple of the heart. Seek for him wherever there are eager souls. There only shall he be found.

Since the first century, people numbering in the millions have made pilgrimages to see the land where I lived and taught. Many candidly are quite disappointed, for Palestine looks a lot like the very place they live—the place from where their pilgrimage began. Where I once taught in open fields, cities rise and guarded borders separate newer nations. Wars and rumors of wars disturb the long-ago serenity that marked the land of my nativity. These "holy land" tours are often hurried and leave the fatigued sighing, "I ran today where Jesus walked." Never take a pilgrimage to find God. God is no more or less likely to be found in Jerusalem than in your hometown. Every land is holy if those who live there hunger for God.

This poor Samaritan woman was simply trying to sanctify her geography. She was saying, "Here on this particular mountain is where we say we ought to worship. This is God's mountain." In fact, she really said, "How can you Jews say that Mt. Zion is the holy mountain, when God clearly prefers our mountain—Mt. Gerizim—as his holy mountain. Come to our mountain; you will find our God right there where we've built his shrine. But on your mountain—never!"

People are always picking out their own special mountain and saying it is God's mountain.

As if this is not bad enough, some even see various cities as central to God's will. Some call God's city Rome, some call his city Istanbul, some Mecca. Make pilgrimages of any sort you like to any city that anyone has called holy. Only disappointment will come. In the end you will discover, as the woman at the well of Sychar discovered, from time to time God shows up in your hometown, right on your block.

Prayer
 Lord Jesus,
 I love your indwelling, never-forsaking presence.
 Wherever I find need of you,
 I there may bow my head and call
  and find you in the only place you may be found,
  my heart.
 I trust my need for you finds warm supply.
 My anguish knows your swiftness of reply.
 Amen.

The Center of Our Worship

John 4:23–24

"But an hour is coming, and now is, when the true worshipers shall worship the Father in spirit and truth; for such people the Father seeks to be His worshipers. God is spirit, and those who worship Him must worship in spirit and truth."

During her Sinai existence Israel learned that God had forbidden the worship of images. God never intended artisans to create statues or paintings of what they supposed he might look like. God issued this second commandment to keep worshipers from imprisoning his cosmic immensity in little plaster molds.

When artists draw an invisible being to make it a visible image, they prevent worshipers from arriving at any conception of their own. The dimensions of God are too immense and his reality too awesome to be limited in one small, human conception.

In Exodus 35, Bezalel is commanded to make the Ark of the Covenant. Great, exact descriptions are given to this goldsmith as to how he shall create the Ark. Obviously my Father is not against art. But with all of this artistic description, the mercy seat of the Ark was to be left empty. This empty seat was to symbolize the earthly dwelling place of God. The mercy seat was literally a seat with nobody in it.

Why?

God is a Spirit—immense, uncontainable, and indefinable. But it is his immensity that makes him omnipotent. He is able to get involved in the littlest places doing the most unbelievable things. Some years ago a great revival broke out in a very small town. Many were being converted and God was adding to the church daily all who would be saved. But those who lived in the larger cities asked, "Why such a small town?"

Once there was a similar revival in the little Samaritan town called Sychar. Of course, everybody asked, "Why not Athens or Thebes?" But then God is a Spirit. He camps invisibly, but in full power, over all the earth. He is ready to reveal his Spirit in large places, as he once did in Jerusalem; he is also ready to do it in small places. Wherever he appears there will be wind and flame. Find the wind and fire, and you will find God. But more than just finding him, you will be thrillingly engulfed in his immensity. Make no pilgrimages where God once was. But where you hear God *is* and *is currently changing the world*, go there. Stand in the gales. Bask in the flame. For God is a Spirit, and those who worship him must worship him in Spirit and in truth.

> *Prayer*
> Lord Jesus,
> I love standing in my small world. For I know it is
>   the very middle of God's immensity.
> No one can ever stand outside of God.
> Not everything that is, is God.
> Such an eastern notion makes every rock and stone
>   the object of some pending idolatry.
> Yet Jesus, you exist, permeating all.
> And I am made to look and bless and see
>   my Maker-King in every flower and tree.
> Amen.

The Most Delicious Food of All

John 4:28–32

So the woman left her waterpot, and went into the city, and said to the men, "Come, see a man who told me all the things that I have done; this is not the Christ, is it?" They went out of the city, and were coming to Him. In the meanwhile the disciples were requesting Him, saying, "Rabbi, eat." But He said to them, "I have food to eat that you do not know about."

There is an exhilaration of the Spirit that surpasses every biological need and appetite. They are to be pitied who see this present life as only a matter of food or clothing. Many live only to gratify such simple and unworthy appetites.

It is possible to be so swept up in eternal issues that we lose all interest in simpler, temporal appetites. Stand by a mountain climber with the thin winds of towering vistas full in your face. Then you will know the kind of thrill that transcends ordinary appetites. Watch some great lover of humanity weeping for some global wound, and you will see an all-consuming appetite. Did he eat today? Perhaps. What we do know is that he had meat to eat that the world did not understand.

Look with me from Calvary and hear me cry, "It is finished!" I had completely obeyed God on Good Friday, and not a single earthly appetite had been served.

There is an intoxicating transcendence that transports the human spirit so that the power of food and drink lose their ordinary hold on us. Consider a missionary who goes to bring the Word of God to some desolate and needy place. This woman may serve alone in a small nation, a long way from the land where she received her calling. She may have lived through many hard times, only slowly making converts. She may even be in a great deal of danger. But she is so in love with the wonderful people she has gone to serve that her difficulties seem unimportant to her. When at last her life is spent, she is welcomed by the angels because of her hunger for the meal she preferred.

She was in love with me and possessed of a great dream. She always felt if she herself were sacrificial enough, she might be able to give just a few more people this life imperishable. Have you ever been fired by some such godly dream? Pray for a consuming calling and such a Christ-filled vision that you might occasionally be completely lost in the glory of what God wants you to do. When you get that involved, you will then be so satisfied with better meat that you will never miss the lesser meals.

> *Prayer*
> *Lord Jesus,*
> *I want to eat better food than that which might*
>   *be served on plates of gold.*
> *I want to watch a child believe.*
> *I want to watch an old man slip from life into eternity*
>   *with a firm smile on his thin lips.*
> *I want to see an old woman*
>   *touch her great-grandchild*
>   *with the fond light of pride shining in her old eyes.*
> *I want to walk where wounded feet have trod*
>   *and reach in joy to touch the face of God.*
> *Amen.*

The Harvest

John 4:35

"Do you not say, 'There are yet four months, and then comes the harvest?' Behold, I say to you, lift up your eyes, and look on the fields, that they are white for harvest."

Evangelism has always been urgent. How can the church ever be casual about its mission to society? On the day I met the woman in Samaria, even my disciples seemed to behave as though they were only on an outing. They had gone into town to buy provisions, as though I had called them to be shoppers instead of evangelists. When they came back and I told them that I had food to eat that they didn't know about (John 4:32), they seemed confused.

Compare the urgency of the church's mission with the work of the farmers. When a farmer's field was ready to be harvested, he quickly set about gathering the grain, lest driving winds or hailstorms destroy an entire year of labor. No good farmer has ever been casual about harvest. Harvest is his income, his living. If the grain is lost, his livelihood is gone and his family will suffer.

Urgency is the matter of God's harvest as well. He loves and desires to save every sinner. I am the Lord of the harvest. In the intervening years since I met the woman at the well, the harvest is going well. Tens of thousands of new churches are being started every year. Much of the globe is coming to faith. The world is turning to faith in me. The harvest is progressing well.

But I must ask you. Are you joyous about all those who are coming to faith? Are you delighted that each hour you have thousands of new brothers and sisters of many colors and language groups around the world? Remember, this harvest is one of utter joy to my Father. Does it not thrill you that these precious ones are finding a more meaningful definition of life?

I pray you, help me with my harvest. Lift up your eyes. I am the hope of this hopeless world. Care about it, for only if you do can you really understand the heart of God. Love all whom I love. Come! We shall love them together.

Prayer
Lord Jesus,
I know God's heart is broken
over all of those who are lost.
But my heart is broken because I have
so little concern about what God cares most about.
Help me to feel the lostness
of the world and to see
God weeping over fields white for harvest.
I would be like you, Lord, so let me reap
and cry about those things that make God weep.
Amen.

Show Business and Human Need

John 4:46–48

He came therefore again to Cana of Galilee where He had made the water wine. And there was a certain royal official, whose son was sick at Capernaum. When he heard that Jesus had come out of Judea into Galilee, he went to Him, and was requesting Him to come down and heal his son; for he was at the point of death. Jesus therefore said to him, "Unless you people see signs and wonders, you simply will not believe."

You must understand that my rebuke was not to the poor man whose son was at the point of death. I was back in Cana, where I had recently made wine from water. I sensed that the poor man's need to save his dying son had alerted the people in Cana, still abuzz about the wine miracle, that I had again been asked to bring about a miracle.

It was here that my heart was most torn. I knew the man was in desperate straits, and yet I had not the slightest desire to offer miracles on demand to gratify those people who wanted me to be some kind of glitzy faith healer. So I said to them frankly, "Unless you people see signs and wonders, you will never believe" (John 4:48).

I fully understood how religious miracles are easily subverted to entertainment. This has always been a key danger in the church. Some churches have gotten into the show biz gospel in an honest attempt to exorcise the demons of congregational boredom from their worship. Then they move from the Spirit's direction to hype. Few of these mean to adopt hype and abandon the Spirit. But in trying to keep things exciting and positive, they trade worship for glitz. They replace genuine adoration with such ordinary things as volume and intensity.

The only foolproof way to know that I am present in worship is to ask a more difficult question: "Is he present in the worship leader?" Worship leaders void of me can become quite proficient at entertainment, but they cannot lead in real adoration.

Salvation is an issue of simple worship; the worship of one person walking and talking with me is the best hope of the lost. Alas, there is not enough power in mere human attempts to bring salvation to a single soul.

I call you to a better hope. Pursue me. Love me. Adore me in the quiet places of your heart. Then those sign-mongers who want to make a religious show the business of the church will be amazed. Worship, and as you do, pray that these sign-seekers will be so needy that mere glitz will not fill their inner hunger. When they see the love of God in the silent center of your life, they may at last cry out for true substance.

Prayer
  Lord Jesus,
  I am needy and I know
    all those with whom I worship are needy too.
  Would you come to us
    and teach us such soul hunger,
    we never can be satisfied with any less definition
    of worship than that
    which starts and ends with you alone.
  Help me to turn apart from glitzy praise
    and meet you at the altar of my heart.
  Amen.

The Greater Miracles Grow from the Lesser

John 4:49–54

The royal official said to Him, "Sir, come down before my child dies." Jesus said to him, "Go your way; your son lives." The man believed the word that Jesus spoke to him, and he started off. And as he was now going down, his slaves met him, saying that his son was living. So he inquired of them the hour when he began to get better. They said therefore to him, "Yesterday at the seventh hour the fever left him." So the father knew that it was at that hour in which Jesus said to him, "Your son lives"; and he himself believed, and his whole household. This is again a second sign that Jesus performed, when He had come out of Judea into Galilee.

A certain Roman official had a son who was dying. The greatest miracle was not that their son came out of a coma. The greatest miracle is that the entire family came to receive imperishable life and immortality.

Be careful in this world lest you celebrate the wrong miracles. The possibility of this grave error is hidden in every public healing service. God's glory can be lost in flashy religious exhibitions that make it possible for the lesser truths to eclipse the greater. Do not spend your lives chasing after faith healers. They sometimes do rather remarkable things; but in offering temporary life, they often play down the greatest miracle of all, eternal life.

Do you not see it! To be born again is not a mere transaction between you and God. When anyone is born again, a genuine miracle occurs. Human destiny changes. Suddenly those who experience my love come to know grace. Their circumstances, however desperate, take on a kind of holy common sense. All of their life's tangled circumstances are suddenly working together because they love God. The immensity of such a great miracle diminishes all lesser ones. For even those who are healed of killing afflictions must face death again sooner or later. But those who know this miracle will never die.

So the official's son was healed and he lived—for a while. But don't miss the central miracle of that day. The father believed. His entire house was saved. That boy is now in heaven forever and will bear you testimony that on that day he received two kinds of life: the smaller, biological kind, and the unthreatenable, eternal kind.

Prayer
Lord Jesus,
I too much treasure
*   treasures which are not.*
Help me to call those miracles of faith
*   the substance of your sacrificial grace.*
Amen.

The Main Thing

Luke 4:16–21

And He came to Nazareth, where He had been brought up; and as was His custom, He entered the synagogue on the Sabbath, and stood up to read. And the book of the prophet Isaiah was handed to Him. And He opened the book, and found the place where it was written,

"THE SPIRIT OF THE LORD IS UPON ME,
BECAUSE HE ANOINTED ME TO PREACH THE GOSPEL TO THE POOR.
HE HAS SENT ME TO PROCLAIM RELEASE TO THE CAPTIVES,
AND RECOVERY OF SIGHT TO THE BLIND, TO SET FREE THOSE WHO ARE DOWNTRODDEN,
TO PROCLAIM THE FAVORABLE YEAR OF THE LORD." *[Isa. 61:1–2a]*

I preached my first hometown sermon among my relatives and acquaintances. In that sermon I said I had come to preach good news to the poor, set the prisoners free, heal the blind, and announce the arrival of grace. The text of my sermon was taken from Isaiah. These ancient words—they were ancient even when I preached them—are the charter of my church. The qualities of the spirit that Isaiah named are still the issues of servanthood that define what a church ought to be.

My Father sent me to tell the prisoners that their release had been secured. Besides giving the poor an inheritance, I came to liberate prisoners, like receiving a letter of pardon from the governor. These prisoners of life walked out of stone walls and iron bars. Their confining gates swung open. Their gloomy dungeons gave way to the outside—to songbirds and sunlight.

And the blind, whose every step was taken in darkness: what of them? What of those who had never seen the food they ate or the lovely faces of the children they had brought into their dark world? Now all is changed! The blind can see!

But the best part of my work was to proclaim the current moment as the year of God's grace. Think of this glorious announcement! No one ever has to wait for the coming of God's grace. It is here. This is the acceptable year of the Lord! This current year! This now!

Prayer
Lord Jesus,
I want to preach the gospel,
liberate captives,
give the blind their sight,
and tell everyone that now is the day
they may be saved.
In short,
This is your work to which my call must cling,
and claim this dream of yours as my great thing.
Amen.

Physician, Heal Yourself!

Luke 4:22–24

And all were speaking well of Him, and wondering at the gracious words which were falling from His lips; and they were saying, "Is this not Joseph's son?" And He said to them, "No doubt you will quote this proverb to Me, 'Physician, heal yourself! Whatever we heard was done in Capernaum, do here in your home town as well.'" And He said, "Truly I say to you, no prophet is welcome in his home town."

Early in my ministry, my enemies began to cry that I was mentally ill. It was a slur of grand proportions to lay on me. I had healed others by common report, but I was called a healer who could not deal with his own mental illness.

My hometown people had watched me grow up and thought they knew me. Their knowledge of me was a kind of containment. How often we limit our world by what we think we know of it. My hometown acquaintances knew me only in a shallow way that kept them from receiving me in any other way. This is familiarity's worst sin: once we define those we know in small ways, we are rarely free to know them by any larger definition.

There are two kinds of repentance. One kind is to feel bad about ordinary moral transgressions. The other is intellectual repentance. Intellectual repentance is our failure to admit that our ideas need an overhaul. The Nazarenes in my hometown committed the second kind of sin and needed the second kind of repentance. They had stamped their feet and said, We know Jesus to be thus and so, and we refuse to know him in any other way. Pride is the real barrier to intellectual repentance. No one likes publicly admitting they were wrong. Most would rather go on being wrong, if only to keep from confessing they are wrong.

That day in Nazareth I learned the pain of ostracism. That day, condemned by my hometown people, I learned the pain of rejection. I hated to hear them scream their errors loudly and collectively. I knew they would later have a hard time changing their minds. They never did—at least most of them. Only a few like James and Jude, my brothers, came to see me later through eyes of full faith. Still, when my family came to me in faith, Nazareth at last found her place in the Kingdom.

Prayer

Lord Jesus,
Help me confess where my loud affirmations
    have proven wrong.
Help me to confess that arrogance
    that condemns all those who will not change
    their minds,
    and thus are powerless to change their destinations.
I'm sorry, Lord, that even when I've lied,
    I find it hard to repent of my pride.
Amen.

Hostility at Home

Luke 4:28–30

And all in the synagogue were filled with rage as they heard these things; and they rose up and cast Him out of the city, and led Him to the brow of the hill on which their city had been built, in order to throw Him down the cliff. But passing through their midst, He went His way.

Most murders occur among friends. Most murdered persons are killed by hands they have once shaken in friendship. So it was that the people I knew best were the first to think of killing me—not in the legal way that Pilate and the midnight mob used, but in an incensed and murderous outrage.

There they were, the people I knew and loved: all our small-town patriarchs, Jacob, Abraham, Isaac, and the entire Nazarene community. There were bootmakers, carpenters, wine vendors, and meat merchants. They had befriended me all through my synagogue years. These were the very ones who had been at my *bar mitzvah*. These were my best friends, who best understood me. Yet in a fit of rage they rushed upon me and in violence pushed me out of the synagogue. At the edge of town they tried to push me over the edge of the precipice. I had gone to those cliffs in my childhood to play with friends.

Crowd concurrence can be deadly. There is a tendency that makes us want to be in agreement with all our friends. But communities, warm as they are, are not generally a good place to grow intellectually or stretch the mind with new ideas. It's too bad too, for if communities could major as much on intellectual freedom as they do on reinforcing prejudices, they might become wonderful centers of human learning.

Unfortunately, we usually discover life-changing truths outside of our narrow provinces. Great truths are rarely discovered in small towns. Small communities derive their warmth from their willingness not to be controversial to each other. They gain their never-changing hometown appeal by never changing their ideas. They do not become warm communities by practicing tolerance. They are good at preserving old traditions, but not at instituting new ones.

My heavenly Father is the God of change. If a thing is boring and static, you may be sure it is not from God.

Consider your community of faith. Can you go there and beg God for new insights into his ancient word? He will give you all the insights you hunger for. Preach the old truths with new insight, but do not preach them too near the precipices of public opinion.

Prayer
Lord Jesus,
I know you are the Way, the Truth, and the Life.
You are the Way of courage,
the Truth unafraid, and
the Life of utter integrity.
Make me brave in my community
to face with grace a fearsome unity.
Amen.

Immediately

Matthew 4:18–20

And walking by the Sea of Galilee, He saw two brothers, Simon who was called Peter, and Andrew his brother, casting a net into the sea, for they were fishermen. And He said to them, "Follow Me, and I will make you fishers of men." And they immediately left the nets, and followed Him.

God's holiest adverb is *immediately. Immediately* describes when and how God is to be obeyed.

Remember my marvelous pun, my humorous and terrifying *double truth,* "follow me and I will make you fishers of men." My earliest disciples were fishers, a noble occupation but one that was far beneath all that God had in mind for them. How could they know the cosmic reasons for which ordinary fishing would lose its hold on their lives? Fishing was life for the here and now. They were signing on to an international team as public speakers and gospel writers. They had always believed they would live and die in the comfortable circle of Capernaum society. They thought they would die and be buried after a lifetime of bending over soggy nets. They believed they would die rehearsing those Old Testament truths that forged their community.

Old Testament was a phrase unknown then, but in time they themselves would create it by creating the New Testament. They could not know all this, for my Father delivers unbearably heavy truths in bite-size precepts. That day all they needed to understand were two words: *"Follow Me."* And they did follow *immediately.* From their little Galilee, they would follow me into bloody arenas and hostile, pagan cultures.

I called Peter that day. His *immediately* ultimately led to Rome itself. In the catacombs of St. Sebastian there is a note scrawled into a soft lava wall. It reads *Paule et Petre provictore,* or *Paul and Peter pray for us.* The words themselves do not prove that Peter was in those very catacombs, but there can be no doubt that Peter died a long way from Galilee. And the reason he marked this world in ways that eluded all his understanding was that he knew the never-look-back-glory of God's holiest adverb, *immediately.*

You have no idea of all that God wants to do with your life. You have no idea of what he has for you to accomplish. If you knew, you would feel you would never be able to do it.

There is only one key issue for you. It lies in the readiness with which you follow God in the moment.

Prayer
Lord Jesus,
Now is when I need to know what you want.
Immediately is the time frame in which I must obey you.
Yes, I am as busy as a fisherman at his nets,
*   but no matter.*
The size of my discipleship has always been
*   my response to your interruptions of my life.*
So here I yield. Come call me and you'll see
*   that I'll do all of it immediately.*
Amen.

The Obligation of Healing

Mark 1:29–31

And immediately after they had come out of the synagogue, they came into the house of Simon and Andrew, with James and John. Now Simon's mother-in-law was lying sick with a fever; and immediately they spoke to Him about her. And He came to her and raised her up, taking her by the hand, and the fever left her, and she waited on them.

To accept any gift from God is to accept the obligation of that gift. Peter's mother-in-law was healed of a critical fever and got up and served those who were guests in her house. She had received the gift of healing and understood that to be well again obligated her to serve others.

There are two kinds of gifts: those that are ornaments and those designed to be used. There are "art" gifts and "tool" gifts. God gives both kinds. He is an artist, and he gives those gifts whose design is to make the world more beautiful. But the gifts of the Spirit are those gifts that are designed to be used in ministry.

Simon's mother-in-law was made well. But her newly made, miraculous health came not so she could luxuriate in feeling good, but so that she could use her new health to serve others. As I called my disciples to be servants, I have also called you to serve. When you have served me, your service will in the end be your gift. Your obedience will at last become the ornament that makes my saving grace a gilded and beautiful thing in the lives of others.

When you are most mature, you will ask at every moment of your walk with me, "Lord, my hands are now free from my last assignment. Tell me, what is my next?" Such lives begin to soar like eagles, yet they are so bound to my pleasure that they never stop and celebrate themselves.

At the end of such service, these serving lives become objects of beauty. Angels are hushed by their obedience. The word *Lord* actually is the chief ornament of their service. Come follow me and join yourself to those who carry basins and towels and seek to serve, always asking in joy, "I have been healed by the Savior; what can I do for you?"

Prayer
Lord Jesus,
I have looked and lived.
I have received your gift of life.
I have looked upon your cross and marveled
    that you paid so great a price for me.
I have been healed by your
    unceasing miracles in my life.
I ask you, now that I have been made new,
    "What is it, Lord, you have for me to do?"
Amen.

Making Demons Mute

Mark 1:32–34

And when evening had come, after the sun had set, they began bringing to Him all who were ill and those who were demon-possessed. And the whole city had gathered at the door. And He healed many who were ill with various diseases, and cast out many demons; and He was not permitting the demons to speak, because they knew who He was.

In my earthly sojourn I was ever torn between the poles of a splendid paradox. I was eager to tell all the world I was God's Son. But I also knew that this eager disclosure must reckon with the critical issue of timing. So I often deferred the joy of revealing my identity so I would not hasten my inevitable crucifixion. I knew if I became too open, those terminal cries of "crucify!" would come too soon. I would then cut short the time I needed to instruct my followers.

But my Enemy knew who I was. So when I cast out demons I would often forbid them to tell what they knew about me. They were eager, of course, to thwart the purposes of God by pushing me toward a premature declaration of my messiahship and death.

Some were amazed that the demons obeyed me. I was not. They always have and they always will. If they could disobey the demand of God, they would be as powerful as God. Christianity degenerates to superstition when it accords Satan such power. Dualism is that false doctrine that teaches that the world is the battleground of a dark god named Satan and a light God named Jehovah. How false! There are not two gods; there is only one. Satan is not a god, nor does he have my power. He has already been judged and is awaiting his final sentence (Rev. 12:12). He is doing a great deal of harm in the world, but only because he goes unchallenged by my all-powerful name.

Allow no dualism in your life. Satan is as subject to me in your age as he was in my own. He must obey me. He has no choice in the matter. He does have great power, but only in relation to you, not me. If you would order him out of your affairs, command him in my name. Silence him in my name as well. He will obey.

As Satan tried to hurry me, he will try to hurry you as well. He will glory in the mistakes you will make when he has tricked you into forgetting that you are my child and that you should dwell confidently in my favor. If he can manage to do that, you will be his for his purposes. Therefore, never give him any entrance to your life. There is not room in your heart for both me and him. Just speak my name in his presence and command him not to speak. He will be silent and you will be free.

Prayer
Lord Jesus,
I want nothing more than
   to understand
   that Satan is mine enemy,
   conquered already by the cross.
I claim that power at every moment when
   he seeks to make me afraid.
I exorcise that foe who bars God's way;
   I know the name whose force he must obey.
Amen.

A Recognition of Godhood

Luke 5:1–8

Now it came about that while the multitude were pressing around Him and listening to the Word of God, He was standing by the lake of Gennesaret; and He saw two boats lying at the edge of the lake; but the fishermen had gotten out of them, and were washing their nets. And He got into one of the boats, which was Simon's, and asked him to put out a little way from the land. And He sat down and began teaching the multitudes from the boat. And when He had finished speaking, He said to Simon, "Put out into the deep water and let down your nets for a catch." And Simon answered and said, "Master, we worked hard all night and caught nothing, but at Your bidding I will let down the nets." And when they had done this, they enclosed a great quantity of fish; and their nets began to break; and they signaled to their partners in the other boat, for them to come and help them. And they came, and filled both of the boats, so that they began to sink. But when Simon Peter saw that, he fell down at Jesus' feet, saying, "Depart from me, for I am a sinful man, O Lord!"

My ministry was and always will be an encounter with the unbelievable. The day I called "Lazarus, come forth!" was like that. The day I stopped the funeral procession in Nain and ordered the young man out of his coffin was also such a day. The day I touched the ten lepers and all of their eroded flesh became new before the wide eyes of the crowd was such a day.

The more things seem explainable, the less I am involved. I feel sorry for those church members who are doing good things but whose lives are quite explainable in human terms. Most of them at the first of their Christian experience knew me well. Miracles were then as customary as prayer. Then somewhere along the way the extraordinary became the customary. By this time they had trained themselves to be content with rigid routines. The electrifying miracles that had first drawn them to me were replaced by the canned and customary. Sadly, they are now at a loss to tell you when the vital Christ they knew at first was replaced by dull religious habits.

Are you at a loss to recall the last time you saw something so wonderful in your life that I was the only possible explanation of it all?

Please, come back to me. End the feeling that you are working hard but achieving nothing. Escape the milieu of these weary, productless apostles. End the feeling that you have fished all night and caught nothing. Take the advice I gave to Peter. Cast out your nets in a better name, and your life will become productive again.

Prayer
Lord Jesus,
I am trapped in mundane churchmanship.
I can't remember when, like Peter,
*   I fell down before your overwhelming power,*
*   amazed at anything out of the ordinary in my church.*
I am too captive to the mundane and the explainable.
Please forgive me.
Baptize me in those things that from your hand
*   are far too wonderful to understand.*
Amen.

Sin and Disease

Luke 5:17–20

And it came about one day that He was teaching; and there were some Pharisees and teachers of the law sitting there, who had come from every village of Galilee and Judea and from Jerusalem; and the power of the Lord was present for Him to perform healing. And behold, some men were carrying on a bed a man who was paralyzed; and they were trying to bring him in, and to set him down in front of Him. And not finding any way to bring him in because of the crowd, they went up on the roof and let him down through the tiles with his stretcher, right in the center, in front of Jesus. And seeing their faith, He said, "Friend, your sins are forgiven you."

Those who saw me daily performing miracles often saw no relationship between physical disease and sin. This paralytic became an opportunity to remind them of the real truth. Do you see the plaintive picture? The house was full. The doorways were jammed. We were talking about the various ins and outs of Jewish theology. Then came this paralyzed man who could not afford theology as a discussion. He was too needy. He could not walk. He had to depend upon friends to carry him to me. They did, but when he arrived he found a heavy discussion in progress. The theology was as thick as the crowd. The paralytic was desperate. His friends, at his encouragement, took the tiles from the roof of the house and lowered him through the ceiling. Soon he was lying directly before me. I forgave his sins. He did not ask me to do it, and the religious leaders were agog that I claimed to be able to do it.

But I reminded them that forgiveness and healing go together. The reason many people are sick is that they languish under heavy guilt that has either created their suffering or contributed to it. In the case of this paralytic, it was definitely so. I could have either forgiven his sin or told him to rise and walk. I dealt first with his sin. If I gave him back his legs and left his heart full of guilt, he would never have been really well.

Have you learned the secret of power that comes from a clean heart? Paralyzed legs are not as big an issue with God as a paralyzed heart. Many people who cannot walk have excellent spiritual standing before my Father.

Are you prevented from full joy because you carry unforgiven sin? Sort out the cause of this paralysis. Is there a grudge you have never been able to forgive? Come to me. Give up your sins, and I will clothe you with a lightness of being. We will know the joy of our open friendship unhindered by any barriers. I will cry, "You are fully mine," and you will reply, "Forever."

Prayer
Lord Jesus,
I am so often a spiritual paralytic.
I can't move freely in my world to win others
because I am too much paralyzed by the very sins
I would like to heal in others.
Please, I beg you,
Cleanse my sins! And when the cleansing's done,
teach my legless soul to serve and run.
Amen.

Spiritual Need and Religious Comfort

Luke 5:29–32

And Levi gave a big reception for Him in his house; and there was a great crowd of tax-gatherers and other people who were reclining at the table with them. And the Pharisees and their scribes began grumbling at His disciples, saying, "Why do You eat and drink with the tax-gatherers and sinners?" And Jesus answered and said to them, "It is not those who are well who need a physician, but those who are sick. I have not come to call the righteous but sinners to repentance."

Religiosity is usually in the way of spirituality. The Pharisees were strict religionists. They knew the rules of faith and practice. They had a Bible-driven way of life. But the Bible alone rarely contents the heart. The religious are too easily content with structures and doctrines. There is nothing that satisfies the spirit except me.

The Pharisees in Levi's house kept their times of worship and their notes on sermons and lectures. But Levi and his group of tax-gathering associates needed God, not religion. Churchmanship can end up in that strict kind of religiosity that loves theology but doesn't care much for God. Spirituality is born in ardor, and ardor is that passion of spirit that cries out its need and wildly celebrates God's successes in life. Here is the checklist that will help you know whether you're spiritual or merely religious.

First, do you feel worse when you realize you're sitting in church with a spot on your suit than when you've passed over an opportunity to help someone in need?

Second, are you faster to criticize the choir for hitting a few sour notes than you are to judge your own religious contentment?

Third, which makes you more angry: being overlooked for a position on the church financial board, or your church's failure to minister in the inner city?

Finally, when you list the things you most like about church, do you start out by listing the church bowling club or its missionary conscience?

The Pharisees at Levi's house loved talking theology, but rarely made friends of people who couldn't. They knew the book of Leviticus backward, but they rarely stopped to talk to the poor.

But in me, the tax-gatherers had a Rabbi who met them Spirit first. The high, unyielding rules of the scribes and Pharisees never came between us. This tax-gatherer, Levi, would ultimately write one of the books of the New Testament. Would he have written it if I had met him with stern religiosity instead of warm spirituality? I think not.

Prayer

Lord Jesus,
Rules are as easy as learning-to-read manuals.
But spirituality comes only from the disciplines of prayer
and Bible reading.
The Pharisees thought that they were doing the excellent work
of studying the Scripture.
But it was the work of the Spirit by which you made
friends of the outcasts.
I want to let your life flow out of me,
with more than dead religiosity.
Amen.

The Obligation of Joy

Mark 2:18–20

And John's disciples and the Pharisees were fasting; and they came and said to Him, "Why do John's disciples and the disciples of the Pharisees fast, but Your disciples do not fast?" And Jesus said to them, "While the bridegroom is with them, the attendants of the bridegroom do not fast, do they? So long as they have the bridegroom with them, they cannot fast. But the days will come when the bridegroom is taken away from them, and then they will fast in that day."

The disciples of John the Baptist and the Pharisees had one thing in common: they were too serious. The Pharisees were especially stern with their religion. They weren't above laughter, but they had to have a very good reason to do it. Their laughter was so infrequent that if you saw a Pharisee doubled over in laughter, you marked the day and hour. You would not likely see it again. The Pharisees were stern because the law was stern. The Pharisees served a stern God. This God from time to time shouted down over the balustrades of heaven, "Are you having a good time?"

If ever a Pharisee felt inclined to answer, "Yes, God, we are!" then their God would shout back, "Well, stop it! Are you religious leaders or not?"

John the Baptist's disciples were also very serious. John was a fiery preacher whose sermons focused on the coming world change.

To them laughter was frivolous because the time was short. Many of John's disciples and most of the Pharisees' disciples did not appreciate the fact that I went to parties. I liked parties. I loved life. I enjoyed my disciples and they enjoyed me. We walked, it seemed, along a million miles of dusty roads, talking and laughing as we went. The fellowship I enjoyed with those men was glorious. In the warmth of our manhood there was so much life to be enjoyed. We laughed as we drank wine and devoured good food. We did this so much that those who laughed less called us gluttons and drunkards (Matt. 11:19).

One of the martyrs would later say, in spite of burning stakes and savage beasts, "Joy really is the most infallible proof of the presence of God." The apostle Paul wrote that we ought to be joyful always (1 Thess. 5:16).

But the hilarity for which we were criticized is characteristic of the joy that should characterize my Kingdom. I am the Bridegroom and the church is my bride. Joy will always be my command to the church. Beware those Christians who do not know how to laugh. They will never come to the marriage supper of the Lamb to enjoy the Bridegroom—only to criticize the guest list.

Prayer
Lord Jesus,
I am here and you are here.
You cannot fail regardless,
*   And I cannot fail when you are*
*   the welcome occupant of the throne of my heart.*
Pardon me if I grand anthems raise,
*   but joy demands that I erupt in praise.*
Amen.

New Wine

Mark 2:21–22

"No one sews a patch of unshrunk cloth on an old garment; otherwise the patch pulls away from it, the new from the old, and a worse tear results. And no one puts new wine into old wineskins; otherwise the wine will burst the skins, and the wine is lost, and the skins as well; but one puts new wine into fresh wineskins."

The word pictures I suggested here were meant to convey the most mighty truth of all: my Kingdom was a new idea. Christianity was not to be seen as Judaism retailored. I did all my preaching among the Jews. I am one myself, and all but a few of those who followed me during my lifetime were Jews. Jews understood that the Messiah would be Jewish. So it was natural for them to assume that I was proposing my new religion as a kind of Jewish reform movement. In their minds they kept comparing what I was teaching with what they had been taught in the synagogues.

In this striking metaphor of new wine, I was telling them that my new faith was such wine. The old wineskins were Jewish tradition. I had no intention of trying to take the rich, pure grace of Christian faith and "Jewish-ize" it with the Haggadah, the Torah, or any of the customary traditions. Those traditions were beautiful. They were strong. They had kept Judaism intact for thousands of years. But in me, God was beginning something brand new. Christianity is not a religion made up from the leftover parts of something else.

Christianity is new wine! Heady new wine, it is! This wine was strong enough to intoxicate the Gentiles to taste and see that God is good. Those who wake up hopeless every morning are included in this. Those who go to sleep despairing every night, night after night, without any hope of eternity: this wine is for them as well.

Imagine a wine so warm and heady that it would draw the nations of the world into a final grand communion. This wine would reach with grace as a drink to strengthen martyrs. This wine would refresh those thirsty for everlasting truth.

This wine was the wine of the New Covenant. It was intoxicating, expansive. It would cause the dreamless to dream again. This wine could be had for merely crying, "I believe." This wine is the glory of heaven. Drink of this salvation; then turn and offer the cup to all.

Prayer
Lord Jesus,
I have tasted your new wine,
    and my mind is drunk with a new delirium.
I am heady with the exhilaration
    that God was in Christ reconciling.
Come wine, addict me to your blest employ.
Inebriate me with narcotic joy.
Amen.

Waiting for the Angels

John 5:1–5

After these things there was a feast of the Jews, and Jesus went up to Jerusalem. Now there is in Jerusalem by the sheep gate a pool, which is called in Hebrew Bethesda, having five porticoes. In these lay a multitude of those who were sick, blind, lame, and withered, [waiting for the moving of the waters; for an angel of the Lord went down at certain seasons into the pool, and stirred up the water; whoever then first, after the stirring up of the water, stepped in was made well from whatever disease with which he was afflicted.] And a certain man was there, who had been thirty-eight years in his sickness.

Catch a glimpse of counterfeit hope. See this poor man who came day after day waiting on a descent of angels into a pool. According to popular lore, whoever first entered the pool right after the angel came would be healed.

How pitiful are the doctrines of the damned. How foolish are their hopes. Here at Bethesda was an odd and tedious superstition. This man had waited on his sluggard angel for thirty-eight years. You can develop quite a grudge against an angel in four decades.

There is a kind of bitterness that comes from watching angels bless everyone but ourselves. Be careful, for there is nothing so everlastingly destructive as bitterness. It grows into a complex and sour entanglement. It wraps its sniveling tentacles around all largesse of spirit.

Bitterness is the grudge of Esau, lying in wait to get even. Bitterness occupied the heart of Judas. Bitterness eats the souls of congregational factions whose unforgiveness destroys the church. One of the New Testament writers reminds us: "Make every effort to live in peace with all men and to be holy; without holiness no one will see the Lord. See to it that no one misses the grace of God and that no bitter root grows up to cause trouble and defile many" (Heb. 12:14–15).

Do you see the image of this root of bitterness? If so, see that it never owns you. Roots of bitterness, like the roots of a tree, thread their way into the soil and intertwine with other roots. It is not possible to pull such a root system out of the ground without destroying all the earth about the tree. Therefore, permit no bitterness to grow in your heart, lest you one day have to tear its roots from your life.

Learn to bless others who have met the healing angel you never found. Learn to rejoice when grace passes close enough for you to see it. I will heal you. You will find my sufficiency so great that you will wonder that you ever thought you needed angels.

Prayer
Lord Jesus,
I must confess, I too have often waited on sluggish angels,
*   trying to get there ahead of the greedier and healthier.*
Forgive me for such selfish spirituality.
I shun the muddy angels in life's pond
*   and hunger for the waiting Christ beyond.*
Amen.

Do You Want to Get Well?

John 5:6–9

When Jesus saw him lying there, and knew that he had already been a long time in that condition, He said to him, "Do you wish to get well?" The sick man answered Him, "Sir, I have no man to put me in the pool when the water is stirred up, but while I am coming, another steps down before me."

Jesus said to him, "Arise, take up your pallet, and walk."

And immediately the man became well, and took up his pallet and began to walk.

The most critical question to those who are sick is, "Do you really want to get well?" It seems an odd question at first. But many sick people have not faced with honesty the fact that they may actually "enjoy" their sickness. Of course, it causes pain and discomfort, but sickness also has its compensations. It always allows the sick to live in the center of commiseration.

Sympathy may not be the best way to get attention, but it is one way. Those who have gotten it for a number of years begin to realize that without it they would have no real means of forcing people to pay attention to them.

So my question to this man who had been sick thirty-eight years was real. Did he really want to quit being the center of attention? All those who carried him to the pool each day were under his command. His sickness became his way to wield power over others.

So I forced him to decide. It was as though I said to him, "I can give you legs and bid you to walk away from this fruitless angel-watching. But, of course, once you start getting about on your own, you will be expected to get a job and enter the dog-eat-dog world. There everyone has enough worries of their own to keep them from continually asking how your spleen is doing or if your arthritis is better. Being whole can set you free, but it will also leave you responsible. Is this what you really want? Do you want to be well?"

The man at the pool, after thinking it over, said *yes*. I made him whole.

The world has never run out of those who are constantly in the process of deciding just how well they want to be.

I want to encourage you to ask yourself, What is the farthest mark of your spiritual maturity? You are most mature when you minister to others in their pain, without reminding them that you yourself have problems.

Remember my cross and renounce all self-pity. Ignore as much as possible your own hurt, and care for the needs of others. To minister to others even when you need ministry is to liberate your soul from small addictions to yourself.

Prayer
Lord Jesus,
I want to use pain to triumph over
my needs to control others,
not as a means to bring that about.
When I hurt, permit me to say, Lord,
That agony where I must often stand
recalls you won while hanging by your hands.
Amen.

Taking the Rest Out of the Day of Rest

Luke 6:1–2

Now it came about that on a certain Sabbath He was passing through some grainfields; and His disciples were picking and eating the heads of grain, rubbing them in their hands. But some of the Pharisees said, "Why do you do what is not lawful on the Sabbath?"

The word *shavath* or *sabbath* is the Hebrew word for the number "seven." But through the ages it has also come to mean "rest."

I did not say, "Come unto me and I will give you leisure!" In fact, if you come unto me, I will not give you more "time off." What I promise is rest. Rest is that deep quality of "rightness" in life. It is not freedom from getting tired but the presence of a joy that removes the ache of meaningless fatigue.

It is not mere toil that causes most to long for rest. It is persons with empty, meaningless toil who cry hardest for my rest.

In classic mythology there is a story of a man named Sysiphus. All through his eternal existence in Hades, he was sentenced to roll a huge boulder up a mountain. Then when he had it at the top, he had to release it and watch it roll down again. Then once more he would go to the bottom and push it up again. This was hell for Sysiphus—not because the work was hard, but because it was pointless.

Salvation is rest, not because it calls believers to leisure but because, for the first time in their pointless lives, souls are able to work hard, believing that what they are doing really matters. They are serving me, and such service is the currency of eternity.

Are you tired? Do you need rest?

Realize that God, as a matter of principle, has established the Sabbath. It is only one day in seven, but it is so much more than that. It is the coming to a quiet place in your life each week and meeting with me for a deep drink of my Spirit. This refreshing will remind you that your Savior meets you in your fatigue. Here those wounds of yours made ragged by the grind at last find healing.

The Pharisees who rebuked my disciples for "threshing" or "rubbing out heads of grain" on the Sabbath were confused. We were having a restful time celebrating God's bounty. Let your own sabbath celebrations bring you laughter, and let holy laughter repair your soul.

Then your Sabbath will restore your weary inwardness. Praise and insight cleanse fatigue, so never miss a chance to take your torn neediness to church. There my sufficiency will meet your need. There you will rest and praise. There I will restore your soul.

Prayer
Lord Jesus,
Help me remember that you, the Lord of Sabbath, said
Come unto me and I will give you rest.
Help me never to be guilty of taking the wonderful, weekly respite of your day
and making it as hassled as all the rest.
And help me see that on such restful days,
I must lay down my toil and be washed by praise.
Amen.

Healing Men or Rescuing Sheep

Matthew 12:9–12

And departing from there, He went into their synagogue. And behold, there was a man with a withered hand. And they questioned Him, saying, "Is it lawful to heal on the Sabbath?"—in order that they might accuse Him. And He said to them, "What man shall there be among you, who shall have one sheep, and if it falls into a pit on the Sabbath, will he not take hold of it, and lift it out? Of how much more value then is a man than a sheep! So then, it is lawful to do good on the Sabbath."

Legalisms are so reflexive, so dull and habitual, that they rarely stop and listen to the imaginations of heaven. The Pharisees publicly agreed that men were more valuable to God than sheep. But they had their set of rules, one of which said: Don't heal on the Sabbath—*period*. There were no pharisaical tables comparing the relative values of sheep and people. But there were many laws, hundreds of them, expanding the fourth commandment. If you were going to keep the Sabbath holy, there were certain things you couldn't do. Healing was one of them.

So it was in my day that the Pharisees said, "Good Jews don't heal on the Sabbath." "Who said so, the Torah?" " No, only very devoted scholars who have studied the Torah." The Pharisees were really saying, "When you get to know God as well as we do, you will be of our opinion."

Remember that legalisms are defined as the words of man added to the Word of God. If God has banned any activity or indulgence and labeled it as sin, then surely it must be so. But what of those activities that some very good friends of God call sin?

All categories of these largely self-righteous laws have sometimes erroneously been added to the Scriptures.

Give yourself only to the greatness of God. Live only for honest joy. Pledge yourself to find the heart of God. Be joyful even in the face of human pettiness. Joy meets God in the moment but holds him forever.

Prayer
Lord Jesus,
Help me to remember I cannot expect
to see you do many great things
if I am always rehearsing little rules
that I am told will please you.
God, I don't want to die having kept your vast freedom
in my little pockets.
I pledge myself to all that's great today,
with nothing small or stingy in the way.
Amen.

The Gentle, Committed Redeemer

Matthew 12:15–21

> *But Jesus, aware of this, withdrew from there. And many followed Him, and He healed them all, and warned them not to make Him known, in order that what was spoken through Isaiah the prophet, might be fulfilled, saying,*
> *"BEHOLD, MY SERVANT WHOM I HAVE CHOSEN;*
> *MY BELOVED IN WHOM MY SOUL IS WELL-PLEASED;*
> *I WILL PUT MY SPIRIT UPON HIM,*
> *AND HE SHALL PROCLAIM JUSTICE TO THE GENTILES.*
> *HE WILL NOT QUARREL, NOR CRY OUT;*
> *NOR WILL ANYONE HEAR HIS VOICE IN THE STREETS.*
> *A BATTERED REED HE WILL NOT BREAK OFF,*
> *AND A SMOLDERING WICK HE WILL NOT PUT OUT,*
> *UNTIL HE LEADS JUSTICE TO VICTORY.*
> *AND IN HIS NAME THE GENTILES WILL HOPE." [Isa. 42:1–4]*

This passage from Isaiah told of my coming and spoke of two clear objectives.

First, I came to present the gentleness of God, in utter humility. This agenda was important to my Father. The world has had its share of warlords who have murdered their way to the chief seats of political kingdoms. But for once in history I would show the world that humility and kindness were the chief agendas of God. No roughshod military maneuvers or murderous tactics would establish the gentle King in his gentle kingdom.

The second agenda was that I should not be deflected from my plan of world redemption. The whole event of human redemption was on a time course that they could not understand.

Paul the apostle understood it perfectly when he wrote, in the words of Jerome's translation, "*in plenitudo temporis*" or "when the time had fully come" (Gal. 4:4). The words of Isaiah stated the immense cosmic purpose of my Incarnation. All that came before it was preparation, and all that came after it was consequence.

Thus my course was set.

Wake every morning to honor my Father's plan. Do not go to sleep tonight without exalting my Father's love. Then, having slept soundly, wake in the morning to praise him yet again. Always keep your alleluias close at hand.

Prayer
Lord Jesus,
How shall I thank you for loving me
enough to buy my soul at Calvary?
The expense was great.
Not that I am worth it,
but that you esteemed me so.
I am redeemed as precious growing seed,
by gentleness that would not break a reed.
Amen.

Clay Leadership

Mark 3:16
And He appointed the twelve: Simon (to whom He gave the name Peter).

Of all those I appointed, it is necessary to begin the list with Simon Peter. How shall I describe Peter, or for that matter any of those I called? They were clay men, unsure of themselves, sometimes bumbling and inept in all they tried to accomplish. But this must be said of them: they achieved in commitment what they may have lacked in polish.

I chose Peter to be my chief disciple. To be sure he could be loud and arrogant, but he was a lover of God. He was so impulsive on the Mount of Transfiguration that he wanted to build three tents and stay there forever. His devotion was reckless but wonderfully warm. I once had to rebuke him for claiming to be able to accomplish more than he could actually perform. But just moments before that he had confessed me as the Christ. He once tried to walk to me on the sea and failed. He once claimed he would never deny me and failed at that too. He failed as much as he succeeded. But he was not the sort to bore an audience or waver in uncertainty. He wasn't always right, but he was never in doubt.

Perhaps that is why I chose Peter as the leader of my church. He had a habit of looking at me with an incredulous, childlike faith. He confessed me in love so often that it was easy to see that his devotion would triumph when his logic could not find a way. And if you could have seen him preaching on the day of Pentecost, you would know why he was so essential to the faith. He was a fisherman destined to outperform the most polished rhetoricians. When he told the truth, hell trembled.

From Pentecost to his martyrdom, his impulsiveness settled into his determination to serve me without any duplicity. How well he at last lived up to all he claimed. And of course, his martyrdom was so confident that it trivialized all his early failures.

Martyrs argue not with their speeches but their blood.

And so he died. From his blood, a river of witness has flowed. The blood of the saints has always nourished the soil of evangelism.

Simon Peter learned at last to back up his testimony with his blood.

Prayer
Lord Jesus,
Peter lures me to be reckless
and impulsive.
He tempts me to say it too fast
and too furiously,
maybe even too insincerely.
Still, I'd rather testify too fast
than never say it at all.
Lord, ask me as you asked him by the sea,
"My fickle friend, do you claim to love me?"
Amen.

The Duffer's Role Models

Mark 3:16–19

And He appointed the twelve: Simon (to whom He gave the name Peter), and James, the son of Zebedee, and John the brother of James (to them He gave the name Boanerges, which means, "Sons of Thunder"); and Andrew, and Philip, and Bartholomew, and Matthew, and Thomas, and James the son of Alphaeus, and Thaddaeus, and Simon the Zealot; and Judas Iscariot, who also betrayed Him.

Consider my disciples. On their backs rested the Christian enterprise.

The Gospel writers have presented them fairly. Each of them is laid out for your scrutiny. Thomas, of course, doubted that I had risen from the dead. James and John were so prejudiced against Samaritans that they wanted to call down fire from heaven on their heads. Their fiery grudges were only exceeded by their ambition: these "sons of thunder" also sent their mother to ask me if they could be my two right-hand nobles when I came into my Kingdom. Matthew was a tax-gatherer, never much respected by the run-of-the-mill Jews in his day. Simon the Zealot and Matthew didn't get along well since the Zealots were committed to destroying the very government that employed tax-gatherers like Matthew. Then there was Judas, the treasurer of our group, whose loyalty degenerated into treachery.

You might look at these men and ask me, "Were these the best applicants you could find to become world changers?" They were indeed. The Gospels let you see them with all their spots and wrinkles. This should keep you from placing them on pedestals so high that their character looks somehow unreachable. The truth is that they were a lot like you. You have their same propensities to success and failure. So if the Kingdom is born in you and if you mark the world for great change, you will find that you must do it with all the same insecurities and self-doubts that they had.

And after all, love is the fuel that drives the Kingdom. I never set out to choose perfect disciples. Instead I chose lovers. How much did they love me? Well, nearly all of them died as martyrs. Most then—died hundreds of miles from their Aramaic homelands. Only love will call people to go such distances and die such deaths.

So they were more extraordinary than they ever knew. Love forged their weakness into steel. They stood at last in the flames, sometimes singing their way into eternity. In Isaac Watts's hymn "Am I a Soldier of the Cross" the martyrs sing, "Must I be carried through the skies / On flowery beds of ease, / While others sought to win the prize, / And sailed thro' bloody seas?" It's a fair question. How would you answer it?

Prayer
Lord Jesus,
I am amazed what ordinary men can do.
I used to believe that there was no real place
    for me in this extraordinary Kingdom.
Now I know the truth:
    Saints were never heroes in their own eyes.
I offer you my own unworthy clay.
Fashion me in manganese today.
Amen.

On Loving Traitors

Mark 3:19
. . . and Judas Iscariot, who also betrayed Him.

Judas ended the list. Being last on the list does not mean that he ever suffered from a lack of love. He did not. He did betray me and end his life with suicide, but his final plight touched the heart of heaven. Judas was not lost because God hated him, but because his self-concern always kept him too much in the center of his own predicament.

Judas was too much into himself. He was so bound up in what he wanted for Judas that he could not focus on what he wanted for me. It wasn't the thirty pieces of silver either. He tried to give that back (Matt. 27:3–5). What he couldn't give back was his broken loyalty.

Judas broke everything and yet never became broken himself.

He broke trust.

He broke faith.

He broke covenants.

He broke every definition of loyalty.

Compare what Judas did on Maundy Thursday to what Peter did on the very same evening. They both denied me. And they both felt bad about what they had done. Peter's weeping at the cock's crow was an evidence that he felt bad. Judas's suicide was an evidence that he also felt bad. But Peter wept in godly sorrow, eager to return to me for healing. Judas's disconsolation never found its object in repentance and confession. He died as he had lived, with too many agendas of his own.

Judas's name has become a synonym for treachery, Christianity's arch monster.

He died outside of grace for exactly the same reason that others do: he never committed his life to my Lordship. Self was his great sin. He lived and died shut up in the narrow walls of his ego.

Come away from Judas and live large. See the world outside your small affairs. That is the world I have died to save, and you must live to serve.

Prayer
Lord Jesus,
You are there when I need you.
Am I there when you need me?
* You have never once betrayed me*
* in the middle of any desperate circumstance.*
Help me never to betray you.
Lord, strengthen me with all that faith's about,
* lest I, in treachery, should sell you out.*
Amen.

Blessed Are the Poor in Spirit

Matthew 5:3

"Blessed are the poor in spirit, for theirs is the kingdom of heaven."

Poverty creates a brotherhood. Those who are poor know it. Their lives are marked by their need. But the poor have one treasure the rich rarely own: they know they need each other. Most of the poor find their needs met by other poor people. The wealthy rarely need anyone. Wealth too often breeds arrogance and a self-sufficiency that needs neither God nor anyone else.

But the poor know no such sufficiency. The poor are more likely to share their last loaf than the rich are likely to give away anything from their full pantries. The wealthy lament the "hard times" as stopovers of ugly necessity, between the good times where they manage to figure out their finances on their own. But the poor, never knowing good times, are much better at giving from their penury than the wealthy give from their abundance.

I once said, "It is hard for a rich man to enter the kingdom of heaven. Again I tell you, it is easier for a camel to go through the eye of a needle than for a rich man to enter the kingdom of God" (Matt. 19:23–24). After meeting a rich man who wanted to be my disciple but simply felt he had too much wealth to give away, I said, "If you want to be perfect, go, sell your possessions and give to the poor, and you will have treasure in heaven" (Matt. 19:21). Alas, the rich rarely value heavenly treasure. They remain addicted to simpler and poorer forms of wealth.

But heaven, to the poor in spirit, is everything. They talk and sing of it in their assemblies. They joyously rehearse their future wealth in eternity. Their need has taught them the warm necessity of bonding to each other in ways that the rich seldom know.

Who, then, is really rich? The poor in spirit! They are the rich of both this world and the one to come. They are the needy rich, and they understand that it is their need that makes them rich. Their poverty accomplishes much. They have so little that they do not hesitate to give it away to gain a coming inheritance. The little they do have is totally available to God. Therefore, they are blessed.

Prayer
Lord Jesus,
Make me destitute of spirit,
So I may treasure that true wealth
that comes from you only.
I want to be so needy that I find
sufficiency in you alone.
My heart is empty-pocketed. So fold
me into riches with your wealth untold.
Amen.

Blessed Are the Gentle

Matthew 5:5
"Blessed are the gentle, for they shall inherit the earth."

The gentle! How long they have suffered at the hands of the fierce and the cruel. If heaven knows any automatic mood, it feels an instant love for all the gentle souls whose quiet natures so often become the targets of the power-mad and depraved. Humanity's inhumanity is the stuff that makes God cry.

But do not see the gentility of the gentle as the result of their victimization by the powerful. No, they were not made gentle by being stripped of power. In the best cases, gentility was not forced upon them, it was an option that they chose. They treasured that open state of living so that no one was afraid of them. No one fears the gentle. We may approach them and draw warmth from their humanity. We never have to fear that they will suddenly become violent.

A child will always guide you to the gentle. No one fools a child. Innocence can guess at once what guilt can never locate: true, approachable kindness. So when a child snuggles in against the breast of a complete stranger, he has flawlessly pointed to gentility.

But if you want a picture of gentility that conquers power, you must go to my cross. There you will see what power can do to the gentle and how gentleness responds. For in that moment when I was naked and bereft before Pilate, I did not accuse in return. I was, as Isaiah said, a lamb before the shearers.

I was gentle. Yet I had the power to knock the world in pieces. I could have called ten thousand angels to destroy the world, but I did not. Gentility is never weakness. It is power under control. Few really gentle people are weak. They have simply learned to subdue their baser nature. They know how badly it feels to be hurt. They have determined that they would rather receive abuse than offer it. They are people of such extraordinary power that you can but thrill at the disciplines they have mastered to become gentle in life.

Your presence in all your relationships is like that of a huge stallion. You may ride it like a warlord, trampling all who get in your way. Or you may choose to be gentle. Those who choose to be gentle have reined the stallion of ego into submission. Their lust for dominance is under control. They have shackled the dragons of heavyhandedness, and their world is blessed. Blessed are the gentle. Blessed. Blessed. Blessed.

> *Prayer*
> *Lord Jesus,*
> *Help me to live so gently*
> *that none are afraid of me.*
> *Help me to lay all needs for power*
> *at your feet.*
> *And when I have placed them there,*
> *I will notice that your feet were wounded.*
> *Then with this offering I will remember*
> *gentility is always at the mercy of despots.*
> *So may your blood remind me of my need*
> *to suffer wounds that others may not bleed.*
> *Amen.*

Blessed Are the Spiritually Hungry

Matthew 5:6–7

"Blessed are those who hunger and thirst for righteousness, for they shall be satisfied. Blessed are the merciful, for they shall receive mercy."

There is no human appetite so glorious to God as the hunger for righteousness. The world is morally needy. And what is righteousness? Righteousness is holiness in longing. And holiness is a hunger to be completed in spirit. It is a craving for wholeness. It is reaching out to the moral God. Blessed are those who care about holiness, for it is the character of God.

But acquiring righteousness is elusive. People are the sum total of their appetites. People talk most about what they most hunger for. If they hunger for material things, they will talk of shopping sprees or the things they own. If they are gluttons, they will talk, even as they eat, of what they have eaten at other times and places. If they are addicted to sexual desires, they will spin endless stories of their caprice and brag of those times they indulged their hearts with the illicit.

Hunger makes us serve ourselves to devour all we are hungry for.

Hunger drives us till we fill our need.

Hunger makes us yearn for what we cannot live without.

And what of those whose affections are hidden in their love for me? These appetites are inward; still, they will speak incessantly of me. Many there are who study my doctrines and call themselves Christian. But few there are who hunger and thirst after righteousness. In such hearts the longing is insatiable. The true lovers of God can never have enough of me.

Hungering after righteousness is a glorious and restless striving. Are you marked by such a hunger? Bless that hunger. In such an acknowledgment lies your appetite for God. Such an appetite is the fulfillment of heaven. It is the only enduring, authentic hope to be found on earth.

Prayer

Lord Jesus,
You were tempted in all ways, yet you lived without sin.
This was not your burden but your desire of joy.
Forgive me for sometimes considering holiness as though it were a headache.
  Forgive me for considering it to be an awful
    but necessary burden.
Help me to hunger for holiness, so that I can claim
    my kinship with the character of God.
Confirm my needy hunger for the light,
    and whet my better unfilled appetites.
Amen.

The Innocence Conferred by God

Matthew 5:8
"Blessed are the pure in heart, for they shall see God."

Innocence is Adam in Eden, newly created to enjoy God forever: still wet and dripping as that divine clay, freshly formed from the mold of God. None has ever taught him sin. Nor has he yet imagined it in his heart. He is a child, a man, both. He loves his Maker with that purity of conscience that has never stopped to play with any notion of betrayal. He is as innocent, holy, and pure as the Creator he adores.

In this innocence he daily meets his holy Maker. He has nothing to hide. He is in love with God, feasting daily on the bread of innocence and utter commitment. Nothing nags his peace. Innocence is rest. Innocence is cleanness. Innocence is a clear, unfogged mirror into which the true believer stares and finds God staring back.

Innocence may be had in two ways. We are born with it. Indeed, we consciously choose to give it up when we sin. Iniquity is the practice of our preferences. Adam, reaching for the fruit of power—the fruit to make one wise—traded his innocence for ambition.

When natural innocence is gone, then the only kind of innocence left is that which I confer upon you by my own sinlessness. In my sinless sacrifice, a new kind of righteousness became possible (Rom. 5). The apostle Paul explained that there is a kind of righteousness beyond the kind we try to manufacture on our own. It is hard work to try to live up to the expectation of the Ten Commandments. Indeed, it is impossible. Since it cannot be done, all our attempts at perfection can only leave us with guilt and failure. But since you cannot perfectly keep the law, you must seek out a kind of righteousness from God that you could never achieve on your own.

To walk in holiness is to take that holy innocence that I achieved and place it in the center of your life. This new kind of righteousness is available to you merely for the desiring. Do you desire it? Will you ask for it so that you may receive it? Will you seek it so that you may find it? Will you knock so that it may be opened unto you?

Be pure in heart and you will know peace. Do you doubt it? Watch a baby sleep. This is the gift I give to the pure in heart. It is as easy as letting me cleanse you. It is as certain as letting me carry the ugly baggage of your yesterdays. It is as free as the wind, as pure as the rain, as real as the earth.

Prayer
Lord Jesus,
I come to you with my fruit half eaten.
I hide the seeds of my disobedience.
And even while I promise you
I will eat the sickly fruit no more,
I am planting yesterday's seeds so I can replenish my guilt
with tomorrow's sins.
Forgive my hypocrisy.
Cleanse me.
Dear Christ, take from my life its very ugly parts,
and furnish me with purity of heart.
Amen.

My Holy and Glorious Peace

Matthew 5:9

"Blessed are the peacemakers, for they shall be called sons of God."

There is a danger in separating quarreling dogs. When hate rages, peacemakers face injury. Peacemaking is what my cross was all about. At Calvary, God and humankind were at odds. It was as though humanity was at war with the Creator. Of course, none would ever say they hated God, but God and humanity were separated over how they felt about me. Most of the human race was either hostile toward me or uncaring. So I came as a peacemaker, a reconciler. I drove my cross between man's horrid apathy and God's raging love. My hands and feet were forever marked by the price I paid.

Take up your cross and continue my work of reconciling. You too must have the courage at times to step between the angry, apathetic world and God's reaching grace. Be prepared to pay what peacemaking costs.

Most people spend their lives dividing their world into friends and enemies. They seem to believe that if only they could eliminate all the people they don't like, all of those left would be their friends. The peacemaker does not serve such myths. He knows the only way to rid the world of his enemies is to rename his foes as friends.

Your antagonists can never be killed in sufficient numbers to rid your world of all your enemies. The key lies in circle-drawing. When people draw against you some hard, exclusive circle, redraw a bigger, more inclusive circle and take them in. A reconciler is one who enjoys the art of large circles. Peacemakers go about looking for angry souls standing in the middle of small, hard circles of spite. When they find these small souls, they draw that circle bigger.

Two soldiers, enemies in humanity's everlasting fray, fell on the same part of a wide battlefield. These wounded, dying foes fell into the same foxhole. Yet as they died the strong lure of family marked their final moments. Each of them drew from their battle clothes pictures of their families in order to take a last, lingering look. Then, though they didn't know each other's languages, each showed the other his pictures. Even though they wore the uniforms of foes, this epiphany of insight taught them that they were not different enough to be enemies. Thus, they died friends. Wherever enemies are dissolved in such acceptance, the Kingdom of God is born.

Prayer
   Lord Jesus,
   I have been a believer all this time,
       but I am still too much the bargain shopper.
   I want a cheap discipleship where I pay nothing down.
   Then I want my daily sacrifice spread over years of very small payments.
   Help me to say the word "Peacemaker" every morning,
       with the understanding of the cost
       I must pay right now.
   Help me to bid all earthly hatred cease
       and draw large circles of enduring peace.
   Amen.

The Witnesses Are the Friends

Matthew 5:10

"Blessed are those who have been persecuted for the sake of righteousness, for theirs is the kingdom of heaven."

The word *martyr* might be defined as "the very best friend God has." The literal meaning of the word is "witness." "Martyr" is the way both God and mortals define the word *witness*. Martyrs know no shallow definition of love. Martyrs make public their allegiance to my name. A martyr will say, "Jesus is Lord" anytime, anyplace, regardless of the consequences. You may stand her at a stake if you wish. But even as you pile the matchwood about her feet she will not change her mind, for she has chosen to wear the high name *martyr*. She will sing her own requiem, embarrassed that she has nothing greater to give God than her life.

There are all kinds of martyrs. Secular people often feel uncomfortable among those who love Christ. Why? The true witness always speaks openly of her love for me. Contempt is sometimes instant toward those who speak of deep things so openly. Do not hide our relationship. Let your witness be the seal of our love. There are blatant symbols for all other kinds of commitment; why not some symbol of our love? Those who are married wear a wedding ring. Soldiers wear uniforms. Martyrs confess, and their confession is the signet of their allegiance.

That which is real cannot be hidden. Great truths have an energy about them that break their confinement in small minds. If you can hide your faith to escape persecution, it is only because your faith is small enough to be hidden.

Take a lesson from children. They love their parents so much that they cannot hide their love. You are my child. Are you afraid of persecution? Does social ostracism frighten you? If so, remember this: Your exclusion or acceptance by other human beings is of no eternal consequence. If you are persecuted for me, you are blessed. I was once persecuted for you. Let your persecutions—great or small—become our fellowship of suffering (Phil. 4:14). The cross you bear for my sake has made us friends forever.

Prayer
> *Lord Jesus,*
> *The next time I tell someone I am a witness,*
>   *help me to remember that* martyr
>   *is the New Testament word for witness.*
> *Upon the force of this better definition,*
>   *help me to kneel and bless your holy name,*
>   *to always be what I so quickly claim.*
> *Amen.*

The Falsely Accused

Matthew 5:11–12

"Blessed are you when men cast insults at you, and persecute you, and say all kinds of evil against you falsely, on account of Me. Rejoice, and be glad, for your reward in heaven is great, for so they persecuted the prophets who were before you."

Before the mob on Good Friday I felt the pain of false accusation. If ever there was a travesty of justice, this was it. Little of all that was brought against me was true. Even above my cross was a sign written in three languages: *Jesus of Nazareth, King of the Jews.* This title of accusation was truer than my enemies understood, for they meant it only as a mockery and slur.

But examine my deportment. I did not rail against the railers. I did not shout against those who shouted. Protesting our innocence, even when it is just, is rarely effective. In the midst of these blasphemous allegations I turned to my heavenly Father. I could hear my Father saying over and over, "The treachery of your accusers is false. You are my only begotten Son, in whom I am well pleased."

It does little good to try to justify yourselves before your accusers. They will only accuse you more. Instead, take your innocence into the prayer closet. Meet me there, and you will enjoy my affirmation even during the accusations. The affirmation of God is sweet in the midst of human treachery. It is the only balm that heals the deepest hurt.

There is a blessing hidden in the pain of ostracism. It is this: Only when you are utterly rejected will you turn to me for friendship. As long as you have one earthly friend who will sympathize with your miserable estate, you will not celebrate my friendship. If you have any human counsel, you will not seek mine. Most people are too easily satisfied with human friends to seek divine friendship.

Can you see why martyrs sang at flaming stakes? In the midst of human contempt, they knew that ostracism is the final friend of faith.

If you could, you would choose a life free of ostracism and criticism. But I would rather you know rejection and need me than to live a life of such wide acceptance that you never seek me. In the ostracism lies your own maturity. What maturity? The unbreakable union of wounded lovers. When I, the wounded King, meet you, my wounded subject, you and I enter into holy union. Seek that union. It satisfies me. Let it satisfy you. Let it symbolize our common love.

Prayer
Lord Jesus,
Thank you for being quietly
 in the middle of raucous accusation.
Help me to take my petty wounds into the closet
 of prayer.
I want to meet you there and linger until I am past all forgetting
 that there is only one tribunal.
It has never been on earth.
It has never been wrong.
I enter into silence, knowing there,
 your Spirit always stirs the waiting air.
Amen.

The Salt and Light People

Matthew 5:13–16

"You are the salt of the earth; but if the salt has become tasteless, how will it be made salty again? It is good for nothing anymore, except to be thrown out and trampled under foot by men. You are the light of the world. A city set on a hill cannot be hidden. Nor do men light a lamp, and put it under the peck-measure, but on the lampstand; and it gives light to all who are in the house.

"Let your light shine before men in such a way that they may see your good works, and glorify your Father who is in heaven."

When my Father created light, he commanded it to be exhibitionist. When the sun shucks off the mists of night, her dark garments fall shamelessly away. Light cannot hide. It is by very nature a showoff. Light tells all. It is the bright braggart—wild and uncontainable—knowing no secrets.

Genesis 1 says it all: *Fiat lux! Let there be light!* With such a mandate given to light, the darkness had no choice but to sneak off to the dingier corners of the universe. Such simple words: *Let there be light.* Yet those words spoke into being a substance that physicists have never explained. This glorious light is the stuff of all cosmic energy. It lets us see the outer growing edges of the cold universe. It gathers its *spectrumized* soul into rainbows and sticks its peacock brilliance into magellanic clouds a thousand light-years wide. But, best of all, light warms, illuminates, discloses, and reveals. It can focus in laser beams of glory to cut the blindness from the blind. It can show a miner his way into the heart of the earth. It lives in seahouses to warn the mariners of reefs. It displays the wonders of the deep and rushes rockets to the edges of the cosmos.

But perhaps the best thing about light is that it rarely serves itself. It fills our world to make vision possible, yet is so transparent that we never see it. It is like the air that fills our lungs with life for scores of years, yet never forces us to acknowledge that it was even there. Light too is there, always serving us with sight yet invisible to the eye.

You are light! When you are filled with my being, you become that brilliance that helps the world locate its value system. You only have to live your life with my light flowing out of you.

Light is ever there, convicting and calling. When you enter a dark but messy room, you do not have to rebuke either the darkness or the mess. All you have to do is to turn on the light. The light will reprimand the mess. Live for me. Then, bathed in full light, some of your world will see well enough to give up its addiction to evil.

Prayer

Lord Jesus,
There is a thin but elusive threshold
between those who are obnoxiously outward about faith
and those who are cowardly and ashamed to bear witness.
Help me not to abuse people with the light,
but help me never to hide it either.
I must remind myself that sight
can't come to those intent on hiding light.
Amen.

Law and Grace: Fast Friends

Matthew 5:17–18

"Do not think that I came to abolish the Law or the Prophets; I did not come to abolish, but to fulfill. For truly I say to you, until heaven and earth pass away, not the smallest letter or stroke shall pass away from the Law, until all is accomplished."

The God of the Old Testament never changed his mind as he wrote the New. Never! Heretics in every era have taught that the Hebrew Scriptures were a mistake that God had to correct later with updated ideas. Not so! The Ten Commandments were not just a set of nervous rules about which God later felt bad. To the contrary, they are as true today as yesterday. Murder is forever wrong. Theft too. Lying, coveting, failing to love God and honor parents—these are sins in any day.

Grace came with me. But I never said that murder was less serious than it had been in the Old Testament. What I was saying was that killing was not simply a matter of murder, but a deeper issue rooted in deviant motives. Obeying the law was good, but hungering after a spiritual nature—where murder was not possible—was even better.

A child who is learning to walk should focus on the path in order to avoid colliding with holes. Why not concentrate on these obstacles? Because the best way to stay upright is to not focus on barriers but on the destination.

The Law was a focus on the obstacles along the pathways of temptation. Grace, on the other hand, is a focus on the destination and the joy we bring by pleasing the Teacher.

In the same way, the man who wants to avoid cheating on his marriage vows should not walk around focusing on all the possible consorts he must be strong enough to refuse. He need only take home flowers once a week and all betrayal will be precluded.

The best way to free your life of sin is not by memorizing a list of all the possible offenses you might commit as you walk about with your head down saying, "No, No, No." Rather, preoccupy yourself with my love. The closer we come together in oneness, the more disobedience will lose its appeal to you. Our friendship will become the chief pursuit of your life. In that pursuit you will not notice that you have overcome your former temptations. You will not really have overcome them. You will have merely walked away from them in pursuit of better values.

Prayer
Lord Jesus,
Help me to follow all the commandments and prove what acts are right,
but help me to follow you to find that life
in which sin is impossible because I hunger too much for your presence.
Help me not to try to arrive at righteousness by quitting what is wrong,
but to arrive there by honoring all that is right.
I cannot conquer sin or struggle through
what I might gain by simply loving you.
Amen.

The Demon's Father

Matthew 5:21–24

*"You have heard that the ancients were told, 'YOU SHALL NOT COMMIT MURDER'
[Exod. 20:13] and 'Whoever commits murder shall be liable to the court.' But I say to you
that everyone who is angry with his brother shall be guilty before the court; and whoever
shall say to his brother, 'Raca,' shall be guilty before the supreme court; and whoever shall
say, 'You fool,' shall be guilty enough to go into the fiery hell. If therefore you are presenting
your offering at the altar, and there remember that your brother has something against
you, leave your offering there before the altar, and go your way; first be reconciled to your
brother, and then come and present your offering."*

The law was right to condemn murder. Still, murder is but the child of anger. If the
law could prohibit anger, murder would never come to be. Murder is only grudge that
loses self-control.

Walk gently in your world. If someone offends you, take charge of that
instantaneous anger that wants to lash back. It is not just that your unbridled temper
might hurt someone else. Your anger can kill you as well. It kills you by first denying you
a focus on the rational and productive. It also kills by leaving your good reputation at the
mercy of your tantrums.

Do not give my Father any gift, be it the gift of your praise or the entirety of
your estate, while you hate another. It is a divided heart that claims to love God while
it hates another. If anyone says, "I love God" and hates his brother he is a liar, for
anyone who cannot love a brother whom he has seen cannot love a God he has not
seen (1 John 4:20–21).

Some Christians sin who freely accept me and join some denomination, only to set
about hating those in other denominations. Denominations are often little more than
bookkeeping clubs, organized to protect someone's vested religious interests. These
privatized Christian groups seem to feel as though I would be one of their particular
group if I were on earth today. Then, smug in their religious club, they set about dividing
my world into needless sects and cults.

Do not separate the Kingdom into small specialized communions. Bless anyone
who loves me in any framework of ministry. Until you can freely give me your gifts in
complete love for everyone, do not give me your gifts at all. I want your love. Give it to
me untarnished by any long-kept grudges, spite, or malice. Then our love will be a
picture of unending grace framed in clean intention.

Prayer
Lord Jesus,
It is the hardest lesson of my life
that I cannot be selective in loving too narrowly.
You have loved too broadly
to permit us the narrow range of our grudges and affections.
Help me not to bring my offering of godly love while I hold in my heart
the stingy littleness of my own contempt.
Help me to lift all of your lovers up
and only then to sip your glorious cup.
Amen.

The Violations of the Heart

Matthew 5:27–28

"You have heard that it was said, 'YOU SHALL NOT COMMIT ADULTERY' [Exod. 20:14]; but I say to you, that everyone who looks on a woman to lust for her has committed adultery with her already in his heart."

People are individual temples. They are the dwelling places of God. The apostle Paul reminds us: "Flee from sexual immorality. All other sins a man commits are outside his body, but he who sins sexually sins against his own body. Do you not know that your body is a temple of the Holy Spirit, who is in you, whom you have received from God?" (1 Cor. 6:18–19). The heart is a person's highest, most sacred altar. Do not profane its holiness even with inner indecency.

Lust is lurid inner commerce. It brings sacred people—other temples of God—into your own private holy place. There it violates them with unseemly fantasies. It coaxes Ashtaroth into the company of the Holy Spirit. It makes a common bed of sin and sanctity. "A man's heart reflects the man" (Prov. 27:19). Do not suppose you may play the saint before the world but live a life of inner license. You may be sure that sooner or later, the inner soul will betray the outer.

There is not room in one heart to contain both an attitude of godly adoration and ungodly fantasies. When you give place to evil imaginings, your own love for God must retreat into the smaller, darker corners of your heart. And if you live too much within this secret lust, you will find that your fantasies compel you to seek open betrayals. You then will disappoint your family. But these earthly disappointments will be but the capstone of what has disappointed your heavenly Father all along.

The heart is the theater of your future. The rehearsal of the drama that you have cherished in private will at last play in the open cinema of your testimony. David once watched Bathsheba at her bath. From this dark rehearsal of lust came his actual adultery. To hide his adultery he later murdered, stole, and lied. He left off being a king and traded that high office for debauchery. Such is the fruit of the permissive imagination. Lust changes kings to gigolos. Then David hid from God. He traded righteousness for license. But every act of outward immorality he first rehearsed in the privacy of his own heart.

What illicit dramas do you rehearse? What images do you play with in the inner cinema of your life? Come to purity. Construct such a large altar in your heart of hearts that there will be no room to build a brothel there.

Prayer

Lord Jesus,
Every soul is sacred.
Every body is a temple.
When my imaginings transgress any sacred being,
my own being trades its gold for lead,
its iron truth for the rotted plaster of decaying sensuality.
Lord, make my fickle heart a worship space,
lest I give lust an easy bedding place.
Amen.

Dividing the Indivisible

Matthew 5:31–32

"And it was said, 'WHOEVER DIVORCES HIS WIFE, LET HIM GIVE HER A CERTIFICATE OF DISMISSAL' [Deut. 24:1,3]; but I say to you that everyone who divorces his wife, except for the cause of unchastity, makes her commit adultery; and whoever marries a divorced woman commits adultery."

To divide anything that longs to be whole sins against unity. To cut the roots of a great tree and separate them from the tree destroys it. For the leaves feed the roots as the roots nourish the leaves. Roots and leaves are vastly different, yet each makes life possible for the other.

Marriage is the grafting of two souls into a wonderful, spiritual interdependency. Life becomes a oneness that did not exist before a promise made a single organism out of separateness. Marital love arrives where the paths of mutual submission meet. When a man and a woman voluntarily surrender their private agendas to each other, each promises enduring commitment to the other's welfare. They vow that in sickness and health, through ultimate trials of soul, they will live for each other.

But if they are not disciplined in their loving, divorce may divide them. The lure of new passions will smother them in the ashes of their lost integrity. Have they not promised "for better, for worse forever"? Then why this voluntary selling of their souls to promote their own private agendas? Did they not agree that they would have no private agendas? Did they not say, What's mine is yours and yours is mine? Now do they dare to take back their words, reschedule their oaths, or sell their secondhand promises to others?

Mark this: There is no such thing as self-seeking love. The two terms cancel each other out. A marriage altar is a union of high promises, not the welding of errant self-interests. So when I said that he who divorces his wife sins, I was really saying this: All breakers of the holy union are committing sins of broken integrity. Think long and hard before you make a marriage promise. Then commit yourself to all you promise. If you say "till death do us part," never make secondary vows with lesser texts. Determine to be a person of integrity.

Prayer
Lord Jesus,
Help me never to join that permissive
war of arrogance
by which the self-excusing
excuse themselves of their integrity.
Help me to honor every vow
and to mean it when I say,
For better, for worse, forever.
Avoiding such poor marriage surgery
is but to keep my vows from perjury.
Amen.

Simple, Uninflated Integrity

Matthew 5:33–37

"Again, you have heard that the ancients were told, 'YOU SHALL NOT MAKE FALSE VOWS, BUT SHALL FULFILL YOUR VOWS TO THE LORD' [Lev. 19:12]. But I say to you, make no oath at all, either by heaven, for it is the throne of God, or by the earth, for it is the footstool of His feet, or by Jerusalem, for it is THE CITY OF THE GREAT KING [Ps. 48:2]. Nor shall you make an oath by your head, for you cannot make one hair white or black. But let your statement be, 'Yes, yes' or 'No, no'; and anything beyond these is of evil."

How odd overstatements sound. Some swear "on their mother's soul." Some swear on "a stack of Bibles." Others "cross their heart and hope to die."

Beware the overstatement! Radical clichés never certify your honesty; they only call it into question. There is a better way to demonstrate trust. Character needs no certification.

Simplicity bears its best message in honor and character. When a good person speaks, he needs to take no special oath to convince you. His unchangeable character has already convinced you.

Lies always need heavy ornamentation to sell as the truth. The heavily ornamental falsehood is rather like a woman who sells a house with many holes in the walls. Rather than mend the walls, she covers each hole by hanging a picture over it. But to make extra sure that the suspecting buyer does not lift the pictures to look for holes, she hangs very big pictures over very small holes. Still she doubts, reasoning that even the big pictures might be moved to look for holes. Then she hangs only huge canvases in heavy plastered frames. Such heavy frames are not needed to keep the buyer from inspecting her integrity. But they are needed in her own mind to be sure she succeeds with her cover-ups.

Such is the nature of oversubscribed oaths. Do not walk into simple conversations with heavy "oathy" frames hung all around your speech. Others will suspect that such large frames cover the holes in your integrity. Look for a simple house—one without any pictures. Then you will know it is a good house, for the clean walls will tell you the seller isn't hiding anything. And when the house is yours at last, enjoy it. But if you accidentally knock a hole in the wall, it is more honest to replaster with repentance than to hang up a lot of suspicious artwork.

Prayer
Lord Jesus,
When you spoke the truth
everyone knew it was the truth
for you are the Truth, the Way, the Life.
Help me to be so filled with you
that any hint of dishonesty
will be dispelled by your presence,
proclaiming itself from inside me.
I want my honesty in full display,
so let my "nay" be "nay," my "yea" be "yea."
Amen.

An Eyeless, Toothless World

Matthew 5:38–42

"You have heard that it was said, 'AN EYE FOR AN EYE, AND A TOOTH FOR A TOOTH' [Exod. 21:24]. But I say to you, do not resist him who is evil; but whoever slaps you on your right cheek, turn to him the other also. And if anyone wants to sue you, and take your shirt, let him have your coat also. And whoever shall force you to go one mile, go with him two. Give to him who asks of you, and do not turn away from him who wants to borrow from you."

Vengeance is shoddy recompense. Getting even barricades the runways of grace. You can hear a vengeful person saying, "Well, I'm usually very merciful, but enough is enough!" Following such a qualification of forbearance, he strikes back.

How often should we turn the other cheek? Peter once asked, "How many times shall I forgive my brother when he sins against me? Up to seven times?" (Matt. 18:21). Peter seemed to imply that there was a legal limit as to how many times one had to turn the other cheek.

There have been some times in history when cheek turning was the only armament of the dispossessed. Before the hordes of armed aggression, the helpless must sometimes die. This dramatic and suffering tactic of cheek turning has become known as passive resistance.

Will such a tactic work? Can the unarmed win by merely dying? At first, it rarely looks like it.

Consider the alternative to cheek turning. Our foes have plucked out an eye, so now they must lose an eye. Then, of course, to really get even they will have to come back to get our remaining eye. Now, blind and chopping at their face, we must go and rip away their final eye. The teeth go next, molar for molar. This is the way warlords play the children's game of "He Hit Me First! I Did Not!"

Are you angry with your offenders? Forgive the offense seven times. Does the culprit charge ever forward, taking advantage of you? Are you tempted to stop being "Mr. Nice Guy" and answer their hate in kind? Turn the other cheek. Begin to pray for them. Bless them with a benediction of kindness. Affirm them. Bake your enemy a cake. Did they smash the cake in your face? Perhaps they would rather have pies. Go again with another offering of peace. Out of pies? Then write them a celebrative poem exalting their goodness. Never give up cheek turning. You will see. In time . . . in time . . . in time.

Prayer
Lord Jesus,
As you have answered all my sin with grace,
  help me to turn to others who need my charity to live.
May I not answer any injustice
  with my desire to make them pay.
Rather, help me to reach in love, to give my enemies
  more than my foes have ever given free.
Indeed, dear Christ, that's how you gave to me.
Amen.

Making Your Enemies Your Neighbors

Matthew 5:43–45

"You have heard that it was said, 'YOU SHALL LOVE YOUR NEIGHBOR [Lev. 19:18], and hate your enemy.' But I say to you, love your enemies, and pray for those who persecute you in order that you may be sons of your Father who is in heaven; for He causes His sun to rise on the evil and the good, and sends rain on the righteous and the unrighteous."

Neighbors and enemies! They earn their labels by living either close to you or somewhere else. The better you know someone, the easier it is to love her and the harder it is to hate her. Most of the wars that have destroyed the world might never have happened if the citizens of the opposing nations were forced to take periodic, long vacations within each other's country. It is much easier to hate strangers than acquaintances, and it is nearly impossible to want to destroy those we know well.

Why do we give so much grace and unlimited forgiveness to those we know? Why do we reserve ill will for those we do not know? It is all part of the geography of loving, and there is but one solution to keep you from hating your enemies: move closer to them. Make them your neighbors. The closer they get, the more they will become real people and the harder you will find it to hate them. Take the following three steps, and you will be able to rid your world of enemies.

First, memorize this proverb of proximity: Since it is harder to hate those close at hand, I will allow no strangers in my world. I will seek to move my distant, doubtful acquaintances more and more toward the center of my life.

Second, begin to pray for all of those you dislike. Such prayers may or may not change the harsh, unlovely qualities of your enemies. But they will change you. After all, the unlovely people that we have called our enemies have often not named us theirs. Since we may have misnamed them, why not simply rename them?

Finally, no one can be your enemy until you say so. No one can wear the title of "foe" unless you agree to it. Your enemies are not God's enemies. Crosses are great places for the crucified to remember that God has no enemies. God has only friends. He loves everyone exactly as he loves you. And when you are most like God, you will find yourself taking every foe captive by the sheer power of your good will.

Prayer
> *Lord Jesus,*
> *I have held my own geography too sacred.*
> *I speak to those at hand*
> *   and say what I will about those who are more distant.*
> *Now I pray you help me in my mind's eye*
> *   to move my distant foes to my proximity.*
> *Help me to see that they, like me, are real,*
> *   with utter problems and demanding pain.*
> *Cause me to name my foes as friends again.*
> *Amen.*

Secret Giving and Open Blessing

Matthew 6:1–4

"Beware of practicing your righteousness before men to be noticed by them; otherwise you have no reward with your Father who is in heaven. When therefore you give alms, do not sound a trumpet before you, as the hypocrites do in the synagogues and in the streets, that they may be honored by men. Truly I say to you, they have their reward in full. But when you give alms, do not let your left hand know what your right hand is doing that your alms may be in secret; and your Father who sees in secret will repay you."

It would amaze you how much you could accomplish in your world if you quit caring who got the credit. Why is it that we want our good works to be noticed? This is especially true in matters of giving. How ego craves the spotlight! Ego begs to be noticed in the church. Many people are motivated to give only if they can be glorified for being sacrificial.

The need to be celebrated for being sacrificial can set in motion a continuing game of one-upmanship in the church. The "how much did you give, dearie?" syndrome leads to high platforms of competition. Considering my gift on the cross, you would think it would be hard to glory in such ordinary things as church offerings or building pledges. Be sure that your pride does not become a pit in the path of your call to Christian service.

There are only two mystiques for the giver. The first is that of intimate blessing. The second is that of proud exhibitionism. The first hides itself, never disclosing what it has given or why. The second glories in the pronouncement of its generosity. Your secrecy about your good deeds causes my Father to become exhibitionist in his blessing.

Your selfless giving is the key to his lavish openness.

To tell whether you are giving in the right way, ask yourself who you really love at the moment of your giving. If your focus is on your gift, the glory you seek is smudged even as you give. You will only give as the Pharisees once gave. But if you bring your gift to him in utter sacrifice, you will feel that your gift is small because of all he has already done for you. You will not then give with ostentation but with a glorious inwardness.

Still, you cannot love and hide your love. All love declares itself with some demonstration. So when you are in love with me, you must bring some gift to the altar. But do it in a way that those who look on will focus on me and not your gift. Then our love will be sealed without ostentation. I will approve your quietly offered gift. It will come wrapped in the simple hush of your gratitude.

Prayer
Lord Jesus,
It is so hard for me to want to hide my piety.
It's just that everyone in the church
    seems to be playing the game, and it is very hard
    not to jump in there and compete.
I want to quit trying to outdo those around me.
Still, I don't want everyone to think I'm a loser.
Help me to give as you gave on the tree
    and to give my all with anonymity.
Amen.

Intimate Prayer

Matthew 6:5–6

"And when you pray, you are not to be as the hypocrites; for they love to stand and pray in the synagogues and on the street corners, in order to be seen by men. Truly I say to you, they have their reward in full. But you, when you pray, go into your inner room, and when you have shut your door, pray to your Father who is in secret, and your Father who sees in secret will repay you."

Prayer is supposed to be conversation with my Father. In truth, public prayers are often little more than people talking to each other under the guise of talking to God. Notice the extra volume in public prayer. Hear the dramatic pauses, the swelling images, and, yes, even gestures. Gestures?

The rules of divine intimacy are roughly the same as that of human intimacy. When a man and a woman share in the deepest act of love, it is called intimacy. But if a third person is admitted to the matrix of their loving, the word *intimacy* immediately changes to *obscenity*. Intimacy by definition is *the loving of two.* So is the definition of spiritual intimacy. Pray in your closet, therefore. Then the agony and longings of your heart, the ardor of your spiritual rapture, your brokenness and need will be heard. The closet is the only place you may be able to tell God everything you are feeling. There no betrayal is possible. In the closet there is absolutely no possibility that some other human auditor will misunderstand your heart. *Only* in the closet can you be absolutely sure that God hears your heart. No words there are misunderstood. There the agony and ecstasy of your soul will speak in wordless yearnings that cannot be uttered (Rom. 8:26). In this intensity of soul, the power of spiritual intimacy is born.

The language of such intimacy is of the Spirit. Sincere praying, in the closet, may be completely wordless. In such time, the reaching heart at last speaks its wordless needs. There my Father hears the heart even before it forms the words.

Use your closet times with my Father in two ways. First, humble yourself in the silence of your closet, while he moves within you—edifying, blessing, rebuking, loving. Your own words will form praise under the utter pressure of your inner joy. Second, never feel obligated to bring a large agenda. Come, and sit and wait unhurried. Then your petitions will not become larger than your focus on God. Learn the patient discipline of waiting and listening plus nothing—not writing, not words, not forced emotion. Just be there in the closet, taking time for God. Your Father in heaven will be faithful to visit you, and the visitation will be glorious.

Prayer
Lord Jesus,
I am afflicted with a busyness
that makes me an infrequent visitor to the prayer closet.
I want to desire you so much
that I find the quiet places in our relationship
altogether welcome.
Meet me when I'm alone and free of fraud,
then ravage me with grace, three-personed God.
Amen.

Words Versus Silence

Matthew 6:7–8

"And when you are praying, do not use meaningless repetition, as the Gentiles do, for they suppose that they will be heard for their many words. Therefore do not be like them; for your Father knows what you need, before you ask Him."

At least half of all praying is listening. It is the best half. It is the listening half that allows the Almighty to implant his counsel directly into your life. When the one praying does all the talking, prayer can become little more than presumptuous monologue. Such praying assumes that God is mute and only people talk.

There are three rules for keeping an empty "chattiness" out of your praying. First, remember who you are praying to. Even most chatty people will get quiet in the presence of true dignity. Let us say you have an appointment with the queen of any earthly nation. In such a moment, almost no one would run on and on, as though he is talking with a peer.

A second rule for getting the chattiness out of praying is to remember to make a distinction between the way you talk and the way you pray. In the whirl and the fury of churchmanship, people often walk into church making conversation. When called upon later to pray in the worship service, they go right on talking to God exactly as they have been talking to their friends at church. God receives from them the same chatty tone in which they relate to everyone in their path.

A third rule may indeed eliminate both others. It is an appeal to what the church fathers called the *otium sanctum*. This is translated as *holy leisure*. This is the leisure that we should use in approaching God. Leisure is time that is unhurried and unstressed.

Consider the way many church people pray. Under the press of all they have to do, they dash in before God's throne. They spill forth the same kind of verbal tornado in which they live. Then, having blurted out their agitated prayers, they hurry back into their hurried world, resuming their blustery way of life. To call frenzied worrying *prayer* is to dishonor prayer.

When you really pray, you must approach God in an unhurried fashion, making a distinct difference from your neurotic agenda. Slow down. Enter his presence in quietness. Garb yourselves in unhurried leisure. Say to God, "My time, all that you want of it, is yours. I have no agenda or schedule more important than you."

Prayer
Lord Jesus,
I'm often all too noisy
in your presence.
I'm confident that the reason we have two ears
and only one mouth
is that you would like us to listen
twice as much as we talk.
If this is so in life, it ought to be more so in our prayers.
I'm too much present in my chatty prayers.
Let me know silence and confirm you're there.
Amen.

Praying Right

Matthew 6:9–15

"Pray, then, in this way: 'Our Father who art in heaven, Hallowed be Thy name. Thy kingdom come. Thy will be done, On earth as it is in heaven. Give us this day our daily bread. And forgive us our debts, as we also have forgiven our debtors. And do not lead us into temptation, but deliver us from evil. [For Thine is the kingdom, and the power, and the glory, forever. Amen.]' For if you forgive men for their transgressions, your heavenly Father will also forgive you. But if you do not forgive men, then your Father will not forgive your transgressions."

If you would pray with power, in every prayer do these four things: Hallow my name, pray for my Kingdom, thank him for your bread, and forgive everyone as lavishly as I have forgiven you.

First, hallow my name. Be reminded every time you pray that prayer is a conversation between friends. But remember too that prayer is the approach of a subject to the King. I have taught you throughout the gospel that God is your Father. Because he is your Father, you need never fear him in approaching him. You may talk to him as friend with friend. But never let your familiarity become so chummy that you see God as a peer. His name *Jehovah* came about as the result of the Jews popularizing *Yahweh,* the covenant name, so it could be spoken aloud. For ancient Jews had such respect for the holiness of God that they believed it a sin to refer to him aloud by using his covenant name, Yahweh. Every time you approach him in prayer, think "Yahweh."

The second thing you should do in every prayer is to pray for my Kingdom. I died to establish that Kingdom. Day by day for the past two thousand years my Kingdom has been adding subjects. Someday when I come again, my Kingdom will be complete.

The third thing you should do is to thank God daily for your bread. Learn to see that your every provision has come from the generous bounty of my Father. Gratitude to God should always mark your life. Never lift your spoon or your glass without breathing a "thank you" for his gifts.

Finally, let your every prayer be a statement of your praise for his forgiveness. Remember, on my cross I forgave your every sin. You have extravagantly received my cleansing. Now, indwelled by this same lavish grace, turn and forgive others, whatever they may have done to you.

Let these four axioms undergird your every prayer. These are the foundations of all prayer. Such prayer will make the world new.

> *Prayer*
> *Lord Jesus,*
> *I hallow God's name,*
>   *I pray for the coming Kingdom,*
>   *I thank you for my daily bread,*
>   *I forgive lavishly.*
> *I want to pray each day as you have taught,*
>   *remembering the price of all you bought.*
> *Amen.*

Secret Self-Denial

Matthew 6:16

"And whenever you fast, do not put on a gloomy face as the hypocrites do, for they neglect their appearance in order to be seen fasting by men. Truly I say to you, they have their reward in full."

The worst form of human bondage may be reputation. The most narcotic of your addictions can sometimes be your need to be the center of attention. This is nowhere more true than in the world of religion.

The appetites for food, lust, and power can become, among the undisciplined, occasions of continual indulgence. The addiction to pornography rises out of the heart unwilling to check its inner gluttonies. The addiction to power, which brutalizes in corporations, comes from the refusal to clear the heart of its ego addictions. Gross obesity rises from other kinds of indulgences. There is only one deliverer from all these excesses: self-denial.

Self-denial is not merely a way to hold your mind in check. It serves your soul too. To say "no" to any appetite is to enter into prayer. Prayer checks these killing indulgences. Finally freed by self-control, you will know the transformed heart. Cleansing your mind of lust leaves your mind clear for the important transactions of life.

A similar danger exists in the power appetite. Those who secretly want to run things must hide their desire to control others. If their power-lust became obvious, they would be rejected. So they become two-souled. They must always appear to be "one of the regular guys" having a good time, while at the same time they carry on their secret agenda of owning others under the pretense of friendship. Powermongers can live this way for so long that they cease to see themselves as they really are. Their defilement is so complete that they continually sin by believing they have some right to control others.

Finally, consider an appetite that is most common among religious people: food. Every way of life, religious or not, has its own addictions. Religious people tend to decry their list of religious taboos with loud sermons. Food, however, is a sin often made legitimate within the church. It is the sin "reserved for the pleasure of the godly." Christians rarely bring it up. Gluttony is a rare sermon topic among those who constantly run to church casserole suppers and ice-cream parties. But every overindulgence should be a matter of conscience. Nothing should be made legitimate that has the power to control us.

Prayer
Lord Jesus,
I want to be as I appear,
for I know that sham is the number one accusation
of all those who are in the church.
No one will hear a thing I really have to say,
while I remain so squarely in the way.
Amen.

Taking Off the Mask

Matthew 6:17–18

"But you, when you fast, anoint your head, and wash your face so that you may not be seen fasting by men, but by your Father who is in secret; and your Father who sees in secret will repay you."

I encourage you to fast. Gluttony shortens life. The conquering of this common passion requires the same submission of ego as the management of any other sin. Fasting may be the only way to rule over appetite. Still, as I reminded the hypocrites of my day, don't allow any form of self-denial to propel you into the center of community esteem. If you fast only in order to advance a godly reputation, you have but denied your food appetite to indulge your power appetite.

Whatever your form of self-denial, keep it to yourself. Deliver your needs to my Father. Begin to talk to him in secret about it. It will become a tryst between the two of you.

The Pharisees fasted so regularly that they never really came to know God. When they fasted, they worked hard to "let it show." They didn't shave or wash their long faces. Their hair was disheveled. Their complexions were wan. They looked dour. All who looked at them were prone to say, "My, what godly men! See, it is clear! They fast!"

The English word *hypocrite* comes from the Greek word *hupocrites,* which means "an actor's mask." This little word is enough to convince us that it is possible to live as a Christian actor in the theater of the church, where every action may be measured not for its inner sincerity but for its dramatic impact. Deny yourselves, but be real when you do it.

The mask is the number one item of dress for many in church. It is also a reason for widespread powerlessness. *Acting* can so much become the group preoccupation in some churches that rarely is anyone whom he appears to be. Many are playing "dress up" to conceal their need or to cloak their private agendas. Seek out some old-fashioned altar in which all members are free to bring their masks and lay them on the altar. Even as they walk away from such old false faces, power will be born in the church. Then I will live again. Among such naked-faced believers, my power will manifest itself in ways they never supposed possible. I will be their God, and they will be my people. Pretense will be gone. Love will be the food of our friendship.

Prayer
Lord Jesus,
A dozen times each day
I put on some mask
which in my heart I believe will
entice others to make over me.
I need a maskless entry into grace,
a way to follow with a naked face.
Amen.

Moth and Rust

Matthew 6:19–21

"Do not lay up for yourselves treasures upon earth, where moth and rust destroy, and where thieves break in and steal. But lay up for yourselves treasures in heaven, where neither moth nor rust destroys, and where thieves do not break in or steal; for where your treasure is, there will your heart be also."

Moth and rust are cancers on endurance. One devours steel; the other, cloth. Rust eats all metal: crowns, thrones, military hardware. Moths do their work in the dank closets of our self-importance. The velvet and ermine of regal dress yield at last to the devouring insects of time.

In bank vaults are the registered collection of things "we would weep to lose." I must ask you this: what would you weep to lose? What do you own that is so dear that you would shrink from every thought of misplacing it?

There is also a vault in heaven to which I invite your attention! It glitters with true wealth. Here, in these endless ranks of eternal safety deposit boxes, lie the enduring things that neither rust nor moths could destroy. Here at flaming stakes the martyrs deposited their unyielding commitment to truth. Here the reformers laid the treasure of their courage. But the best treasures of heaven are not historically grand. Here a child, suffering from the quarrels of her divorcing parents, lays her insecurity in tears. Here a minister abused by wealthy parishioners has laid those needs that no one in the church ever stopped to ask about. Here the dying inmate laid his years of crying in the dark, where none could see. Here the thief on the cross, criminal that he was, laid down his fleeting life to take it up as jewels in another world. Here Magdalene wept out her need for full forgiveness, and the glittering diamonds of her repentance were safely stored to be opened in better times.

Lay your best treasures in my heavenly vault. Take charge of your ego. Rust is expected to be heavy during your lifetime. Moths will be frequent. Therefore, do not store up treasure on earth.

Prayer
> *Lord Jesus,*
> *There is but one kind of valuable.*
> *There is but one place to store my valuables.*
> *In the vaults of heaven*
> > *where all the best treasures are kept,*
> > *there are glittering shelves*
> > *of simple things:*
> > *virtue, self-sacrifice, commitment.*
> *I want to lay up treasures all untold,*
> > *as things that never can be bought with gold.*
> *Amen.*

Strangling Worries

Matthew 6:25–33

"For this reason I say to you, do not be anxious for your life, as to what you shall eat, or what you shall drink; nor for your body, as to what you shall put on. Is not life more than food, and the body than clothing? Look at the birds of the air, that they do not sow, neither do they reap, nor gather into barns, and yet your heavenly Father feeds them. Are you not worth much more than they? And which of you by being anxious can add a single cubit to his life's span? And why are you anxious about clothing? Observe how the lilies of the field grow; they do not toil nor do they spin, yet I say to you that even Solomon in all his glory did not clothe himself like one of these. But if God so arrays the grass of the field, which is alive today and tomorrow is thrown into the furnace, will He not much more do so for you, O men of little faith? Do not be anxious then, saying, 'What shall we eat?' or 'What shall we drink?' or 'With what shall we clothe ourselves?' For all these things the Gentiles eagerly seek; for your heavenly Father knows that you need all these things. But seek first His kingdom and His righteousness; and all these things shall be added to you."

Worries and anxieties distract our focus on all things important. Get yourself a single focus on one important thing. Keep it there, and the trivial things that distract you will take a lesser place. The mind is a very narrow channel. It permits us to think of only one thing at a time. There is not room in a single mind for both purposeful thinking and trivial self-concern. The mind too often occupies itself with trivia. Which functions shall we attend? What shall we eat when we get there? Can we eat that much and stay on our diet? If we eat the main course, can we really eat those fatty desserts? If we don't eat, will we appear ungracious? If a simple dinner invitation can engender so many questions, consider the anxieties you feel about clothes. Many spend their lives buying clothes, washing clothes, putting them on, primping before mirrors, and receiving the compliments. We want to look just right for the just-right occasion. The formal event, the wedding, the funeral, or the governor's reception: such events wrap the psyche in so much concern about our appearances that we are paralyzed.

While we agonize over appearances, the flowers in the field blanket the hillside in that natural beauty that comes from God. Effortlessly they grow.

Remember the flowers and put to death all those cares and concerns that have been strangling you for years. Remember this: The word *anxiety* comes from an old Latin word *angere*, which means "to strangle or to choke." The word *worry* comes from another ancient word, *wyrgan*, which means "to strangle or to choke." Worry and anxiety strangle the single focus. But on the other hand, a single focus on the Kingdom will strangle worry and anxiety. The recipe of personal peace is simple. Be like the wildflowers. Think *only* about what God wants. Be truly free.

Prayer
Lord Jesus,
Let me see the wildflowers in December,
for it's then I have the hardest time remembering
that you naturally clothe the world in beauty.
All those things that choke and strangle me
remind me where my focus ought to be.
Amen.

Today Is the Only Place We May Live

Matthew 6:34

"Therefore do not be anxious for tomorrow; for tomorrow will care for itself. Each day has enough trouble of its own."

Those who live only for today are foolish, for eternity is long. But those who are so consumed by future fear that they cannot make the moment meaningful are equally foolish. You cannot live in tomorrow. It is a locked land. Its walls are so high that you cannot see over them. Don't waste time trying to guess what's behind the high, thick walls of tomorrow.

There is but one way to get ready for tomorrow. Live today. Today is the porch of tomorrow. Things are never as good today as they could be. We are prone to lament, "If only I were doing better in this area or that, I would be truly happy. I wish tomorrow would come so I could see how life will turn out." Rarely liking where we are, we are still unable to figure out where we would like to be.

What is this present moment really for? It is for meeting God. You cannot undo the past by lamenting how you wished you had met God more frequently back there. Nor can you stalk him in your tomorrow. If you would know him at all, today is the only day you have to take care of the matter.

The present moment is the only address you have. Embrace the now. It is glorious. *Now* is the only address you can fully own. Plow the present moment and sow it with tomorrow's harvest. Plant what you will, or let it lay fallow with dreaming. You may conquer a habit in the present land of *now*. You may apologize to a wounded ally and restore a golden friendship only in the time at hand. You may call to God even now and ask his blessing on your visions. *Now* is rich with possibility.

The gold lies in today. All other prospecting is fruitless. The treasure of now lies under your feet. Dig down, now. It is a mistake to presume that the gold you must dig for today will lie near the surface tomorrow. The gold is in the moment. Meet God, now. Dig.

Prayer
Lord Jesus,
I have wasted so much of my life
worrying about problems that never came.
I have counted so much on the mine I thought I would discover,
I never saw the gold about my feet.
I want today to be defined in grace,
so that tomorrow has its proper place.
Amen.

How Do You Like That?

Matthew 7:1–2
"Do not judge lest you be judged. For in the way you judge, you will be judged; and by your standard of measure, it will be measured to you."

Have you ever heard vindictive children fighting? With his little fist one child will strike the other and say, "How do you like that?" The other, not to be outdone, will double up his little fist and strike back, crying, "And how do you like that?"

The game persists through life. From childhood we are taught not to let anyone get the best of us. More than that, we are taught that to stay on top, we must get the best of others. The older we get, the less prone we are to hurt others with our fists. We graduate to more mature kinds of playing "How do you like that?" Some grown-ups lash back with judgment, and others slap with gossip.

These judgments, once dispersed, are impossible to gather back up. During medieval times gossip was often called "regathering feathers." In those days pillows were stuffed with feathers. Gossip was seen as the event of taking one of those feather pillows to the steeple of the church and ripping it open. Just as those minute feathers would settle out and over the entire community, the villagers could see that they could never be gathered again.

So it is with hasty judgments. You can never regather all your "How do you like thats." They exist to wound and destroy for life. Do not hide behind the cliché that "sticks and stones can break the bones, but words can never hurt you." How false! It is words that hurt the most. Words destroy and cut into the soft, tender flesh of our self-respect. Sticks and stones bruise outwardly, but words can excise the heart and leave life shattered for years.

Do not judge. It is quite possible that the ones you would like to judge are wrong, but leave their assessment and criticism to God alone. After all, is it fair to level criticism at those who are clearly guilty? They may deserve it, but remember that they may not know me as Savior. Be generous with those who have not called me Lord.

Will judging others ever make you feel better about yourself? In cutting others down, will you really rise in your own gloating self-esteem? No. It is a sad and spurious self-esteem we try to gain by judging others.

There is a better recipe for feeling good about yourself. Love those you would like to judge. Loving is a dear physician, who treats the soul with instant health. When you affirm others, a wonderful therapy will heal your own soul. Instead of seeing the faults in others, you will see *your* own. Then the judgment you would have given others will touch your own belligerence with grace. No one else will be injured, and you will be healed.

Prayer
Lord Jesus,
I give up this foolish game of one-upmanship.
"How do you like that?" is not an appropriate game for those
*   who've seen the cross.*
I must not measure others as their judge.
Come heal my caustic soul of every grudge.
Amen.

Abundance

Luke 6:38

"Give, and it will be given to you; good measure, pressed down, shaken together, running over, they will pour into your lap. For by your standard of measure it will be measured to you in return."

As you give, you will be blessed. Earth's shabby banking is done only in the small ciphers of doubting disciples with grudging mathematics.

Here is the truth behind the banking of the heart. God ordained people to be happy only when they are channels of wealth and not repositories. How many millionaires have you known who wrote books on the meaningful life? That's because meaning for some millionaires consists only in how much they own. Yet happiness, like meaning, always eludes them. They cannot be happy with what they have because it only reminds them of how much they still do not possess. Ask a millionaire how many dollars it would take to make him truly happy and he will answer, "Just one more."

So those who appear to have all really have nothing, because they never have quite enough. Those missionaries who serve in the poorest of world countries have experienced a glorious phenomenon. They must be very careful in complimenting the slender holdings of a family in their flock. For if they compliment some poor family's single possession of worth, the family will likely give them whatever they have complimented. What's a missionary to do? To receive this single, prized possession seems to completely disinherit their impoverished benefactors. Still, the only way for the poor to feel rich is to see themselves as the channel of wealth. Do you want real treasure? Give till you feel wealthy. To feel really rich, you may have to give a lot.

Remember Good Friday. All I owned was taken away. Even my coat became the sport of gamblers. Some say I died naked and bereft. Nonsense! What I really owned was being held on deposit just one world away. I had given everything to gain the treasure I sought most: my Father's pleasure.

Do you want such treasure? Then rehearse the art of giving. Use the biggest scoop you can find to shovel your resources into the treasury of God. Then stand back and wait for the avalanche of blessings.

Prayer
Lord Jesus,
I do not want to save and scrimp my way
*   to utter poverty of soul.*
I'd rather teach my world that to have everything
*   is to give it all away.*
Only what I keep will make me poor.
Here! Take my bank account of poverty.
I trade it all for heaven's currency.
Amen.

Seeing Well Enough for Eye Inspection

Matthew 7:3–5

"And why do you look at the speck that is in your brother's eye, but do not notice the log that is in your own eye? Or how can you say to your brother, 'Let me take the speck out of your eye,' and behold, the log is in your own eye? You hypocrite, first take the log out of your own eye, and then you will see clearly to take the speck out of your brother's eye."

How clear are other people's faults and how obscure our own. Once a blind man, having a heavy schedule for the day, rose early. He had gotten dressed so quickly that when he stepped out into the morning commerce, he still had his comb sticking in his hair. As he walked through his world, he began to condemn the loud talk of the people around him. He congratulated himself that he was not as ill-tempered as the quarrelsome hagglers in the marketplace. He felt good in his heart that he was not as boisterous as those who pushed and elbowed their way around him. He enjoyed feeling superior to those he secretly condemned.

While he thus gloried in his own intellectual superiority, he ran his hand across his hair to discover, with horror, that he had left his comb in his hair when he had dressed to go to work. He was suddenly washed with healthy shame. It is dangerous to try to pick the speck out of others' eyes with the logs of condemnation in our own.

Let us talk about healthy shame. Healthy shame is not that which we seek to project on others, making them feel guilty because they lack our excellence. Healthy shame is that which we inflict on ourselves. The sweetest words in the ears of our heavenly Father are, "Oh, God, forgive me for being so much less than I supposed myself to be." When you are busy criticizing someone else's faults, remember that there could be a comb in your hair.

Remember the elegant church lady who had a louse on her hat? She was in her own mind the very picture of cultural refinement. In her icy sophistication, she presumed herself queen of all the "underlings" in her church. Her presumption held no mercy for the unsophisticated. But a small insect—vile and unacceptable—cavorting on the brim of her ego eradicated her right to judge.

So let us be careful in our practice of Christian opthamology. Blind opthamologists can complicate the saving work of God. We are never doctor enough to pick a speck from the blinded eyes of others! It takes a good eye to see what's wrong with a bad one.

Prayer
Lord Jesus,
I must confess the sin
of trying to help others see
when I can't read your eye chart.
How arrogant I have been
in presuming my vision clear enough
to prescribe glasses for others.
Wash my clouded sight with honest mind,
and give me grace to see I too am blind.
Amen.

The Aesthetics of the Sty

Matthew 7:6

"Do not give what is holy to dogs, and do not throw your pearls before swine, lest they trample them under their feet, and turn and tear you to pieces."

Hogs are not good at aesthetics. A pigsty is a poor place to have your pearls evaluated. Understand spiritual values for what they are. Many is the young college woman who, entering the instruction of an avant-garde professor, must listen while the worldly-wise philosopher shreds her Christian worldviews. She then leaves class emotionally destroyed. All that she learned to cherish in church has been dragged through the sloughs of academic logic. She weeps in shame that she has no answers to offer the intellectual assassin of her faith.

Further, she remembers her parents and how they too believe all that the professor has scoffed at. Now she must also despise what her parents have taught her, or even worse, what she believes her parents are. Her mind gathers its hurt against her parents' naiveté. How could they have believed such simple, unprovable doctrines? Worse, how could they have taught her such "nonsense"?

What can regather such a heart? What will put Humpty Dumpty back together again? There is but one great doctrine. Keep your pearls out of pigpens. Swine are not jewelers. Feel only pity for those who try to make the great mysteries of faith perform for polygraphs. Mystery cannot be explained in any of the halls of logic. Do not take your treasures to the sty. Pigs do not esteem elegance.

Do not misunderstand me. Scholars are not pigs in the sense of their worth to God. God loves atheists with the same ardor that he loves the redeemed. But scholars may be pigs in the sense that their value system has not kept touch with the mystery of godliness. A pig's chief crime is not that he doesn't recognize the wealth of pearls, but that he is addicted to his love of the sty. Pigs are by nature pigs. They cannot transcend their piggyness to contemplate beauty and meaning. Every pig has a narrow focus that never moves beyond loving the mire that cools him and the swill that makes him fat. Academic atheists have stayed too long within the confining boundaries of their little sciences.

Truth is vast, and nobody's a specialist at everything. A janitor who prays is a better person to learn faith from than a physicist who doesn't. A doubting biologist may be less a specialist on the mystery of godliness than a praying child. Your pearls are your faith. Never give it to those who do not treasure pearls.

Prayer
> Lord Jesus,
> I want to meet the atheist who challenges me
>   and my faith
>   as someone whose knowledge only qualifies him to speak narrowly.
> I want never to forget he may be too focused on academic logic
>   to have the whole picture.
> And old men who have prayed through pain and night
>   are scholars with another kind of light.
> Amen.

Truth Hunger

Matthew 7:7–8

"Ask, and it shall be given to you; seek, and you shall find; knock, and it shall be opened to you. For everyone who asks receives, and he who seeks finds, and to him who knocks it shall be opened."

There is but one appetite that supremely matters: seeking after God. There is but one eternally damning human sin: not seeking after God. The apostle Paul wrote, "The wrath of God is being revealed from heaven against all the godlessness and wickedness of men who suppress the truth by their wickedness, since what may be known about God is plain to them, because God has made it plain to them. For since the creation of the world God's invisible qualities—his eternal power and divine nature—have been clearly seen, being understood from what has been made, so that men are without excuse" (Rom. 1:18–20). Do not think the apostle too harsh. Those ignorant of God commit the same sin as those who know him. It is not the sin of being ignorant that condemns humankind before the throne of God. It's the sin of being content in ignorance.

The sin of the lost is the sin of the saved. It is the sin of the lost not to seek to understand more about the God they do not know. It is the chief sin of the saved not to want to understand more about God than they do know. The ignorant, according to the apostle, are not damned because of their ignorance. They can look around and see that the world has been made by the Creator. Seeing the little and the obvious, they sin by not wanting to know more about God. Both the saved and the lost are too content with their partial knowledge.

The world perishes not because grace is in short supply, but because it considers grace of no importance.

What do you suppose God has been doing all through the long centuries? He has been sitting upon the throne, waiting for the hungry rap of those who genuinely desire him.

Come to him asking. He has answers that will turn your questions into doorways of everlasting truth.

Come to him seeking. He will not hide himself.

Come knocking. He is standing at the door, eager to open it and fold you into the glory of his presence.

See how quickly God answers. It is because you are hungry to know me, find me, and enter my embrace. Such simple hungers wake the angels to dancing. Hurry, then, to my Father! Ask. Seek. Knock.

Prayer
Lord Jesus,
Do you hear my feeble knocking?
  I have always knocked too lightly,
    afraid I would wake God from his napping
    and find him irritated with me.
Oh, may I delight Him by eager knocking.
I'll loudly rap, create a noisy din,
  to hear my Lover cry, "My child, come in!"
Amen.

The Golden Rule

Matthew 7:12
"Therefore, however you want people to treat you, so treat them, for this is the Law and the Prophets."

It has been well said, "If the mothers of the world were allowed to plan the battles, all wars would cease." Most of the pain inflicted on the weeping is ordered by people who have none. The depraved evils of the Inquisition were ordered by healthy priests. Witch-burnings seem fun only to those who hold the matches. Sadism is enjoyed only by torturers who are getting a warm bath and a neck-rub every night.

Once in a land ruled by a tyrant, a young field worker committed an indiscretion during a state harvest. The boy had stolen a handful of grain for his starving parents. When he was caught, he was sentenced to die in a small bamboo cage. In this cage he could neither comfortably stand nor lie down. Cramped into this fetal position he died, whimpering for water and covered with ants and his own excrement. Death was the only mercy he could pray for. His weeping parents, for whom he had stolen the grain, looked on from a distance, praying for him to die.

Would you understand the true meaning of the golden rule? Don't seek an ethicist to explain its high morality. Such atrocities will exist as long as there are people. Study the injustices that others bring upon you. Celebrate that pain. Only as you suffer from pain will you learn the golden rule. Then you will not nurture vengeance so that you may someday get even. Your hurt will teach you a generosity of spirit. You will determine never to be that kind of person. You will resolve never to inflict on anyone else what you have suffered.

To the suffering parents of the youth who stole grain for them, I offer my own mother's understanding. She, like them, once watched her son die. She felt the sword that Simeon predicted thirty years earlier. Her suffering at the cross pierced her own soul through (Luke 2:35). Ah, poor suffering parents, it is the pierced who understand the piercing. It is only the wronged who know how grievous wrong really is. Let hurt be your teacher. Then what others have done to you may cause you to pledge with honest tears: I will never, never, never do that to another.

Prayer
  Lord Jesus,
  Let me live in continual rehearsal
    of those hurts I've felt at other's hands,
    not to get even with the world
    but so that my memory will make me be an agent of gentle love.
  I prize the scars from conflicts I've not won
    and pledge: No wounds like mine to anyone.
  Amen.

Two Roads

Matthew 7:13–14

"Enter by the narrow gate; for the gate is wide, and the way is broad that leads to destruction, and many are those who enter by it. For the gate is small, and the way is narrow that leads to life, and few are those who find it."

It's easy to tell if you're on the road to heaven. The way is not crowded. The broad road, on the other hand, is full of people whose values are less than admirable. Further, the broad road is marked with the spirit of a parade.

Rehearse the way of discipline. The words *disciple* and *discipline* come from the same word. Grace is God's gift to you, but your gift to him is discipline. Grace, being God's part, is easy for you, while it cost God everything. I came to earth and died to pay the price for your salvation. Grace, like any gift, is free to the receiver. But oh, how such gifts cost the giver!

Discipline is your gift to God. For the gift of discipline that you give God means that all the prayer, ministry, and sacrifice you give him comes from your own desire. God will never put a revolver to your head and order you to pray, read the Bible, or minister to others. If you ever do these things, they will come from your overwhelming desire to please God.

Many sing "Amazing Grace," but few have the honesty to sing "Amazing Discipline." Yet it is discipline that is truly amazing, for disciplined believers are hard to find. They are as rare as diamonds.

Apart from the size of the crowd on the road, there is one other infallible guide to distinguishing the roads between heaven and hell. The road to heaven is rigorous and requiring. The discipline of holiness causes the road to rise in steep ascent. The broad road that leads elsewhere is comfortably wide and gradual in its descent.

The disciplines of the narrow road are crammed with meaning. So come to the upper road. The altitude is glorious. The mists roll back enough to let you see the towers of heaven through the undiluted light. The music swells even as you climb. You have my promise: at the end of the road are God's grand gates. Those gates swing open just beyond the gold pavilions.

Prayer

Lord Jesus,
Conversion is that fork where routes divide.
I'm glad I took the road less traveled.
For the journey is direct
    to the only place where I can live forever.
I bask in golden light and thinner air,
    I see sometimes that city built foursquare.
Amen.

The Art of Fruit Inspecting

Matthew 7:15–20

"Beware of the false prophets, who come to you in sheep's clothing, but inwardly are ravenous wolves. You will know them by their fruits. Grapes are not gathered from thorn bushes, nor figs from thistles, are they? Even so, every good tree bears good fruit; but the bad tree bears bad fruit. A good tree cannot produce bad fruit, nor can a bad tree produce good fruit. Every tree that does not bear good fruit is cut down and thrown into the fire. So then, you will know them by their fruits."

It is often said that Christians are not permitted to be judges, only fruit inspectors. There is some truth in this skewered proverb. How are a judge and a fruit inspector different? A judge makes rulings and offers stern sentences and reprimands. A fruit inspector merely acknowledges that the quality of the fruit passes or fails.

Do not be misled. There is no Christianity without values. Some deeds are bad and some good. Some are sinful and some not. In this moral-less world, some will tell you that you must decide on your own which values are right and which are wrong. But it is not so. There is right and wrong. Wrong things, willfully committed, are sins. They resulted in my death. You must repent of those wrong things if you hope to acquire the life of holiness.

There are things that are always wrong and things that are always right. There are values that are always bad and those that are always good. God gave his Ten Commandments so that you do not have to decide your own moral code. Those values are constant from generation to generation, century to century, millennium to millennium. So you do not have to work very hard to tell if a person is moral or immoral. A good person always produces good fruit. Such a person is like a good tree. Commend the tree. Eat of that fruit. Desire to be like that tree.

It has been well said that we are what we eat. If you sample the illicit or the lurid, you will become what you eat. If you eat pornography, you will become a person driven by unmanageable lust. If you eat power, you may end up destroying those you encounter with your own possessive agenda. The key is your diet. Never taste what you do not want to become. Eat only what is good.

Prayer
Lord Jesus,
Knowing right from wrong is not the hard part.
It is eating what I know is good for me that seems so difficult to do.
I want to please you by distinguishing right from wrong.
I want to ingest only that which I know is good for me.
This is the feast the hungry heart knows best,
the wondrous, holy fruit of righteousness.
Amen.

What's Done and What's Named

Matthew 7:21–23

"Not everyone who says to Me, 'Lord, Lord,' will enter the kingdom of heaven; but he who does the will of My Father who is in heaven. Many will say to Me on that day, 'Lord, Lord, did we not prophesy in Your name, and in Your name cast out demons, and in Your name perform many miracles?' And then I will declare to them, 'I never knew you; DEPART FROM ME, YOU WHO PRACTICE LAWLESSNESS.'"

Heaven is not achieved by chanting a Christian mantra. Nor does anyone arrive there because of some "magic" spirituality. Some use religious words as though they believe that their sacred rhetoric will swing open the gates of heaven.

There are no special deeds that will achieve heaven, either. Even ministry to the sick or the imprisoned will not. There are those who have performed such deeds in the name of social agencies or service clubs.

Heaven knows only one language that will offer admittance. It is the language of relationship. Heaven opens to those who transcend their confidence in special words and deeds. Heaven is achieved by longing. Those who run through the high gates with open arms are welcome. These don't want to be celebrated for the ministry they have given God. Their need recommends them simply because they are unfulfilled without him. They have never sought heaven as a way out of the maze of their lower choices. These see heaven as the dwelling place of God. Where God dwells in his fullness is the only place they would ever want to live.

Those who call me "Lord" to flatter me will never find my acceptance. On the contrary, those who call me "Lord" out of utter need and acceptance will be welcome in heaven forever. Those who have ministered in my name will, of course, find heaven a delightful place to live.

Consider heaven's code of acceptance, and distinguish between being loving and lawless. For there are those who all through their lives did good things for bad reasons. They wanted to find people who would make over them for their heroic and showy goodness. These people shall not live in heaven.

Heaven is for those who saw a needy world and agreed to be my hands and feet in ministry. These have but to whisper my name and the angels will come to attention.

Prayer
Lord Jesus,
When I say "Lord," help me to mean
    "I love you."
When I tell anyone of the good I've done,
    help me to say,
    "It is for Him alone my life knows any merit."
I want to live my life so that my every word
    seems like an anthem offered to my Lord.
Amen.

Making the Wisdom of Christ Life's Foundation

Matthew 7:24–27

"Therefore everyone who hears these words of Mine, and acts upon them, may be compared to a wise man, who built his house upon the rock. And the rain descended, and the floods came, and the winds blew, and burst against that house; and yet it did not fall, for it had been founded upon the rock. And everyone who hears these words of Mine, and does not act upon them, will be like a foolish man, who built his house upon the sand. And the rain descended, and the floods came, and the winds blew, and burst against that house; and it fell, and great was its fall."

No building or life is more secure than its foundation. When the great cathedrals were built, their transepts often rose fourteen stories above the cathedral floor. The buildings took centuries to complete. Only the descendants of those who began the church ever saw it brought to completion. A whole generation of foundation building was required before the superstructure of the church was ever started. Some foundations required eighty years to build. The builders wanted to be sure the foundations went down far enough into the ground to support walls and roofs that would not be complete for centuries.

To be sure, it is more exhilarating to set the capstone on a spire eight hundred years later. It is more fulfilling to cry, "It is finished!" than "It has begun." Still, if those who laid the foundations did not take their work seriously, there would have been no finishing cry later.

Do you love to worship me? Do you find great exhilaration in singing my praise? Praise is the pinnacle work of the Christian life. But do not despise the foundational work of discipleship.

Without foundations, all the exhilaration of your private worship and praise will be a soil too spongy on which to build the higher towers of adoration. The sand beneath undisciplined holiness will dissolve, and you will fail.

Dig down into your soul with the spade of Bible reading and prayer. Then pour the steely strata of studied endurance under your frail life. Reinforce your foundling hopes with the iron rods of discipline. Then will the tower of joyous praise rise above the strong foundations of your inner life. Then the world will look at you and see me.

Prayer
> *Lord Jesus,*
> *I want to be sure*
>   *I base my towering dreams upon*
>   *deep and secure foundations.*
> *Help me see that*
>   *my life can only reach as high up*
>   *as your power reaches down, making certain the piers*
>   *of my insecurity.*
> *I laid my dreams as one foundation grand,*
>   *I set a granite pier in unsure sand.*
> *Amen.*

God Has Visited His People

Luke 7:11–16

And it came about soon afterwards, that He went to a city called Nain; and . . . behold, a dead man was being carried out, the only son of his mother, and she was a widow; . . . He felt compassion for her, and said to her, "Do not weep." And He came up and touched the coffin; and the bearers came to a halt. And He said, "Young man, I say to you, arise!" And the dead man sat up, and began to speak. And Jesus gave him back to his mother. And fear gripped them all, and they began glorifying God, saying, "A great prophet has arisen among us!" and, "God has visited His people!"

Have you wept because of loss? You did not weep alone. My Father cries when you cry. In heaven my Father will at last wipe away all tears.

I was torn by the grief of the little woman I saw one day in Nain. Bent by despair, she followed the coffin of her son. Her shoulders were rounded, heaving with the convulsions of her brokenness. Her pain stabbed at me. She was a widow who had already wept at the grave of her husband. Now she was grieving again.

I acted.

I had the power to do it, for God holds the power of life, and I am his only begotten Son. It was easy for me to say, "Young man, I say to you, arise." He did.

How odd to see a corpse sit up, surrendering his stillness. He stared, blinking into the sunlight, to make his eyes adjust. He smiled. That smile sent chills down the spines of all who followed the coffin. They gasped in fear. The uncanny event froze the crowd and raised the hair upon the neck.

Their fear gave way to wonder as he swung his legs over the side of the coffin and stepped down onto the ground. Their awe was swallowed up in joy and wild applause as he approached his mother. The deadness in her came suddenly alive. A great gift had been given to her.

Someone cried, "God has visited his people." Rejoicing broke around the miracle. Grief had taken off its muddy boots, and human joy danced cleanly in the streets.

Have you grieved? Are you now in grief? Remember, you are not alone. God loves a broken heart. Someday he will say to the loved one you have lost, "Arise." For everyone over whom you've cried will one day be restored to you. And God will wipe away all tears, and you will sing throughout the endless years of eternity, "Indeed, God has visited his people."

Prayer
Lord Jesus,
I have wept at many gravesides.
Yet because of your victory
*   I've never had to sorrow*
*   as those who have no hope.*
I cannot wait till I caress the skies,
*   to hear you command, "I've come! Arise!"*
Amen.

Are You He?

Luke 7:18–23

And the disciples of John reported to him about all these things. And summoning two of his disciples, John sent them to the Lord, saying, "Are You the Expected One, or do we look for someone else?" And when the men had come to Him, they said, "John the Baptist has sent us to You, saying, 'Are You the Expected One, or do we look for someone else?'" At that very time He cured many people of diseases and afflictions and evil spirits; and He granted sight to many who were blind. And He answered and said to them, "Go and report to John what you have seen and heard: the BLIND RECEIVE SIGHT, the lame walk, the lepers are cleansed, and the deaf hear, the dead are raised up, the POOR HAVE THE GOSPEL PREACHED TO THEM. And blessed is he who keeps from stumbling over Me."

There is only one way to determine if I am the Christ. You must pull the answer from your heart. "What if? What if this Jesus is not the Christ? What if I am forever locked away and cannot serve that cause for which I was born? If Jesus is not the Christ, and I never get out of this prison, what has been the purpose of my life?" These were John's questions in prison.

So John sent his disciples to ask, "Are you he?" He knew, of course, that the question could only be answered either yes or no. I was the true Christ, but I could not convince him with a mere "Yes, sir, I am! I would swear it on a stack of Torahs!" I knew I could not answer this question for John. John had to answer this question for himself. My being the Christ is the faith question that no one can answer for another. Each person must believe or disbelieve, find or lose the affirmation within his own soul.

"Are you he?"

I answered the only way I could. "Look around you, John. See what may be seen and then decide yourself. Wherever I pass, I leave the cold, dead world in a state of resurrection. The crippled run. The mute are singing. The dead are spoiling the dignity of their funerals by leaping from their caskets. The poor, who rarely get any good news, have the good news preached to them regularly. Prisoners are free. Joy is camping in the souls of the disconsolate. You tell me, John: am I he?"

Have you ever had doubts about me? I cannot answer you any more than I could answer John. When doubts come, do not ask me if I am the Christ. Look around you. You were once self-willed with no hope. You were once living only for your crumbling career. Once your life was out of control and going nowhere. Sin clotted your soul with dark entanglements.

Now you are free. Now you have hope.

Tell me, am I he?

Prayer
Lord Jesus,
I am grateful
*   that your life is real enough*
*   to supply all the evidence I need to trust*
*   you most implicitly for life.*
I see all that you've done in grace achieved
*   and I cry out in faith, "Lord, I believe."*
Amen.

A Voice for the Ages in a Desert Place

Luke 7:24–28

And when the messengers of John had left, He began to speak to the multitudes about John, "What did you go out into the wilderness to look at? A reed shaken by the wind? But what did you go out to see? A man dressed in soft clothing? Behold, those who are splendidly clothed and live in luxury are found in royal palaces. But what did you go out to see? A prophet? Yes, I say to you, and one who is more than a prophet. This is the one about whom it is written, 'BEHOLD, I SEND MY MESSENGER BEFORE YOUR FACE, WHO WILL PREPARE YOUR WAY BEFORE YOU.' I say to you, among those born of women, there is no one greater than John; yet he who is least in the kingdom of God is greater than he."

John was a rustic trumpet at the end of a grand oratorio. Prophets long before John had announced my coming. This symphony of the prophets resounded with the plaintive poetry of Jeremiah and the high literature of Isaiah. Elijah wrote no literature. Still, my Father chose Elijah's rural demeanor in the form of John the Baptist to walk once again the wilderness of Jordan. John was an evidence that my kingdom would be born among the rustic.

In his own estimation, John was the least of all these prophets. What the other prophets had seen only in the distance, John announced to be here already.

I praised John as the greatest of all who were ever naturally born, but with this reservation; it could be that you were born to be even greater. The key to your exaltation lies in your "leastness." Do you want to know the farthest reaches of my love and own a pedestal in heaven above all the prophets? Then find a wilderness where you may know and love God. In such a desert place, desire to be nothing that I may be all.

Desire oneness with my Father. Out of this craving will come your self-definition—your assignment. We cannot find our calling while we seek some personal platform of recognition. There are two kinds of gifts we should want to give God. The second and most inferior are these gifts we take from our material blessings to offer Him. The first, and much preferred, is the gift of our yieldedness.

This was John's primary gift, his yieldedness. His fiery sermons, his royal rebukes to Herodias, his self-deprecating dress or diet: these courageous gifts grew out of John's need for God. From these gifts came a greatness he never saw. Be blind to your own excellence, and your usefulness will never be measured.

> *Prayer*
> *Lord Jesus,*
> *Make me a lonely trumpet*
> *to sound out unmistakably my yieldedness.*
> *Life exists to tell the world*
> *you are God's only Son*
> *and, best of all,*
> *my glorious Lord.*
> *Rejoice, all you who hurt, the Savior comes.*
> *Look, all you blind, and all you feeble, run.*
> *Amen.*

Children Playing with the Jewels of God

Matthew 11:16–19

"But to what shall I compare this generation? It is like children sitting in the market places, who call out to the other children, and say, 'We played the flute for you, and you did not dance; we sang a dirge, and you did not mourn.' For John came neither eating nor drinking, and they say, 'He has a demon!' The Son of Man came eating and drinking, and they say, 'Behold, a gluttonous man and a drunkard, a friend of tax-gatherers and sinners!' Yet wisdom is vindicated by her deeds."

There are times when the majesty of God comes to the spiritually immature—like children who greet magnificence with hopscotch. John was a man of God who heralded my coming. Yet some of those who heard him announce my Kingdom said he had a demon. In this criticism God's reaching love was despised.

John lived a solitary life of committed prayer. He lived alone in the jungles of the Jordan. He never drank wine or ate rich foods. He was committed to the simple life. The Pharisees criticized his holy and separated life.

I, on the other hand, lived in towns and cities. I lived in the middle of crowds of people so that I could reach to save them. Both John and I were criticized. Because I loved immoral party-goers, I too was called a sinner.

How did I view these phony critics of reality? They were like children who were playing marriage and funeral. Real weddings and real funerals are times of utter commitment and finality. But children in every generation sometimes dress up in their parents' clothing to make pretense at marriage or death.

While I walked on earth, the Pharisees looked past my Incarnation and judged me by the mere rules of human convention. I endured it all. I had to become a man. It is impossible to save the blind unless you understand the night. Nor could I redeem the immature without walking in the midst of children.

The Pharisees thought themselves scholars but would not look beyond the rigidity of their stingy doctrines. While they played their churchy games, I came among them, died, and rose again. And yet they were so preoccupied with their consuming petty theologies that they never saw me.

Are you open to those great truths that shatter your comfort level? Love what is holy. Never play petty games when human redemption is at stake.

Prayer
Lord Jesus,
How wondrous free is your salvation.
I cost you all,
*   but you came to me completely packaged*
*   in your costly grace,*
*   yet altogether free.*
I want to praise the bearer of such grace,
*   not play like children in the marketplace.*
Amen.

The Sin of Seeing God
and Remaining Unchanged

Matthew 11:20–21

> *Then He began to reproach the cities in which most of His miracles were done, because they did not repent. "Woe to you, Chorazin! Woe to you, Bethsaida! For if the miracles had occurred in Tyre and Sidon which occurred in you, they would have repented long ago in sackcloth and ashes."*

Here is a tale of three cities: Chorazin, Bethsaida, and Capernaum. These infamous towns saw the hand of God and remained unchanged.

I walked through many cities and tried to touch their deadness with life. Yet many of these cities remained unchanged. Cities are unfeeling centers of humanity where people are murdered on the streets and their cries for help or pity go unheard.

I walk daily in every city. Everywhere I go I find a calloused urban hardness. What shall we say to this?

Woe to you, Chorazin, Bethsaida, Capernaum.

Woe to you, modern cities of unfeeling people.

A compassionate woman once rescued a sick young homeless woman and took her into her small home to nurse her back to health. The nurse often kissed this young woman as though the power of her affection alone might heal. As she ministered with such kisses she would often say to herself, "Who knows how much healing there is in a kiss of pity? Who knows but by such a kiss I may bring both rescue and new usefulness to such a one?" On one occasion as she kissed this fevered young woman, the patient came to awareness. She spoke from her delirium. "I thank you," she wept, "nobody's done that since my mother died."

Ministry to those who need God is the only evidence the needy may have that there actually is a God. Yet the busy and self-important come and go unchanged.

Woe to you, Chorazin, Bethsaida, Capernaum!

Woe to all other cities who are only Chorazin, Bethsaida, and Capernaum, named something else! It is a sin to know that I am in your streets, saving and healing, and yet to remain unchanged.

Prayer
Lord Jesus,
Help me look upon
the world of beauty that's fashioned
in your holy fingers
and promise you
beneath such canopies of nature
I'll never doubt you.
Help me see what
beautiful souls you fashion from
ugly but repentant lives.
And seeing all you have made evident,
I can but bid my sinful soul repent.
Amen.

The Easy Yoke for the Weary Soul

Matthew 11:28–30

"Come to Me, all who are weary and heavy-laden, and I will give you rest. Take My yoke upon you, and learn from Me, for I am gentle and humble in heart; and YOU SHALL FIND REST FOR YOUR SOULS. For My yoke is easy, and My load is light."

Are you weary? Are you worn with a draining fatigue of soul that never seems to be relieved? Are you sick and tired of being sick and tired? Come unto me; I am the Sabbath Christ. I want to infuse you with such strength that you will understand the truth of Isaiah's words: "Those who hope in the LORD will renew their strength. They will soar on wings like eagles; they will run and not grow weary, they will walk and not be faint" (Isa. 40:31).

As I have told you where to find rest, I can also tell you why you are tired. You are tired because you stand beneath your yoke alone. You push against the heavy chafing wood all by yourself. You claim I am your Lord, but you are too much lord of your own burdensome affairs. A certain Bedouin once thought to save his camel by carrying himself the burden he would have put on his beast. Are you like that heavily laden man? Are you struggling to carry the heavy bundles of your own grief to save the back of God? Oh, how foolishly you seek to spare God such labor. Lay aside the heavy gatherings of your own agendas. Put down this minute your staggering determination to be "self-made." God longs to give you a joyous lightness of being.

Cast all your cares on me, for I care for you (1 Peter 5:7). Do not struggle with your yoke alone. Above all, lay aside the heavy burden of getting ahead. It is too much for you, and it is pointless. Stop bragging that you are a self-made person. This boast alone causes your struggle. My yoke is easy, my burden light.

Come to me and feel the strain of your struggles flow away. Dissolve your struggles in my sufficiency. Say like the refreshed apostle, I truly can do all things through Christ who strengthens me (Phil. 4:13). Then will you sing with new strength, "My God will meet all your needs according to his glorious riches" (Phil. 4:19). The yoke is not only light. It is pure joy. Both his manna and my joy are fresh every morning.

Prayer
Lord Jesus,
So often I am soul fatigued
and bear a lonely, heavy yoke.
How needy. How lonely.
How much I long for your renewing strength.
When trial and turmoil crowd me with distress
help me to fly to you, to accept your rest.
Amen.

Gratitude in Tears

Luke 7:36–38

Now one of the Pharisees was requesting Him to dine with him. And He entered the Pharisee's house, and reclined at the table. And behold, there was a woman in the city who was a sinner; and when she learned that He was reclining at the table in the Pharisee's house, she brought an alabaster vial of perfume, and standing behind Him at His feet, weeping, she began to wet His feet with her tears, and kept wiping them with the hair of her head, and kissing His feet, and anointing them with the perfume.

When we understand our unworthiness and God's great grace, we weep. We cannot help but prostrate ourselves before our benefactor and let our tears give witness to our gratitude. Consider this woman. Her moral reputation was poor. She had crashed a party given by those who were above her social caste. Then she dared to come in among the elite and wash my feet with her tears.

Those who were there saw her as contemptuous. But blessed are the needy, for they are so overwhelmed by the goodness of God that they must shout their alleluias openly. One thing is sure: to feel sinfulness washed with the forgiveness of God leaves no one silent. Touched with such a lightness of being, we must all wake the town and tell the people. We must "crash the party" and praise him who is the great Forgiver.

Propriety and true joy are rarely found in the same place at the same time. Nor are high liturgy and utter brokenness. But God inhabits the real far more often than the rehearsed. So the sinful woman came, overwhelmed by a loving God who had forgiven her. Her alleluias were unstoppable.

I much enjoyed her unwelcome presence among the Pharisees. They were all set to talk theology with me when she broke into the room. She *did* theology. *Talking it* was not enough for her. I am sure that had she not come, we would have talked about the theological ins and outs of intellectual forgiveness and thankfulness. The Pharisees would have used the right footnotes and quoted the right sources.

But triumph held the day! Real sin and real forgiveness interrupted their academics. All who were there learned sin and forgiveness as more than doctrine.

How is it with you? Are you as interested in a religious discussion as you are in God? Would you rather teach a lesson on forgiveness than have it ravage you with open praise?

Prayer
  Lord Jesus,
  I want to be
    more exhibitionist in my
    repentant heart.
  Not to be sharing for
    the sake of showiness
    but to let everyone know
    how glorious it is to be forgiven.
  I must declare your grace with gratitude
    and let my thank yous be my attitude.
  Amen.

The Women of God

Luke 8:2–3

And also some women who had been healed of evil spirits and sicknesses: Mary who was called Magdalene, from whom seven demons had gone out, and Joanna the wife of Chuza, Herod's steward, and Susanna, and many others who were contributing to their support out of their private means.

Every day women were the most consistent of my supporters. Luke's glorious Gospel begs us to shout of the triumph of those women who supported me.

I do not want to speak of angry feminism in this day. Often women have a right to be angry, for they have been pushed aside and held down in a long-dominated masculine world. But for the moment let's not any of us talk—men or women—of seizing all we have a right to seize. Instead, let us talk about the voluntary laying aside of those things that we have the right to own.

Here is the glory of the women in Luke's Gospel. More than all the other Gospel writers, Luke seemed to sense their utter importance to my life and ministry. Why were these women so important? Because they were willing to lay down their lives for my sake. They did not argue their right to run the Kingdom of God. They simply demonstrated the submission that ought to belong to either gender.

Consider my mother, Mary. While she is not mentioned in Luke 8, so much of Luke's Gospel is clearly privy to information only my mother could have known: the birth stories, the reaction of the Nazarenes. So it is not unthinkable to see Luke's Gospel as Mary's Gospel—at least in part.

So then let us not speak of the great men of God without speaking of the great women of God. It is even as Paul says in Galatians 3:28–29: "There is neither Jew nor Greek, slave nor free, male nor female, for you are all one in Christ Jesus. If you belong to Christ, then you are Abraham's seed, and heirs according to the promise."

Disciples come in both genders! So do martyrs. Those who really love me offer only their commitment as credentials. Never is their gender a barrier to ministry.

Prayer
Lord Jesus,
I know so many women
who follow you in utter adoration.
They have surrendered all,
yet often they have struggled
with their self-esteem.
Father, forgive us when we fail
to honor those whose gender
has sometimes relegated them to second class.
Help me to see that you do not see men and women
as separate kinds of people to be loved in separate ways.
That's how I want to see all people,
just like you do.
The church must gather for your adoration
and cast before your cross discrimination.
Amen.

Distinguishing Good and Evil

Matthew 12:22–26

Then there was brought to Him a demon-possessed man who was blind and dumb, and He healed him, so that the dumb man spoke and saw. And all the multitudes were amazed, and began to say, "This man cannot be the Son of David, can he?" But when the Pharisees heard it, they said, "This man casts out demons only by Beelzebul the ruler of the demons." And knowing their thoughts He said to them, "Any kingdom divided against itself is laid waste; and any city or house divided against itself shall not stand. And if Satan casts out Satan, he is divided against himself; how then shall his kingdom stand?"

I consider the casting out of demons to be the most significant of my miracles. Consider the space that is given to exorcisms in the four Gospels. Demons represent the unlawful incursion of Satan into the sanctity of the human soul. Every human life is sacred. Everyone is made by my Father to celebrate his holiness. What right does the Enemy think he has to invade those lives so loved by God?

It is a confused state of thinking that cannot distinguish good and evil. If a thing is evil, it is not from God. If it is good, it can be from nowhere else. But as simple as this rule is, good men and women sometimes believe that they can do some temporary evil which will, in the end, bring about everlasting good. Do not believe it. No good end ever came from evil means.

The crusades were the monumental failures of those Christians who believed they could make war to establish peace. Pious Christian warriors felt that if they waged death with great effectiveness, they could bring forth life. They tortured unbelievers to the point of madness to get them to confess Christianity. Being flayed alive, many cried out that they did believe in me. The horror of these forced confessions still mark the earth with old, undying hatreds.

It is Satan's greatest lie that he can help us, through acts of evil, to arrive finally at good. Never adopt such logic. Good fruit cannot come from a corrupt tree.

Only righteousness can come from God. The Pharisees were wrong. I could never be so filled with Satan that I would do God's will.

Stand up to your temptations in the power of God. When you have finished, angels will come and minister unto you (Matt. 4:11). You may not see them, but they will be there.

Prayer
Lord Jesus,
I want to avoid
the idea that I can trade
some little lies
to buy some greater truths.
Help me to be a person
who never attempts
to arrive at constant values
with flexible righteousness.
Hell's darkest demons spend the coins of soul
as currency to purchase my control.
Amen.

The Unforgivable Sin

Matthew 12:30–32

"He who is not with Me is against Me; and he who does not gather with Me scatters. Therefore I say to you, any sin and blasphemy shall be forgiven men, but blasphemy against the Spirit shall not be forgiven. And whoever shall speak a word against the Son of Man, it shall be forgiven him; but whoever shall speak against the Holy Spirit, it shall not be forgiven him, either in this age, or in the age to come."

The greatest sins are sins against love. The greatest love is the love of God. Therefore, the unforgivable sin—the greatest sin—is the sin against the love of God.

But what has the Holy Spirit to do with this unforgivable sin? He is the indwelling God. He woos the hearts of human beings in the name of Almighty love. He knocks in my name to seek entrance to your heart. He desires to live in you. To refuse to let him in is the sin of inhospitality to God.

Walk outside on any starry night. Look up into the face of a thousand, unnamed galaxies and sun systems. Realize that he who made all this made you as well. He made you for himself. Tell me now, what right have you to refuse such a grand God his entrance to your lowly heart? What right have you to say no to your Father? Indeed, I stand at the door and knock; if anyone hears me and opens the door, I will come in (Rev. 3:20). Yet nations refuse me, churches refuse me, and individuals refuse me.

Would you refuse me too? To leave me standing outside, while the Spirit begs entrance, is a dangerous refusal. Hell rarely begins in grand and blatant blasphemy but in weak intent. It is not belligerent atheists who fill the halls of hell. It is the good men or women who wanted to know God, but believed that knowing him sometime later would be soon enough. It is the someday saint who arrives in eternity still saying, "Not today, God."

Can you not see this? Blasphemy against the Holy Spirit is not usually some grand and single moment of cursing God. No, it is rather a thousand small denials of "Not now, please." These tiny Lilliputian threads at last stake us down just inside the gates of hell.

Are you guilty of saying no to God? Are you forever slapping the gentle fingers of a reaching Father? He will not enter your heart without your open invitation. Hell has but a small population of grand blasphemers. It is filled mostly with warm procrastinators who never saw their weak intentions as dangerous.

Prayer
Lord Jesus,
The road to eternal separation
rarely begins when we order
Jesus from our lives.
The final barring
of our souls from heaven
comes as we ignore the quiet
rapping of the gentle hand of love.
The only sin beyond the Savior's face
is that which will not yield to love and grace.
Amen.

The Jonah Sign

Matthew 12:38–40

Then some of the scribes and Pharisees answered Him, saying, "Teacher, we want to see a sign from You." But He answered and said to them, "An evil and adulterous generation craves for a sign; and yet no sign shall be given to it but the sign of Jonah the prophet; for just as JONAH WAS THREE DAYS AND THREE NIGHTS IN THE BELLY OF THE SEA MONSTER, so shall the Son of Man be three days and three nights in the heart of the earth."

The hunger to see convincing miracles is always born in the weakness of faith. "Give us a sign," said the Pharisees. "Please, pull some divine rabbit—even a little one—out of your celestial hat and we will believe."

I wanted to say to them, "Yes, magic will convince you, but for how long? Till you doubt another time and need another trick? Will there ever be rabbits enough in my hat to keep you forever running back for more?"

I think not.

"Here only is my sign," I said to them. "As Jonah was in the belly of a huge fish for three days and nights, so shall the Son of Man be in the heart of the earth."

My words were cryptic to them then. Only after that first tomb-splitting Easter would they understand. In the meantime, I refused to give them what they wanted so I could give them what they needed. What they needed was not signs. Signs are like fireworks exploding against a dark sky. We love them. They bring the "oohs and aahs" from spectators. Sadly, however, we are unable to recall their precise form once the sky is black again. We strain to try and "re-feel" what cannot be refelt.

So instead of signs, I have given you one great truth. I am that truth. Those who trust in me and in all I am will be saved. My presence may at times seem less immediate than you would like. When you are torn with grief, I may seem out of reach. Have you not had such moments when you cried and I seemed not to answer?

Of course you have. I ache for you at such times. But do not despair. For in these reaching, racking moments of your awful aloneness, your need will always bring me close. And my closeness will reward you not because you saw a miracle, but because you trusted what cannot be seen.

Faith alone saves, not signs. Therefore, when you pray and cannot feel my nearness, keep on trusting. I will come. Until that time, I give you only that same sign I gave the sign-mongers of the first century—the sign of Jonah. I was dead in the cold earth and came forth in triumph. Behold, I am alive forevermore! Such a sign is all you need. An eternal promise from an eternal Savior is better than a temporary trick.

Prayer
Lord Jesus,
Require our faith.
We want to see these things
that require the deliciousness
of trust.
But we are so frustrated by our doubts.
Excise our fears and drive the demons out.
Amen.

Filling the Cleansed Heart with Clean Things

Matthew 12:43–45

"Now when the unclean spirit goes out of a man, it passes through waterless places, seeking rest, and does not find it. Then it says, 'I will return to my house from which I came'; and when it comes, it finds it unoccupied, swept, and put in order. Then it goes, and takes along with it seven other spirits more wicked than itself, and they go in and live there; and the last state of that man becomes worse than the first. That is the way it will also be with this evil generation."

To exorcise a host of heavy demons brings on a marvelous buoyancy. But beware the exhilaration that comes from this new cleanness. Emptiness is never the point of God's cleansing. He empties us of evil only to fill us with himself. It is a mistake to celebrate too fast or too long that good clean feeling you had when first you came to know me.

See your longing soul as a well-bucket that can be lowered on a long rope in order to bring up clear, cold water from the depths. Neither the bucket nor your soul can be filled beyond the capacity of your emptiness. If you lower the pail into the deep water full of rocks, when you draw it forth you will bring up both water and rocks. If you would have the rising bucket completely full of water when you bring it up, it must be completely empty when you send it down.

God cleansed you so that your emptiness may become a vessel for his use. He wants to refresh the world through your life. God never wants you to celebrate your emptiness but your coming fullness. Only if your cleansing comes with a yearning to be filled can you ever serve him.

Do you see that exorcisms may heal you either terminally or temporally? The choice is yours. If the demons that leave your life are not replaced by his fullness, they will be back. Have you not known some outstanding convert, some secular hero, who came to me purged of a squalid lifestyle? For a while, such cleansed souls acquire more adulation than they received when they were secular heroes. But soon Christian ego only takes the place of the celebrity ego, and no real filling of God takes place. Soon the original devil is back with seven of his friends. Not only is faith abandoned, but the glory of the testimony is gone as well.

Come to me and be clean. Do not leave the altar too soon. Send down the bucket of your need into my cold, deep, pure supply. Let the rope lengthen and descend ever so slowly into the deep influx of God. Then will your empty soul fill with godly substance; and the world that reaches out for my Father will find him in the middle of your life.

Prayer
> *Create in me a clean heart, O God,*
>   *and renew a right spirit within me.*
> *Cast me not away from your presence*
>   *and take not your Holy Spirit from me.*
> *Purge me with hyssop, and clean shall I go.*
> *Wash me, and I shall be whiter than snow.*
> *Amen.*

Who Is Your Family?

Matthew 12:46–50

While He was still speaking to the multitudes, behold, His mother and brothers were standing outside, seeking to speak to Him. And someone said to Him, "Behold, Your mother and Your brothers are standing outside seeking to speak to You." But He answered the one who was telling Him and said, "Who is My mother and who are My brothers?" And stretching out His hand toward His disciples, He said, "Behold, My mother and My brothers! For whoever does the will of My Father who is in heaven, he is My brother and sister and mother."

Families feel together the sting of public scandal. My family knew from the first my own unique role in human redemption. They felt a strong sense of rebuke when so much negative community conversation broke all around me. Still, when the storm of criticism gathered around my ministry, they came to "take me home." "Take me home" really meant "shut me up."

Good Friday was especially hard on them. No one likes to have a convicted felon in the family. I understand how they felt, and yet I yearned for their affirmation in my time of rejection. When the family understands, one can bear all that must be borne. Given a good home life, a person can endure anything.

I experienced much rejection in my life, but none of it hurt more than the knowledge that my family refused to have confidence in me. Judgments within the family are the most damaging to our development.

When families reject us, there is but one alternate course: we must widen our families to those who will accept us and those who will affirm us. It was neither to hurt my mother or my siblings that I turned to the crowd to ask, "Who are my brothers, my sisters, my mother? Who is my family? Those who understand and do the will of God, who reached to me in confidence and faith."

Where do you go to church? Do you prize that church? Let it be your family at those moments when you are emotionally needy. At those moments when you are emotionally secure, let your church be the place where you become a part of the larger family. Be a mother to the orphans, especially on holidays. Be a quiet friend to grieving widows, especially on Memorial Day. The needy believers of your church are your family. They have given to you in your need; give unto them as well. These are your family. Love them. Reach out to them.

Prayer
Lord Jesus,
It is hard to be a Christian
among those who really know us.
But help me see my own family
as a wonderful gathering
of all the best folks I know.
May all of us within our homes
see all your children as our family
and celebrate your love eternally.
Amen.

The Mystery Is for Those Who Are the Trustees of Truth

Matthew 13:10–11, 13

And the disciples came and said to Him, "Why do You speak to them in parables?" And He answered and said to them, "To you it has been granted to know the mysteries of the kingdom of heaven, but to them it has not been granted. . . . Therefore I speak to them in parables; because while seeing they do not see, and while hearing they do not hear, nor do they understand."

Often my Kingdom stories seemed to befuddle those who wanted pat answers. Parables hold a double power. They put into flesh and bone those commandments some would not hear if they were not in story form. Stories rivet the attention, while precepts plunge people into boredom. If you would teach and hold interest, tell stories. Wrap your greatest truths in "once-upon-a-times" and all will hear you gladly. There is no truth too heavy to bear if you can put it in a story.

Why did I deliberately cloak the message of the Kingdom in these elusive stories? Because the same parables clearly understood by my friends befuddled my enemies. I quoted the prophet Isaiah: "You will be ever hearing but never understanding; you will be ever seeing but never perceiving. For this people's heart has become calloused; they hardly hear with their ears, and they have closed their eyes. Otherwise they might see with their eyes . . ." (Matt. 13:14–15).

My stories held the magic of mystery. After my ascension the story impulse continued. The stories of my life and resurrection were called Gospels. The stories within the Gospels were called parables. The stories of the young church were called the Acts of the Apostles. And best of all, the story of your own affair with me is called your personal testimony. My church has ever gathered around the Apostle's Creed, which is a story confession, recounting how I was born, lived, died, rose, and am coming again.

Story is the teaching method of the Kingdom of God. Eyes grown blind in studying narrow precepts will miss much. The singsong repetition of legal codes will never hold the unfolding of the mystery of those kingdom stories that the church still gathers to celebrate.

The story redeems. The story praises. The story instructs. The great "once-upon-a-times" of the Gospels are but God's carriages of truth, in which the needy, at last, come spellbound into my presence.

Prayer
  Lord Jesus,
  Your parables
    were narrative wrappers
    in which you packaged
    your eternal truth.
  I want to make your kingdom stories grand
    as sleeves of love that hide your wounded hands.
  Amen.

The Roadside Soil

Matthew 13:18–19
"Hear then the parable of the sower. When anyone hears the word of the kingdom, and does not understand it, the evil one comes and snatches away what has been sown in his heart. This is the one on whom seed was sown beside the road."

The birds came and devoured the seed that fell beside the road. This devoured seed was emblematic of Satan's determination to stop all growth in the Kingdom. But do not give the devouring birds your focus. The central symbol of this parable is the seed, for each seed contains a small plant eager to reproduce itself. Warmed by sunlight, such tiny seedlings are driven sunward by a single dream: they must mature to keep their kind alive upon the earth. This power of their zeal to reproduce we can only call plant power.

Consider plant power.

A seed, though tiny, has only to drink the smallest sip of water to be moved by a kind of drivenness. It will reach upward for sunlight even though it has been planted underneath solid stone. It will burst through tarmac and split pavement. It will, with small but certain force, dislodge foundation stones. This unrelenting life force of the seed is born in its need to reach the sun.

Here lies the parable within the parable. The power of the seed is contained in its "seeing" itself as a full-grown plant bearing seeds of its own. Can any seed lament its size? Does a seed inside a redwood cone lie on the ground beneath the tree that spawned it and despair? Does it look at a giant redwood and lament, "I could never be that!" No! It handles the issue of its own becoming by taking one step at a time: a little earth, a little water, a little time. Never letting the size of its destiny challenge the immediate moment, it puts first things first. It splits its jacket and sends out only a tiny thread of life that longs for *treedom*. Then presto! One hundred years! A tree! And somewhere from its towering branches it drops a cone, whose eager seeds begin their patient yearning to be trees themselves.

But what of the seeds dropped by the wayside? Poor seed. No destiny for this small seed. It is eaten quickly by the birds of the air. No growth. No maturity. No destiny. Satan can stop the Kingdom growth within any life. He can destroy that power of all spiritual growth that neither martyrdom nor threat can end. He devours the destiny of those who will not find a life within the nourishing of better soil.

Prayer
> *Lord Jesus,*
> *You loved the hardened souls,*
>   *those whom life had toughened*
>   *with stony states of heart.*
> *The hardened sometimes need a gentler touch.*
> *I want a better soil than roadside clay,*
>   *that I may grow like Christ without delay.*
> *Amen.*

The Place of Rootlessness

Matthew 13:20–21

"And the one on whom seed was sown on the rocky places, this is the man who hears the word, and immediately receives it with joy; yet he has no firm root in himself, but is only temporary, and when affliction or persecution arises because of the word, immediately he falls away."

There are places where the seed falls where the soil is shallow of root. There is enough earth to warm the seed and enough moisture to entice it to grow. It springs up quickly. But there is not enough earth to give it root. When the sun rises, the new sprout of promise is scorched and lost.

Rootlessness is the curse of the church. There are too many churches that keep up an appearance of good nourishment but whose roots are shallow. Amos the prophet wrote of that spiritual shallowness that would characterize the Kingdom at the end of time. "'The days are coming,' declares the Sovereign LORD, 'when I will send a famine through the land—not a famine of food or a thirst for water, but a famine of hearing the words of the LORD. Men will stagger from sea to sea and wander from north to east, searching for the word of the LORD, but they will not find it. In that day the lovely young women and strong young men will faint because of thirst. They who swear by the shame of Samaria, or say, "As surely as your god lives, O Dan," or, "As surely as the god of Beersheba lives"—they will fall, never to rise again'" (Amos 8:11–14).

The hunger of the human heart for the knowledge of God is immense. The root of this nourishment is the Word of God. Yet there is in every age, as the prophet suggests, a famine for the hearing of the words of the Lord.

Consider all the hungry worshipers whose churches do not nourish them with the Scriptures. The members of these churches usually know they are hungry. They do not always know what to do with their hungers. The prophet describes their searching: they fly from church to church, from new idea to new idea. They try out each new "ism" and read hungrily through every new manual of discipleship, but they never stay with any new idea long enough to put down roots. Soon their frantic search ends in spiritual anemia and death.

Seek me on your own within the Word. But seek me beyond the hassled, hurried searching that ends in spiritual death.

Prayer
Lord Jesus,
The life of Christ
    is needed in the shallow,
    secular souls I see along the way.
Help me to nourish
    those whose shallow soil
    holds no nutrition
    in which their souls can grow,
Because those so weakly nourished in the root
    die quickly as they're trodden underfoot.
Amen.

Spiritual Death by Strangulation

Matthew 13:22

"And the one on whom seed was sown among the thorns, this is the man who hears the word, and the worry of the world, and the deceitfulness of riches choke the word, and it becomes unfruitful."

When the vitality of your life is choked by worldly cares, it is usually the result of your choices. The thorns of your circumstances do choke, but only when you give them permission to do it.

Consider two people who embrace Christianity at the same time. One of them goes on to live a powerful life, while the other winds up a hypocrite or drop-out. Both of their destinies are a matter of their individual choices. At every juncture of our lives we choose our futures and our moods. No one ever forces us to laugh or weep, we consciously choose mirth or gloom.

Are you sweltering under despair? Blame it not on your circumstances. Happiness is an option; so is despair. If you are dominated by darkness, you have given gloom the right to camp in your soul by saying yes to the darkness. You can as easily order gloom from your soul by saying no to the darkness. Thorns do strangle, but only with your permission.

Would you argue that moods cannot be so easily written off? Would you protest that your particular circumstances forced themselves upon you without your permission? Do you feel that life hurled the stones at you too fast for you to dodge them all?

Job had his moments of despair. Still, he did not always allow his moods to own the day. When he had every right to choose the no option, he said yes and cried, "Though he slay me, yet will I hope in him" (Job 13:15).

Let your tears become your counselors. Then confess, "Lord, I know this pain has come from you. Teach me your triumph. Teach me that crosses are often the result of overwhelming and crushing circumstances. But even on your cross, you did not complain of life's unfairness. Nor did you let despair steal from you the certain knowledge of your destiny. Lord, help me when my vision blurs with weeping, never to let my own cross make me bitter with hopelessness."

Prayer
Lord Jesus,
Stress kills those beyond your help,
and keeps all those with your
love looking too low.
Like empty husks I see them row on row,
those choked by their consent who will it so.
Amen.

The Good Earth

Matthew 13:23

"And the one on whom seed was sown on the good soil, this is the man who hears the word and understands it; who indeed bears fruit, and brings forth, some a hundredfold, some sixty, and some thirty."

The good earth in this parable of soils is that which takes root, nurtures, and produces a thousand grains of wheat. Each stalk of wheat was once just a seed. Did the seed that produced a hundred other seeds ever struggle to outsucceed the less productive seeds? Did the tiny seed ask how it could become the tallest and the richest through competition? Of course not. It merely took life one step at a time, while God supplied the sun and water.

But the good soil did produce. This must also be said of good people. There is a yearning in every noble life to produce something of value. Which of us do not want to feel like we are creating something worthy from the substance of our lives?

Artifacts are bits of cultural bric-a-brac that describe for us what the former inhabitants of the earth were like. These bits of pottery or rusted implements were created out of the human need to produce something. With their making of such artifacts these ancient souls would say, "This is of me—mine—I made it." Now such ancient artists are gone, and only that which they made told us they ever existed.

My Father loves people unconditionally, whether their lives ever produce anything or not. But people who never take pride in making something useful have a longing to say, "Here's what's issuing from my life." To create is a part of the *imago dei*, the image of God. The universe and all that is in it says God is the Maker. But this is the heart-cry of every human soul: "See, I am a maker too. Behold what issues from my life. My life draws meaning from the good things it produces."

The good soil in my parable knows the pride of taking something little and being willing to be the matrix for the creativity of God. Think about the product of one little grain of wheat: one little seed taking off its coat and going to work. This self-replicating seed pushes through its tiny little filament stalk 100,000 times the substance of its flimsy self until it has made a huge plant. Not even the brightest person in the world can explain the miracle of harvest, but even the dullest may enjoy bread.

> *Prayer*
> *Lord Jesus,*
> *I want to feel your power*
> *stirring in my life.*
> *I want to create something beautiful*
> *that I may leave it here*
> *to point others to eternity and truth.*
> *In what I make, I want to know the worth*
> *of what you felt creating heaven and earth.*
> *Amen.*

Weeds

Matthew 13:24–30

He presented another parable to them, saying, "The kingdom of heaven may be compared to a man who sowed good seed in his field. . . . But when the wheat sprang up and bore grain, then the tares became evident also. And the slaves of the landowner came and said to him, . . . 'Do you want us, then, to go and gather them up?' But he said, 'No; lest while you are gathering up the tares, you may root up the wheat with them. Allow both to grow together until the harvest; and in the time of the harvest I will say to the reapers, "First gather up the tares and bind them in bundles to burn them up; but gather the wheat into my barn."'"

In the final harvest of all the good we have produced will be some weeds. The weeds were never honest. The weeds took advantage of the soft earth that was cultivated for the sake of the grain. When the grain was fertilized, the weeds ate up nutrients never intended for them. They devoured the same sunlight meant to nourish the grain.

Weeds!

It is not possible to grow much grain without them. The question is how to get rid of weeds. If you try to crush them beneath your heel, you will also crush the tender plants. Do not try to pull the weeds out, lest you uproot the grain.

The way to handle weeds is to let them grow till harvest. Then they may be burned up when the grain is harvested.

Fire is the final test of all that is usable or not. In the New Testament my customary word for hell was *Gehenna*. Gehenna grew out of the Hebrew word *Hinnom*. Hinnom was a valley once used by pagans for child sacrifice in fire. But by New Testament times the place had become a valley where the city trash was burned. By New Testament times it was merely called Gehenna, the trash dump outside Jerusalem. Visitors and citizens coming in and out of this city could never remember entering or leaving Jerusalem that they did not see the thin tendrils of smoke rising from this burning trash dump. In Gehenna the fire never stopped—the smoke was there forever.

But what is the trash to be put in such fires? God will burn the refuse to make room for the valuable.

It is right to be concerned with the presence of weeds in your fields. But let your concern be healing as it directs you to a better way of life. Focus on the grain. My Father, in time, will deal with the weeds. In the final writing of your life, the weeds will be forgotten. It is the grain that will commend you to God. And God will welcome you into my eternal presence.

Prayer

Lord Jesus,
No flawlessness can come to any life.
And so I must live with
all the warts and wrinkles
of my own imperfect life.
I give to you the grain fields of my deeds.
Receive the grain; eliminate the weeds.
Amen.

The Mustard Seed Kingdom

Matthew 13:31–32

He presented another parable to them, saying, "The kingdom of heaven is like a mustard seed, which a man took and sowed in his field; and this is smaller than all other seeds; but when it is full grown, it is larger than the garden plants, and becomes a tree, so that THE BIRDS OF THE AIR *come and* NEST IN ITS BRANCHES."

Growth is the principle of all that is healthy. If something is getting bigger and if it is not diseased, it is of God. This mustard seed, like the seeds of grain I mentioned in many other parables, contains a life principle. This mustard seed, like a grain of wheat, holds within its speck of near invisibility a very little plant yearning to grow. Once it germinates, it will become a tree so huge that the birds of the world can rest in its branches. Between the microscopic speck of a mustard seed and the adult tree it produces is the dynamism of God.

My church has grown slowly from a tiny little seed of its beginning. The warm soil of Calvary and the balmy winds of Pentecost nourished my infant church. Now it stretches its arms around the globe. This is true of the individual church as well. Here in the local church the mustard seed must be the example. I intended the local church to grow. Not every great church is a big church, but every great church is a growing church.

It is possible to make a fetish out of church growth. Is the church not sometimes guilty of using marketing and advertising tactics that seek to make it bigger without making it great? Of course, many do. But wherever my Spirit is given full rein to act in individual ways with individual congregations, it will grow.

What of those churches that cannot grow much because they are in areas where the population is declining? There ministers and people should allow the mustard seed of growth to enlarge their hearts. Members of these growth-locked congregations can learn to serve beyond the borders of their declining communities. In a rural or isolated community when the church cannot get bigger by adding members, the members should at least be getting bigger in their understanding of my mission to the world beyond its walls of the church.

The Kingdom is to grow. Growth is the destiny of the healthy church. Praise is its energy. Joy marks the journey.

Prayer
Lord Jesus,
help me to see
that a child which will
not grow may be very loved,
but it is not healthy.
Help me to earnestly desire
to mature to ever greater
levels of responsibility
and understanding.
I want to know the joy of destiny
that grows and hungers for maturity.
Amen.

The Yeast

Matthew 13:33–35

He spoke another parable to them, "The kingdom of heaven is like leaven, which a woman took, and hid in three pecks of meal, until it was all leavened." All these things Jesus spoke to the multitudes in parables, and He did not speak to them without a parable, so that what was spoken through the prophet might be fulfilled, saying, "I WILL OPEN MY MOUTH IN PARABLES; I WILL UTTER THINGS HIDDEN SINCE THE FOUNDATION OF THE WORLD."

The yeast represents pervasive transformation.

Oddly, this process describes all that God touches, even to the least of my disciples. Yes, the yeast of God's all-pervading Spirit fills your life. If the size of your compassion and your heart of adoration is not growing, you frustrate the yeast of the Spirit. Selfish Christians sometimes try to keep God and their church in stingy little boxes of sameness. These who fear the pervading and transforming work of God need to check up on their state of heart. Miniaturizing God till he slips comfortably inside a zippered Bible misses him altogether. God has never been fascinated by miniature believers who are content to live in littleness. It is against the nature of the Spirit. When the yeast permeates, the loaf must grow.

All the attributes of God enlarge with the loaf. The courage it takes to speak to town-hall assemblies is an evidence of the growing soul. So ask yourself, "Am I getting bigger? Bigger in understanding? Bigger in adoration? Bigger in courage to infiltrate political structures with an honest value system?" Do not be afraid! Do not champion the *status quo*. A content mind in a content little system, practicing the contented rules of churchmanship, can never be much like God.

Prayer
Lord Jesus,
It is your nature
to fill all the universe.
And in your growing presence
I can see
that you must live and grow
inside of me as well.
Grow inside my life till all can see
the size of grace and your immensity.
Amen.

The Treasure and the Pearl

Matthew 13:44–46

"The kingdom of heaven is like a treasure hidden in the field, which a man found and hid; and from joy over it he goes and sells all that he has, and buys that field. Again, the kingdom of heaven is like a merchant seeking fine pearls, and upon finding one pearl of great value, he went and sold all that he had, and bought it."

Imagine some farmer on a nameless day of backbreaking effort. He stumbles through ground too dry. His oxen use their brambled tails to swat at flies. The merciless sun draws the sticky sweat from every pore of his body. Salty perspiration runs into the corners of his eyes, stinging them with fire. Round and round the chocolate fields he plows. His earth-stained hands now wrap the cracked reins around the split wood handles of the plow. He stumbles again and again down another endless furrow. He turns the dry earth even as it furnishes him a shallow ditch in which to walk.

Then in the middle of this staggering humdrum the old plow strikes something hard. Dry, hot sparks jump like flint from the earth. The plow stops. The oxen will not budge. He must remove the flinty rock that has the plow hung. But as he goes to remove the rock, he can see it is not a rock. It is an iron box. He pries it from the earth. He beats its rusty hinges till they split away. The box is open!

There greets him a huge and fiery, glittering treasure of gold and silver and precious gems. He quickly burrows back into the earth and hides the treasure. He quits plowing for the day. He puts the oxen in the barn. He barely takes time to clean the field grime from his sweaty body.

Let the humdrum be condemned forever! There is a treasure in his field! Only it is not his field—it belongs to another! He is only the sharecropper. He hurries to the registry with the last of his world's goods and buys the field.

Now is he truly rich.

His humdrum is hallowed forever!

"Mine, mine, mine!" he cries. From that moment on he is rich because he owns that field. To own the field is to own the treasure.

Remember the humdrum in which you lived? Remember how I came to you with great treasure? Remember your excitement? Remember how you cried, "Mine, mine, mine"? You were refreshed by grace. You were made rich by my sacrifice. Your life since then has been a living demonstration in my grace. Your emptiness found fullness. Your endless plowing in the infertile furrows of your life yielded treasure.

Prayer
Lord Jesus,
When first I found you
  Joy was my unforsaking companion.
The treasure from the field
  was buried in my heart of hearts.
All that I'd come to own at last owned me.
Praise swelled the anthem of my liberty.
Amen.

The Fine Art of Rebuking
the Winds of Fear

Mark 4:37–41
And there arose a fierce gale of wind, and the waves were breaking over the boat so much that the boat was already filling up. And He Himself was in the stern, asleep on the cushion; and they awoke Him and said to Him, "Teacher, do You not care that we are perishing?" And being aroused, He rebuked the wind and said to the sea, "Hush, be still." And the wind died down and it became perfectly calm. And He said to them, "Why are you so timid? How is it that you have no faith?" And they became very much afraid and said to one another, "Who then is this, that even the wind and the sea obey Him?"

Awakened on the high sea, I stared into dark waves and roaring winds. Then I looked into the faces of my disciples. They were terrified. I am the Christ, and fear in my presence is inappropriate. One of those who grew so fearful in the face of the encroaching storm was John, who would later write, "Perfect love drives out fear" (1 John 4:18). He learned this great truth that night on the furious sea. Notice, he did not say that courage casts out fear. Only love does that.

Once fear owns the human mind, courage is almost impossible to pluck up. But love can do it every time. A child may lay in the dark and fear those unreal predators of darkness. But let her father walk in the room and the child is suddenly made bold—because in the presence of love, fear is driven out.

What of all the stories in which thin, frail women lift giant boulders or heavy fallen beams off their children in wild, extraordinary circumstances? In ordinary days such mothers could in no way perform such Herculean feats. But motivated by love, the strength is there, put there by that immense love that casts out fear.

For all those troubled disciples on Galilee, I ordered the storm from the sea. It seemed no miracle to me; I had made the sea and the waves. They were mine. The seas must grow quiet and whimper at my command.

The real miracle that day was that I calmed the inner storms of their frightened souls. With maturity, these disciples would learn that no heart is large enough to contain both terror and my presence. If I am really there, fear must move out and make a place for peace. The storms upon the wild and outer seas of your life cannot threaten you either. Let me live fully in your heart. The storms must stay outside you. The only fear you then will have to conquer lies in the weather of your heart.

Prayer
Lord Jesus,
Why do I always run
  before the storms?
Why do I not remember my
  heavenly Father's love?
I rebuke my fears and
  cleanse my trembling heart.
I welcome in a love that's ever warm
  and, with it, you who sleeps amid the storms.
Amen.

Legion: The Many Faces of Fear

Luke 8:26–30

And they sailed to the country of the Gerasenes, which is opposite Galilee. And when He had come out onto the land, He was met by a certain man from the city who was possessed with demons; and who had not put on any clothing for a long time, and was not living in a house, but in the tombs. And seeing Jesus, he cried out and fell before Him, and said in a loud voice, "What do I have to do with You, Jesus, Son of the Most High God? I beg You, do not torment me." For He had been commanding the unclean spirit to come out of the man. For it had seized him many times; and he was bound with chains and shackles and kept under guard; and yet he would burst his fetters and be driven by the demon into the desert. And Jesus asked him, "What is your name?" And he said, "Legion"; for many demons had entered him.

When I came to the region of Gerasa I met Legion, the monstrous demoniac. He was an unkempt giant who frightened both children and adults. In his fierce rage he had broken chains. His huge hulk made the world tremble.

My Father is called the Creator. Satan is often called *Abaddon* in the Hebrew and *Apollyon* in the Greek. Both of these words simply mean "the Destroyer." A creator finds great joy in making things. A destroyer finds his great joy in destroying them. My Father created the universe day by day with great satisfaction. After every day's redeeming work he said, "It is good." Then on the seventh and final day of that great creative epoch, he rested. Such a beautiful new world required a Sabbath of joyous celebration.

The enemy celebrates no such Sabbath. Creativity calls for rest and assessment. A destroyer never needs to stop and rest. The destroyer can never be happy until chaos and utter destruction own the day.

So it was with Legion. God made him whole and clean. But the destroyer had come. Now he is broken, mentally splintered, and possessed of dark forces. Now he raves in the unholy caverns of his hollow mind. And like all who are under Satan's power, he is also afraid. Terror is Satan's favorite instrument of torture. Fear is the chisel that splits all confidence apart. It is the hammer that drives the crushing, splitting wedge of hate.

When I saw Legion, he seemed an overpowering monster. But I saw what others could not. I saw this huge man not as an ugly threatening ogre, but as a child terrified of the hellish fiends inside him.

I want to heal you too. I want to take your irrational fears and cast them out. I want to take your financial and employment fears and cast them out. Your family fears, your health fears, your future fears—I want them all. Is your name Legion too? If so, stand still and I will cast out all that makes you seem fierce when in actuality you are only afraid.

> *Prayer*
> *Lord Jesus,*
> *I see you and submit.*
> *The enemy is seeking to destroy*
>   *every beautiful value of my life.*
> *I shall know peace and everything will be well*
>   *when you cast out these ugly dogs of hell.*
> *Amen.*

Pork Therapy

Luke 8:32–35

Now there was a herd of many swine feeding there on the mountain; and the demons entreated Him to permit them to enter the swine. And He gave them permission. And the demons came out from the man and entered the swine; and the herd rushed down the steep bank into the lake, and were drowned. And when the herdsmen saw what had happened, they ran away and reported it in the city and out in the country. And the people went out to see what had happened; and they came to Jesus, and found the man from whom the demons had gone out, sitting down at the feet of Jesus, clothed and in his right mind; and they became frightened.

The demons on the day of Legion's healing begged to be sent into a herd of pigs. Why pigs? Because all demons are homeless, and in their homelessness they fear having to return to the abyss. So I responded to their request and gave the demoniac a visible evidence that the demons were gone. Legion beheld the pigs rush over the precipice and perish in the sea. Their wild behavior was a powerful evidence to him that he had been healed.

The glory of the cross is not just that I save, but that in my dramatic dying I have certified my salvation in your confident security. It is not so much your being well that heals you. It is your knowing you are well that heals.

Consider two patients cured of an incurable disease. In the one case the doctor says, "You are free of this disease forever." In the other case the doctor says, "You are free of this disease forever, I think." The lack of certitude in the second patient is a cancer all its own—a cancer of anxiety that eats at peace.

Peace is not merely having the demons gone. Peace is *knowing* the demons are gone. It is in watching them perish forever that the cleansed know they are truly clean. There are two certifications of peace that should teach you confidence. First, "You will know the truth, and the truth will set you free" (John 8:32).

The second and grandest "knowing" is that security which knows no threat, "And this is the testimony: God has given us eternal life, and this life is in his Son. He who has the Son has life; he who does not have the Son of God does not have life. I write these things to you who believe in the name of the Son of God so that you may know that you have eternal life" (1 John 5:11–13).

These great Scriptures are to you as pigs plunging over a precipice. Trust what you know of grace. You have seen Calvary. Know for sure you are healed.

Prayer
Lord Jesus,
The certainty of healing
  is your greatest gift.
Such security is forever.
In watching every plaguing devil go,
  I praise you that I know, I know, I know.
Amen.

The Non-Exotic Assignment

Mark 5:18–20

And as He was getting into the boat, the man who had been demon-possessed was entreating Him that he might accompany Him. And He did not let him, but He said to him, "Go home to your people and report to them what great things the Lord has done for you, and how He had mercy on you." And he went away and began to proclaim in Decapolis what great things Jesus had done for him; and everyone marveled.

"Go home!" I said to Legion. "There, tell your countrymen what great things have happened to you." It was not what Legion wanted to hear. He wanted a more exotic assignment, a Christian adventure. Still, he did obey.

Why did he dread those words, "Go home and tell"? Because home was where they knew him well. Naturally he did not want to go back where everyone knew him. He wanted to go and make converts among those who didn't know him, because there the baggage of his past would not be a problem. Besides, witnessing to those we haven't met carries the intrigue of newness. In the process of meeting someone for the first time, there is some possibility they will hear us. But going home holds no such intrigue. There we must shout our witness across the high walls of harsh familiarity.

I was shortly to go home to Nazareth, where my lofty claims were met by, "Isn't this the carpenter's kid?" Everyone owns less respect in the home country than elsewhere. Still, home has two great advantages. First, hometown folks will hear a family member before they will hear a stranger, however exotic. And second, a family member can get inside the inner sanctum of the familiar far faster than a stranger.

Genuine change is more easily recognized by those inside the family than those outside. If you doubt this, remember the impact my own family had on the world. My mother believed and obviously furnished some information to Luke for the writing of his Gospel. My brother James believed and became head of the church in Jerusalem. My brother Jude believed and became one of the writers of the New Testament. My faith was not widely accepted in Palestine, but it was deeply believed by my family, who surprised themselves by becoming world-changers.

The impact I made on my family was echoed in Legion's life. He went home. The change in him was so profound among those who had known him that his influence was incredible. My assignment to Legion is my assignment to you: I'm sending you home too. Go home, where the changes I have produced in your life will be everywhere evident. Go home, to those who are skeptical of what you say you have become because they know what you used to be. It is because they know what you used to be that they will have trouble believing what you say you've become. But if you are really changed, you will impact them in ways no stranger ever could.

Prayer
Lord Jesus,
I need to remember
home is where it's easy to go
but hard to bear witness.
I want to live my life impeccably,
witnessing your love unto my family.
Amen.

The Importance of Public Confession

Luke 8:43–47

And a woman who had a hemorrhage for twelve years, and could not be healed by anyone, came up behind Him, and touched the fringe of His cloak; and immediately her hemorrhage stopped. And Jesus said, "Who is the one who touched Me?" And while they were all denying it, Peter said, "Master, the multitudes are crowding and pressing upon You." But Jesus said, "Someone did touch Me, for I was aware that power had gone out of Me." And when the woman saw that she had not escaped notice, she came trembling and fell down before Him, and declared in the presence of all the people the reason why she had touched Him, and how she had been immediately healed.

I felt her hand that day as one reaching out to me in earnest need. In her reaching desperation, I felt healing power in vast amounts flooding out of me to meet her needs. I felt her lingering, hungry touch.

I stopped and said (not overforcefully, for she was not far away), "Who touched me?" It seemed a foolish question in such a large crowd. Everybody had touched me. Still, the woman whose frail arm had struck out through the massive people-wall knew I meant her. She had been healed. She knew it instantly. I knew it too.

At my question the world around her stopped. I stopped. The crowd stopped. She came timidly and tremblingly, owning up to her healing. I rather forced her to acknowledge that she had been healed. It was not my intent to call her forth and to brutalize her fragile spirit. Still, a huge principle was at stake for the Kingdom. People are never free to receive great things from God and slink back into the crowd without acknowledging God's gift.

The Kingdom I died to found has but one tactic of enlistment and growth: confession. Unless those who receive grace acknowledge what they have received, the Kingdom will not grow. The heart of the Christian faith is confession.

Many are prone to ask me, "Well, do I have to confess Christ to be converted? Can I not be saved without this showy declaration?" Confession is the primary witness to the authenticity of my presence in the life. If a man and a woman marry in secret, their marriage is not lawful. Civil law declares that two people called *witnesses* must sign the marriage document. These witnesses must declare by signature that they heard and saw the couple make their life promises. The marriage is otherwise not lawful. If there are no witnesses, there is no marriage.

In the same way, you may not touch me secretly and keep secret all you've received from my Father. This poor woman intended to take my healing as an unacknowledged gift. Had she succeeded, it would not have been a gift I gave but one she stole.

Are you open about what I have given you? Have you acknowledged me before people so that I may acknowledge you before my Father, who is in heaven? (Matt. 10:32).

Prayer
Lord Jesus,
I have received in private your salvation
    but I bless you publicly for all your gifts.
I met you in a darksome, lonely place,
    to publicly exalt your saving grace.
Amen.

The Dangers of Familiarity

Mark 6:1–3

And He went out from there, and He came into His home town; and His disciples followed Him. And when the Sabbath had come, He began to teach in the synagogue; and the many listeners were astonished, saying, "Where did this man get these things, and what is this wisdom given to Him, and such miracles as these performed by His hands? Is not this the carpenter, the son of Mary, and brother of James, and Joses, and Judas, and Simon? Are not His sisters here with us?" And they took offense at Him.

I began my ministry by going to Nazareth to preach.

"Read for us!" they cried. "Yes, Jesus, read for us!"

I wanted to, and yet felt some reluctance to read to all my old childhood teachers. At last I walked to the front of the synagogue and stood. A leathery old rabbi picked up the scroll of Isaiah and brought it to me. I unrolled it slowly while a hush fell over the little congregation. Then I stopped unrolling the scroll and I read:

"The Spirit of the Lord is upon me,
  because he has anointed me to preach good news to the poor.
He has sent me to proclaim freedom for the prisoners
  and recovery of sight for the blind,
  to release the oppressed,
  to proclaim the year of the Lord's favor" (Luke 4:18–19).

Then I set down the scroll and said, "Today this scripture is fulfilled in your hearing" (Luke 4:21).

This was truth as truth should be proclaimed. My words were joined to God's ancient and holy words. It was right to join them, for they were all God's words. The prophecy for which all Judaism had waited had come true. Truth was joyously set free in my hometown.

But all would learn that day that when God makes a claim, however joyous, the truth of it is left in human hands for judgment. And these, my hometown friends, who might have made Nazareth the cradle of Christianity, were skeptical. They fidgeted in doubt. They grew angry. They cast off faith. They left the world's greatest truth to be decided by others, who trusted me more because their hearts were larger.

Prayer
  Lord Jesus,
  I want to have a ready response
    in the face of every skeptic.
  I want to proclaim you
    in full belief and utter open courage.
  You perfectly interpreted God's Word.
  I now, in perfect faith, must call you Lord.
  Amen.

The Limiting Littleness

Mark 6:4–6

And Jesus said to them, "A prophet is not without honor except in his home town and among his own relatives and in his own household." And He could do no miracle there except that He laid His hands upon a few sick people and healed them. And he wondered at their unbelief. And He was going around the villages teaching.

No prophet in his own hometown is capable of honor. He cannot achieve great things there. The unbelief of those who know the prophet will keep great things from happening. Now consider the cost of my rejection in Nazareth: I could do for them no mighty work because of their unbelief.

Have you ever stopped to consider the cost of unbelief? Kingdoms fall. The sick die needlessly. The brokenhearted commit suicide. Orphans grieve. Widows live disconsolately.

Faith, like a grain of mustard seed, can move mountains. Yet hometown skeptics can prevent miracles. No mustard seed could grow in Nazareth.

However, before you are too severe on these Nazarenes, consider the price of unbelief in your life. Do you not see how even the most ordinary crisis evokes the same response in you? Crisis comes and instead of meeting it with faith, you crumble in your fear. You check your bank account to see if you can handle the crisis financially. Then you tell your poor, weak, human friends of the severity of your crisis.

"Poor thing—we pity you!" they say. Their pity is worthless, yet you treasure it. Then you cry and they console you. Then you check with your family, and they too offer condolences which you receive. You check with other resource people. Your counselor says the problem is too severe for him to lend you counsel. You call your banker, who says your situation is too risky for him to help.

Alas, when you have tried every other avenue, it suddenly occurs to you that you are a Christian. Then finally you turn to me for help. Going last where you should have gone first, you find me all-sufficient. Then you believe. Gratefully, at long last, you trust. I destroy the crisis. How costly is unbelief?

So it was in Nazareth. They wanted me to do at home what I had done elsewhere. But at home they tied my hands with skepticism before they begged me to demonstrate my power. I had no choice but to go to proclaim my full Messiahship to those whose hearts were large with faith. I am able to meet your every need. Give me your trust and stand back.

Prayer
Lord Jesus,
So much I might
have meant to you is past.
I cannot scrape it back together for a second pass.
I held you at arm's length knowing that
God's deeds are snatched by one foul, petty thief—
that bandit known to God as unbelief.
Amen.

Venturing into My Sufficiency

Luke 9:1–3

And He called the twelve together, and gave them power and authority over all the demons, and to heal diseases. And He sent them out to proclaim the kingdom of God, and to perform healing. And He said to them, "Take nothing for your journey, neither a staff, nor a bag, nor bread, nor money; and do not even have two tunics apiece."

I once sent the twelve out on a preaching tour with no supplies. I gave them no money or extra clothing to carry with them. I wanted them to learn what I already knew: to have the means to do my work without needing me almost always leads to doing it without me.

To have sufficient means to accomplish something great in my name often ends in pride for having achieved some goal on your own. Self-reliance is easily subverted into self-seeking. The best way to avoid self-seeking is to avoid acquiring material things that tempt you to become self-reliant. This is why I asked my disciples not to take anything with them on the preaching tour: not a cane, not money, not even an extra shirt.

When Francis of Assisi began to take the Kingdom of God to the poor and the mentally ill, he dressed only in haircloth and begged his bread from door to door. In begging his bread he remained dependent on simple fare. Begging is not an occupation one brags about. So there grew up around his begging an institution of mercy that could not be credited to his own clever achievements. Only when God is all you have will he get the credit for all you accomplish.

How often has a small church preached and achieved some glorious dream. When they began that dream, they were pure of heart and willing for God to have all the credit. But once they "succeeded," they thought they had to adopt an operating budget. Next they hired a large staff. Little brass plaques rose beside pulpits and organ pipes. The great stained-glass windows contained leaded-in, colored panels with the names of those generous Christians who had made the splendor possible.

All that happens in some churches is fully explainable in terms of human resources. But here and there, some churches exist who have not forgotten their call to servanthood. These still gird their waists with towels and carry the basin of ministry into the world they are called to serve. They have no money, no power members, not even the greatest of preachers. They walk in their world simply—no staff, no bag, no bread, no money. They depend on me and me alone. They are a Pentecost in embryo. Their ensigns are fire and wind.

Prayer
Lord Jesus,
We have planned too well for success.
We have read every manual on the subject.
We have laid by us in store the necessary finances.
We have secured the pledges,
*   and we have the signatures of the significant*
*   all filed away on faith-promise cards.*
But we shall fail without a Christ desire,
*   achieving nothing without wind and fire.*
Amen.

The Double Obligation

Matthew 10:14–16

"And whoever does not receive you, nor heed your words, as you go out of that house or that city, shake off the dust of your feet. Truly I say to you, it will be more tolerable for the land of Sodom and Gomorrah in the day of judgment, than for that city. Behold, I send you out as sheep in the midst of wolves; therefore be shrewd as serpents, and innocent as doves."

Never forget the bottom line as you minister: you are not accountable for any supposed failure to any human court. Nothing I have called you to do in my name will be dismissed as trivial in that world to which you are headed. If you are rejected in your attempt to preach the truth, the truth that caused your rejection will not be judged on this earth. Those who reject your preaching must themselves face the last tribunal.

Never despair over rejection. The greatest truths are regularly rejected. I told my disciples as they began their preaching tour, If you are cast out of any city, do not try to barge back into it compelling them to listen. Just "shake the dust off your feet." Why? Because those who hear the truth need to remember that the truth of the gospel is not an option left up to human caprice. The shaking of the dust off your feet will remind them of their obligation to hear. The gospel has always carried this double obligation. It obligates the saved to tell the message and the lost to listen. Pity the complacent saved, who will not tell the saving story. Pity the complacent lost who will not hear it.

But in this double obligation, important as it is, never merely count your converts to measure your success. Truth is its own reward. Once you have told the truth, you have succeeded. Telling the saving truth is your responsibility. Doing the saving is mine. Counting converts is unnecessary. It is an unworthy bottom line on earth and unessential in heaven. So do not grow neurotic trying to be a Savior yourself. That is my title; I will do that work. That should take quite a load off your mind. You are only responsible for telling the truth. So tell it! If thousands are drawn to the faith, you will succeed. If you are crucified for telling it, you will still have succeeded.

Still, tact is the lubricant of the good news. Tact does not mean you flatter people so they will like you. "Shrewd as serpents, harmless as doves!" This is the rule. Be shrewd like the snake, whose lowly existence makes it mandatory for him to keep out from under people's boots. Snakes know the principles of their own survival: keep to the side of the path, avoid the crushing commerce. But also be like a dove. These gentle creatures make no one afraid. Their softness invites all to know them.

Prayer
Lord Jesus,
I need to learn to travel
through my world negotiating the hostile traffic
and the crowds of skeptics.
Help me to learn the difference between tact and cowardice.
Help me feel the obligation to tell the truth
and to understand the obligation of my listeners to hear it.
Responsibility is served, it seems,
when I but preach the truth, and you redeem.
Amen.

The Inner Voice

Matthew 10:17–20

"But beware of men; for they will deliver you up to the courts, and scourge you in their synagogues; and you shall even be brought before governors and kings for My sake, as a testimony to them and to the Gentiles. But when they deliver you up, do not become anxious about how or what you will speak; for it . . . is not you who speak, but it is the Spirit of your Father who speaks in you."

My presence within you was never intended to lie inoperative. There are those who want God's Holy Spirit to reside within them like a pink and pleasant coma.

My inner presence is neither sweet nor sleepy. I am a raging fire. I am a restless cry within your breast. I am not the passive indweller. I am the Roar of Life, the Morning Thunder, the Lightening of life eternal. To permit me in your life is to dissolve your ego in the acid of power. Then if you have to go before Caesar, do it in confidence. Pity him if he judges you. For anyone who judges you must later reckon with the Spirit of God.

Do you wish to make demons flee at your command? Then greet them with that power—God's power, not your own—that resides in your heart. Set the roaring God free within you. Let Him force these threatening serpents back into the abyss. God will cap them in steel and bury them forever in the deepest part of hell from which they came: all of this at your command.

What is it that makes you afraid?

I told my disciples of the fear they would feel when they came before human tribunals and were forced to answer. I reminded them that in their hour of need they would meet my sufficiency. The principle will never change. You have the same wonderful indwelling Spirit that they had. It is human to be afraid; but to be paralyzed by your fear, while I indwell your life, is a denial of my power. It is ungodly to be a Christian and appear weak.

Fear no longer.

Open your heart. The enemy will see and flee before the formidable power in your heart.

Prayer
Lord Jesus,
Help me remember that when I trusted you,
*   you filled my life with force.*
I could never face a single threat
*   with which you could not successfully cope.*
And here I am; my heart of Spirit-steel is made.
Begone, poor hell! For I am unafraid!
Amen.

The Only Enemy

Matthew 10:28

"And do not fear those who kill the body, but are unable to kill the soul; but rather fear Him who is able to destroy both soul and body in hell."

Do you think you have many enemies? You do not. You have only one. This should simplify your discipleship and eliminate your hating anyone. Never dislike anyone. Remember, those qualities in them that have raised your antipathy are only facets of your one predictable enemy. So much of the hate we allow in our lives is aimed at those who are under the control of Satan. Satan's behavior in the lives of others should never cause us to dislike them.

I encouraged my disciples never to fear earthly potentates who possessed the power to make them martyrs. Satan was the only person they had to fear. We should never hate those persons under the control of Satan simply because we have perceived some evil in them. Anyone who is already on the way to hell bears burdens enough without their having to carry our additional censure.

So the next time someone offends you, hold your anger in check. A pleasant smile will better serve. The next time you are tempted to return someone's slur, do not reciprocate in kind.

You can see that Satan already has them in his kingdom. Surely you can concede that it is he and not them who is your enemy. Better it is to serve God. Better it is to dress daily for combat with this enemy. Each morning, "Put on the full armor of God so that you can take your stand against the devil's schemes. For our struggle is not against flesh and blood, but against the rulers, against the authorities, against the powers of this dark world and against the spiritual forces of evil in the heavenly realms" (Eph. 6:11–12).

Consider Paul's final advice on how to handle the only enemy you have. "Stand firm then, with the belt of truth buckled around your waist, with the breastplate of righteousness in place, and with your feet fitted with the readiness that comes from the gospel of peace. In addition to all this, take up the shield of faith, with which you can extinguish all the flaming arrows of the evil one" (Eph. 6:14–16).

Prayer
Lord Jesus,
How I need to know there is
but one enemy.
It simplifies my battle strategy
to know that you are Lord of everything
and certainly the Lord of my single enemy.
I offer unto you my enemy,
whom you once vanquished, that I might be free.
Amen.

The Value of You

Matthew 10:29–31

"Are not two sparrows sold for a cent? And yet not one of them will fall to the ground apart from your Father. But the very hairs of your head are all numbered. Therefore do not fear; you are of more value than many sparrows."

One of the leading causes of suicide is the obsessive feeling that no one really cares about us. In this awful sense of abandonment we feel all alone in our pain. Finally, we lament that God neither knows nor cares about us. However they are written, almost every suicide note bears the cry, "Good-bye, cruel world! You never cared that I lived, and the roar of your senseless apathy is more than I can bear."

This empty world might deserve such epitaphs if we were not so radically loved. But love is the anthem of God whose music drowns out the awful roaring of our self-pity. God cries louder through our despair: "You are mine. You are not here by accident. I know your name. I know all about you. I have counted the hairs on your head. I keep books on every aspect of my world. I know the number of pebbles on the slopes of every mountain, the number of corpuscles in each newborn baby. I know exactly how many sparrows there are on the earth. As each new one hatches, I log its number in the *Book of Sparrows*. When one falls to the earth, never to rise again, that event is also noticed and recorded. If I am so thorough with sparrow counting, you may be sure I know you. Do not withhold yourself from my love. You are worth many sparrows."

Once a little girl committed suicide by drowning herself. Life had become too much for her, and she had attached a note to her clothing before she threw herself into the river. The muddy waters of the river had not obscured the words of her note: they read in faded letters, "I haven't a friend in the world: nobody cares for me."

It was not true. I cared.

An elderly woman was found dead in her small cubicle. By the time she was discovered, she had been dead some weeks. There was a journal by her bedside that contained the same entry, day after day: "No one cares, no one came today . . . No one cares, no one came today . . . No one cares, no one came today. . . ."

Not so!

The hair-counting, sparrow-loving God cares. Come to him. Celebrate your place and importance in the world. If you do this, you will never write your own disconsolate note. You are loved too much to write such notes.

Prayer
Lord Jesus,
I know I am loved.
I know that you constantly care.
I know the world is not as meaningless
*   as some imagine it.*
Accepting your enduring love for me,
*   I'll never ask, To be or not to be?*
Amen.

Saying Who We Are

Matthew 10:32–33

"Everyone therefore who shall confess Me before men, I will also confess him before My Father who is in heaven. But whoever shall deny Me before men, I will also deny him before My Father who is in heaven."

Christians compose a kingdom designed to march by one simple principle: confession. Confession is the willingness to own up to who we are. Wherever Christians confess, the kingdom of God advances. Where Christians do not confess, the Kingdom of God loses its compassion and service.

This simple technique of life or death should surprise no one. Throughout our lives we make our way into every social situation simply confirming or denying who we are. We are quite open in stating the obvious issues of our identity: our employer, our family heritage, our hometown. But in stating the inward issues of our lives, we sometimes become reticent.

The only way a community becomes a community is for its various members to openly admit their connection to it. In needy communities, membership can become redemptive. When a man says, "Hello, I'm John. I'm in trouble!" he has stated his identity both in terms of his need and of his place in that community.

So to say, "Hello, I'm John Doe. I believe in Christ!" pulls our confession out into the center of scrutiny. Our confession automatically turns some on and some off. But one thing is sure: none are neutral to this confession. Some will consider your openness valiant. Others will think of you as a person to be avoided. Some will admire you; others will see you as irrelevant.

Heaven knows of no private conversions. Civil courts know of no private weddings. If a couple is going to claim to be married, there is a high demand that they be willing to file the civil contract at the courthouse. Their public acknowledgment of love is mandatory, or a wedding cannot occur. In the same way, public acknowledgment is necessary for a believer to claim that she is a Christian.

I make this promise to you: I will confess you as openly as you confess me. If you admit to your office group that you and I are friends, then I'll admit the same to the hosts of heaven. But if you are ashamed of me in your carpool or your country club, then I will not tell anyone in heaven either. I will be as open about our friendship as you are.

> *Prayer*
> *Lord Jesus,*
> *So often, when I might easily*
> *   tell my world about our friendship,*
> *   I do not.*
> *In the midst of all your blessings,*
> *   I act as though I have provided my own good fortune.*
> *Forgive me.*
> *So let me clearly shout in every street,*
> *   "I have a friend I wish that you could meet!"*
> *Amen.*

The Jangling Jesus

Matthew 10:34–37a

"Do not think that I came to bring peace on the earth; I did not come to bring peace, but a sword. For I came to SET A MAN AGAINST HIS FATHER, AND A DAUGHTER AGAINST HER MOTHER, AND A DAUGHTER-IN-LAW AGAINST HER MOTHER-IN-LAW; *and A MAN'S ENEMIES WILL BE THE MEMBERS OF HIS OWN HOUSEHOLD [Mic. 7:6]. He who loves father or mother more than Me is not worthy of Me."*

There is a certain jangling that can come to a family when a member confesses that I am Lord. How often do you hear of someone who comes to faith in me, only to find himself excluded from his entire community and family?

One very famous man admitted for years that he was an atheist, with no belief whatsoever in Jehovah, the God of Abraham, Isaac, and Jacob. His parents wanted him to abandon his atheism, but he would not. In spite of his atheism, his family loved him and included him in every social event in their home. Then, one day, in a moment of utter need, he was confronted by a Christian who led him to believe in me. He was wonderfully converted and went home to bring the news to his parents. "Father," he freely admitted, "You were right. There is a God. You must be very happy indeed, for at last I can accede to all that you ever wanted for me. I now wholeheartedly believe in Jesus, and I want to give him my life as a minister in the church."

But they were unable to rejoice. It was the *Jesus* part that troubled them. They would have much preferred their son to have died in atheism than to come to believe so much in Jesus that he would become a preacher.

For all who wish to follow me, there is a price to be paid—sometimes within the family. I want to create unity around the joy of common faith. But until that faith is common, my presence often creates only destructive quarrels and inward division.

May your confession be compassionate within your family. Find the grace to say, "I will never cease to love you, dearest family, for you are indeed bone of my bone and flesh of my flesh. But I will never be able to stop loving my Savior either, for in him is life and meaning and hope for eternity. I would give my life to bring peace to our home, but I will never—I can never—surrender my Savior to achieve it. Please understand me, I beg you. I need your love and your understanding, but I also need Jesus." Perhaps with such honesty, my peace may become acceptable within your family. Then who knows but that those who at first scorned your love for me will at last themselves come to love me?

Prayer
Lord Jesus,
I need your peace.
I also need my family.
Help those tensions born to me
  from this double love
  cause me to serve them more readily
  as I move inward in my
  relationship with you.
I must admit to your love for me
  and own this faith within my family.
Amen.

The Great Paradox

Matthew 10:38–39

"And he who does not take his cross and follow after Me is not worthy of Me. He who has found his life shall lose it, and he who has lost his life for My sake shall find it."

All that you will finally hold in your limp, lifeless hand is what you have given away. There is nothing you can cling to or hold on to forever. The number one rule for saving anything is relinquishment. Relinquishment is letting go of something we treasure in order to hang on. It is the ancient conundrum of a child with his hand caught in a bottle of peanuts. Setting himself free is simple. He may retract his hand from the jar anytime he wishes. He has but to release his handful of peanuts.

"Mine!" is an early word in every human vocabulary. We learn to possess and define our possessions quite early. With this early bluster we begin to create a grand illusion that we can own and hold to whatever we wish for as long as we wish. Unfortunately, we cannot. Death is the great disinheritance. All our "mines" become someone else's. Often the act of transferring them, even by will or estate, is a matter of the greedy heirs huddling around the sickbed of the fading tycoon. They gather, circling, waiting for the pulse to stop. Then they will become the owners of that cache of goods over which the deceased man has cried "mine" all of his life. Then they will start crying "mine" over it themselves. Then their inheritors in turn will wait for their pulse to stop. On and on runs the dark comedy of human ownership.

Most people spend their lives pursuing the same brief spasms of claiming such ownable stuff. "I want to live my life, my way!" shouts the teenage prodigal as she stomps out of the house. "What right do you have interfering in my life!" screams the about-to-be divorcée. In each of these cases, the person is trying to claim clear-cut ownership of herself.

Luke wrote of the early church, "All the believers were one in heart and mind. No one claimed that any of his possessions was his own, but they shared everything they had . . . those who owned lands or houses, sold them, brought the money from the sales and put it at the apostles' feet, and it was distributed to anyone as he had need" (Acts 4:32–35).

Those in the early church had learned that they not only saved their souls by relinquishment, they established the Kingdom. Clinging only challenges waiting inheritors to cry "mine" once death has weakened your grasp. All that is truly valuable can only be owned by relinquishment.

Prayer
Lord Jesus,
I hold so tightly to my little trinkets
and grip my inheritances.
I want to learn what my natural inclinations
cannot teach me:
To have, I must let go.
I beg you take and use my life today
and pry my grasping fingers from my way.
Amen.

The Noble Friend

Matthew 14:1–11

At that time Herod the tetrarch heard the news about Jesus, and said to his servants, "This is John the Baptist; he has risen from the dead; and that is why miraculous powers are at work in him." For when Herod had John arrested, he bound him, and put him in prison on account of Herodias, the wife of his brother Philip. For John had been saying to him, "It is not lawful for you to have her." And although he wanted to put him to death, he feared the multitude, because they regarded him as a prophet. But when Herod's birthday came, the daughter of Herodias danced before them and pleased Herod. Thereupon he promised with an oath to give her whatever she asked. And having been prompted by her mother, she said, "Give me here on a platter the head of John the Baptist." And although he was grieved, the king commanded it to be given because of his oaths, and because of his dinner guests. And he sent and had John beheaded in the prison. And his head was brought on a platter and given to the girl; and she brought it to her mother.

It was said of one of the martyrs, beheaded for his faith, "We have not such another head to be cut off!" So often in human courts the noble are extinguished by the ignoble. When John was killed, Herod unquestionably beheaded his better. And in the long course of history, greatness has often been made the sport of some lewd dance.

Thus John died.

The lips that announced my kingdom were silent. The voice that once thundered "Repent!" was stopped. John had condemned the sins of royalty, those complicated adulteries that often describe the lives of those who rule the land poorly. The powerful are often rich enough to think they owe the world no apology for their risqué lives. But catch the final and pitiable pilgrimage of John's disciples. They came and carried away their master's remains and buried them.

Who's to know what they must have felt as they carried their master away from the site of his execution? They must have known that the curtain had come down upon a major participant in the theater of redemption. Now he who made the canyons of Jordan tremble with the sheer power of his message was gone. The overture of God's great symphony was over, but the real music of redemption was just beginning.

I was already set for the difficult music of Good Friday. I, too, would die and complete the music this glorious prophet began. Together, his overture and my symphony would set the galaxies alive with the greatest and most redeeming music the world has ever known.

Prayer
Lord Jesus,
John was faithful unto death,
completing all you asked of him.
I want to fulfill every last thing you have for me as well.
I want to die only when it may be said of me
that all you laid before me I have done,
I waged the war of faith till it was won.
Amen.

Good Grief

Matthew 14:13

Now when Jesus heard it, He withdrew from there in a boat, to a lonely place by Himself; and when the multitudes heard of this, they followed Him on foot from the cities.

Grief is that music of the soul that turns our affections from the earth so that they may fly upward toward the Father. Grief is music? Yes, but heavy music. The day I heard of John's death, I left the city. I walked out into the countryside to a very lonely place. My mind was numbed by grief. I had lost a wonderful friend. I thought of how John once preached fearlessly by the river, his brow shining with the light of God. I thought of how he preached unapologetically the honesty of his convictions.

The issue of our first meeting would not leave my mind. Back then John had seen me on two successive days. He had been reluctant to baptize me, only agreeing to it after I insisted on it. I thought of how the voice out of heaven had called out over the river, "This is my beloved Son!" I thought of how John had called out upon seeing me, "Behold the Lamb of God!"

The wilderness was often my retreat. Now in my grief it was especially so: it was easy to be alone with my Father in the wilderness and to sort through all that it meant to be the Son of God. There I had first gone after my baptism to fast for forty days. During those days, I had talked to the Father about his exact plan of redemption. Now I was back, alone again. I was sorting through John's life and death. John was but thirty-one years of age, and yet in so short a time he had completed all that God had given him to do. Now he was gone. In an equally short span of time, I too would be back in heaven. Yet I would remain forever the fount of all consolation. I was the Son of Man who could rule over every grieving human heart with full understanding.

Have you faced the loneliness of the desert place? When will you leave the madding crowd to get in touch with the meaning that only my Father can give? John the Beloved would later testify of the glorious end of all grief: "And I heard a loud voice from the throne saying, 'Now the dwelling of God is with men, and he will live with them. They will be his people, and God himself will be with them and be their God. He will wipe every tear from their eyes. There will be no more death or mourning or crying or pain, for the old order of things has passed away'" (Rev. 21:3–4).

Do you grieve even now? Find yourself a desert place. There I will meet you as my Father met me. Someday I will wipe away all your tears. Until that time, I will sit with you as you grieve.

Prayer
Lord Jesus,
I have lost a friend to death.
Indeed, I have lost my best friend to death.
But he came back from death.
It is you, Lord Jesus.
You have marched through that undiscovered country
*   and taught me not to fear.*
I want to meet you in the lonely hour
*   and feel the pulse of resurrection power.*
Amen.

Nothing Must Be Lost

John 6:4–13

Now the Passover, the feast of the Jews, was at hand. Jesus therefore lifting up His eyes, and seeing that a great multitude was coming to Him, said to Philip, "Where are we to buy bread, that these may eat?" And this He was saying to test him; for He Himself knew what He was intending to do.

Philip answered Him, "Two hundred denarii worth of bread is not sufficient for them, for everyone to receive a little."

One of his disciples, Andrew, Simon Peter's brother, said to Him, "There is a lad here who has five barley loaves and two fish, but what are these for so many people?"

Jesus said, "Have the people sit down." Now there was much grass in the place. So the men sat down, in number about five thousand.

Jesus therefore took the loaves; and having given thanks, He distributed to those who were seated; likewise also of the fish as much as they wanted. And when they were filled, He said to His disciples, "Gather up the leftover fragments that nothing may be lost." And so they gathered them up, and filled twelve baskets with fragments from the five barley loaves, which were left over by those who had eaten.

On the day I multiplied the loaves, Andrew brought a little boy to me. Five biscuits and two fish was his lunch. It wasn't much, but he surrendered it freely to me.

Wonderful things began to unfold. As his little lunch slid through my fingers it was replicated into more and more. I handed his little lunch to my disciples and in their fingers it expanded once again. And so on, ever and anon, the child would say, "Those are my loaves. Those are my fish!" But bit by bit, he grew silent. With the wonder of so many sharing his small lunch, he at last wistfully admitted, "That's not my loaves and my fishes anymore."

There is an economy in all my Father undertakes. He does not create anything to be disposed of without being used. The deserts and seas, the ice caps and steaming geysers exist in just the right combination to be sure that nothing on earth is ever lost. There will be no waste. The fish and loaves were passed. All took of it, ate of it, and laughed and yet feared what they were beholding. It was the kind of meal one is afraid to eat and yet the kind of meal that must be eaten for the sheer wonder of it. But what began with five loaves and two fishes ended up in twelve baskets.

The twelve baskets full meant that each of the disciples would have a basket for his journey. The loaves and the fishes are not just a sign of God's wonderful and lavish grace; they are a sign that God is an economist. They are evidence that nothing is to be lost.

Prayer
Lord Jesus,
Help me to celebrate
your lavish provision for all who follow you.
Help me also to remember that
you gave so much and still required
that nothing be wasted.
I want to give with generosity,
yet celebrate it economically.
Amen.

The Risk

Matthew 14:24–25, 28–33

But the boat was already many stadia away from the land, battered by the waves; for the wind was contrary. And in the fourth watch of the night He came to them, walking on the sea. . . .

And Peter answered Him and said, "Lord, if it is You, command me to come to You on the water." And He said, "Come!" And Peter got out of the boat, and walked on the water and came toward Jesus. But seeing the wind, he became afraid, and beginning to sink, he cried out, saying, "Lord, save me!"

And immediately Jesus stretched out His hand and took hold of him, and said to him, "O you of little faith, why did you doubt?" And when they got into the boat, the wind stopped. And those who were in the boat worshiped Him, saying, "You are certainly God's Son!"

God loves the risk-taker. What Peter was really doing that stormy night was begging, "Lord, bid me do the impossible! I'm tired of always doing things I can explain." Before you set out to reprimand Peter's "weak faith," please remember that he was the only one who got off the boat that night.

He was doing well too, till in his pride he forgot that the enabling factor in his sea stroll was the power of God. He got a little too self-congratulatory. A huge dark wave came between us. His firm pride jellied into fear, which caused him to look down. Then his faith fled and he began sinking into the sea. He knew the utter horror of feeling the water come over his sandals, then his ankles. At last he stumbled forward to his knees, falling headlong into the tumbling water, crying, "Lord, save!"

And so I did.

But the glory of that night held a lesson he would never forget. "All things really are possible to those who believe." Only one mortal, Simon Peter, ever walked on water. He didn't walk far. But he walked.

Are you weary of doing the explainable? Are you worn out with church work, which has become too little church and too much work? Wouldn't you like, just once in your life, to do something so outstanding that it cannot be explained apart from me? Then get ready to risk yourself. Get ready to say with a bowed head, "God, if it is you, bid me walk to you on the water!"

> *Prayer*
> *Lord Jesus,*
> *I want just once in my life*
> *to walk on water, so to speak.*
> *I want to fix my eyes on you and sprint across*
> *the sea of Galilee.*
> *I want to fall before some burning bush*
> *whose fire I did not light.*
> *I want to gather manna and toast*
> *for some atheists I've been dying to have over for breakfast.*
> *I beg you to do within my life today*
> *some deed I can explain no other way.*
> *Amen.*

The Humanitarianism That Obscures God

John 6:24–27

When the multitude therefore saw that Jesus was not there, nor His disciples, they themselves got into the small boats, and came to Capernaum, seeking Jesus. And when they found Him on the other side of the sea, they said to Him, "Rabbi, when did You get here?"

Jesus answered them and said, "Truly, truly, I say to you, you seek Me, not because you saw signs, but because you ate of the loaves, and were filled. Do not work for the food which perishes, but for the food which endures to eternal life, which the Son of Man shall give to you, for on Him the Father, even God, has set His seal."

I fed the multitude because they were hungry. There is no joy quite so fulfilling as knowing that you have given the hungry a filling meal. I could have done this every day of my ministry. In fact, my entire saving mission could have easily been turned into one huge cafeteria service. I could have faced the north and said on any given Thursday, "Let every pantry for a hundred miles be instantly filled." Then I might have faced the other directions and done the same. Why did I not do it? Because, I realized, the supply of bread is a kind of addiction. To give a man a slice begs a whole loaf the next time. Furnish one loaf to a starving man, and he will soon seek to own the bakery.

You may wish to argue the point. "May we not give anyone a slice of bread in the name of God?" Well, I had given them bread in the name of God, and they came by force to make me a king (John 6:15). They really didn't want a king; they wanted an unending meal ticket. They didn't want me as the Lord of life but Lord of the larder. Bread given, even in the name of God, quickly becomes the god of the hungry. The hungry worship in bakeries more readily than in temples.

Much of the interest that many citizens show in Christian conversion is motivated by the notion that Christians can get rich by claiming Christ.

There is a powerful attraction in the loaves that perish. There is music in the notion that to know Christ is to fare well. But beware: literal bread—the bread that perishes—is bread too little. Most who get all the material loaves they want no longer feel a need for the Bread of Heaven.

The people were poor. When I gave them bread, I did something you could call humanitarian. But alas, much of the time humanitarianism leads to that practical atheism that claims to believe in the Bread come down from heaven, while it puts all of its emphasis on the kind you can toast.

Prayer
Lord Jesus,
Here I am in utter need.
I want to get on in the world
    and earn my own daily bread—lots of it.
Frankly, Lord, the church is a place
    I can meet the right people to help me buy the bakery.
So move my stomach farther from my heart
    and help me learn to tell the two apart.
Amen.

The Manna Eaters Are All Dead

John 6:30–35, 49–50

They said therefore to Him, "What then do You do for a sign, that we may see, and believe You? What work do You perform? Our fathers ate the manna in the wilderness; as it is written, 'HE GAVE THEM BREAD OUT OF HEAVEN TO EAT'" [Exod. 16:4].

Jesus therefore said to them, "Truly, truly, I say to you, it is not Moses who has given you the bread out of heaven, but it is My Father who gives you the true bread out of heaven. For the bread of God is that which comes down out of heaven, and gives life to the world."

They said therefore to Him, "Lord, evermore give us this bread."

Jesus said to them, "I am the bread of life; . . .

"Your fathers ate the manna in the wilderness, and they died. This is the bread which comes down out of heaven, so that one may eat of it and not die."

Miracles fascinate, but often only for a moment. Consider the Exodus. God did wonderful things. Water gushed from rocks and bread fell from the skies. The children of Israel marveled at the manna—bread come down from heaven—for only a little while. All too soon they were grumbling that it was not very good bread after all. The children of Israel wept again and said: "If only we had meat to eat! We remember the fish we ate in Egypt at no cost—also the cucumbers, melons, leeks, onions and garlic. But now we have lost our appetite; we never see anything but this manna!" (Num. 11:4–6).

Moses rebuked them and told them God was about to give them quail: "'Consecrate yourselves in preparation for tomorrow, when you will eat meat. The LORD heard you when you wailed, "If only we had meat to eat! We were better off in Egypt!" Now the LORD will give you meat, and you will eat it. You will not eat it for just one day, or two days, or five, ten or twenty days, but for a whole month—until it comes out of your nostrils and you loathe it—because you have rejected the LORD, who is among you . . .'" (Num. 11:18–20a).

When the children of Israel disputed with God over manna, they proved exactly what I said to Satan in the wilderness temptation: "Man does not live on bread alone" (Matt. 4:4).

There is a hunger that drives the human spirit. It is a hunger for meaning. When people find no meaning for their lives, they despair. There must be many in your circle of need who have never tasted this better bread. You know this glorious loaf. Indeed, you hold it in your hand. Please give it to them. It is the only Bread that matters.

> *Prayer*
> *Lord Jesus,*
> *I have tasted this joyous bread.*
> *The living loaf is mine.*
> *Help me never forget that the bread*
>   *is not mine to enjoy in the presence of the starving.*
> *There I must share it or be false to all whose meaning-hunger*
>   *leaves them weak and dying all around your church.*
> *I must divide my loaf and pass it on*
>   *to all the meaning-starved whose hope is gone.*
> *Amen.*

Interiorizing the Eternal Bread

John 6:51–55

"I am the living bread that came down out of heaven; if anyone eats of this bread, he shall live forever; and the bread also which I shall give for the life of the world is My flesh."

The Jews therefore began to argue with one another, saying, "How can this man give us his flesh to eat?" Jesus therefore said to them, "Truly, truly, I say to you, unless you eat the flesh of the Son of Man and drink His blood, you have no life in yourselves. He who eats My flesh and drinks My blood has eternal life, and I will raise him up on the last day. For My flesh is true food, and My blood is true drink."

This teaching sets forth the cost of discipleship. Consider the physical parallel for a moment. You may set a hot loaf of freshly baked bread before a starving man; and if he chooses not to eat it, he will die as surely as though there were no bread at all. Bread must be consumed to furnish life.

Just so, you may put my atoning sacrifice—my broken flesh and my spilled blood— before a man who is perishing in his sin and self-will. Unless he eats that flesh and drinks that blood—that is, unless he accepts my sacrifice—he will never have real life.

But there is in all this a stern call to discipleship. I was not merely inviting the lost to be saved. I was reminding them of the cost of that salvation. Appropriating the saving power of my cross meant that there was an equal cost for the believer. My dying presaged their own. I would pay the price of a martyr to furnish eternal life.

Those who take the wine and bread in Communion symbolize that they have already taken me into their lives. In this simple ritual, they agree that saving humankind is costly work. The communion ritual is a kind of string around the human finger. As often as people lift the cup and taste the loaf, they remember the length to which divine love went in order to save. But you are also to remember that you agreed to my Lordship in the process of becoming a Christian. When you said "Lord," you received me into your life with the understanding that I had the right to ask anything of you. Indeed, once you say the word "Lord," there is nothing unreasonable that I can ask. Then the very requiring of your soul is my right. You surrendered your will in breathing that one simple word. Your desires then and there were yielded unto me.

Therefore to eat my flesh and drink my blood is to participate in this double submission. My life belongs to my Father. He required the salvation of the world through my submission. I now require your own. I paid my price obediently. Do not spend your own life shopping for cheaper ways to redeem your world.

Prayer
Lord Jesus,
I want to be all that you require.
I want to give all that I implied
when first I called you Lord.
I eat your flesh and drink your blood, O Christ,
aware of the expense in sacrifice.
Amen.

No Other Options

John 6:60–62, 66–69

Many therefore of His disciples, when they heard this said, "This is a difficult statement; who can listen to it?" But Jesus, conscious that His disciples grumbled at this, said to them, "Does this cause you to stumble? What then if you should behold the Son of Man ascending where he was before?" . . .

As a result of this many of His disciples withdrew, and were not walking with Him anymore. Jesus said therefore to the twelve, "You do not want to go away also, do you?" Simon Peter answered Him, "Lord, to whom shall we go? You have words of eternal life. And we have believed and have come to know that You are the Holy One of God."

First memorize, then celebrate, Peter's rhetorical question, "Lord, to whom shall we go?" It is a question to be answered by all. Where can one go to find enduring meaning? To the latest guru of moral feather-bedding? To the enchantress of some New Age massage parlor? To contemplate a lotus leaf or read the latest self-help author? The demands of my narrower way are difficult, but there is no other.

The world I invaded at Bethlehem was not so large as it has since become. Then travel was arduous and slow. Any trip could require weeks and sometimes months to make. The driving hope of all who traveled was finding a possible shortcut that would allow travelers less time en route and more time at their destination. But it is not the geographical shortcut that most marks the human pursuit, but the philosophical shortcut. Seekers are always looking for a way to meaning that moves past the arduous disciplines of study and meditation. Everyone wants the most meaning that can be purchased for the least amount of discipline.

Union with me holds the greatest of human meaning. There is no easy way across the great deserts of sects and cults in the search of this meaning. So my message of hope does not fall easily on the ears of casual seekers. It was not an easy message to deliver to my disciples. It was not an easy message for them to receive. But it was an honest message. The human hunger for meaning is a wide continent of discipline that has to be crossed. Eternal life is the gift of commitment.

That day Peter summed up the heart of the gospel. "To whom shall we go?" has but one answer. Shortly after my ascension he said it in yet another way: "Salvation is found in no one else, for there is no other name under heaven given to men by which we must be saved" (Acts 4:12).

Prayer

Lord Jesus,
I realize that you alone
    are our passage through the iron gates
    of death.
I praise you, for I live.
Without you no one would.
So here I stand in the gilded light of day
    and bless one truth: There is no other way.
Amen.

Hiding from God in Church

Mark 7:9–13

He was also saying to them, "You nicely set aside the commandment of God in order to keep your tradition. For Moses said, 'HONOR YOUR FATHER AND YOUR MOTHER'; and 'HE WHO SPEAKS EVIL OF FATHER OR MOTHER, LET HIM BE PUT TO DEATH' [Exod. 20:12; Deut. 5:16]; but you say, 'If a man says to his father or mother, anything of mine you might have been helped by is Corban (that is to say, given to God),' you no longer permit him to do anything for his father or his mother; thus invalidating the word of God by your tradition which you have handed down; and you do many such things as that."

It is possible to hide from God inside his temple. The Pharisees were masters at this. They had the Torah that required them to obey. But they preferred to focus on their own set of legalisms that allowed them to wriggle out from under the heavier requirements of God. Their own set of rules got close to God's. In fact, some of them sounded as though God had written them. Still, the Pharisees were able to get around dealing with the big commandments of God by focusing on their own smaller legal code.

Hiding from God in church is really quite easy. In church your religious words fly so fast that it can appear that you are really involved with God. The truth is that your rhetoric becomes *a* god that keeps you from having to really deal with *the* God. Ritual so encrusts you that you never have to face the terror of meeting God in church. The high, cold, liturgical hymns and basso recitations have such a delicious religious sound that they become the substitute for an encounter.

Liturgy is not the only way you protect yourselves from an encounter. Some of you turn to "busianity," under which you also hide. Lest you should risk meeting God in the quiet center of your adoration, you turn your religious "busyness" to a high r.p.m. You fly at your churchy agendas so fast that you are not able to touch God in the whirl of your high-velocity programs. Soon you do not expect to find God in church. What you do expect is the elusive appearance of devotion, the theological chitchat, the unceasing rhetoric, and the dervish of high-speed programs. All these things make it seem that you know God, without the slightest danger that you have ever had to face Him.

But do not be deceived. You can only know me in that blessed leisure that never hurries your prayers—in that special quiet that knows only the noise of rushing wind. The joy of faith is only to be found in the far side of hurried, barren, arid protocol.

> *Prayer*
> *Lord Jesus,*
> *I've gone to church so often,*
>   *so filled with inner noise,*
>   *only to be met with so much outer noise,*
>   *that I sometimes go for weeks*
>   *in only a noisy empty walk with you.*
> *But the religious discord is especially thick.*
> *I find I can hide from you in this dense religious noise.*
> *Therefore,*
>   *Destroy the noise with some encounter true,*
>   *where I can never hide myself from you.*
> *Amen.*

O God, Have Mercy on All of Us Outside the Loop

Mark 7:24–30

And from there He arose and went away to the region of Tyre. And when He had entered a house, He wanted no one to know of it; yet He could not escape notice. But after hearing of Him, a woman whose little daughter had an unclean spirit, immediately came and fell at His feet. Now the woman was a Gentile, of the Syrophoenician race. And she kept asking Him to cast the demon out of her daughter. And He was saying to her, "Let the children be satisfied first, for it is not good to take the children's bread and throw it to the dogs."

But she answered and said to Him, "Yes, Lord, but even the dogs under the table feed on the children's crumbs." And He said to her, "Because of this answer go your way; the demon has gone out of your daughter." And going back to her home, she found the child lying on the bed, the demon having departed.

Beyond the circle of those who think they are special to God are the outcasts. Listen to the plaintive voice of those who know the sting of this word *outcast*. For to wear this word is to wear the pain that knows no balm for the longing, no friend who will touch, no counselor who will hear.

When the poor woman asked me about exorcising her daughter, I used the harsh words by which my race often referred to Gentiles: "dog!" The prejudices of my people had been filtered through a thousand years of anti-Semitism, even when I walked the earth. There were Jewish anthems that expressed themselves in such masculine prayers as, "Lord, I thank thee that I am not a Gentile, a dog, or a woman!" So when I said to the woman, ". . . it is not good to take the children's bread and throw it to the dogs," I was reflecting the strong racial exclusion that my race often expressed toward the others.

If God is God, he will never exclude any who cry out to him in need. Here was a woman who reminds us all that a loving God would not pick out some to call children and others to call dogs. Her tears touched me. Her need overwhelmed me. I healed her daughter, and all of those in her hometown must surely have realized that Christianity would never be a religion that would pick some people to love and others to condemn.

A great philosopher was once asked, "What is the ugliest word in the human language?" The philosopher answered in a single word, "Exclusive!"

The Syrophonecian woman brought the ugliness of that word home to my disciples. To be excluded is to be victimized by all that is ugly and unkind. Look around you. Has anyone come through your door at church? Was he alone? New in the city? Starved for anyone to say hello or, "I love you"? Then remember that I am the inclusive Christ. If you would be my friend, you must be his.

Prayer
Lord Jesus,
I would never consciously exclude
anyone from your grace.
Help me to look around that I might see
these lonely ones who crave a family.
Amen.

How Much Do You Have?

Matthew 15:32–35

And Jesus called His disciples to Him, and said, "I feel compassion for the multitude, because they have remained with Me now three days and have nothing to eat; and I do not wish to send them away hungry, lest they faint on the way." And the disciples said to Him, "Where would we get so many loaves in a desolate place to satisfy such a great multitude?" And Jesus said to them, "How many loaves do you have?" And they said, "Seven, and a few small fish." And He directed the multitude to sit down on the ground.

God needs a starting point to multiply anything we hope to be. Remember mathematics: zero times anything is still zero. You never have to give God much to see it increase, but you must give him all. From a few biscuits and a few fish, God proved himself the adequate caterer. He even gave them better, newer loaves, and sweeter, fresher fish. But then that's God's nature, to improve our resources with his ever-renewing Spirit.

But God will not multiply what we will not surrender. He only needs a fish and a biscuit to make a banquet, but he must have at least that much. Remember the grand rule of heaven's currency: "Give, and it will be given to you. A good measure, pressed down, shaken together and running over, will be poured into your lap. For with the measure you use, it will be measured to you" (Luke 6:38).

A little girl in a popular fable had a mother whose face was hideously scarred by an old injury. As the girl grew older she became increasingly ashamed to be seen with her mother, whose monstrous form often caused those they met on the sidewalk to skulk across to the other side of the street. She would find reasons not to accompany her mother or be seen outside with her. When she grew older, she married and moved away.

Her mother fell into hard times, but the girl—now a married woman—tried to forget all the unpleasant memories and thus refused to have anything to do with her mother, even though her mother was often hungry and alone. One day as she was rifling through her mother's things, she came across an old diary that described the fire that had swept their home when she was a child. Suddenly as she read the entry, she saw that her mother had become terribly burned by trying to save her life. She realized that she had gained redemption through her mother's scars. She was washed with shame. What was once hideous became beautiful in her sight. She at long last gave to her aging mother the kind of flamboyant love recorded long before in the old woman's scars.

If you were to see my hands, you might consider them ugly. They are very scarred; I'm sure you know why. Considering what I gave, may I ask what you are willing to give? You have only a few loaves and fishes? Lay them on the altar of God, and stand back. With such a gift, grace feeds a world.

Prayer
Lord Jesus,
I am selfish.
I haven't much and yet I cling to it
as though its small substance were of consequence
in eternity.
Help me to give you my small loaves and fish,
and multiply them any way you wish.
Amen.

Slowly Arriving at Sight

Mark 8:22–25

And they came to Bethsaida. And they brought a blind man to Him, and entreated Him to touch him. And taking the blind man by the hand, He brought him out of the village; and after spitting on his eyes, and laying His hands upon him, He asked him, "Do you see anything?" And he looked up and said, "I see men, for I am seeing them like trees, walking about." Then again He laid His hands upon his eyes; and he looked intently and was restored, and began to see everything clearly.

If you found me in a single, brilliant flash of grand repentance, be patient for those who found me in some slower way. Remember the man whose sight came in two stages.

A certain publican named John once received my gift of life in a remarkable conversion experience. As he put it, "The Lord Jesus came into my life and set my whole nervous system afire. I was saved and I knew it. It felt like squirrels were running up and down my spine!"

In his circle of new Christian friends, that was a welcome testimony. He always described his conversion in the same way, saying "his nervous system was afire and it felt like squirrels were running up and down his back." In time, John the publican became an evangelist. There was always great excitement in his meetings. Indeed, the only thing predictable in one of John's meetings was his methodology. He always treated all of his altar inquirers the same. After he evangelized a sinner, he always asked them the same question: "Sister, was your whole nervous system afire? And did it feel like squirrels running up and down your back!" Those who grudgingly confessed the running-squirrel sensation were freely welcomed into John's church. But if they were saved without it, they remained suspect in John's judgment.

One day John led a brother to Christ and then asked, "Did you feel the running squirrels?"

"No," replied the somber convert. "I feel nothing. But I know that Christ is in my life. I know that when I have studied more, I shall apprehend even more of Christ."

"Oh, pshaw!" cried John. "You feel nothing? No squirrels, no Christ!"

"But may I not experience Christ gradually?"

"No squirrels, no Christ," insisted John.

"Please, I beg you. Wait on me. In a month I may know him as you do!"

"No squirrels, no Christ," said John. "Find another church who can tolerate such shoddy, gradual salvation."

And so he did, but something beautiful in the Kingdom is broken when a brother with a different experience is shunned. Please celebrate those blind ones who, being healed, see instantly. But offer those your patient love who come more gradually to light.

Prayer
  Lord Jesus,
  I want to give you the freedom
    to call all the blind to sight
    in any way you want to heal them.
  I came so quickly and so readily to light,
    help me be patient with the slow of sight.
  Amen.

The Confession

Matthew 16:13–16

Now when Jesus came into the district of Caesarea Philippi, He began asking His disciples, saying, "Who do people say that the Son of Man is?" And they said, "Some say John the Baptist; and others, Elijah; but still others, Jeremiah, or one of the prophets." He said to them, "But who do you say that I am?" And Simon Peter answered and said, "Thou art the Christ, the Son of the living God."

There is but one confession for the church: "Thou art the Christ, the Son of the living God." This remains the Christian church's official confession.

The variety of opinions that were circulating about me during those days when I walked the earth has not changed.

To the philosopher, I will be the essence of cosmic truth.
To the educator, I will be a great Teacher.
To the hungry, I will be the Bread of life.
To the thirsty, I will be the Living Water.
To the lonely, I will be the Friend.
To the confused, I will be the Counselor.
To the scientist, I will be the source of universal order.
To the musician, I will be all cosmic harmony.
To the poet, I will be transcendent love.
To the artist, I will be true beauty.

But amid all these various ways of seeing or thinking of me, the world will need the clarifying word—that wonderful insight and definition—that Peter offered that day in Caesarea Philippi: "You are the Christ!"

Peter's confession is to be yours. For your own sake cry, "I believe that thou art the Christ, the Son of the Living God!"

Prayer
Lord Jesus,
I would not confess myself as adequate,
   my needs are too great.
I would not confess my friends as adequate,
   they have too often been unable to meet my needs.
Nor would I confess my church as adequate,
   for sometimes when I've needed them they've forgotten me.
So here and now I cry, "Thou art the Lord!"
   I hide my life in thee, Incarnate Word.
Amen.

The Church Triumphant

Matthew 16:17–18

And Jesus answered and said to him, "Blessed are you, Simon Barjona, because flesh and blood did not reveal this to you, but My Father who is in heaven. And I also say to you that you are Peter, and upon this rock I will build My church; and the gates of Hades shall not overpower it."

In these words I have hidden the church's confidence: "the gates of hell shall not overpower it." Does such a statement seem too strong? Can you think of times when you needed the church and it seemed to let you down?

From time to time I too have been disappointed in the performance of my church. But look beneath her institutional sins and see all that she has accomplished.

She has taken education around the world. She has advanced the human condition. She ultimately abolished slavery and child labor laws. She smashed into caste-locked lands with social freedom. She taught the Romans the evils of infanticide. My church established hospitals, orphanages, and asylums. My church has brought food and shelters to the inner city. In short, my church is glorious! In fact, it is ever stronger day by day.

The church is not weak. Indeed, she is the church triumphant. She has ever marched to the great hymn:

> The church's one foundation is Jesus Christ her Lord;
> She is His new creation, by Spirit and the Word:
> From heav'n He came and sought her to be His holy bride,
> With his own blood He bought her, and for her life He died.
>
> Elect from every nation, yet one o'er all the earth,
> Her charter of salvation, one Lord, one faith, one birth;
> One holy name she blesses, partakes one holy food,
> And to one hope she presses, with every grace endued.
>
> 'Mid toil and tribulation, and tumult of her war,
> She waits the consummation of peace forevermore;
> Till with the vision glorious, her longing eyes are blest,
> And the great church victorious shall be the church at rest.
>
> (Words by Samuel J. Stone)

The gates of hell shall not prevail against my church.

Prayer
Lord Jesus,
How wonderful it is to know
that in linking my littleness to your great church,
I will never cease to move in a direct line
to the perfect and completed center of your historical purposes.
Above the smoke of Armageddon's hour,
the towers of the church will rise at last with power.
Amen.

The Authority in Faith

Matthew 16:19
"I will give you the keys of the kingdom of heaven; and whatever you shall bind on earth shall be bound in heaven, and whatever you shall loose on earth shall be loosed in heaven."

Before I rose above Mt. Olivet in my ascension, I called for the execution of God's world plan. The keys of the kingdom of God belong to my church. Consider the power of these keys. They were meant to unlock souls in Satan's dungeons of deception. These keys were created to open the chasms of dark fear to the glorious light of God. These keys were meant to unchain the souls sweltering under oppressive governments. These keys were meant to unbolt science and literature and art.

Is spiritual understanding locked to you? Use the keys.

Is power in prayer locked to you? Use the keys.

Would you be free of some conforming passion? Use the keys.

Is your heart locked in hardness? Use the keys.

The stewardship of these keys I commit to my church. I once lamented over Jerusalem, "If you . . . had only known on this day what would bring you peace . . ." (Luke 19:42). Jerusalem lived without sensing the great place that she might have held in the plan of God.

Jerusalem's sin has become the sin of the church in every age. I pity my church. She seems to have forgotten the stewardship that is hers. Heaven might spread its colonies throughout earth if only the church would remember her commission.

I told my disciples long ago: "He who listens to you listens to me; he who rejects you rejects me; but he who rejects me rejects him who sent me" (Luke 10:16).

You have the keys! Use those keys, and hell itself will tremble. Together we will exalt my Father's plan.

The commission is yours.

The glory will be mine!

Prayer
Lord Jesus,
I know I spend so much of my time
doing so little.
I am the tender of trivia,
when I ought to use the keys
and make hell tremble.
Help me use the keys of destiny
and unlock hell and make it bow to thee.
Amen.

Getting the God-View

Matthew 16:21–23

From that time Jesus Christ began to show His disciples that He must go to Jerusalem, and suffer many things from the elders and chief priests and scribes, and be killed, and be raised up on the third day. And Peter took Him aside and began to rebuke Him, saying, "God forbid it, Lord! This shall never happen to You." But He turned and said to Peter, "Get behind Me, Satan! You are a stumbling block to Me; for you are not setting your mind on God's interests, but man's."

The greatest stumbling block to the discovery of God's will may be the failure to get the God-view of your circumstances. Peter followed me through times of my burgeoning popularity. He was convinced that the Kingdom that I represented would continue to be as popular in the future as in the past. We had known some criticism, but for the most part we had known large crowds and wide fame. The Kingdom was heady, popular work for my starstruck followers. They wanted this popularity to go on forever.

Peter believed that I would be king, and he and all of the rest would be the newly appointed dukes and earls of my new kingdom—big shots of reputation.

Now came the hard truth. All that we had experienced would soon fall upon hard times. I would die; they would be scattered. In time the world would be a better place to live. But the change would come only after they had endured great trials that drove them to their knees in fear.

The good things God has planned for his children will only come after the heart is purified. Most of the time that purity is attained through suffering rather than compliments. If you were lured into conversion by anyone who promised you a bed of roses, remember my rebuke to Peter. It is not my intention to make your life easy, but beautiful—not fun, but usable—not pleasant, but meaningful.

See the God-view of all that I require. The God-view is somewhat like your own except that instead of looking from the present and trying to guess what the end will be, God looks from the end and sees how the present circumstances fit in. It is much more gratifying to look back and see how all things were working together to produce your ultimate glory than it is to look ahead and wonder what some particular moment means. Walking into an uncertain future is easier if you remember that no step you take in the darkness will be taken alone.

Prayer

Lord Jesus,
I will not make demands upon you
    that you must make my life beautiful and simple.
I rather shall require of my own self
    that obedience which trusts you in the dark places,
    knowing you will be there.
I fear to walk alone in garish light.
I'd rather walk with you in the demon's night.
Amen.

Life's Bottom Line

Matthew 16:24–26

Then Jesus said to His disciples, "If anyone wishes to come after Me, let him deny himself, and take up his cross, and follow Me. For whoever wishes to save his life shall lose it; but whoever loses his life for My sake shall find it. For what will a man be profited, if he gains the whole world, and forfeits his soul? Or what will a man give in exchange for his soul?"

There's only one treasure you can't afford to lose: your soul. It is easy to forget the value of this asset. Your soul is so naturally a part of you that you forget its nondemanding existence. Your soul is there, like a part of your body that is healthy and without pain. As long as that part of your body works well, you need not pay it heed. It is like a good, well-functioning leg. It is equally indispensable. You cannot do without it. It is just there; *it is you.*

The Bible says that when God created Adam, God breathed into Adam the breath of life and he became a living soul—*a nephesh* (Gen. 2:7). The Bible does not say that Adam *had* a soul but he *was* a soul. The *nephesh* is our true being, our true self. We lose our authenticity, our *genuine being,* when we lose our *nephesh.*

Therefore, when I ask, "What shall it profit to lose your soul?" I am really referring to the loss of your *self.* If throughout your life, you serve only some never-ending list of wants, you will likely amass a great deal of goods. But there are two ways you lose your soul. The first and most obvious is the grand way. This grand loss comes at the hour of death when the real you, your living being, your *nephesh,* perishes (John 3:16) and is gone forever. Death is indeed a grand disinheritance. The final gates of life are so narrow that only the most unencumbered of souls may pass through it. Those that are encrusted with self-importance, greed, and years of self-will cannot squeeze through the portals.

The most general way that souls are lost is through the gradual erosion of being. True being, real *nephesh,* is like a sandbar that the tides of our *too-good-to-resist-good-deals* and the storms of our *must-have-indulgences* erode, swallowed up in the dark seas of death.

The majority of those who lose themselves are dead long before they reach the final gates. There is very little of them left to die when the time comes. They have become nothing more than the sallow-eyed and sunken remains of their selfish choices. How poorly they bargained their lives. They kept pursuing what they wanted, following their own desires until they were but the shadows of their chase. The grand mansions of eternity receded at last, beyond the walls they would not climb. They are lost!

Prayer
Lord Jesus,
I pray that I may learn the
simple dignity of the word no.
It is not a long word, but a hard word to speak
when the pressure of my appetites is full upon me.
Unless I can learn this simple syllable of denial,
I will in time be unable to locate myself.
I want to learn the art of self-control,
lest I should gain the world and lose my soul.
Amen.

The Law, the Prophets, and Grace

Mark 9:2–4

And six days later, Jesus took with Him Peter and James and John, and brought them up to a high mountain by themselves. And He was transfigured before them; and His garments became radiant and exceedingly white, as no launderer on earth can whiten them. And Elijah appeared to them along with Moses; and they were talking with Jesus.

The Mount of Transfiguration was a summit of realms. There shall not be such a meeting again. The two who appeared with me had been gone for a long time. Elijah must be listed among the greatest of the prophets. He did not die, but was taken bodily into heaven (2 Kings 2:11). Moses did die and was buried in Moab (Deut. 34:5–6).

Moses had shaped the heart of Israel by giving them the Ten Commandments. He had also formed the heart of the Hebrew faith by writing the first five books of the Old Testament. These five glorious books contained the story of the formation of Israel. Indeed, these books record the creation of the entire cosmos. But they contained also the law—the Ten Commandments, laws that had forged a huge assembly of wondering nomads into the most influential nation of history.

Elijah represented the prophets. He was without a doubt the most exotic of all the prophets. And who were the prophets? They were the aloof, often single, always fiery and passionate preachers. They formed the caste of interpreters of the will of God for the kings and the nation. They were often maltreated and abused and sometimes martyred. But they could always be depended upon to tell God's truth, even when those truths were inconvenient or unpopular. The prophets represented God on earth. These courageous preachers had God's ear, and all who claimed to love God knew it was unwise not to listen.

On the mount I represented grace. Grace was about to dawn upon the earth. Grace was the heart of a glorious new relationship! The law of Moses—never to be transcended—was about to be upgraded by the notion that God could redeem human beings on the basis of my sacrifice. Grace meant there was no hierarchy of approach. There was no veil in the temple, no Jews, no Gentiles. The God of grace would be accessible to all.

On the Mount of Transfiguration the law of Moses, the prophecy of Elijah, and grace eternal sat together in counsel. Moses laid his laws at my feet on that mountain. Elijah put his special revelations into my hands. Grace was on the way. I was its sentinel.

Prayer
Lord Jesus,
How grateful I am for the Ten Commandments,
and even more grateful that I don't have to keep them all perfectly
to go to heaven when I die.
How grateful I am for the prophecies of those special men of old
who spoke so often for a less accessible God,
and even more grateful that I can come to you directly for insight
without waiting for special revelation.
Mostly I am grateful for that special place
your sacrifice provided me in grace.
Amen.

Replying to Majesty with Silence

Mark 9:5–7

And Peter answered and said to Jesus, "Rabbi, it is good for us to be here; and let us make three tabernacles, one for You, and one for Moses, and one for Elijah." For he did not know what to answer; for they became terrified. Then a cloud formed, overshadowing them, and a voice came out of the cloud, "This My beloved Son, listen to Him!"

It is impossible to miss Peter's love for the mountaintop religious experience. Peter desired to prolong the best of religious experiences. The joy of a great experience with God causes people to want to cling to the compelling warmth of the mystery. Miracles father a mysterious addiction to their unworldly glory. Who would want to leave God when his awesome presence is so real? We cannot escape the desire to capture these overwhelming moments and keep them for seasons of our own special enjoyment.

But Peter had a valuable lesson to learn.

There is but one reply to majesty—silence. Mark said that Peter got chatty because "he did not know what to say" (Mark 9:6). When you are so overwhelmed with the reality of God that you don't know what to say, say nothing. Keep all your words to yourself in grand moments, lest they betray your shallowness.

Now see Simon Peter! He is ever talkative and not very comfortable in the dignity of God. Now he is in on the highest of high-level meetings. No human councils or senates could ever compare with this high-level meeting. The summit of all earthly ages met in council. Yet Simon Peter talks! He would do well to remember, "Be still, and know that I am God" (Ps. 46:10).

Would you, yourself, find the heart of God's majesty? Then do not try to talk your way into the holy quiet of his engulfing splendor. Rather, learn the art of silence. Then you may live in the joy of his presence.

Prayer
Lord Jesus,
Most of us are so ill at ease
in the center of your throne room
that we forget that your majesty is grander than
our pettiness.
I want to wait in silence at your chair
to see the splendor of your royalty in prayer.
Amen.

The Imperative Valleys

Luke 9:37–43a

And it came about on the next day, that when they had come down from the mountain, a great multitude met Him. And behold, a man from the multitude shouted out, saying, "Teacher, I beg You to look at my son, for he is my only boy, and behold, a spirit seizes him, and he suddenly screams, and it throws him into a convulsion with foaming at the mouth, and as it mauls him, it scarcely leaves him. And I begged Your disciples to cast it out, and they could not."

And Jesus answered and said, "O unbelieving and perverted generation, how long shall I be with you, and put up with you? Bring your son here." And while he was still approaching, the demon dashed him to the ground, and threw him into a convulsion. But Jesus rebuked the unclean spirit, and healed the boy, and gave him back to his father. And they were all amazed at the greatness of God.

The Mount of Transfiguration was such a glorious experience that Peter in exuberance cried out, "Let us put up three shelters" (Mark 9:5). He wanted to stay forever! Only the shallow of soul would not feel the urge to camp in the middle of such a spiritual experience. But the thirst for those ultimate religious experiences can mislead. These wonderful satisfactions can lead people to quit loving God and begin to love experiencing God. They will lead people to build tents on mountaintops and refuse to get involved in the needy affairs of the valley below.

Nothing is more inherently selfish than that utter longing for the mountaintop religious experience. Whole armies of Christians go to church, seeking a feel-good Christianity. The choral anthems of adoration are traded for emotive, religious ditties. The worshipers touch each other; they clamp their eyes shut, weep, laugh, and enjoy. No one would want a religion void of emotion, but beware the temptation to make emotional experience the god of easy Sundays. In a cold world where faith is scorned, it is easy to mistake the warmth of worship as the goal of our lives. God is the goal of life. Emotion may be the result of our meeting with God, but it is never the goal of it.

On the day we came down from the mountain of transfiguration into the real world, there were needs to meet. On the mountaintop we had basked in the realities of God. But in the valley we met a plaintive man in utter need. His only son was demonic. In touching the boy and driving out the demons, my disciples learned the glory of the Kingdom. The victory is often in the valley. Mountaintops without ministry are irrelevant.

> *Prayer*
> *Lord Jesus,*
> *I must confess my utter need*
> *to "feel" your stirring in my heart to live.*
> *I must be where I can feel you take possession*
> *of my nervous system and "bless" me with the actual*
> *experience of the mountaintop.*
> *But help me lay aside my need to feel,*
> *that I may touch and love and heal.*
> *Amen.*

Feeding the Demons of Our Lives

Matthew 17:19–21

Then the disciples came to Jesus privately and said, "Why could we not cast it out?"
And He said to them, "Because of the littleness of your faith; for truly I say to you, if you shall have faith as a mustard seed, you shall say to this mountain, 'Move from here to there,' and it shall move; and nothing shall be impossible to you. [But this kind does not go out except by prayer and fasting."]

Once in an ancient kingdom there lived a man who kept a serpent. No one knew he had the serpent, for serpents were illegal. Still, there was something deliciously beautiful about the beast. It was almost iridescent and seemed lit from the inside out. When he stroked it in the darkness, it would draw near to him. The snake at last possessed the man's senses.

The serpent could only be hidden for a while, for it grew large. It was at last common knowledge that the man had the beast. At length the man became afraid of it. One night as he slept, the beast circled its coils quietly around him. He woke and saw that he was trapped. He began to cry for help. The villagers heard his cry and came to help him. But fearing the size of the monster, they laid aside their sticks and stones, knowing they were not able to overcome it.

Finally the village counselor told them why they could not kill the serpent. "You cannot help the poor man because each of you are keeping little serpents of your own. Bring your own secret serpents to the square, and we shall have a serpent killing! Do not think you can kill *beyond* you what you will not kill *within* you!" They came and set their own serpents down in the sunlight.

"Kill them without mercy; do not show them pity lest your pity allow them to live. Remember, you too can become what lives in the cave!" said their counselor.

Thus they began to stomp the creatures, who begged most pitifully to be spared. But the villagers did not listen. Soon the serpents were all dead. "Now you may advance on the great serpent in the cave," said the counselor. But when they arrived to kill the great serpent the beast was dead already, and the poor man whom he had nearly destroyed came out of the cave befuddled. "The monster is dead," he confessed. "I am free."

"Not quite," said the counselor. He reached into the man's pocket and pulled out a very small serpent and threw it on the ground. "Here is the offspring of that which you have slain." The man looked down at his very small foe.

"Do not think of this serpent as small. Remember what it soon will be. You know what to do," said the counselor. Indeed he did. He placed his heel on the head of the tiny thing and crushed it.

"Now you are free!" said the counselor. And so he was.

Prayer
Lord Jesus,
Help me never give those demons place
lest I nourish them by my approval.
I want to say to each small sin, "I charge
'Begone you fiend!' lest it with time grows large."
Amen.

The Greatness beyond Competition

Luke 9:46–48

And an argument arose among them as to which of them might be the greatest. But Jesus, knowing what they were thinking in their heart, took a child and stood him by His side, and said to them, "Whoever receives this child in My name receives Me; and whoever receives Me receives Him who sent Me; for he who is least among you, this is the one who is great."

Competition is a common sin among those who aspire to leadership in my church. Consider the greatness that lies beyond competition: it is the greatness of servanthood. Servants seek not to control but to enable others to become all they can be.

Servants live their lives in a way that says, "If you want to find me, do not seek me on some pedestal of power. Rather, seek me beneath your own feet, for that is where you'll find me." Does this seem demeaning? It is not. It is the very code by which I lived when I came to earth. In me God, the Father, was saying, "If you want me, look for me not in the lofty skies but in the needy dusty towns of Palestine."

For you see, God has no competitors. Therefore, I did not come to earth to be president of anything, but the servant of all. So while "how to overcome your competition with brilliant success" is a major theme on earth, it holds no fascination in heaven. I was not born in Bethlehem to give Caesar a run for his money. Still, Caesar has nowhere near the historical reputation that I have. Yet all I came to do was serve.

Do not tell God all your plans for success. If you want God's approval, humble yourself and serve others. Then you will gain the same rapt attention of the angels that I received when I reentered heaven.

Heaven has never been much impressed with the question "Who shall be greatest?" It more esteems the plaintive question of the disciple who asks, fearfully lest he drop the prize, "Point me, dear Christ, to some path of servanthood. If I cannot live like you, I will not live at all."

Prayer
Lord Jesus,
I don't want to be greatest anywhere,
unless it be the greatest in bearing all you ask.
Give me no prize
unless it be the prize of standing in your presence.
May I take off my earthly, foolish crown
and at your feet lay egotism down.
Amen.

Making Room for All Confessors

Mark 9:38–40

John said to Him, "Teacher, we saw someone casting out demons in Your name, and we tried to hinder him because he was not following us." But Jesus said, "Do not hinder him, for there is no one who shall perform a miracle in My name, and be able soon afterward to speak evil of Me. For he who is not against us is for us."

How easy it is to grow stingy with grace. How easy it is to take personal empires and break them down into tiny little provinces of "like us" and "not like us." None should take something as vast and diverse as the Kingdom of God and splinter it into a million little provinces of special-interest bishoprics. Beware all who want to start even more new partitions in my already too-divided Kingdom. It is too cosmic and beautiful to wear such small, unlovely divisions.

Instead of being proud of your small Christian species, learn to celebrate all who bear the cross. Be made rich by the variety. Bless your inclusiveness. Never "smallify" great truths by keeping them in little packages at the center of your private experience.

John, son of Zebedee, wanted to be sure he was certifying the Christian faith and keeping everyone in the one true doctrinal camp. O for the divine thump on the skull! It can set us free of narrow exclusivism of rigid provincialism. How glorious it would be if all Christians could swallow this infernal urge to "call down fire on Samaritans." You are far more drawn together by your common hatreds than your common loves. You develop far more pride when you examine your differences with others than when you consider your similarities. You are made larger in your own eyes by contrasting yourselves with weaker brothers than you are by wanting to be like them. Thus, if you really want to develop corporate pride and "make your church grow," you have to keep quoting the statistics on how poorly your competitors are doing.

In fact, in American suburbs my heart is broken by large, competitive churches who wouldn't dare be friends for fear of losing their competitive edge. Their gloating, church-growth spirit makes their megafellowships erupt in megapraise with the most minimal examples of what the church should really be doing to follow me.

I beg you, love your brothers and sisters in other fellowships. Cease calling down fire from heaven on believers who worship me in ways different from your own. Rather, bless all who love me. Then I will send down fire to warm the unconverted world.

Prayer
Lord Jesus,
I will not think so much of my church
that it keeps me from thinking well of all churches.
I will not call down fire on those beyond the borders of my church,
unless it be that Pentecostal fire that quickens all churches.
I have no brother-censure, no blame.
I send no fire, yet crave your holy flame.
Amen.

Disciples of the Dipper

Mark 9:41

"For whoever gives you a cup of water to drink because of your name as followers of Christ, truly I say to you, he shall not lose his reward."

If you are a disciple, consider a tenet of grace: hospitality. Always cherish the unsolicited knock at your door. Is anyone there who is thirsty? Get your dipper ready! Be generous to any who stumble in out of the desert. Are you a sister of ministry, a brother of the dipper?

Water is a symbol of hospitality. Why water? Because even the poor can own water, and therefore even the poor have much to offer the desert wayfarers.

Hospitality involves a willingness to see people in a new way. It is the ability to smile when need comes bounding into your tightly scheduled day. It baptizes your interruptions as opportunities.

Do you protest that you have nothing to offer them? Nonsense! You have water! When you give a thirsty person that dipper of water, you take your place in that long-standing honor roll of the lovers of God. Does water seem too little a thing to celebrate? Remember that when I was on the cross, every fiber of my dying body was in need. I cried, "I am thirsty!" (John 19:28). They gave me only vinegar. My cry was for water.

The thirsty are all around you.

Extend the cold, sweet dipper.

Water makes the world rich.

It is the best refreshment at any occasion.

Prayer
Lord Jesus,
I once thirsted in the barren land,
where I lived a barren life.
I cried, "I thirst,"
and you were there with water.
I drank, never to thirst again.
I want to live with like fidelity
and prize the gift of hospitality.
Amen.

To Offend the Process of Spiritual Growth

Mark 9:42

"And whoever causes one of these little ones who believe to stumble, it would be better for him if, with a heavy millstone hung around his neck, he had been cast into the sea."

God is a sculptor. He fashions every piece of willing marble into his image. This is particularly true of little children. They are easily misled, easily shaped into monstrous human forms by adults who will not permit God to do his work. To take a child and shape it like yourself without any reference to God delays the finishing work of God. Your interference can be costly.

Once a deposed king and queen were executed by insurgents. The same conquering revolutionaries took the surviving son to a lonely cell to brainwash the boy with the new harsh doctrines of conquerors. They forced the boy at swordpoint to say he hated his parents. They made him denounce his father by calling him a "former aristocrat and tyrant." Then they compelled him to call his mother a "former debaucher and prostitute!" Finally the tyrants forced the prince to say he was glad his dead parents were in hell. They made him cry before the crowds, "I spit upon their graves!"

Woe to all who mistreat children. The millstone is ready for such as would offend these little ones. Why? Because children have no advocate on earth. A mother may torture her own young, and who will defend and protect her little ones from her abusiveness? A father may secretly abuse his own daughter, and none will ever know the child's inner pain. These little ones will weep in the dark, unable to understand. Have you ever watched a child rebuked or beaten in public? Their broad eyes narrow to slits of confusion. Their humiliation by the people they love best becomes an unthinkable ulcer in their tiny hearts. In their childish minds they feel it is all their fault; if only they "try to do better," they may stop the flow of terror. Heaven reaches out to such children even as it scorns those who hurt them.

The millstone is waiting for all who abuse God's lovely little ones. Heaven has keen ears. When frightened children whimper, the waiting recompense of heaven records their cries and waits.

Prayer
Lord Jesus,
Help me to be a friend to every child I meet.
In a day so filled with cruel souls,
*   so many children carry scars of unthinkable pain*
*   and horrible abuse.*
I want to be like you are, Christ above,
*   and show each child the riches of your love.*
Amen.

Appetite Management

Mark 9:43–48

"And if your hand causes you to stumble, cut it off; it is better for you to enter life crippled, than having your two hands, to go into hell, into the unquenchable fire [where THEIR WORM DOES NOT DIE, AND THE FIRE IS NOT QUENCHED.] And if your foot causes you to stumble, cut it off; it is better for you to enter life lame, than having your two feet, to be cast into hell, [where THEIR WORM DOES NOT DIE, AND THE FIRE IS NOT QUENCHED.] And if your eye causes you to stumble, cast it out; it is better for you to enter the kingdom of God with one eye, than having two eyes, to be cast into hell, where THEIR WORM DOES NOT DIE, AND THE FIRE IS NOT QUENCHED" [Isa. 66:24].

Addiction is the result of choices. Let all enslaved by any passion remember this: you once controlled the addiction that now controls you. You once encouraged those foundry devils even as they forged the chains of your bondage.

A certain man made frequent business trips to many cities, indulging in illicit trade. His devious business seemed innocent enough at first. His indulgence never threatened his reputation. He was sensible about his taste. But his appetites could not remain forever distant. At last he took into his home those indulgences that spoiled life in distant cities. Now he cannot stop. He dare not really consider what he has become. When his passion lies spent, he thinks of lost freedom. He remembers that day so long ago when he was free to choose—long ago, before his choosing passed the point of no return.

Now, while you are free, you can destroy your own poor choices. Deny the little things that grow to monsters of abuse. Do it! For if you wait you will die slowly, a thousand times for each of your permissions. Then your permissions will gather against you. They will bully you and shove you into endless need and shame, a desperate if temporary hell. Therefore, if your hand or foot or eye leads you into such fire, cleave the offense. Cut it all away. There is a worse fate than being an amputee.

> *Prayer*
> *Lord Jesus,*
> *there are so many things that seem so innocent*
>   *and so controllable.*
> *How I hate the freedom they assess*
>   *because I will not speak my "Nays"*
>   *as loudly as I grin my sweet "Why nots?"*
>   *I will beware the devil forging chains*
>   *lest he should buy my mind and own my brain.*
> *Amen.*

The Power of Agreement

Matthew 18:19–20

"Again I say to you, that if two of you agree on earth about anything that they may ask, it shall be done for them by My Father who is in heaven. For where two or three have gathered together in My name, there I am in their midst."

The closet is the place I long to meet you. People never get to know me unless they are prepared to pay the price of praying alone. Only in praying alone to me can you know the intimacy of real love. I will not disclose myself fully to more than one person at a time. Those who have written of my fullest love and best explained my nature to the world were not strangers to the prayer closet. There they met with me in secret, and my Father who sees in secret rewarded them openly (Matt. 6:6).

But praying knows another kind of power. That force is born when you meet with another Christian. In the company of a friend the art of intercession can be honed. Two or three together can powerfully address the needs of life. Find a small, two-person altar. Mark the need. Agree in prayer. You may be sure that I will be there.

Ask what you will according to God's will, for "the world and its desires pass away, but the man who does the will of God lives forever" (1 John 2:17). Paul reminded us not to "conform any longer to the pattern to this world, but be transformed by the renewing of your mind. Then you will be able to test and approve what God's will is—his good, pleasing, and perfect will" (Rom. 12:2). Always ask according to God's will. Remember my agonizing prayer in Gethsemane: "not my will, but yours be done" (Luke 22:42). In Gethsemane my human reflex was to get around the cross painlessly. But even there I sought God's will. What the Father wants is always the last, best guide to honest praying.

Besides asking for what you want within the Father's will, you must also ask without wavering (Heb. 10:22–23) in your confidence that God really can do all you ask. "Is any one of you in trouble? He should pray. Is anyone happy? Let him sing songs of praise. Is any one of you sick? He should call the elders of the church to pray over him and anoint him with oil in the name of the Lord. And the prayer offered in faith will make the sick person well; the Lord will raise him up" (James 5:13–15).

Let your need to be alone with me nourish you with inwardness. Then join your life, renewed by our private conversations together, into the life of another. You will enjoy the abundance such prayer always asks.

Prayer
Lord Jesus,
I want to meet with two in the full confidence
that when I do, there will be three.
Indeed, I want to meet with three in the full confidence
that when I do, there will be four.
Then will I see your power and record the fame
of all that is when two stand on your name.
Amen.

The Level Ground at the Foot of the Cross

Matthew 18:21–30

Then Peter came and said to Him, "Lord, how often shall my brother sin against me and I forgive him? Up to seven times?"

Jesus said to him, "I do not say to you, up to seven times, but up to seventy times seven. For this reason the kingdom of heaven may be compared to a certain king who wished to settle accounts with his slaves. And when he had begun to settle them, there was brought to him one who owed him ten thousand talents. But since he did not have the means to repay, his lord commanded him to be sold, along with his wife and children and all that he had, and repayment to be made. The slave therefore falling down, prostrated himself before him, saying, 'Have patience with me, and I will repay you everything.' And the lord of that slave felt compassion and released him and forgave him the debt.

"But that slave went out and found one of his fellow slaves who owed him a hundred denarii; and he seized him and began to choke him, saying, 'Pay back what you owe.' So his fellow slave fell down and began to entreat him, saying, 'Have patience with me and I will repay you.' He was unwilling however, but went and threw him in prison until he should pay back what was owed.

The church is the forgiving colony of the forgiven. Nothing is more contradictory than a Christian who will not forgive. Remember how needy you were when you first wept over the state of your sin? My forgiveness touched you with a kind of joy. Why, then, would you ever hold anyone accountable for their offenses?

Therefore I call you to the cross. Stand there and gaze up at me in wonderment and sing that gracious grace that asks these four questions:

> Have you been to Jesus for the cleansing pow'r?
> Are you washed in the blood of the Lamb?
> Are you fully trusting in His grace this hour?
> Are you washed in the blood of the Lamb?
>
> (Elisah A. Hoffman)

Then when you have answered these four questions, rebuke all your self-righteousness with this hymn:

Forbid it, Lord, that I should boast, save in the death of Christ, my God;

All the vain things that charm me most, I sacrifice them to His blood.

All who have been forgiven must forgive. To have life eternal is to enter the fellowship of the forgiving forgiven.

(Isaac Watts)

Prayer
Lord Jesus,
Your cross, the faithful, all-forgiving cross,
never stops forgiving me.
Shall I then lose patience with those
I must repeatedly forgive?
No, if I repeatedly am graced by heaven,
I shall forgive then seventy times seven.
Amen.

Blessing Rejection

Luke 9:51–56

And it came about, when the days were approaching for His ascension, that He resolutely set His face to go to Jerusalem; and He sent messengers on ahead of Him. And they went, and entered a village of the Samaritans, to make arrangements for Him. And they did not receive Him, because He was journeying with His face toward Jerusalem. And when His disciples James and John saw this, they said, "Lord, do You want us to command fire to come down from heaven and consume them?"

But He turned and rebuked them, [and said, "You do not know what kind of spirit you are of; for the Son of Man did not come to destroy men's lives, but to save them."] And they went on to another village.

It is difficult to answer harsh rejection with a blessing, but this is the Kingdom requirement. It is human to want to answer injury with injury. It is fun to play God, especially if you have the earthly power to do it.

Calling down fire from heaven upon your enemies is the abscess of a hurt soul. Were even the worthiest of Christians granted the power to make sinners pay for their harsh ways, lightning would be more frequent upon the earth. So God retains this power to protect the earth from the endless temper tantrums of the insulted.

Harshness should be answered with blessing. Remember the sins of Balak? He tried to hire the Moabite prophet, Balaam, to curse Israel (Num. 22–24). But each time Balaam stood to curse Israel, only blessings came out of his mouth.

So will it be when you walk closely with me. Your love for me will so weld us in purpose and insight that you will be unable to call down fire on anyone.

The urge to get even with our critics comes from a shallow walk of faith. Those who love God more are less apt to call down fire. As believers mature in their Christian life, unbridled anger disappears. As the believer's temper comes beneath my feet, their use of instant lightning bolts is less frequent.

How should you handle rejection? Without a haughty sense of judgment. Those who may deserve your harshness are also those most in need of your good will. Lightning was not heaven's answer when you needed grace. Make love your reply to the noisy and sometimes nasty Samaritans on your pilgrimage.

Prayer
Lord Jesus,
When I am angry, my anger is the evident token of my depravity.
I want to learn not to answer hostility in kind.
I want to bless my gainsayers.
I want to look out from my own cross
    and forgive my executioners.
Help me to answer hate with warm reply,
    a dying soul who's watched the Savior die.
Amen.

Following When You Don't Know the Destination

Luke 9:57–58

And as they were going along the road, someone said to Him, "I will follow You wherever You go." And Jesus said to him, "The foxes have holes, and the birds of the air have nests, but the Son of Man has nowhere to lay His head."

The key to your obedience in following me lies not in finding out where I am going. The key lies in following me even when you have no idea where I am going. The will of God is not a road map and timetable on which your entire course and estimated time of arrival are clearly marked. Faith is a pilgrimage for pilgrims who are willing to get their travel plans one day at a time.

"By faith Abraham, when called to go to a place he would later receive as his inheritance, obeyed and went, even though he did not know where he was going. By faith he made his home in the promised land like a stranger in a foreign country; he lived in tents, as did Isaac and Jacob, who were heirs with him of the same promise" (Heb. 11:8–9). All should follow me in dependency, knowing that God will sometimes not reveal the next step until we take it. "All these people were still living by faith when they died. They did not receive the things promised; they only saw them and welcomed them from a distance. And they admitted that they were aliens and strangers on earth" (Heb. 11:13).

Abraham confessed that he was a pilgrim in a strange land. He followed, believing that God would point out the next step of his journey. Remember the instruction to the priests who bore the ark of the covenant through the Jordan when it was at flood stage? "And as soon as the priests who carry the ark of the LORD—the Lord of all the earth—set foot in the Jordan, its water flowing downstream will be cut off and stand up in a heap" (Josh. 3:13).

The secret of crossing the Jordan was in advancing on the river. It would remain a river until the priest's feet touched the water. Only then would the river retreat.

To follow God is always to opt for the art of the confident nomad. God owns the trip. The travel plans are his. The map will be given only after you have begun the journey.

Prayer
Lord Jesus,
Help me to walk by faith.
It is not a great light that pierces far ahead
into the darkness.
But it is adequate for me and the step I now take.
So call me and send me into any night.
I'll wait till morning for tomorrow's light.
Amen.

The Sin of Playing Light with Urgency

Luke 9:59–60

And He said to another, "Follow Me." But he said, "Permit me first to go bury my father."

But He said to him, "Allow the dead to bury their own dead; but as for you, go and proclaim everywhere the kingdom of God."

The sin of being trivial with urgent matters comes from misunderstanding how earnest my Father is about saving the world. Do not think me harsh for saying to this young man, "Let the dead bury the dead!" In actuality, his father was quite alive. Therefore, he was really saying, "I'll be your disciple someday. But right now I feel an obligation to take care of my father until he dies. After that I will come and follow you!" It was not the young man's concern for his father that I was rebuking but his apathy concerning the urgency of the kingdom.

The kingdom of God is urgent business. It is not a matter that Christians can casually ignore. Too many of my followers slouch before this urgency in lackadaisical discipleship. The church, it seems, will always be there. If they miss worship this week, they can always go the next. If they forget to take their offering to the altar this Sunday, they can make it up on the next.

Do not presume that you have unlimited time. *Urgent* is the kingdom's big word. The word *saved*, which all the world needs, is a demanding word. I called myself *Savior,* which has a desperate ring to it. John the Baptist cried the urgency of the kingdom in his Jordan River warning: "Repent—now, right now, it is most urgent—for the kingdom of God is at hand."

Kingdom business must be taken seriously. My church once understood this. The evidence of the church's depravity is that she now considers the urgency of evangelism to be melodrama. I beg you to see that God weeps when souls enter eternity without me. Care! Now! Urgency cannot postpone its compassion.

> *Prayer*
> *Lord Jesus,*
> *Every moment lost for your purpose*
> *is time unreclaimable in my life.*
> *I want to be sure I do not presume upon the day.*
> *I come to you in my insurgency*
> *accepting every kingdom urgency.*
> *Amen.*

Decidophobia

Luke 9:61–62

And another also said, "I will follow You, Lord; but first permit me to say good-bye to those at home." But Jesus said to him, "No one, after putting his hand to the plow and looking back, is fit for the kingdom of God."

You can be everything I have called you to be. You can achieve all that I have called you to achieve. But you must start as young as possible, decide once, and don't look back.

A thin and starving youth was told by a plump visitor that there was food in the East. His portly bearing made the thin and hungry lad believe. The visitor told the lad that he had only to choose the proper road through the forest to arrive at the land of plenty. Hungry but hopeful, the starving boy started out. He came at last to the fork in the road. Both of the roads were marked by a single sign, "At the end of this road lies the Land of Abundance—choose recklessly!"

But the starving man could not be induced to choose recklessly. He sat long, pondering the fearful outcome of choosing too fast. He finally took the road to the left. He walked a good ways down it before his fears led him to return to the starting point, and he walked the first road once again. Ultimately discouraged on that road, he returned again to the second road, feeling that the reversal of his reversal had been wrong.

After weeks of starving and thinking it through, he was still at the fork in the road. Looking down the road to the left he saw a plump visitor coming toward him. "Ah," he thought, "The left road was obviously the road to the Land of Abundance." He was about to run down it when he suddenly saw another person coming down the road to the right; it was another plump visitor. Now he was confused. Both of the portly visitors came upon him at once.

"But," he asked, "down which road lies the Land of Abundance?"

"It would not have mattered; either road would take you there," they both replied. "But you cannot save what you will not risk. At the final end of either road is abundance."

"Am I too weak or too thin? Should I set out at once?"

"Not too thin, only too old. Look at yourself." One of them handed him a mirror.

In the glass before him appeared an old and ugly face. He was wrinkled and haggard. "You have spent your foolish years in redeciding. Courage is the servant of decision—doubt is the thief of years."

Prayer
Lord Jesus,
I am in need of knowing
*   not whether my road is the right one,*
*   but that I may keep walking down it that*
*   until you whisper in unmistakable tones,*
*   I must consider some other way.*
And thus I set myself free from all dread:
*   I'll once decide and then I'll move ahead.*
Amen.

The Christ-filled Life Refreshes the World

John 7:37–38

Now on the last day, the great day of the feast, Jesus stood and cried out, saying, "If any man is thirsty, let him come to Me and drink. He who believes in Me, as the Scripture said, 'From his innermost being shall flow rivers of living water.'"

In the writings of John I have rehearsed what the Water of Life does for the drinker. But a better question might be, "What does the drinker do for the world?" This world can be an arid, dying place, but here and there the parched planet owns a lovely stream—a green oasis of refreshment—in the center of those lives whose love for me is unquestioned.

Consider the witnesses: out of their inmost being flows living water.

The water of life that each of these has brings its refreshment to all they touch. Each prizes it because it sparkles with eternity. Through these water bearers, redemption becomes a roaring current that cleanses the world they serve. Their all-perceiving eyes see the light that others somehow miss. What deep humility prevents them from seeing any virtue in themselves?

Worship me. The water redeems, and those who distinguish themselves as great Christians love to hang around the waterworks. They must taste the saving stream each moment, or they fear they will become as barren as the world they want to refresh. They are so much in love with me that they grow addicted to the cold, clear, spiritual abundance flowing from my being.

Your life contains mine, does it not? Hopefully, you are lost in the rapture of the water.

Seek me with all your heart as you pass through the world. Behind you, the area through which you passed will blossom with life—the life that comes from the refreshing waters of your own inmost being. The world will bless you for that transforming grace you never saw. And yet it came from you, without the slightest suspicion that life sprang up all around you in the unseen wake of your obedience.

Prayer
Lord Jesus,
I want to pass through the deserts of human relationships
leaving them touched by the fertility of your grace.
I want to so adore you that I am totally blind to any part I play
in making the dead human wilderness a place of greening eternity.
And so within my inmost being here
touch death with life and barrenness with cheer.
Amen.

The Fine Art of Turning Outward
Judgment to Inner Honesty

John 7:53–8:7

And everyone went to his own home. But Jesus went to the Mount of Olives. And early in the morning He came again into the temple, and all the people were coming to Him; and He sat down and began to teach them. And the scribes and the Pharisees brought a woman caught in adultery, and having set her in the midst, they said to Him, "Teacher, this woman has been caught in adultery, in the very act. Now in the Law Moses commanded us to stone such women; what then do You say?"

And they were saying this, testing Him, in order that they might have grounds for accusing Him. But Jesus stooped down, and with His finger wrote on the ground. But when they persisted in asking Him, He straightened up, and said to them, "He who is without sin among you, let him be the first to throw a stone at her."

It is only possible to be hard on the sins of others by not being honest about our own. Therefore every harsh judgment is a testament to ego.

What was it that I wrote in the sand that day? I wrote words that the prostitute might not understand, but her accusers did. They had not committed adultery; that was her sin. But oh, they had been adulterous with holiness! They had been so professional in the practice of their rank religiosity that the stench of their hypocrisy rose constantly to heaven.

"Stone her, if you are sinless," I cried.

The old Pharisees left first that day. May God be praised for the honesty of old men. They had already picked up rocks, eager to get rid of the woman and so to rid the world of sinners. They had stoned many others before. It was all a part of their harsh campaign to cleanse the land of evil. And the Mosaic law was on their side: "If . . . the charge is true and no proof of the girl's virginity can be found, she shall be brought to the door of her father's house and there the men of her town shall stone her to death. She has done a disgraceful thing in Israel by being promiscuous while still in her father's house. You must purge the evil from among you" (Deut. 22:20–21).

Remember this. If you are torn between doing what you know to be right and what you know to be loving, do what is loving first. If you are torn between your convictions and your compassion, be compassionate first. If you can't tell whether you should throw stones at a sinner or embrace her, ask yourself how it was that God first greeted you: with rocks or love?

Prayer
  Lord Jesus,
  I had been caught at sin by Calvary love.
  There was not the slightest question of my guilt.
  I deserved death, but was given life.
  Now shall I be harsh to others who are unquestionably guilty?
    I think not.
  I shall reach out with grace as it atones,
    embracing need while dropping all my stones.
  Amen.

The Obligation That Follows Forgiveness

John 8:8–11

And again He stooped down, and wrote on the ground. And when they heard it, they began to go out one by one, beginning with the older ones, and He was left alone, and the woman, where she was, in the midst. And straightening up, Jesus said to her, "Woman, where are they? Did no one condemn you?" And she said, "No one, Lord." And Jesus said, "Neither do I condemn you; go your way. From now on sin no more."

Once when a little boy was drowning, he began to cry out hopelessly for help while he thrashed in the water. A man who was passing by saw his trouble and leaped into the water to save him. When he had placed the little boy safely upon the beach, the boy said, "Thanks, Mister!" His benefactor replied, "Don't mention it ever again. Just be sure that you were worth saving."

It is said that for the rest of his life, every year on the anniversary of that date, the boy sent a letter thanking the man. The boy never ceased to see that each successive year of his life was a gift given to him by his savior.

The question "Have I been worth saving?" presupposes the obligation of grace. In the case of the woman taken in adultery, she finished out her life under my unceasing mandate of renewal: "Go and sin no more!"

In the strictest sense of the words, she could not do as I commanded. No one can live life without sin. But she could stop the kind of sin for which she had been arrested. Further, the actual command not to sin was given so she would never forget the cost of her redemption. *Grace* means *gift*. Gifts are free, but only to the receiver. They are always terribly expensive to the giver. What I gave her that day would cost me my life. In the process of considering her sin, she needed to ask what her forgiveness had cost my Father. "Go and sin no more" is a command that causes one to consider the nature of the sin and to remember its cost.

Grace is lavish and is always there. Still, we are never to count on its abundance as though our sins do not matter. Paul wrote: "What shall we say, then? Shall we go on sinning so that grace may increase? By no means! We died to sin; how can we live in it any longer?" (Rom. 6:1–2). It is great joy to meditate on the fact that the cross is all-sufficient in its lavish forgiveness, but let none play in caprice before the cross.

Go and sin no more! See that you are worth the saving! Reckon yourself dead to sin, but alive in Christ (Rom. 6:11).

Prayer
Lord Jesus,
My sin was so costly
that you spent your all to forgive it.
Help me to beg forgiveness for caprice,
lest Calvary go on and never cease.
Amen.

The Great "I Am"

John 8:54–59

Jesus answered, "If I glorify Myself, My glory is nothing; it is My Father who glorifies Me, of whom you say, 'He is our God'; and you have not come to know Him, but I know Him; and if I say that I do not know Him, I shall be a liar like you, but I do know Him, and keep His word. Your father Abraham rejoiced to see My day, and he saw it, and was glad."

The Jews therefore said to Him, "You are not yet fifty years old, and have You seen Abraham?" Jesus said to them, "Truly, truly, I say to you, before Abraham was born, I am." Therefore they picked up stones to throw at Him; but Jesus hid Himself, and went out of the temple.

The initials of God are YHWH. These four Hebrew letters form the consonants of the word for *Jehovah* or *Yahweh*. The word is as old as the Hebrew language itself.

This name for God came in an ancient encounter at a burning bush. There God gave Moses the assignment to go into Egypt and liberate Israel.

Thus the name YHWH was born. The God of Israel is the "I am" God of all being. This God is pure Being—Being irreducible and all-powerful. *Yahweh* is a "breathy" kind of word. When said aloud, it sounds like the blowing of the wind. It may be that this powerful "storm-driven" word for God came directly out of Israel's sojourn in Sinai. There in the desert, Israel heard the wind blowing night and day. In those fearful days when they traveled from Egypt to Canaan, they lived in tents. The wind was always there. Like God himself, it never ceased. Sometimes this wind became a knifing storm of hot sand that cut their flesh and lashed their tents. In this fury God became the restless and breathy *Yahweh*, the God of the storms.

This was the same name I gave the Pharisees that day. They did not miss the significance of the way I used the word. The word was life and was preexistent, as I was. In this word I let the Pharisees know that I had been alive before the Hebrew faith itself.

If you would make the metaphor complete, read Acts 2. For there I came in symbol as the great "I Am" God. I filled my church with the ancient sound of the desert, the sound of a mighty rushing wind (Acts 2:2) and the great "I Am," as full, pure Being was now blowing life into the church.

Come stand in this wind with the breath of God full in your face. See, I indwell you! I am ready now with the power to create newness in your world, wherever I touch it. Yield to the wind. Desire it.

Prayer
Lord Jesus,
I love you not because
you are the great "I was"
or because you are the great "I will be"
but because you are the great "I am,"
contemporary with every generation
and, best of all, my ever-present Lord.
You are the wind of my endeavor.
Empower me, breath of God, forever.
Amen.

Dealing with the Forces of Darkness

Luke 10:17–20

And the seventy returned with joy, saying, "Lord, even the demons are subject to us in Your name." And He said to them, "I was watching Satan fall from heaven like lightning. Behold, I have given you authority to tread upon serpents and scorpions, and over all the power of the enemy, and nothing shall injure you. Nevertheless do not rejoice in this, that the spirits are subject to you, but rejoice that your names are recorded in heaven."

The Book of Job opens on that day when "the angels came to present themselves before the LORD, and Satan also came with them. The LORD said to Satan, 'Where have you come from?' Satan answered the LORD, 'From roaming through the earth and going back and forth in it'" (Job 1:6–7). There is a restlessness in the devil's heart that keeps him pacing the earth, fruitlessly plotting the overthrow of the children of God. This ravenous pacing never ceases. "Be self-controlled and alert," wrote Peter. "Your enemy the devil prowls around like a roaring lion looking for someone to devour" (1 Pet. 5:8).

These two simple rules must be yours. Always stand against the devil, keeping him outside your life. You can do this by "overlaying yourself with the armor of God." Satan is here on earth, committed to the destruction of every virtue and the shredding of every belief. The battle is never easy, so dress for the fray: "Put on the full armor of God so that you can take your stand against the devil's schemes. For our struggle is not against flesh and blood, but against the rulers, against the authorities, against the powers of this dark world and against the spiritual forces of evil in the heavenly realms" (Eph. 6:11–12).

But it is not only important to be "overlaid by the armor"; we must also be "indwelled by the Spirit." For there is only one thing worse than fighting Satan on the outside of you, and that is fighting him on the inside of you. "If . . . the light within you is darkness, how great is that darkness!" (Matt. 6:23). That is why James encouraged us never to permit the devil entrance to our inner lives: "Submit yourselves, then, to God. Resist the devil, and he will flee from you. Come near to God and he will come near to you" (James 4:7–8a).

When you are "overlaid and indwelled" you are prepared to experience the same wonderful victory that the apostles had. When they returned from their preaching tour, they actually felt themselves triumphing over Satan. I said to them that day, "This authority is yours, for I beheld Satan fall as lightning from heaven."

There is nothing remarkable in this. It happens to all who are "infilled and overlaid." So claim your birthright of power. Live the victorious life. Do not be surprised that even the demons will obey you. They will. They have no other choice.

Prayer
Lord Jesus,
I want to live in the world
aware of two realities:
yours and the enemy's.
I cannot live realistically if I forget
that either source is real.
Help me to know, then, how I may define
the power and inner victory that are mine.
Amen.

6-15-01

The Good Bad-Guy

Luke 10:25–37

And behold, a certain lawyer stood up and put Him to the test, saying, "Teacher, what shall I do to inherit eternal life?" And He said to him, "What is written in the Law? How does it read to you?"

And he answered and said, "YOU SHALL LOVE THE LORD YOUR GOD WITH ALL YOUR HEART, AND WITH ALL YOUR SOUL, AND WITH ALL YOUR STRENGTH, AND WITH ALL YOUR MIND; AND YOUR NEIGHBOR AS YOURSELF" [Lev. 19:18; Deut. 6:5].

And He said to him, "You have answered correctly; DO THIS, AND YOU WILL LIVE" [Lev. 18:5]. But wishing to justify himself, he said to Jesus, "And who is my neighbor?"

Jesus replied and said, "A certain man was going down from Jerusalem to Jericho; and he fell among robbers, and they stripped him and beat him, and went off leaving him half dead. And by chance a certain priest was going down on that road, and when he saw him, he passed by on the other side. And likewise a Levite also, when he came to the place and saw him, passed by on the other side. But a certain Samaritan, who was on a journey, . . . came to him, and bandaged up his wounds, pouring oil and wine on them; and he put him on his own beast, and brought him to an inn, and took care of him. . . .

"Which of these three do you think proved to be a neighbor to the man who fell into the robber's hands?" And he said, "The one who showed mercy toward him." And Jesus said to him, "Go and do the same."

The evil at the heart of prejudice can mark those who are whole as it does those who are flawed. Prejudice camps throughout the human race. "Listen," says prejudice, "some guys are always good guys, but some guys are always bad guys!" Always? Are not the bad guys sometimes good and the good guys sometimes bad? "No," replies prejudice. "Some guys are always good, and some guys are always bad."

Of course, it goes without saying that the speaker is one of the good guys and has long known what is so bad about the bad guys. The bad guys are lazy. All bad guys? Well, most of them. The bad guys are always quarrelsome, and they drink too much. Further, the bad guys are immoral and have too many children. But worst of all, the bad guys can't be trusted. None of them? Mostly not.

It is always the good guys who make such assessments. Generation by generation they teach these doctrines to their children. By the time their children are five or six they have learned how to spot and hate bad guys. Thus evil passes from generation to generation.

The bad guys deserve a second chance. They are not as bad as you think. Nor are the good guys as good as you suppose. Every bad guy is but another soul in need of grace, and every good guy is just a soul in need of honesty.

Prayer
Lord Jesus,
I know there is so much right in those who are wrong
and so much wrong in those who are right,
that we would be wise to cease our hate.
And so may I love all as heaven would,
and for your sake, call every bad guy good.
Amen.

For Heaven's Sake,
Let the Dishes Go, Martha

Luke 10:38–42

Now as they were traveling along, He entered a certain village; and a woman named Martha welcomed Him into her home. And she had a sister called Mary, who moreover was listening to the Lord's word, seated at His feet. But Martha was distracted with all her preparations; and she came up to Him, and said, "Lord, do You not care that my sister has left me to do all the serving alone? Then tell her to help me."

But the Lord answered and said to her, "Martha, Martha, you are worried and bothered about so many things; but only a few things are necessary, really only one, for Mary has chosen the good part, which shall not be taken away from her."

It is easy to major on minors. Martha was the world's greatest hostess and housekeeper. Mary wasn't. Martha saw the cobwebs that Mary never could see. Martha hated it when the house wasn't in order, and Mary hated it when her life wasn't.

Into the world of these very different sisters I came along. Mary liked to sit with the men because she thought the men talked about important things. Martha was trying to be the perfect hostess to all thirteen of us when we stopped in at their house in Bethany.

When Martha's frustration reached its peak, she blurted out to me—but really more to Mary, fastidiously listening to me teach—"Lord, tell *Queen* Mary to help me with the serving."

Martha wanted me to rebuke Mary. Instead, I rebuked Martha: "Martha, you are worried and bothered about so many things; but only a few things are necessary, really only one, for Mary has chosen the good part. . . ." If you are a fussbudget, you need to remember that sometimes God himself may be in your midst. When that happens, let the linens go and the dishes as well. Give yourself to the visitation of God, for you know not when he will come again. It could be while you are dusting the furniture, God will come and go and you will have missed the day of his visitation. If you make no place for him in your heart, he will not sit long at your table.

Prayer

Lord Jesus,
Often I am so busy just getting ready.
I get ready to meet you in church.
I get ready to study you in Bible class.
I get ready to meet you at the Easter service.
I'd like to quit getting ready to meet you
    and spend a little time with you.
While the Martha in me hurries to be neat,
    the Mary longs to listen at your feet.
Amen.

Persistence in Prayer

Luke 11:5–8

And He said to them, "Suppose one of you shall have a friend, and shall go to him at midnight, and say to him, 'Friend, lend me three loaves; for a friend of mine has come to me from a journey, and I have nothing to set before him'; and from inside he shall answer and say, 'Do not bother me; the door has already been shut and my children and I are in bed; I cannot get up and give you anything.'

"I tell you, even though he will not get up and give him anything because he is his friend, yet because of his persistence he will get up and give him as much as he needs."

God answers all prayers. He sometimes says, "Yes!" He must at times say, "No!" And he often says, "Wait with me a while!"

If your prayers are marked by weariness, ask yourself how long you have waited, continuing in steadfast confidence in God. Are you so tired that you will wait no more? Do not make up your mind that God has been unfair to make you wait so long for the answer. Remember that God himself has often waited on you. In fact, he has long postponed my return: "The Lord is not slow in keeping his promise, as some understand slowness. He is patient with you, not wanting anyone to perish, but everyone to come to repentance" (2 Pet. 3:9). To all who had long ignored God's grace, Paul wrote of the eager process of those who are waiting on God, "You who are trying to be justified by law have been alienated from Christ; you have fallen away from grace. But by faith we eagerly await through the Spirit the righteousness for which we hope" (Gal. 5:4–5). Waiting is the watchword for both Christians and their heavenly Father.

Waiting is the wordless part of the language of prayer. "Elijah was a man just like us. He prayed earnestly that it would not rain, and it did not rain on the land for three and a half years. Again he prayed, and the heavens gave rain" (James 5:17–18a). Prayer is not to be taken up only for a restless moment and laid aside. Prayer is both the issue of waiting on God and the promise of the Father. It is the expected work of the Christian: "Devote yourselves to prayer, being watchful and thankful" (Col. 4:2). Waiting is the currency of faith with which we purchase the joy of life. Waiting with God is being with God, and being with God can be never tedious or laborsome.

My Father intends waiting to be sweet work. He treasures the wait because it keeps the two of you together until the answer comes. It is like blessed detention by an old friend. Waiting is the overture of God.

Prayer
Lord Jesus,
I have not waited on you in prayer
so much as I have waited with you in prayer.
Of course you answered.
You always do.
I am not only richer for the answer,
I am richer for the wait.
I do not wait to force an answer out of you.
For waiting is a pleasant thing to do.
Amen.

Prayer: Asking for Good Gifts

Luke 11:11–13

"Now suppose one of you fathers is asked by his son for a fish; he will not give him a snake instead of a fish, will he? Or if he is asked for an egg, he will not give him a scorpion, will he? If you then, being evil, know how to give good gifts to your children, how much more shall your heavenly Father give the Holy Spirit to those who ask Him?"

A good parent does not give a child a cobra if he has asked for a fish. Nor does he give a child a scorpion if the child has asked for a boiled egg. Good parents always act to protect their children. In a nursery all sharp corners are padded, all sharp blades are taken out of the play areas. Children are given an environment that cannot hurt them.

But the lesson on prayer that God's children need in this generation is the lesson of what to ask for. The "health-wealth" gospel has led many to ask God for those glitzier gifts that enhance life with material things. Such prayer asks too directly for snakes and scorpions. Those who seek material gifts from God often quote Psalm 37:4: "Delight yourself in the LORD and he will give you the desires of your heart." Then they ask, "Is the Bible true or not, dear sister. You have only to name your desire to claim God's gift!"

Popular preachers often encourage listeners to pray for the material blessings they desire: lands, money, houses. "My Father loves me so!" I once said, "Seek first his kingdom and his righteousness, and all these things will be given to you as well" (Matt. 6:33). But this does not mean things like estates or jewels or rich holdings. Do not seek God so that you may have things.

Now regarding Psalm 37:4, the question must be asked, "If you really are *delighting* yourself in the Lord, why am I not the delight of your heart? Why would such poor temporary heavens as new homes or riches be your delight?" The true believer will find little fascination in such material things.

Couple Psalm 37:4 to James 4:2: "You do not have, because you do not ask God." If this still seems a little too name-it-and-claim-it, then add James 4:3: "When you ask, you do not receive, because you ask with wrong motives, that you may spend what you get on your pleasures!"

Here's what may be named and claimed: the Holy Spirit. If you ask God for him you may be sure you will receive him. His indwelling presence will then make you rich in both this age and the one to come. Enjoy his fullness! All else that you might ask for are by comparison but snakes and scorpions.

Prayer
Lord Jesus,
I beg you.
Give me nothing of what I ask
    if what I ask obscures my need for you
    and feeds my lust for things.
I know the lust for riches teaches its gluttonies
    unto the soul.
And so I beg,
    withhold all greed lest such amenities
    obscure the glory of the Trinity.
Amen.

Lunching with Pharisees

Luke 11:37–39

Now when He had spoken, a Pharisee asked Him to have lunch with him; and He went in, and reclined at the table. And when the Pharisee saw it, he was surprised that He had not first ceremonially washed before the meal. But the Lord said to him, "Now you Pharisees clean the outside of the cup and of the platter; but inside of you, you are full of robbery and wickedness. You foolish ones, did not He who made the outside make the inside also? But give that which is within as charity, and then all things are clean for you."

Consider long if a Pharisee invites you to lunch. He will probably not be seeking the pleasure of your company. He may only be buying your meal to push his viewpoints. Most Pharisees never quite learn the difference between theology and a hang-up. Such lunches lead to dogmatic indigestion. Before you are through the appetizers, he will be instructing you on how you might improve your walk with God, which, when achieved, will look remarkably like his own.

A certain Pharisee once lectured me on the subject of unwashed hands. I decided to move the issue from cleanliness of hands to the cleanliness of the heart. The heart's an area where the uncleanness can remain while the hands are washed a thousand times. "For out of the heart come evil thoughts, murder, adultery, sexual immorality, theft, false testimony, slander. These are what make a man 'unclean'; but eating with unwashed hands does not make him 'unclean'" (Matt. 15:19–20).

The Pharisees were prone to divide the world into two kinds of sin: the kind you would get caught at and the kind you couldn't. The kind you can get caught at are called "kosher" sins, such as not washing your hands. But the sins you can't get caught at are "mental-attitude" sins: hate, envy, lust, resentment, jealousies, pride, grudge, spite. How deceitful are these inner sins! Those who commit only these inner sins often celebrate their self-righteousness while consigning kosher sinners to condemnation.

The Pharisees thought my hands needed washing when really it was their hearts that needed scrubbing up. But God rarely is invited to swab the dark interiors of the human heart.

Prayer
Lord Jesus,
I have paid far too much attention
to issues of propriety
and far too little to the important issue of my inner life.
May I forget my hands and learn to pray.
Cleanse me, O God, and know my heart today.
Amen.

Front Row Seats

Luke 11:43

"Woe to you Pharisees! For you love the front seats in the synagogues, and the respectful greetings in the market places."

Religious exhibitionism is a form of showmanship. Once during Holy Week, a prominent cleric traveled through a wide country. He had arranged, somewhat elaborately, that everywhere his retinue came to rest, he would be met by a seminarian who would allow him to "wash his feet." In every city a great hubbub gathered around his arrival. His humility soon became the focus of every region of the country. Soon all who saw him came to believe they had seen a true man of God.

There was once an order of nuns who refused to take baths without being fully robed. When asked why, they would say, "Ah, the great God can see through bathroom walls!" And, of course, to their own view of piety it was important not to be naked in the presence of the living God to whom they had devoted their lives in service. And yet there was a hint of religious exhibitionism in their odd doctrine. For some reason they never seemed to see the illogic of a God who could see through bathroom walls but not robes.

The Pharisees were masters of the religious exhibition. They loved the front row seats at the synagogue. There is nothing wrong with taking the seats if your motive is to hear or see better. But they took the seats because they wanted to make doubly sure that no one ever had to ask whether or not they were in church.

They loved being called "doctor" in the marketplace. I was a "field rabbi," as they like to call me. I was not properly educated or schooled in the endless volumes of formal theology that belonged to these temple graduates. When these scholars spoke for God, they did it with swelling academic authority. They were not so much admired for loving God as knowing about God. "Holier than thou" is the final trap of exhibitionism.

No wonder Paul said, "Knowledge puffs up, but love builds up" (1 Cor. 8:1b). It is no sin to know a great deal. The world owes much to authentic Christian scholarship. The Bible itself is a wonderful testimony to scholars who work tirelessly to make God's word accessible to the world. Learn all you can about the Bible, and study the language and theological disciplines that will help you have an informed faith. But walk wide around academic pride. It might have you sitting on the front row and insisting that people call you "Doctor." Faith is easily subverted to exhibitionism. Honest adoration sits further back in church.

Prayer
Lord Jesus,
Help me to never learn a thing rather than
surrender my authenticity to pride.
Help me to ask myself why I'm sitting so far forward
in the church service.
Help me to wonder why I feel so badly
when others criticize something I said in the Bible class.
Could it be that I've traded love for pride?
I must surrender self and not insist
on things that make me exhibitionist.
Amen.

Killing Prophets, Building Tombs

Luke 11:47

"Woe to you! For you build the tombs of the prophets, and it was your fathers who killed them."

It is easy to honor old truth and celebrate the old tellers of it. But it is sometimes difficult to celebrate those younger tellers of newer truth. It is almost impossible to honor those who tell the truth to one's own generation. Some today get very upset with hearing that I am the Son of God. This truth raised my cross when it was told.

One generation builds the mausoleum of those prophets they martyred because they would not tolerate the truth those prophets told. The next generation willingly gilds that monument. One generation creates martyrs; the next decorates their shrines with adoration. The time between the killing generation and the worshiping one always illuminates the real truth.

Have you ever said to yourself, "If I had been alive in Jesus' day, I would have seen all the miracles that he performed and I would have believed. How dull the apostles or the Pharisees must have been. For they saw it all and yet they doubted." Do not hastily bless yourself or castigate my contemporaries. After all, you have the blessing of twenty centuries of historical perspective. You came so late in time that you are able to see how it all worked out. Perspective clarifies the tiresome work of sorting through reality.

To my disciples and to the Pharisees, there was no perspective. Everything I said back then was a new idea. They had no books they could read to confirm it. There were no corner churches that assumed it to be so. They had to hear my truth and assess it. Then and there, they either believed it or denied it. If they believed, they became disciples. If they doubted, they considered raising the very tomb their children would later decorate. But they had to make up their mind while swimming in the middle of it all.

When you tell your non-Christian friends about me, be patient. They may have to wrangle it through while you wait. It is too new to them to evaluate on the spot. That which you have so long believed may try their souls. Wait therefore till the light has fully come. Truth must sometimes whisper, or its noisy approach will deafen all.

Prayer
Lord Jesus,
The Pharisees may have built the tombs of earlier ages,
*   and they may have reacted to your truth as new truth.*
But help me see that at least they did not take it for granted.
They struggled and doubted and died.
They might have struggled and accepted and lived.
But they did struggle.
I do not want a faith of quick caprice
*   while others swim to faith through bloody seas.*
Amen.

The Moral Motivator

Luke 12:1–3

Under these circumstances, after so many thousands of the multitude had gathered together that they were stepping on one another, He began saying to His disciples first of all, "Beware of the leaven of the Pharisees, which is hypocrisy. But there is nothing covered up that will not be revealed, and hidden that will not be known. Accordingly, whatever you have said in the dark shall be heard in the light, and what you have whispered in the inner rooms shall be proclaimed upon the housetops."

If an angel came to you tonight and said, "Tomorrow morning God will print in the paper every sin you have not confessed," what would you do? Would you not name those sins in a private place and quickly beg my cleansing? Beneath our churchly exterior hides demons so wanton and ugly that we would scarcely be able to enter the community again if they were published.

Yet the statement "be sure your sins will find you out!" has a way of becoming all too true. Once at a huge pastors' conference an old man stood to speak a word of warning to the youthful young ministers in his charge: "This is a day when ministers are increasingly irresponsible with their sexuality. It is a fight for all men in ministry. I would like to tell you that I have lived free of these kinds of struggles, but the truth is that I have known such struggles in my time. I would also like to tell you that for all of my years of serving Christ, it was the rich infilling of the ever glorious Spirit of God that allowed me to refuse the evil and choose the good. In actual truth, the thing that has helped me preserve my morality across the years was that I just kept hearing Jesus say, 'What you have whispered . . . in the inner rooms will be proclaimed from the housetops'" (Luke 12:3).

How wise is this advice. Hiding your sin is not possible for long. Soon all that you practice in the inner rooms will be rooftop proclamations. Remember my words and let them be your counselor in fear and the reward of your vigilant purity: "There is nothing concealed that will not be disclosed, or hidden that will not be made known" (Matt. 10:26).

Come therefore to that open life that hides nothing in darkness that it would not surrender in sunlight. To have purity of heart is to desire one thing: my kingdom. If your heart is single, your body will be full of light. What is then declared from the housetops will be only what you have kept in open, inner integrity.

Prayer
   Lord Jesus,
   I want to learn the art
      of living in such openness
      that all that is in my heart
      is what people believe is there.
   Help me to keep my soul in purity
      so shouts from the rooftops can't dishonor me.
   Amen.

Epitaphs

Luke 12:16–21

And He told them a parable, saying, "The land of a certain rich man was very productive. And he began reasoning to himself, saying, 'What shall I do, since I have no place to store my crops?' And he said, 'This is what I will do: I will tear down my barns and build larger ones, and there I will store all my grain and my goods. And I will say to my soul, "Soul, you have many goods laid up for many years to come; take your ease, eat, drink and be merry."'

"But God said to him, 'You fool! This very night your soul is required of you; and now who will own what you have prepared?'

"So is the man who lays up treasure for himself, and is not rich toward God."

Above the sprawling cemetery across the fields he once owned, one can still see the huge barns of a huge fool. His stone reads:

Here lies a poor man, six feet down
He had ten barns outside of town.

Building bigger barns uses up a lot of days. And yet why is it that when you complete a new barn, you somehow feel better off? You feel more secure. It never seems to occur to you that building barns does not provide security; it only uses up your years.

Psalm 90:12 reminds us: "Teach us to number our days aright,/that we may gain a heart of wisdom." The three haunting words of my parable are: "this very night!"

We are in a long running battle with the clocks. We will not beat the clocks. But oddly, barn building is the frequent weaponry of our futile assault on the clock. "This very night" refers to that time which stops the clock. It is the cry at midnight. It is the falling curtain on the scene of history. It is that hour when all the banks are finally closed: no more deposits and no more withdrawals.

Do not be like the foolish man. There are no barns big enough that you can use them to store grain to be used after you're dead. So if the three important words in this parable are "this very night," the nine most foolish words must be "Soul, take your ease, eat, drink and be merry."

You must live in reference to the clocks. You must never presume upon the moment; the clocks will run on. But remember Belshazzar on the night his kingdom fell. He was at a party, assuming he had all the time in the world. Suddenly he saw the scrawling fingers of a man's hand writing his judgment on the wall. He had profaned God (Dan. 5), but he could not profane time. We may race with time, but it's a race that time will win.

Prayer
Lord Jesus,
There is no security except in you.
There are no banks wealthy enough
*   and no barns big enough to compensate*
*   for a self-indulgent life.*
Therefore I come to you remembering,
*   I must not live presuming on the time.*
Each final moment awaits some final chime.
Amen.

Anticipation

Luke 12:35–40

"Be dressed in readiness, and keep your lamps alight. And be like men who are waiting for their master when he returns from the wedding feast, so that they may immediately open the door to him when he comes and knocks. Blessed are those slaves whom the master shall find on the alert when he comes; . . .

"And be sure of this, that if the head of the house had known at what hour the thief was coming, he would not have allowed his house to be broken into. You too, be ready; for the Son of Man is coming at an hour that you do not expect."

Anticipating the Kingdom is the work of the Kingdom. Anticipation is glorious. Ask children near Christmas. Waiting for tomorrow makes your today all neurotic and fidgety.

Yet it should not be. Anticipation knows no boredom. It is eager to experience what is on the way. What you had yesterday is museum stuff. What you have today has quickly bored you. But what is on the way? How shall you hurry sundown so that tomorrow will arrive early to delight you?

Don't think you held all of the glory of Christianity when you were born again. Anticipate tomorrow, for tomorrow you will know the very fullness of our final togetherness. Tomorrow holds the completion of our friendship. It is a glory so marvelous that its wonder will amaze you for eternity.

Anticipation is the work of Christmas, the children's glory. My second coming will bring that utter reunion, of being known even also as we are known (1 Cor. 13:12). It will be the ultimate banquet, the marriage supper of the Lamb (Rev. 19:7). You already have the invitation. There is only one other obligation: Anticipate. Be ready.

How will you know when the time is near? Where you see the vultures gathered together, you will know where the carcass is (Matt. 24:28). Do not be hoodwinked by bogus information. "If anyone says to you, 'Look, here is the Christ!' or 'There he is!' do not believe it. For false Christs and false prophets will appear and perform great signs and miracles to deceive even the elect. . . . So if anyone tells you, 'There he is, out in the desert,' do not go out; or, 'Here he is, in the inner rooms,' do not believe it. For as lightning that comes from the east is visible even in the west, so will be the coming of the Son of Man" (Matt. 24:23–27).

My coming will be as unmistakable to the true believer as it will be welcome. Pay attention. Watch. Do not despair. Heaven is as eager as you are for the great reunion of the ages. I am coming. We shall meet soon in a volley of international hallelujahs.

Prayer
Lord Jesus,
I am waiting, but I can hardly wait.
I am rejoicing, but rejoicing is not enough
   to signal my joy.
I want to read my place card
   at the marriage supper of the Lamb.
Come even now, Lord of time's sweet end,
   and let the party of the age begin.
Amen.

Why Bad Things Happen
to Good Galileans

Luke 13:1–5

Now on the same occasion there were some present who reported to Him about the Galileans, whose blood Pilate had mingled with their sacrifices. And He answered and said to them, "Do you suppose that these Galileans were greater sinners than all other Galileans, because they suffered this fate? I tell you, no, but, unless you repent, you will all likewise perish. Or do you suppose that those eighteen on whom the tower in Siloam fell and killed them, were worse culprits than all the men who live in Jerusalem? I tell you, no, but unless you repent, you will all likewise perish."

In a fit of anti-Semitic rage, Pilate had killed some worshipers with the animals that they were sacrificing. "Why?" is always the question after some horrible slaughter like this. "Why," we want to know, "do bad things happen to good people?"

It is the theme of the Book of Job. The madness causes us to want to know why we are the recipients of terrible pain or bereavement we do not deserve. Not only are we at a loss to explain the undeserved pain that comes our way, we are also hard pressed to figure out why the wicked prosper. Job long ago asked the same questions.

"Why do the wicked live on,
    growing old and increasing in power?
They see their children established around them,
    their offspring before their eyes.
Their homes are safe and free from fear;
They spend their years in prosperity
    and go down to the grave in peace.
Yet they say to God, "Leave us alone!
    We have no desire to know your ways.
Who is the Almighty, that we should serve him?" (Job 21:7–9a, 13–15a)

On one of the "normal" days of my life, a tower collapsed and killed eighteen people. There is little use in asking if this happened because the victims were worse sinners than those who survived them. Likely not. The explanation is probably simple. There were too many people working on the flimsy scaffold.

So how are we to explain it all? "The sweet by and by" is sweet partly because full understanding will then be ours. There in that distant realm is the only place where all sums shall be totaled in the proper, logical columns. Until then, love God, bless your crucifiers, and listen for the sound of distant trumpets.

Prayer
Lord Jesus,
I do not understand why good things happen to bad people
    and bad things happen to good people.
But I am glad, Lord Jesus, that grace happened once for all people.
If God himself was not immune from pain,
    let's bless life's riddles and begin again.
Amen.

God's Definition

John 9:1–3

And as He passed by, He saw a man blind from birth. And His disciples asked Him, saying, "Rabbi, who sinned, this man or his parents, that he should be born blind?" Jesus answered, "It was neither that this man sinned, nor his parents; but it was in order that the works of God might be displayed in him."

Theologians can argue their definitions of God very effectively. "God is the sum of all," they say. Or "God is the first cause behind all effects!" Or "God is the force behind all living things." Or "God is the ground of all being!" These are the kind of God definitions that theologians offer. But when God writes his own definition, he writes it in terms of the unexplainable mysteries of his goodness. Consider the man born blind.

Never cease to glorify the God who writes his own definition in the unexplainable acts of his goodness. James wrote: "Every good and perfect gift is from above, coming down from the Father of the heavenly lights, who does not change like shifting shadows. He chose to give us birth through the word of truth, that we might be a kind of firstfruits of all he created" (James 1:17–18). Do you see the glory of this term "Father of lights"? When my Father wants to write his definition in something other than a great miracle, he writes it in the stars. Stand out under a canopy of night fire and doubt, if you can. But if you have any conscience at all, you must hear God's definition, hanging in a million glittering, sun systems just above your head. He writes it on the very scroll of space: "The heavens declare the glory of God; the skies proclaim the work of his hands" (Ps. 19:1).

So view the night sky and let the "Father of lights" define himself. Then run to the biblical miracles and, having seen them, affirm their glory. You can do nothing else but stand back in awe and cry: "See, here is God. The sea is cut into roaring walls of water. See, here is God; the dead Messiah is alive! See, here is God; he is defined in this bewildered blind man, who was born in darkness but now lives in light." In lives like his God writes his definition.

On that occasion the disciples asked me why the man was born blind. Was he a sinner? Were his parents? Yes, of course, everyone is a sinner. But God is still looking for desperate, lonely, and despairing places to write his definition. And when he does, all who see it say, "Now I know who God is!"

Prayer
Lord Jesus,
In every sunrise God defines himself.
He writes his name on every blade of grass.
He endorses every petal of a rose.
He forms the stars into constellations that stretch across the sky
*   spelling out "Jehovah Is!"*
And, as if this were not glory enough,
*   his definition comes in all that is good but unexplainable.*
His miracles befuddle history,
*   defining God as glorious mystery.*
Amen.

The Man Who Knew One Thing

John 9:24–28, 34

So a second time they called the man who had been blind, and said to him, "Give glory to God; we know that this man is a sinner." He therefore answered, "Whether He is a sinner, I do not know; one thing I do know, that, whereas I was blind, now I see."

They said therefore to him, "What did He do to you? How did He open your eyes?" He answered them, "I told you already, and you did not listen; why do you want to hear it again? You do not want to be His disciples too, do you?"

And they reviled him, and said, "You are His disciple, but we are disciples of Moses."...

"You were born entirely in sins, and are you teaching us?"

The inquisition of the man born blind provides a splendid contrast between the educated, who knew many things, and a simple man, who knew only one thing. The formerly blind man knew only that he could see. But they did seem to resent him for being so know-it-all about the one thing he knew.

A fanatic is often defined as someone who can't change her mind and won't change the subject. The man born blind gets fairly close to this definition. But it is hard not to admire people who know one thing and are sure about it. First of all, the man born blind is living in the joy of his relationship with me. Joy is truly authentic when you cannot lay it aside to become rational and academic. When you come suddenly to sight, it is hard to set the wonder of it aside. Neither is it possible to live comfortably with those who have always been able to see. For them light is so "old hat" that they have lost interest in it.

Herein is the glory of my church. Those who have newly come to me cannot quit talking about the wonder of their salvation. Those who have been Christians for years can grow academic in their discipleship. Older Christians can get quite involved in the topography of the Sinai Peninsula. But the new Christian knows only one thing: light. He marvels that older Christians can spend so much time talking about how to organize lay involvement or what color the church carpet should be.

Even as the new Christian looks around the congregation, he fears that one day he may become as sterile in his faith as those he beholds. He scorns the notion that he too may one day be dead to wonder. But for the moment, he has the whole church gloriously edgy. He knows one thing and he will not quit talking about it. Whereas he was blind, now he sees. It is enough for him.

Prayer
Lord Jesus,
I have been a Christian a long time now,
    and I sure do know a lot of things.
I sometimes wish I knew less and felt more.
I liked me better when I felt like singing more
    and had much less interest in understanding.
I want again to love as I did first
    when everything I was was joy immersed.
Amen.

One Door to Abundant Living

John 10:9–10

"I am the door; if anyone enters through Me, he shall be saved, and shall go in and out, and find pasture. The thief comes only to steal, and kill, and destroy; I came that they might have life, and might have it abundantly."

Heaven is the ultimate place of union with foreverness. Heaven is that wonderful place of promise where tears are illegal and joy is customary. This final glory exists for all Christians who long for that wonderful world where all things are possible with God. This great new life of grace is approached through a single door called salvation. There is no other way into grace. And once you pass the door, you will find my sufficiency in large supply. Abundance is the only fair word to describe it.

The question is, "What is abundance?"

The word sounds materialistic. It sounds as though salvation is the way into riches and all those things you could possibly want to own. But the word is greater than that. Abundance is that inner certainty that all you will ever need has been supplied in myself; it is that complete feeling that just comes, not because you are guaranteed a lot of good things. As I said to Martha and Mary of Bethany, these things cannot be taken away (Luke 10:42).

Abundance is the reality of completion that comes not from having but being. The word may come closest to the idea of being "furnished" with all that is necessary to find each need supplied and the strength for coping with each situation.

For Paul, abundance came not merely in having what he needed, but in the special power to live without many things that he presumed he needed: "I am not saying this because I am in need, for I have learned to be content whatever the circumstances. I know what it is to be in need, and I know what it is to have plenty. I have learned the secret of being content in any and every situation, whether well fed or hungry, whether living in plenty or in want. I can do everything through him who gives me strength" (Phil. 4:11–13).

It was Paul's overwhelming conviction that my abundance was adequate for all of his need and for the needs of everyone in the church. He further testified to the Philippians, "My God will meet all your needs according to his glorious riches in Christ Jesus" (Phil. 4:19). This, then, is my promise of abundance. Inwardly you will grow old with the assurance that nothing can happen to you beyond the Father's love and care. All that you need, he will provide.

Prayer
Lord Jesus,
I am grateful to you, the Door,
* for all good things.*
I am never in need beyond
* your assurance that what might be defined as a need*
* can often be lived without.*
All things I have reach to eternity.
Your grace each day comes so abundantly.
Amen.

Security

John 10:27–30

"My sheep hear My voice, and I know them, and they follow Me; and I give eternal life to them, and they shall never perish; and no one shall snatch them out of My hand. My Father, who has given them to Me, is greater than all; and no one is able to snatch them out of the Father's hand. I and the Father are one."

All through life you want to know that the sun will come up tomorrow and that all will be well when it does. Paul said that all things work together for good to them who love God and are called according to his purpose (Rom. 8:28). One of the greatest saints of God said that all shall be well, all shall be well, and all manner of things shall be well. All of these statements tell you that you want to feel a sense of peace in the world.

Peace is the sister of assurance. You have peace when you know that the assurance you seek tomorrow is already on the way today. You must know about God too. You must know that his love is not fickle (as mere human love sometimes tends to be). You want to know that his saving grace doesn't depend on how well you are doing at conquering the sin in your own lives. Peace comes from the knowledge that tomorrow is guaranteed.

But the kind of security I offer is that spiritual security that knows no threat of condemnation. I save everyone who calls upon me, and I save forever. Indeed, I keep those I have saved in such security that they cannot ever be lost. Do you understand just how secure you are? I have given you eternal life. I picture you as an acorn held deep within my coiling fingers. But your security does not end there. My hand is held in my Father's. To tear you from my hand, my hand would first have to be torn from my Father's hand. Since that is impossible, you are saved beyond all possibility of being lost.

You are my sheep. You belong to me; I bought you with a price (1 Cor. 6:20); and I own you. I will always own you. I will never give you up. You are secure in my keeping to the edge of eternity and beyond. Rest in me, for there is nothing that can separate us. Cast yourself on Paul's promise: "Who shall separate us from the love of Christ? Shall trouble or hardship or persecution or famine or nakedness or danger or sword? As it is written: 'For your sake we face death all day long; we are considered as sheep to be slaughtered.' No, in all these things we are more than conquerors through him who loved us. For I am convinced that neither death nor life, nor angels nor demons, neither the present nor the future, nor any powers, neither height nor depth, nor anything else in all creation, will be able to separate us from the love of God that is in Christ Jesus our Lord" (Rom. 8:35–39).

Prayer
Lord Jesus,
How glorious it is to know for sure
that as you died for sure,
I am saved for sure.
How grateful I am for the certainty
that certainty is the only way I can live.
How glorious is the knowledge that is so—
to know we know and shall forever know.
Amen.

Herod and the Unhurried Purposes of God

Luke 13:31–35

Just at that time some Pharisees came up, saying to Him, "Go away and depart from here, for Herod wants to kill You."

And He said to them, "Go and tell that fox, 'Behold, I cast out demons and perform cures today and tomorrow, and the third day I reach My goal.' Nevertheless I must journey on today and tomorrow and the next day; for it cannot be that a prophet should perish outside of Jerusalem. O Jerusalem, Jerusalem, the city that kills the prophets and stones those sent to her! How often I wanted to gather your children together, just as a hen gathers her brood under her wings, and you would not have it!

"Behold, your house is left to you desolate; and I say to you, you shall not see Me until the time comes when you say, 'BLESSED IS HE WHO COMES IN THE NAME OF THE LORD'"[Ps. 118:26].

Cities are often the unfeeling gathering places of very feeling people. Cities can be very intimidating. Still, Herod's threats were not going to intimidate the well-planned course of my saving sojourn. *Fox* was the word with which I labeled Herod. It was not profane or obscene. He did have red hair, being an Idumean, but my calling him a fox had nothing to do with the color of his hair. A fox is an animal of little significance, wily but unimportant.

The problem was that Herod had no real idea of how utterly insignificant he was.

God's plan of redemption had been on humanity's drawing board for ages. There was no earthly potentate, including Caesar himself, who could alter it. Paul testified that this was not a haphazard event. "When the time had fully come, God sent his Son, born of a woman, born under law, to redeem those under law, that we might receive the full rights of sons" (Gal. 4:4–5). Further, John called me the "Lamb that was slain from the creation of the world" (Rev. 13:8).

So when you recall my Jerusalem lament, "O Jerusalem, Jerusalem!" recall also that some of my last earthly words to my infant church were: "Stay in the city until you have been clothed with power from on high" (Luke 24:49). Christianity was born an urban religion. It never called its disciples to meditate on mountaintops alone, but to enter the cities and cry for human desperation.

Live for me in the city! Serve me there! In the city, put your obedience to use. If you would honor me, love God and the city.

Prayer
Lord Jesus,
I want to feel that sense of redemptive schedule to my life
that you felt in yours.
I don't want people or circumstances to hurry me past
the complete doing of your will.
I want to call your urban mercy down
and summon you to weep in my hometown.
Amen.

Never Switch Place Cards

Luke 14:8–11

"When you are invited by someone to a wedding feast, do not take the place of honor, lest someone more distinguished than you may have been invited by him, and he who invited you both shall come and say to you, 'Give place to this man,' and then in disgrace you proceed to occupy the last place. But when you are invited, go and recline at the last place, so that when the one who has invited you comes, he may say to you, 'Friend, move up higher'; then you will have honor in the sight of all who are at the table with you. For everyone who exalts himself shall be humbled, and he who humbles himself shall be exalted."

There is a strange custom among aggressive guests at fine dinners. They often arrive at the banquet early to circulate among the tables, studying place cards. If they find their own card too far toward the rear of the banquet hall, they will trade it with one closer to the front. This maneuver moves them close enough to catch the eye of the really important people at the head table. Then with a smile or an aggressive handshake, they are less likely to be forgotten during the next round of social promotions.

Humility is accepting your place card where you find it. Humility is not being glad you are a long way from the head table, but neither is it getting pushy with your anonymity. Humility never cries, either in the presence of God or those we consider better than ourselves, "Oh, to be nothing, nothing." For the Christian, humility is bringing your life next to mine and noting the differences. Only the most impious can stand next to me and say, "Jesus, you and I are both really something!" Your sheer proximity to me should hush all arrogance.

But if you think you are more special than the world might agree to, here are three simple rules that may help all who could be chronically arrogant. First, try standing next to me. If this fails, ask yourself, "Even though I am truly great, how can I best fold myself into a larger world of interpersonal relationships? Would others not accept me better if I were a little less obviously great?" If this fails, go directly to your knees and ask God to help you locate those weaknesses that seem hard for you to find on your own.

If you put into practice these three rules for humbling yourself, you will never be guilty of switching place cards.

Prayer
Lord Jesus,
Help me to isolate all the things
that you might ask me to do,
which I still feel inwardly I'm too good to do,
and after a brief repentance,
get busy doing them.
Remembering that you died in naked shame
should strip all self-importance from my name.
Amen.

Deferred Payment

Luke 14:12–14

And He also went on to say to the one who had invited Him, "When you give a luncheon or a dinner, do not invite your friends or your brothers or your relatives or rich neighbors, lest they also invite you in return, and repayment come to you. But when you give a reception, invite the poor, the crippled, the lame, the blind, and you will be blessed, since they do not have the means to repay you; for you will be repaid at the resurrection of the righteous."

Life can become an endless cycle of competition and repayment. Many live life with no other seeming purpose than that of being sure no one gets ahead of them. Are you playing the social game? John took you out to dinner, so you must give him a Christmas present. Mary sent you a sympathy card, so you mustn't forget her birthday. "You've been to our house three times now. Why, pray tell, haven't you ever invited us over?"

There is a kind of credit-and-debit sociology that majors on this "bookkeeping of the heart." Remembering who bought lunch last or who owes who the coffee at break time is hard work.

There is a way to stop such never-break-even accounting. Do nice things for those to whom any idea of return is impossible. Start inviting people over who could never invite you back. Give to those who cannot give to you in return. Offer gifts without a name tag, and wonderful things happen. The recipient has no hope of replying to your gift with debit and credit bookkeeping.

A young woman once received an expensive coat from a very expensive shop. Someone in her church had noticed that she had no warm coat to protect her from the fierce winters where she faithfully served. But the coat came with no name tag, so there was no one to thank. She could but wear the coat and enjoy its warmth. I found this young woman confessing to me her thanks for my provision. She would say, "Jesus, you have provided richly for all my needs. I give thanks to you alone, for I know not who else to thank."

But one other curious thing occurred. Not only did I get the thanks for the young woman's anonymous coat, but not knowing who to thank, she became thankful to even the most meager souls in her church, "just in case" her rich gift had come from their penury. Great is the gift of anonymity.

Prayer
Lord Jesus,
For me
*   you paid a debt you didn't owe*
*   because*
*   I owed so much I couldn't pay.*
I know I will be most like you
*   when I learn to pay for others*
*   what they shall be unable to repay on their own.*
Your rich expenditure at Calvary
*   is teacher unto all in penury.*
Amen.

The Wideness of Grace

Luke 14:15–23

And when one of those who were reclining at the table with Him heard this, he said to Him, "Blessed is everyone who shall eat bread in the kingdom of God!"

But He said to him, "A certain man was giving a big dinner, and he invited many; and at the dinner hour he sent his slave to say to those who had been invited, 'Come; for everything is ready now.' But they all alike began to make excuses. . . .

"And the slave came back and reported this to his master. Then the head of the household became angry and said to his slave, 'Go out at once into the streets and lanes of the city and bring in here the poor and crippled and blind and lame.'

"And the slave said, 'Master, what you commanded has been done, and still there is room.'

"And the master said to the slave, 'Go out into the highways and along the hedges, and compel them to come in, that my house may be filled.'"

Let us forget about those for whom this great dinner was prepared. Let us look at the reassigned guest list, the army of the socially condemned. Watch them enter the resplendent dining hall: the legless man who has for years begged in the forum; the old woman, bent by years of street brooding; the boy in the rolling chair, whose own head has traveled long beneath the eye level of those on the sidewalks; the bleary-eyed wino, whom the world no longer sees; and the beggar, a heap of rags in the hedges.

Now grace has made them rich; they are summoned to a house whose stately ivory porticoes further diminish their shy estate. These rag piles in search of majesty stare as the chandeliers lower and the candles are lit. Then the slaves help all of them to the regal dining chairs. The chandeliers shine down on vases gorged with roses. The wine is poured. The pheasant is served.

The old woman hides her bread sack, green with its mold and contagion. The beggar with the tin cup cannot even see his lifted glass, for his tears blur his vision. The roving violinist circles the table playing a plaintive melody—but what is it? Oh yes, now they recognize its lovely words:

> Amazing grace! how sweet the sound, That saved a wretch like me!
> I once was lost, but now am found, Was blind, but now I see.

The story is your story, isn't it? Were you once in the hedges? Were you not once low in your self-impression? Then, when you least expected it, you were banqueting on grace.

Has it been a long time since then? Then set the table and get ready for a new round of alleluias. The table shall be filled again. In my house every cup is joy, and every roving violinist plays "Amazing Grace."

Prayer
Lord Jesus,
I lived so long in hedgerows
that I knew at once the ivory porticoes
must harbor your sweet presence.
I beg your grace shall let me ne'er forget
the night my need and your abundance met.
Amen.

The Single Focus of Saving Love

Luke 14:26–27

"If anyone comes to Me, and does not hate his own father and mother and wife and children and brothers and sisters, yes, and even his own life, he cannot be My disciple. Whoever does not carry his own cross and come after Me cannot be My disciple."

Do not misread this great hyperbole. I am not championing hatred. It is never right to hate anyone—your family, friends, or even yourself. But when the single focus of your life is in place, what is given to me will make all lesser passions seem like hate.

"Dear friends, let us love one another, for love comes from God. Everyone who loves has been born of God and knows God. Whoever does not love does not know God, because God is love. This is how God showed his love among us: He sent his one and only Son into the world that we might live through him. This is love: not that we loved God, but that he loved us and sent his Son as an atoning sacrifice for our sins. Dear friends, since God so loved us, we also ought to love one another" (1 John 4:7–11). In this brief hymn of five verses the word *love* is used eleven times. You must not suppose that I could ever teach you hate.

But because of your great love for me, some of the attention you once gave to family and friends may appear apathetic to them. You do not hate them. But you are so focused on divine love that you may seem to them too absorbed in grace.

But to anyone who has seen you bearing your cross, you will be seen at the very epicenter of my love. For you cannot bear a cross of your own volition without leading all who see you to be touched by the single focus of my love.

Cross-bearing is the farthest step of volitional love. See me at my crucifixion. At Calvary I knew a horrible but delicious obedience. No one took my life; I laid it down. It was an act of love.

So will cross-bearing be for you. You will not ever be able to love my Father and hate anyone else. The ardor of your worship with your singleness of heart will cause my love to spill over into your every relationship.

Prayer
Lord Jesus,
I want to take up my cross
as an evidence of all that I feel for you,
and may such love bless all I touch.
Here is the zenith of that love which is true:
I take my cross to follow after you.
Amen.

Planning the Christ Life

Luke 14:28–33

"For which one of you, when he wants to build a tower, does not first sit down and calculate the cost, to see if he has enough to complete it? Otherwise, when he has laid a foundation, and is not able to finish, all who observe it begin to ridicule him, saying, 'This man began to build and was not able to finish.' Or what king, when he sets out to meet another king in battle, will not first sit down and take counsel whether he is strong enough with ten thousand men to encounter the one coming against him with twenty thousand? Or else, while the other is still far away, he sends a delegation and asks terms of peace. So therefore, no one of you can be My disciple who does not give up all his own possessions."

The undisciplined life is not worth living. At the outset of your pilgrimage, seek discipline.

Self-discipline is not something we discover in a happenstance moment of giddy worship. How I wish it were that easy. It is not. Look at those ministers who have built empires of vast acceptance; the prevailing mood of their service seems always happy and casual. It would be easy in such circumstances to assume that to be Christlike, you have only to be transported by emotive feelings. You have but to hold up your hands, clamp your eyes shut in prayerful intention, and be slain by raw emotion. Then you will automatically give up your wealth and follow me.

Do not believe it. Spiritual moods of any sort rarely result in discipline. To walk in discipline, count the cost as an architect plans a great building. Measure the strength of all that you are doing, like a general going to war.

There are many who say that I can't have literally meant this commandment. "After all," reasoned one "near" Bible scholar, "if everyone sold everything that they had, who would buy it?" But let not such faulty logic wean you from the strength of my calling.

What I have asked of you will require everything. When will you give me all? How will you give me all? The answer to all of these questions lies in daily surrender. If on any single day you say to me, "Oh, Christ, today I give you some but not all," that day will be lost to you. No partial gift can evoke the maturity that at last comes to the committed life. Only the committed life is worthy.

Prayer
   Lord Jesus,
   I will not be like those
      who seem to believe that the planned
      life is an accidental state we trip over
      during our jubilant worship.
   I offer unto you the lion's share,
      to make relinquishment my daily prayer.
   Amen.

Lost

Luke 15:1–6

Now all the tax-gatherers and the sinners were coming near Him to listen to Him. And both the Pharisees and the scribes began to grumble, saying, "This man receives sinners and eats with them."

And He told them this parable, saying, "What man among you, if he has a hundred sheep and has lost one of them, does not leave the ninety-nine in the open pasture, and go after the one which is lost, until he finds it? And when he has found it, he lays it on his shoulders, rejoicing. And when he comes home, he calls together his friends and his neighbors, saying to them, 'Rejoice with me, for I have found my sheep which was lost!'"

A woman once lost her wedding ring. It was encrusted with diamonds and made entirely of platinum and gold. She deeply grieved its loss. But her grief did not focus on how much the diamonds or precious metals were worth financially. She thought of all the ring stood for. She thought of her wonderful thirty-year marriage and how her husband had faithfully stood by her during a long illness. Even as she searched for the lost ring, she saw only the beloved face of her husband. Sometimes that face was young—her handsome young bridegroom. Sometimes that face was bowed in saying a simple grace over their meals.

In the course of days, she found the ring. It was wedged oddly upright between two sections of floor tile. She called her next-door neighbor. She called her friend of twenty years who lived across town. She called her maid of honor from a wedding three decades past!

When they arrived, she embraced them all in joy. They were all wonderfully affirming. Then she did a curious thing. She put the wedding ring back in its old box and set it in the center of the table. Then they all sat down around the small table, joining hands. The woman prayed, thanking God for her good husband and their long marriage. Only when the prayer was done did she reach for the box. All of the friends expected her to put it on again. But she did not.

"One man put this on my hand thirty years ago," she said. "He'll be home tonight. He can put it on again." And again they rejoiced.

How the woman felt about that ring is how God feels about sinners. He made them for himself. He longs to find them, to set them in joy in the company of angels and rejoice. For all his longings are satisfied only when lost sinners are found and celebrated in his presence.

Prayer
Lord Jesus,
I must remember
   how you considered me dear when I was lost.
I want to remember all of those
   I know who are lost to every purpose you hold for them.
They might become the center of heaven's rejoicing,
   if only I will help them find you.
Dear Christ, I want to help you find the lost,
   remembering they're redeemed at lavish cost.
Amen.

Ungodly Presumption

Luke 15:11–14

And He said, "A certain man had two sons; and the younger of them said to his father, 'Father, give me the share of the estate that falls to me.' And he divided his wealth between them. And not many days later, the younger son gathered everything together and went on a journey into a distant country, and there he squandered his estate with loose living. Now when he had spent everything, a severe famine occurred in that country, and he began to be in need."

There is a destructive principle among some youth. They want to hurry time and buy up all of life at once. They so often greet life with the cry, "Give me my share . . . now!" They want to hurry their way to some exalted station in life.

What the younger son did not see in the case of my parable was that his father's continuing love for him had created the false illusion that he had a legitimate share of his father's estate coming. But what had he done to merit this share? The fortune was his father's. The estate was his father's. The home where he grew up, the garden where he played, the food that he ate, and the clothes that he wore: all of these things were his father's. So it was with utter presumption that he cried: Give me my share!

It is a similar presumption toward God that causes people to say, "God, give me heaven when I die." Why? Do they deserve it? Which angels are their special friends? How did they come to such a deserving place?

Presumption is a great sin against the price I paid to buy everyone a place in heaven. There is but one ticket to heaven. So if you want to go to heaven when you die, then you must do more than demand it. Grace exists to give to you what has been purchased at an awful cost.

It is sheer presumption to cry, "Give me my share!" It is wiser to cry, "Father, what must I do to be saved?" (Acts 16:30). The answer to that question is printed across the portals of the eternal city.

Prayer
Lord Jesus,
In this world everyone seems to think
*   that heaven is a mandated right they have.*
Help me never to wake up a single morning
*   but that I pray,*
I am redeemed by grace, therefore I sing,
*   God gave. I had no right to anything.*
Amen.

Your Need and God's Supply

Luke 15:17–21

"But when he came to his senses, he said, 'How many of my father's hired men have more than enough bread, but I am dying here with hunger! I will get up and go to my father, and will say to him, "Father, I have sinned against heaven, and in your sight; I am no longer worthy to be called your son; make me as one of your hired men."' And he got up and came to his father. But while he was still a long way off, his father saw him, and felt compassion for him, and ran and embraced him, and kissed him. And the son said to him, 'Father, I have sinned against heaven and in your sight; I am no longer worthy to be called your son.'"

Can you see the waiting father in my story? Every day he stands looking down that long and empty road where his lost son disappeared so long ago. His old eyes strain to see through the wavy vision of the desert heat bouncing off the sun-baked paving.

"Will he never come?" asks the father inside his longing heart. How he strains to catch sight of him—that lanky, hungry shadow, breaking the thin horizon—his son, coming home.

Shall there be no rebuke? Much of the family fortune is gone. The good name has been slandered. There is no hope of recovering all the son has lost. The father is old. His plain life has known few delights since his boy left home.

Besides, what father ever gets so old that even an old son does not remain a baby in his memory? It is no mere bedraggled vagabond, unkempt and unshaven, that he awaits. This keeper of swine is his son.

And so he waits.

And how in truth is the rebel? Gone is his arrogant presumption. Gone is the cry, "Give me my share of the estate!" Now all he wants is to come home. He will not ask to live in the big manor house where he grew up. All he wants is to live in the shed with the field hands. All he wants is gruel for breakfast and an occasional chance to see his old father's head above the garden wall. If he is allowed to say "Father, forgive me," this will be meaning enough for him.

The tears, the laughter, the joy of encircling completion! Need and longing love are well met. Joy owns the day!

Prayer
Lord Jesus,
I remember coming down that long road,
wondering about the nature of your Father.
Would he take me back?
Would he forgive me for all that I had done?
Could I expect to know his grace?
Then heaven's sweetness out of all control
circled me in love and claimed my soul.
Amen.

The Joy of Union with Christ

Luke 15:22–24

"The father said to his slaves, 'Quickly bring out the best robe and put it on him, and put a ring on his hand and sandals on his feet; and bring the fatted calf, kill it, and let us eat and be merry; for this son of mine was dead, and has come to life again; he was lost, and has been found.' And they began to be merry."

See their eager union. The old man cannot believe his eyes. There is someone in the road. Yes, he is tall and like his son. Is it? . . . No, it is not . . . Yes, it is!

The old man has not run in years. But his steps are too hurried to be called walking. It is said that old men have not much dignity when they run. But dignity does not matter. The old man's son is in the road ahead! He runs!

The young son cares not for dignity either. He, too, drops his filthy coat and his rotten rucksack. He runs. They collide in grace. They embrace! "Father, I am undeserving of your love. Make me but a field worker!"

The father cannot forgive him fast enough. His tears forbid the possibility of words. How can he forgive when he cannot even speak? He is mad with joy! They weep and the wordless things they want to say will not come, but they cannot stop loving.

When joy will let the old man speak again, he says to the gathering servants, "Don't just stand there! Get a robe for this, my naked son! And you run to the house; get my father's ruby ring. He gave it to me shortly before he died to preserve our family name forever. I have treasured it but never worn it. Today I will put the idle relic to good use. And you who tend the kitchen, kill the brown calf and set the table with the silver."

The son is so overwhelmed he cannot speak. "No, I do not deserve this. I have hurt you too much. I have sinned against heaven and in your sight. I am not worthy to be called your son!"

"Nonsense, boy! Your repentance has made you worthy! I would have died if you had not come. I love you!" And while they stare at each other in disbelief, the homecoming is prepared. The entire manor rejoices. But no one's joy is greater than the father's. The boy is home. The world is whole. There is a new name, a new robe, a new ring. Restored love has been crowned with a circlet of gold.

Prayer
Lord Jesus,
Heaven is full of those
who once were so loathsome
to themselves
that the only thing they could do in your presence
was to weep of their unworthiness.
I was one of them.
How glorious to find my soiled clothes
were instantly replaced by ring and robe.
Amen.

The Sin of Elder Brothers

Luke 15:25–32

"Now his older son was in the field, and when he came and approached the house, he heard music and dancing. And he summoned one of the servants and began inquiring what these things might be. And he said to him, 'Your brother has come, and your father has killed the fattened calf, because he has received him back safe and sound.' But he became angry, and was not willing to go in; and his father came out and began entreating him. But he answered and said to his father, 'Look! For so many years I have been serving you, and I have never neglected a command of yours; and yet you have never given me a kid, that I might be merry with my friends; . . .'

"And he said to him, 'My child, you have always been with me, and all that is mine is yours. But we had to be merry and rejoice, for this brother of yours was dead and has begun to live, and was lost and has been found.'"

An odd thing begins to happen as believers serve their church more and serve their God less. The shift of their affection is so gradual that they often do not see it. But they finally give the church the love they once gave to God alone. The only way you can be sure that you have not made this mistake is to ask yourself, "What evidences are there in my current discipleship that I belong to God alone?"

The church will receive all the love and service it can get. It may give no assurance in return that those who give it so much are really appreciated. In matters of crisis the church will dismiss the love of its "smaller" members as less important in favor of some of its more "significant" members. This state of rejection can be very hard on those who are excluded. In such moments the disenchanted may leave the church for the rest of their lives.

The church is not God. It isn't even the repository of God's grace. Those who remember this do not lose their faith when disenchantment comes. Those who do forget it often settle down to an embittered life of discouragement that leaves them passing God in the dark without speaking.

This kind of resentment is the sin of the elder brother. The elder brother resented that glorious music and dancing that welcomed his sinful brother home. Elder brothers are so embittered that they often can't rejoice when the lost are found.

Elder brothers grieve the heart of the waiting Father!

Elder brothers swelter in continual hurt because in learning how to bear a grudge, they forget how to be a bearer of grace.

Prayer
Lord Jesus,
Forgive me if I have eyes
but cannot see the spiritually needy.
Forgive me if I have arms but will not use them
to readily embrace penitents.
Make me a soul whose hand became God's glove
to touch those souls as only God would love.
Amen.

Shrewd Discipleship

Luke 16:1–8

Now He was also saying to the disciples, "There was a certain rich man who had a steward, and this steward was reported to him as squandering his possessions. And he called him and said to him, 'What is this I hear about you? Give an account of your stewardship, for you can no longer be steward.' And the steward said to himself, 'What shall I do, since my master is taking the stewardship away from me? I am not strong enough to dig; I am ashamed to beg. I know what I shall do, so that when I am removed from the stewardship, they will receive me into their homes.'

"And he summoned each of his master's debtors, and he began saying to the first, 'How much do you owe my master?' And he said, 'A hundred measures of oil.' And he said to him, 'Take out your bill, and sit down quickly and write fifty.' Then he said to another, 'And how much do you owe?' And he said, 'A hundred measures of wheat.' He said to him, 'Take your bill, and write eighty.'

"And his master praised the unrighteous steward because he had acted shrewdly; for the sons of this age are more shrewd in relation to their own kind than the sons of light."

This parable is not meant to endorse shady business but to illustrate that Christians are often not good stewards of their resources. The owner's compliment of the servant's shrewdness was not a commendation of evil dealing. Rather, the affirmation was a compliment of his survival savvy.

The unjust steward freely admitted that he didn't want to dig ditches and he was too ashamed to beg. Knowing what he didn't want to do, he asked himself how he could use his brain to make the future work for him.

Unfortunately, many Christians have never asked themselves how they could make the future work for themselves. Because they do not plan for the future well, they waste the present moment.

Please remember that God gave you a heart so that he could build his throne there. He wants to rule your life and all your circumstances. But he gave you a head so that when you have walked a mile in pain, you would remember not to take that path again. When options come your way that would make the kingdom work better, you may need to leave your quiet altar and do some honest, healthy planning with some of the time you might have used to pray. If you are wise in serving God, you will certainly hear the owner of your vineyard say, "Well done, good and faithful servant! You have been faithful with a few things; I will put you in charge of many things" (Matt. 25:21a).

Prayer
Lord Jesus,
I want to use my heart
* to hold your heart-sized throne.*
But I want to use my head,
* to be sure that I do not stumble into heaven*
* clutching the remnants of unwise bargains*
* because I would not act more intelligently.*
I want to use my head for business art
* and keep your throne within my heart of hearts.*
Amen.

Reversed Priorities

Luke 16:19–24

"Now there was a certain rich man, and he habitually dressed in purple and fine linen, gaily living in splendor every day. And a certain poor man named Lazarus was laid at his gate, covered with sores, and longing to be fed with the crumbs which were falling from the rich man's table; besides, even the dogs were coming and licking his sores.

"Now it came about that the poor man died and he was carried away by the angels to Abraham's bosom; and the rich man also died and was buried. And in Hades he lifted up his eyes, being in torment, and saw Abraham far away, and Lazarus in his bosom. And he cried out and said, 'Father Abraham, have mercy on me, and send Lazarus, that he may dip the tip of his finger in water and cool off my tongue; for I am in agony in this flame.'"

Consider Lazarus. Hell had been his customary way of living. He needed medical attention, but rarely got it. He needed food, but little of it came his way. He was always cold and shivered in the shadows of the rich man's house. He begged the table scraps that fell from the rich man's table.

The rich man was entirely consumed by those affairs and arrangements that occupy rich men. He rarely noticed Lazarus, that crumpled pile of rags, surrounded by the dogs who licked his sores. But the dying time comes to all. Do not confuse the real issue of this story. Lazarus went to heaven, not because he was poor or covered with sores. He went to heaven because he loved God.

Conversely, the rich man went to hell not because he was rich. He went to hell because he had too much seen himself as God. He had never really needed that God who was the only resource the poor man had.

Imagine going from a leprous and vile existence into the presence of God. Imagine also going from a splendid silver-spoon and gold-plate existence to the flames of hell. With no hope of heaven, the rich man learned begging—that horrible and dehumanizing art that Lazarus had practiced to stay alive in the shadows of his marble mansion. He begged water from the man who had once begged his table crumbs. But he was told that water is not a possibility in Hades. Then he begged for the return of Lazarus to tell his surviving relatives of hell. But Father Abraham told the rich man regrettably that resurrected beggars are not as good at evangelism as he supposed them to be.

And so the story ends. Heaven is still heaven. Hell is still hell. Hopelessness and bliss are forever. Faith, not wealth, is the key to life eternal.

Prayer
Lord Jesus,
Heaven must be as filled with intelligent beggars
*   as hell is with the unwise wealthy.*
Help me never to condemn the tycoons of hell,
*   nor forget to exercise that love that never sees beggars as beggars.*
I pray that when I come to heaven's gate
*   befriending beggars will have made me late.*
Amen.

Serving the God of Children

Luke 17:1–2

And He said to His disciples, "It is inevitable that stumbling blocks should come, but woe to him through whom they come! It would be better for him if a millstone were hung around his neck and he were thrown into the sea, than that he should cause one of these little ones to stumble."

Have you not heard the adage, "Never hurt a child." The history of humankind is a never-ending tale of brutality to children. Only in recent times have laws protected them. In earlier ages and civilizations children suffered unimaginable horrors. The most desirable children were often thrown screaming into the fiery arms of some pagan god or goddess. Unwanted babies, on the other hand, were left on mountainsides or in forests to die or be devoured by wild beasts. Children were often sold by needy and unfeeling parents into slavery. It was common in war to kill the children of the enemy to intimidate them into surrender.

History is an unending saga of children abused, tortured, and forgotten. Children in our contemporary culture are treated little better. They are herded through divorce courts, bewildered by having to choose whether they like Mommy or Daddy best as their custody parent.

But all of these abuses begin in the same way. Child-suffering begins with the simple idea that children are less important than adults. That idea was behind what happened the day that my disciples began rebuking the mothers for taking my important time with children. This inherently ugly notion has left children defenseless in the world. I rebuked the disciples for rebuking the mothers. For a moment I stopped the all-important business of healing and preaching.

And while they thought I should have ignored the children to do "truly important things," I did one of the most important things that can be done: I took the children in my arms and blessed them. In their simple, believing faces I saw what I would most like to have seen in the disciples' faces: love, trust, and an overwhelming desire for God.

Do you need me as a child needs a mother's love just to exist? If not, don't try to become more adult so you can understand the mysteries of God. Try to be more like a child—trusting, needy, believing—for of such is the kingdom of heaven.

> *Prayer*
> *Lord Jesus,*
> *Help me to look in every childish face*
>   *and see the future.*
> *Help me to see in those*
>   *same faces the coming possibilities of grace.*
> *Help me to see I have an obligation to bless the children*
>   *that I know*
>   *so that the world may have its best chance*
>   *of meeting you.*
> *I must remember you were once a child,*
>   *Dear Christ of power, My Savior meek and mild.*
> *Amen.*

The Sicknesses God Intends to Use

John 11:1–7

Now a certain man was sick, Lazarus of Bethany, of the village of Mary and her sister Martha. And it was the Mary who anointed the Lord with ointment, and wiped His feet with her hair, whose brother Lazarus was sick. The sisters therefore sent to Him, saying, "Lord, behold, he whom You love is sick." But when Jesus heard it, He said, "This sickness is not unto death, but for the glory of God, that the Son of God may be glorified by it." Now Jesus loved Martha, and her sister, and Lazarus. When therefore He heard that he was sick, He stayed then two days longer in the place where He was. Then after this He said to His disciples, "Let us go to Judea again."

Lazarus had a serious sickness. His soul was troubled. His sisters were so concerned that they summoned me to come. They became critical when I didn't hasten to their need. But in my reasons for the delay was a truth that I wanted everyone to understand: "This thing is from me—my glory is hidden in the pain." At every juncture of suffering, remember this.

Lazarus's pain, like all pain, held a great lesson. Pain is an ego-packager. Pain shuts us up within the tiny prison of ourselves. It builds an impenetrable shell of ego. Even the most selfless people, under the suffocating thrall of pain, cease looking outward and begin focusing inward. Many very radiant Christians in the last stages of cancer are so smothered by pain that they don't want to see anybody else. They don't even want their best friend in the room with them. They can, in such straits, become harsh and ugly. They may hurt so much that they pray to die. They welcome the sweet silence that only death can bring to their screaming nervous systems.

Why did I tarry when my friends in Bethany were in such straits? Mary and Martha and Lazarus were about to learn the incredible power of God. But they would only learn it after they had crossed the deep chasm of despair. Once the pain had been faced down, then they would finally be able to see me as the all-sufficient Savior. Then they would know the glory they could not know while they were focused entirely on their own suffering.

Pain is the pilgrimage, and someday you will be the pilgrim. At such a moment, close your eyes and rehearse earth's only common sense. It is heaven's wisest proverb: "This thing is from me—my glory is hidden in the pain."

Prayer
  Lord Jesus,
  So often I have wept
    because I didn't understand
    that your ways are higher than mine,
    your thoughts are loftier,
    your reasons more inscrutable.
  I thank you that the darkest threads of strife
    point to those golden threads that gild my life.
  Amen.

Venturing into a Doubtful Future

John 11:14–16

Then Jesus therefore said to them plainly, "Lazarus is dead, and I am glad for your sakes that I was not there, so that you may believe; but let us go to him." Thomas therefore, who is called Didymus, said to his fellow disciples, "Let us also go, that we may die with Him."

It was no secret that I was not well liked in Jerusalem. Bethany was uncomfortably close to the capital. Thomas was always doubtful and a bit pessimistic, but his fears of being caught in Jerusalem with me were very real. I decided to go to Jerusalem. I was advised by all not to go. Thomas did not support my decision, but he did not turn back. When he said, "Let us go and die with Jesus" he was cynical, but he was also making a statement of real commitment.

I knew what I was going to do. All of those I had so far raised from the dead were from cities far to the north of Jerusalem. But I was going to do something that would have Jerusalem caught in the grip of wonder. In fact, Mary and Martha and Lazarus were so well known in Jerusalem that this resurrection, far more than all of the others, would stir up a commotion that would leave even the officials of Judaism wondering if I might not be the Messiah (John 12:9–10). I knew that after his resurrection many would be stopping by Lazarus's house to see how he was feeling, particularly all those who had gone to his funeral.

So even though Thomas knew what the disciples were risking to follow me to Jerusalem, he did not know that what I was about to do would plunge my final weeks of ministry into an odd intermingling of turmoil and victory.

Discipleship is a covenant of following, no matter what. Thomas came along with me to the capital city because it was his nature to follow. That's what he saw to be the purpose of his life. His mind was firm. His life held no meaning apart from me. He might be insecure about it—he might even doubt the outcome—but he did not forget that disciples follow, regardless. Thus it must be for all who take up their cross. Sometimes it means following me into desperately dangerous territory. But those who know the word *disciple* always remember its definition. If *immediately* is God's adverb, the disciples' adverb must surely be *regardless*.

Prayer
Lord Jesus,
I don't feel much like following
  when I know it's risky.
Help me to remember that risk
  is the job description of my calling.
I am called to be a disciple
  with all that it entails.
I want to follow even when I fear.
Unless I do, you have no disciple here.
Amen.

If Only You Had Been Here, Lord

John 11:17–21

So when Jesus came, He found that he had already been in the tomb four days. Now Bethany was near Jerusalem, about two miles off; and many of the Jews had come to Martha and Mary, to console them concerning their brother. Martha therefore, when she heard that Jesus was coming, went to meet Him; but Mary still sat in the house. Martha therefore said to Jesus, "Lord, if You had been here, my brother would not have died."

Do you not feel the sting in Martha's rebuke? Have you yourself spoken those words somewhere along your needy pilgrimage? Maybe it was one of those times when you felt that heaven was deaf when you walked through some crisis seemingly alone.

After Lazarus died, Martha was angry. When she saw me again, she didn't even say hello. She blurted out, "Where have you been anyway? He's dead now, you know. If you had come earlier, maybe not, but now . . ." Martha's attitude is common among believers in pain or grief. But be careful about harboring grudges toward God. It may sometimes seem like I'm not around in your hour of need, but I am. So I was in Martha's case. In fact, since I had first heard of her need, I thought of very little else. I had sent her name up to my Father with the plea that he surround her with his love. And you can be sure of this: I have never loved you any less than I loved Martha. I give you the same assurance that I will always be with you.

Martha made a mistake in judgment. My heart of prayer was constantly directed toward her during her crisis. Do you feel abandoned? Remember that I am always there, whether or not your emotions agree to it. When your inner turmoil will not confirm my presence, yield to the promise alone.

I have always been faithful to you. I will never forsake you. I have never castigated you with some unseen grudge. It is not possible for me to hate you. I settled all that, long ago, when the nails were in my hands. Learn Job's great pledge and make it your daily prayer in times when you feel all alone: "I know that my Redeemer lives" (Job 19:25). Say it again and again until you believe it. And when you do at last believe it, keep on saying it so that you may never doubt it.

Prayer
> *Lord Jesus,*
> *At those times when I cried out to you*
>   *and felt the heavens were closed,*
>   *it was always because I forgot to see you*
>   *praying for me before your Father.*
> *In need I come to you.*
> *O please forgive,*
>   *for I know now that my Redeemer lives.*
> *Amen.*

The Resurrection and the Life

John 11:22–27

"Even now I know that whatever You ask of God, God will give You."

Jesus said to her, "Your brother shall rise again." Martha said to Him, "I know that he will rise again in the resurrection on the last day."

Jesus said to her, "I am the resurrection and the life; he who believes in Me shall live even if he dies, and everyone who lives and believes in Me shall never die. Do you believe this?" She said to Him, "Yes, Lord; I have believed that You are the Christ, the Son of God, even He who comes into the world."

Death is the final frontier. I came to help you cross it. I said this any number of times to Martha and, indeed, to them all. But it was hard for them to see before my own resurrection how very powerful this force was. Lazarus was my chance to try out Martha's resurrection theology.

There is an easy contentment in talking about theology. When anyone in the family dies, the parson comes over with a little theology, and he reminds us that the dead will be raised again at the last trumpet (1 Cor. 15:52). But it is sometimes just grief therapy: a kind of saccharine chitchat that goes along with funeral dinners. If indeed the trump sounded right then, the good reverend might spill the food all over himself in the discovery that his words were instantly truer than he ever dreamed possible.

So let us remember that Martha knew what had happened to her brother. She was, however, not ready to see her theology come alive before her very eyes. And when I walked to the door of the tomb and ordered the stone rolled away, she was very quick to remind me that theology was one thing, but no good in the face of anything really practical. As she so candidly put it, "Lord . . . by this time there is a bad odor, for he has been there four days" (John 11:39).

Theology rarely goes where things have a bad odor! Yet Martha and all the company who were at hand were about to see that the perishable can be changed to the imperishable and mortality can be changed to immortality (1 Cor. 15:53).

I cried, "Lazarus, come out!" (John 11:43). Of course he did. He had no choice about it. God is my Father. Whatever I speak will be. So mark this down the next time you're reading theology. It's nice and as true as the paper it's printed on. But when I command anything to be, it must occur. At my word stones become bread, storms quiet, paralytics run. Martha learned the dead cannot sleep when I have ordered them awake.

Prayer
　Lord Jesus,
　When the trumpet blows,
　　may I understood the glorious horror
　　of all that made the hair raise on the necks
　　of those who knew the wonder of Lazarus's obedience
　　to your voice.
　I look forward to it all,
　　for there are so many I want to see alive again.
　Yet you I would see first, beyond this strife,
　　to praise thee more, thou Resurrected Life.
　Amen.

What Makes God Cry?

John 11:35
Jesus wept.

There is but one thing that causes the heavens to erupt with joy: faith. There is but one thing that makes heaven weep: unbelief. I wept that day because I saw that Mary and Martha had accepted me as the Christ of theology, but not the Lord of faith.

Yes, I wept.

I weep still when I stand beside the despairing who sorrow hopelessly in my presence. They may quote the Bible by memory and minister in my name, but if they despair in my presence, they do not really believe. And their unbelief makes heaven weep.

I had one other such experience on the Emmaus road. I walked along with two disciples and consoled them because they felt so everlastingly bad about my death. As we walked, they gloomily recounted the hopeless tale of their poor Messiah.

"Well, is it possible that this Jesus is alive?" I asked them.

"No, he was crucified, you know. Grisly death! He hung there till he gasped his last. Poor fellow, his mother was there too," they ran on.

"Well, did he not say he would rise again?" I asked.

"Oh, yes," they replied, "back when he felt better. But, of course, he changed his mind when they held him down and nailed his hands."

"Nailed him down! I heard that he walked to his cross and lay down upon it and willingly stretched forth his hands and feet. I heard that no one took his life but that he laid it down (John 10:17–18). Who knows? If he laid it down, maybe he can take it up again. After all, he once said, 'I am able to destroy the temple of God and rebuild it in three days' (Matt. 26:61), didn't he?"

"Well, yes, my good fellow," they said, "but he meant it only in a metaphorical and wholly existential sense. You see, resurrection is a mystical truth. You mustn't get too literal about all this."

Well, having just risen from the dead, I was not so mystical as they supposed. I didn't weep for their unbelief. My resurrection was too joyous for me to reply to them as lightly as I had to Mary and Martha.

Have you ever been guilty of the sins of Lazarus's sisters? Have you ever adored me as the textbook Christ and rejected me as the living Lord? Cultivate a living faith. Practice believing, lest when you need to, you can't.

Prayer
Lord Jesus,
Help me to remember
that I am saved forever because you can do unbelievable things.
Do some for me
so often that I will never doubt the divine possibilities
of all my mundane days.
You speak and corpses lift their heads,
and they must live who thought that they were dead.
Amen.

Gratitude Is an Attitude

Luke 17:11–17

And it came about while He was on the way to Jerusalem, that He was passing between Samaria and Galilee. And as He entered a certain village, ten leprous men who stood at a distance met Him; and they raised their voices, saying, "Jesus, Master, have mercy on us!" And when He saw them, He said to them, "Go and show yourselves to the priests." And it came about that as they were going, they were cleansed.

Now one of them, when he saw that he had been healed, turned back, glorifying God with a loud voice, and he fell on his face at His feet, giving thanks to Him. And he was a Samaritan. And Jesus answered and said, "Were there not ten cleansed? But the nine— where are they?"

Thank you are those magic words that lubricate all relationships. As with lepers, so with all of life. Yet they are scarce indeed. Something rather remarkable happened to these lepers. I remember them as they looked longingly and in need. Their rags proclaimed them outcasts and they stood at quite a distance. They were used to being pelted with stones when they came too close to the healthy. They often cried with raucous throats, "Unclean!"

They were so afflicted that their pitiful plight arrested my concern. Nothing so appeals to my Father as those who are hopeless, for their needs are unmistakable. Lepers died lepers—hated, feared, despised. They just died, that's all. So they had nothing to risk and everything to gain by asking for my mercy. There was no human reason that I should reply to their need. Nobody felt sorry for lepers, nobody cared. They really were not viewed as human. So nobody would have blamed me for not paying the slightest attention to them.

But grace loves the hopeless, so I sent them to the priest to claim their cleansing. It was an old Jewish ritual proscribed by law. Once the priest said you were clean, then you were clean.

But on the way to the priest, they all discovered that they were cured.

One of the ten came back to thank me. He was, of course, a Samaritan. As if being a leper wasn't bad enough; being a Samaritan leper was doubly bad. Yet it was he who returned to say thanks.

I was touched that he came back. I always wondered why the others never came. I still wonder that today. I have saved millions and for each of them made eternity a sure thing. I rarely find those who, having been saved, consider their salvation an issue of gratitude for very long.

Prayer

Lord Jesus,
I came to you when I was hopeless,
    and grace stopped to care for me.
It is even as the old hymn says,
    "My sins were washed away
    and my night was turned to day."
And so my grateful praise shall ever be
Thanksgiving till I reach eternity.
Amen.

The Intentional Heart

Luke 18:1–7

Now He was telling them a parable to show that at all times they ought to pray and not to lose heart, saying, "There was in a certain city a judge who did not fear God, and did not respect man. And there was a widow in that city, and she kept coming to him, saying, 'Give me legal protection from my opponent.' And for a while he was unwilling; but afterward he said to himself, 'Even though I do not fear God nor respect man, yet because this widow bothers me, I will give her legal protection, lest by continually coming she wear me out.'"

And the Lord said, "Hear what the unrighteous judge said; now shall not God bring about justice for His elect, who cry to Him day and night, and will He delay long over them?"

The intentional heart is one who cries out for what it really wants. Such intention in prayer is the pleasure of God. Do not underestimate the force of the person who prays unceasingly. These dedicated people do not change God's mind about anything. For in God there is no fickle variableness or shadow of turning (James 1:17). For God is unique and unlike people. "I the LORD do not change" (Mal. 3:6).

God will not change his mind, though we pray again and again. Still, God's blessing is always granted at the end of your faithful praying. It was not that your prayers changed God's mind, but your intentional heart that achieved, by its desire, what had been God's holy will all along.

In my story there is a widow who needs the judge to notice her and protect her. Widows in every age often live without protection. The widow in my story came to the judge again and again, and her persistence opened up the judge's heart, from which his miraculous protection flowed. Did the widow's petition transform the judge? Not at all. He had within him the empathy of justice all along. But the widow's unceasing cry did at last release his answer.

Learn to pray without ceasing. Your prayers will delight your waiting Father. Then the unceasing intention of your own yearning heart will release all those wonderful things God has held for you all along.

Prayer
Lord Jesus,
I do not want to die and suddenly
    discover that many of those gifts you had for me
    went totally unclaimed
    because I would not ask.
You have said that we have not
    because we ask not (James 4:2).
And so I beg you,
    Release those things you're holding just for me
    and teach me how to pray unceasingly.
Amen.

In the Absence of Faith

Luke 18:8b

However, when the Son of Man comes, will He find faith on the earth?

Apostasy is the sin of rejecting faith. It may be committed though some grand and showy defiance. Some loud nihilists have challenged God—if he exists—to throw them into hell. But most people usually abandon faith without such grand pronouncements. Jude spoke of people who once appeared to believe and later were judged for their apparent unbelief: "Though you already know all this, I want to remind you that the Lord delivered his people out of Egypt, but later destroyed those who did not believe. And the angels who did not keep their positions of authority but abandoned their own home—these he has kept in darkness, bound with everlasting chains for judgment on the great day" (Jude 5–6).

The greatest impetus to abandoning faith begins with trading the God of requirement for the God of good deals. The culture may be caught up into making God easy for those who can't take him the way he is. God must be "user-friendly." We are encouraged to preach the God of butterflies since he is so much more easily approached than the God of the fiery furnace. "There is no use scaring people," say the God marketers. "Just put God in blue cellophane and shrink-wrap him with plush toys and nature calendars."

Leaving church on a casual, sunny Sunday makes it hard to believe that Jeremiah wept over the hard requirements God had for Jerusalem. John the Baptist talked of the coming apocalypse as snakes fleeing a wildfire. These days God has become a joyous and jovial Jehovah, bearing a "lite" message for his "lite" people. The desperation in this issue is this: what will the lite people hand down to their children? In the little synagogue at Nazareth I once memorized the first five books of the Bible. It is unthinkable that sermons often ignore Scripture these days.

Could it be that Jews have traditionally believed that it was their responsibility to pass their faith on to the next generation? Unless Christians do that, when I, the Son of Man come, I will not find faith on the earth. I will find only party caps, horns, and whistles scattered among the church pews. These artifacts may be the last will and testament of churches who found ways to be completely full of completely empty people.

Prayer
Lord Jesus,
I want to follow God
    exactly as he is.
I want the faith with all of its difficult
    demands unchanged.
I want to study hard to know faith's worth,
    that you may come and find faith on the earth.
Amen.

Eye to Eye with God

Luke 18:9–14

And He also told this parable to certain ones who trusted in themselves that they were righteous, and viewed others with contempt: "Two men went up into the temple to pray, one a Pharisee, and the other a tax-gatherer. The Pharisee stood and was praying thus to himself, 'God, I thank Thee that I am not like other people: swindlers, unjust, adulterers, or even like this tax-gatherer. I fast twice a week; I pay tithes of all that I get.'

"But the tax-gatherer, standing some distance away, was even unwilling to lift up his eyes to heaven, but was beating his breast, saying, 'God, be merciful to me, the sinner!'

"I tell you, this man went down to his house justified, rather than the other; for everyone who exalts himself shall be humbled, but he who humbles himself shall be exalted."

Those who bring their sin to God, eye to eye, in chatty conversational repentance make two mistakes. First, they have misunderstood the holiness of God. Second, they have not grasped the nature of repentance. God is so holy that Moses, in looking upon God's face, experienced so much glory that his face shone (Exod. 34:29). Moses was afraid to look upon the holiness of God.

Consider the second mistake, wherein is the presumption of the Pharisee. He had not learned the difference between a *testimony* and a *bragimony*. A testimony focuses on what God is doing in our lives. A bragimony centers on all the great things that people do for God. See how secure the Pharisee is in his opinion; he thanks God that he is not a swindler or an adulterer or even a tax-gatherer. His self-congratulatory posture is remarkable. He feels he has repented all that's really necessary.

The most grievous sin of the Pharisees may be that they believed themselves completely free of any major sin. They seemed to believe their sins were small and of no real consequence to God. Privately, most people are not so impious as to say they have never done anything wrong. They admit they have "goofed up," "flubbed," and "boo-booed." Still, they are not really sinners. After all, nobody's perfect.

The problem with getting people saved in this generation is that it's almost impossible to get them lost. Spiritual neediness is no longer a category. People rarely feel guilty over their sins. Judgment is out of fashion.

So the Pharisee is the perfect role model for this current time.

But consider the publican, the tax-gatherer. He feels the weight of his sin so much that he cannot lift up his eyes to heaven. He prays, "Lord, be merciful to me, a sinner!"

It's the publican who goes to his house "justified," and not the Pharisee.

Prayer
Lord Jesus,
Help me to remember
how good it feels to feel clean.
Then help me to remember,
I can only know this cleansing
when I come to you dirty.
Give me the cleansing born in honesty.
Wash me, O Lord, from my iniquity.
Amen.

Human Oneness

Matthew 19:3–9

And some Pharisees came to Him, testing Him, and saying, "Is it lawful for a man to divorce his wife for any cause at all?" And He answered and said, "Have you not read, that He who created them from the beginning MADE THEM MALE AND FEMALE, and said, 'FOR THIS CAUSE A MAN SHALL LEAVE HIS FATHER AND MOTHER, AND SHALL CLEAVE TO HIS WIFE; AND THE TWO SHALL BECOME ONE FLESH'? Consequently, they are no longer two, but one flesh. What therefore God has joined together, let no man separate."

They said to Him, "Why then did Moses command to GIVE HER A CERTIFICATE OF DIVORCE AND SEND HER AWAY?"

He said to them, "Because of your hardness of heart, Moses permitted you to divorce your wives; but from the beginning it has not been this way. And I say to you, whoever divorces his wife, except for immorality, and marries another woman commits adultery."

"What about divorce?" the Pharisees asked me. I wanted to get them to see that what they were really talking about was adultery. I wanted them to see that in the original creation, God made one man and one woman. When a man and a woman marry they are to be like that original couple. Adam was not free to decide capriciously that he had found some unforgivable flaw in Eve and to go out looking for her replacement.

These two were to be one flesh. This "one flesh" is not a statement of sexual union. It is the image of spiritual togetherness created by God. It was not intended to be interrupted by human legalisms. Moses gave Israel some permission concerning divorce. But it was a concession that grew out of their hardness of heart. Hardness of heart is the fruit of human selfishness. Most divorces gather themselves around this inflexible selfishness that uses marriage rather than serves it.

Men and women begin to endanger a marriage when they say, "You don't satisfy me anymore." There is the even worse accusation, "You don't make me happy!" What utter selfishness such statements contain. It is as though others exist only to gratify our ego. Who exists to make anybody happy? Happiness comes from the heart that declares itself happy. "Happy" is something you give to someone else, not something you require. Two become one flesh in marriage. Those having achieved this union should never seek to end the oneness, for it is God's gift.

Prayer
Lord Jesus,
In whatever conflict arises in our home,
help me to remember that you love my mate
in exactly the same way you love me.
If you love my mate that much,
maybe I could learn to love as I have been loved
and forgive as I have been forgiven.
Give me redeeming love for this my spouse
and make an honest temple of our house.
Amen.

The Gift of Focus

Matthew 19:10–12

The disciples said to Him, "If the relationship of the man with his wife is like this, it is better not to marry." But He said to them, "Not all men can accept this statement, but only those to whom it has been given. For there are eunuchs who were born that way from their mother's womb; and there are eunuchs who were made eunuchs by men; and there are also eunuchs who made themselves eunuchs for the sake of the kingdom of heaven. He who is able to accept this, let him accept it."

Sexuality is a gift to be shared, but only by two. Sometimes this gift given by God is given back to him as celibacy. Whether sexuality is shared between a man and a woman or a gift given back to God in surrender, the purpose of either marriage or a view of celibacy is focus.

A young minister once sat talking with a nun. The young minister had on his wedding band, and the nun commented on its beauty. "Oh, I have been married ten years now and I have a wonderful mate," the young man said.

"I have been married to my Lord for fifty years," said the old nun. "I too have a wonderful mate." Then she slipped her old and gnarled hand out of her ample sleeve.

"My mate really adds a lot to my ministry and gives me many ideas on how to help others," said the young minister.

"Even so, is mine!" said the nun.

"My mate walks with me through all the people problems and all the turmoils of my ministry," said the preacher.

"And my mate has guaranteed that he will never leave me nor forsake me," said the woman, looking fixedly down at her wedding band.

"And I know my mate in that sweet communion of lovers when we are both alone and we know that wonderful closeness," he said.

"I, too, meet my lover daily in aloneness, and he gives me all his love to strengthen me for the journey," said the woman.

Then the minister realized that for both, sexuality was a gift. The old nun celebrated her sexuality and returned it to God. The minister, too, along with his wife, celebrated his sexuality and submitted it as an offering to God. Their very different consecration of their sexuality gave both nun and preacher the same thing: a focus in ministry.

Prayer
Lord Jesus,
Help me to see that sex,
like every human appetite,
is given by God.
Kept as it is meant, it blesses.
Abused by any faulty definition,
it can be squarely in the way of God.
May all who have received rise up and bless
this gracious gift of human tenderness.
Amen.

The Children

Mark 10:13–16

And they were bringing children to Him so that He might touch them; and the disciples rebuked them. But when Jesus saw this, He was indignant and said to them, "Permit the children to come to Me; do not hinder them; for the kingdom of God belongs to such as these. Truly I say to you, whoever does not receive the kingdom of God like a child shall not enter it at all." And He took them in His arms and began blessing them, laying His hands upon them.

Children have often been seen as "in the way." My disciples rebuked the mothers of Israel for bringing their children to me for a blessing. Here they made the typical adult mistake of considering the really important concerns of this life "adult stuff." "Kid stuff," by contrast, is usually seen to be trivial.

But I wanted the world to know that children are the stuff of the real Kingdom. Not only are they the best at modeling innocence and trust, they are also an evidence that Christianity really is going somewhere. A church with no children is like a room with no windows. As adults grow old, they tend to trap their faith within the tastes and preferences of their own generation. Without children, they take their rehearsed (and often traditional) values to the grave. Children, naive as they are, pass faith on to the next generation. That's why the psalmist wrote:

> Sons are a heritage from the LORD,
>   children a reward from him.
> Like arrows in the hands of a warrior
>   are sons born in one's youth.
> Blessed is the man
>   whose quiver is full of them. (Ps 127:3–5a)

My disciples ignored one other value on the day they rebuked the mothers. Children have a way of being much more tedious to others than they ever are to their own mothers. A child is the choicest possession of a mother. So when they brought their children to me, they were offering me the finest thing they had to offer. Naturally, I blessed them as the precious gifts their mothers so freely gave me. But I blessed them even more as models of innocence and devotion.

If you would really know me, watch a child worship me and worship as she does. If you would really pray, listen to a child pray and do it as he does. If you want to know what holiness is, listen to a child confess, then desire the life that is pure.

Prayer
Lord Jesus,
I want the little children
*   whom I see as peripheral in my vision*
*   to be more central in all I do.*
Cleanse my heart of sin, I beg of you,
*   and help me pray and praise as children do.*
Amen.

One Very Small Thing

Mark 10:17–23

And as He was setting out on a journey, a man ran up to Him and knelt before Him, and began asking Him, "Good Teacher, what shall I do to inherit eternal life?" And Jesus said to him, "Why do you call Me good? No one is good except God alone. You know the commandments, 'DO NOT MURDER, DO NOT COMMIT ADULTERY, DO NOT STEAL, DO NOT BEAR FALSE WITNESS, Do not defraud, HONOR YOUR FATHER AND MOTHER.'"

And he said to Him, "Teacher, I have kept all these things from my youth up." And looking at him, Jesus felt a love for him, and said to him, "One thing you lack: go and sell all you possess, and give to the poor, and you shall have treasure in heaven; and come, follow Me." But at these words his face fell, and he went away grieved, for he was one who owned much property." And Jesus, looking around, said to His disciples, "How hard it will be for those who are wealthy to enter the kingdom of God!"

So many would like it if heaven were achieved by good morals. In fact, like this rich young ruler, most like to think of heaven as granted or denied on the basis of our behavior. They want it to be a matter of the balance on the scales. If your good works outweigh your bad works, heaven is for you. If not, it's not.

So here is a man whose balances look good. He is ready immediately to go to that heaven where the gates swing open for good morals. But when he told me that he was good at the commandments, keeping every one, I knew that he was breaking one—even as he told me how good he was at being good. Still, within his own relativistic framework of expectation, he was doing reasonably well. Compared to tyrants and mass murderers, he was as moral as a messiah. Compared to the true Messiah, however, he more resembled tyrants and mass murderers. I tried to get his mind off his own goodness, which is nobody's guarantee of heaven.

"I have kept the commandments," he said, in effect. "Is there anything else, Lord?"

"Actually, there is one other very small thing you must do," I replied. "Sell all you own and come follow me."

For most who consider following me, there seems to be a pre-set limit to the price they are willing to pay. When I hung on the cross, God's pockets were truly empty. When I died for your sins, heaven's treasury was depleted. I gave all. Now the requirement for all of my disciples is matching funds. If you come telling me how much you have done and how moral you are, I can only bid you to consider my cross and ask if you are not seeking grace at a bargain. Heaven is never a matter of rule-keeping. It is an issue of relationship. Relationship is everything, and every authentic relationship is based on sacrifice.

Prayer
> *Lord Jesus,*
> *Help me remember*
> *that what I own*
> *I have committed unto you.*
> *With hands turned up I offer you my gift.*
> *It isn't much, and yet it's heaven's thrift.*
> *Amen.*

The Enrichment of Depletion

Luke 18:25–30

"For it is easier for a camel to go through the eye of a needle, than for a rich man to enter the kingdom of God." And they who heard it said, "Then who can be saved?" But He said, "The things impossible with men are possible with God." And Peter said, "Behold, we have left our own homes, and followed You."

And He said to them, "Truly I say to you, there is no one who has left house or wife or brothers or parents or children, for the sake of the kingdom of God, who shall not receive many times as much at this time and in the age to come, eternal life."

To all outward purposes, sacrifice looks as though it steals our substance and disinherits us. But do not accept this at face value. Rather, make sacrifice the definition of your life.

Do not lay up for yourselves treasures on earth but in heaven. Peter once reminded me how much they had sacrificed just to be disciples. But I reminded Peter that all that was given up on earth were riches deposited directly into heaven's account.

Did you notice that I also said, "Peter, you will receive it all back, now, as well as in the age to come"? Not all that you sacrifice is stored in eternity. Some of those wonderful things are bestowed on you right here on earth. For instance, in surrendering life to me, you become part of a wonderful believing community right here in the present. Have you considered the riches that are contained in the worship service of your own church? You gave up all, and instantly became friends with a community of sacrifice and glory. Give yourself to that community and you will discover that those around you have repaid you in friendship for all you ever gave to me. It is a rich man or woman who can say, "I follow Christ, and look at this wonderful community of support and relationship I have purchased with my obedience!" It is a wonderful thing to have friends, committed to the same values and living in the same kingdom.

To be a Christian involves great sacrifice. But when you are sacrificing for a great cause, joy comes from knowing that the sacrifice is little compared to the blessing. To surrender all may seem a great cost, but behind total surrender is total blessing.

The rich man's real problem was that he put monetary price tags on everything he touched, and then decided which items in life were really a bargain. If he had less money he would have had to learn to evaluate his world as the poor do. Those things of most value cannot be priced. They cannot even be bought and sold. They are matters of the heart, too valuable to be evaluated.

Prayer
Lord Jesus,
My sacrifice is rather reminiscent of that old hymn:
"What shall I give you, Master?
Thou, who gavest all for me?
Shall I give less of what I possess,
Or shall I give all to thee?"
Here is the little bit I am. Please see
it isn't much, and yet it's all of me.
Amen.

Playing Fair with God

Matthew 20:1–15

"For the kingdom of heaven is like a landowner who went out early in the morning to hire laborers for his vineyard. And when he had agreed with the laborers for a denarius for the day, he sent them into his vineyard. And he went out about the third hour and saw others standing idle in the market place; and to those he said, 'You too go into the vineyard, and whatever is right I will give you.' And so they went. Again he went out about the sixth and the ninth hour, and did the same thing. And about the eleventh hour he went out, and found others standing; and he said to them, 'Why have you been standing here idle all day long?' They said to him, 'Because no one hired us.' He said to them, 'You too go into the vineyard.' And when evening had come, the owner of the vineyard said to his foreman, 'Call the laborers and pay them their wages, beginning with the last group to the first.'

"And when those hired about the eleventh hour came, each one received a denarius. And when those hired first came, they thought that they would receive more; and they also received each one a denarius. And when they received it, they grumbled at the landowner, saying, 'These last men have worked only one hour, and you have made them equal to us who have borne the burden and the scorching heat of the day.' But he answered and said to one of them, 'Friend, I am doing you no wrong; did you not agree with me for a denarius? Take what is yours and go your way, but I wish to give to this last man the same as to you. Is it not lawful for me to do what I wish with what is my own? Or is your eye envious because I am generous?'"

Blessed are those who are so generous, they enjoy seeing a competitor praised. Most Christians want grace to be given to others so long as they get all that's coming to them. Much of the personal misery people feel does not come because they feel that God hasn't been good to them, but because they feel he has been doing even more for someone else.

God always plays fair with his world. But few souls really want God to treat them fairly. They want God to give them special treatment, to make over them, giving them gold while dispensing rocks to their enemies. The more this dangerous game is played, the more the spoiled person desires to be pampered by heaven. Pretty soon these grace-requiring Christians are not very generous to each other. They are often very critical.

A temperate theologian once became aggressive about ridding the entire world of drink. She was most censorious to all who did drink and vowed that the world must soon come to her discipline of abstinence. A cheerful and pleasant sister, after reaping her scorn, said, "Well, Jesus turned water into wine. How do you feel about that?"

"I know," said the woman, "but I would have thought a lot more of him if he hadn't!" A censorious spirit may at last approach blasphemy. And the dour saint may never surrender that eternal scowl.

Prayer
Lord Jesus,
help me to be generous,
for I have received so generously.
Help me never grudge your charity
because you give to others and not me.
Amen.

The Lavish Nature of Grace

Matthew 20:16
"Thus the last shall be first, and the first last."

This parable of the vineyard illustrates the demanding nature of law and grace. It wasn't that those workers hired early in the day were treated unfairly. They were not. But when they came to collect, they acted as though they had been. Everybody got paid the same. It is mere propriety that suggests that there should be different pay scales for different hours spent on the job.

The vineyard workers who had worked all day completely missed the point. It is true that they had been there longer. But they should not have acted as though they were being cheated. They should have celebrated the wonderful privilege of knowing the vineyard owner longer.

Can you remember who my first disciple was during my three-year ministry? It was Andrew (John 1:40). Now can you recall who was the last disciple who came to believe in me before my death? It was a thief on the cross. Some three years elapsed between this first believer and the last. Is Andrew to resent the thief because he got to go to heaven just the same as Andrew? Certainly not. The length of the walk that gets you to heaven is also a part of the pay.

The first shall be last and the last first.

It is my Father's will that all who follow me remember that the issue of lastness or firstness has to do only with human arrogance and presumption. Those who think they are first are the most likely to wind up last. Those who believe that they could not possibly be at the head of the line are very likely to be first. Why? Both the arrogant and the humble usually suffer from poor vision. There is a haughty blindness in those proud believers that causes them to be so unaware of their weaknesses that they assume that they have none. Likewise there is a delicious blindness in the humble that causes them to be unaware of their strengths. The proud rarely see those shortcomings that might enable their repentance. The humble rarely see those strengths that so endear them to God.

Both are likely to be surprised on Judgment Day—the last-place proud who thought too much of themselves and the first-place humble who were forever blind to their virtues. Seek every morning to learn what is God's requirement for that day. Let your inward hunger answer Micah's question: "And what does the LORD require of you? To act justly and to love mercy and to walk humbly with your God" (Mic. 6:8).

Prayer
Lord Jesus,
In that great reversal of spiritual positions,
*   help me not to be surprised*
*   wherein I stand.*
Help me never to congratulate myself
*   for anything I think I am,*
*   but to remember to be with you*
*   is joy redeemed by time,*
*   to enter grace though I be last in line.*
Amen.

Redeeming Hiddenness

Luke 18:31–34

And He took the twelve aside and said to them, "Behold, we are going up to Jerusalem, and all things which are written through the prophets about the Son of Man will be accomplished. For He will be delivered to the Gentiles, and will be mocked and mistreated and spit upon, and after they have scourged Him, they will kill Him; and the third day He will rise again." And they understood none of these things, and this saying was hidden from them, and they did not comprehend the things that were said.

The finished will of God concerning you is sometimes so hidden that you cannot see it, even though you search for it repeatedly. Much of this has to do with your inability to see your final position in grace. I have hidden it all through the Bible to encourage you to seek in the Scriptures an understanding of what your future will be like. In the pages of the Bible, there are many images of your final state. There are pictures of the great white throne (Rev. 20), the last trumpet of God (1 Cor. 15), the second coming (1 Thess. 4), and the last judgment (Matt. 25). Do not try to wrest from my Father's hands the exact nature of your final state. Such a fruitless quest—on which all too many get sidetracked—thwarts your interest in the right-now.

Never forget that the pilgrimage is not the same as the destination. You are to walk in humility and devotion. You will not be just walking with me, you will be going somewhere with me. No truly great Christian has ever lost perspective of this double track. They saw always, just over the horizon, the crystal empire where God rules. They saw me standing at the right hand of that throne. Sometimes when the way was truly desperate, that vision made them keep on being faithful to their daily walk. Remember Stephen at his stoning? Why was it he saw the heavens opened when he stood before his accusers? Because he had so often lived with that vision, when his life was more certain.

As you walk through the battlefield, look out and see the wounded. Then bandage their injuries. You will be dead of heart if some of those wounds that you bandage do not remind you of my own scars. You must also beware that you do not become content doing good. Those who do no longer think of me; they cease being Christian and are merely humanitarian. Do good works, but do them in my name. If they only lead you to think about doing more good works, you will be serving humankind, not my Father.

That day when I told my disciples the future, they were so imbedded in the present that they could not see the big picture. Their lives were too secure in the popular acceptance I was enjoying at the moment. My looming, desperate Calvary and their need to be strong in the coming crisis was lost to them. And they fled before it when it came. Use some of the present moment to contemplate your finished state. Be ready for the future into which I am sending you.

Prayer
Lord Jesus,
I have in my daily round of service
looked often upward and seen
that final union of our lives.
The work I know I must someday complete
I hope to lay as a prize before your feet.
Amen.

The Dangerous Longing for Special Position

Mark 10:35–37

And James and John, the two sons of Zebedee, came up to Him, saying to Him, "Teacher, we want you to do for us whatever we ask of You." And He said to them, "What do you want Me to do for you?" And they said to Him, "Grant that we may sit in Your glory, one on Your right, and one on Your left."

I know of few longings more dangerous than that of longing for prestige. James and John were presumptuous enough to believe that somehow they had an edge on personal advancement in my Kingdom. Ambition is perilous within the church. Untold harm has been done in church councils and great denominations because those who should have been content to serve became possessed of a need to control.

Virtually no church is safe from power struggles. Often men and women who are "little" in corporate structures have seen the church as a reasonable playing field where they may be king or queen for a season. These power-hungry souls at first polarize congregations and later paralyze them. They divide them into small partisan groups. Then, having divided, they set out to conquer.

Many small congregations have been so shattered by partisan politics that they lose all interest in ministry.

The hardest thing about this is that such people rarely see themselves as a problem. They may wreak havoc in the church, but all the time they are doing it they believe they are "committed and unafraid to take a stand." They often sense that they are not well liked, but they believe that it's because they are "true to God and will not put up with Satan and all his works."

Examine your life. Is there any part of it where you hold a desire to "be somebody" rather than to "serve someone"? Have you ever been caught up in the drive to "bring efficiency" to the church's affairs? Do you ever catch yourself thinking, "If only I had the power, I'd purge this church of evil"?

It is with such little privatized viewpoints that good people are misled. Hide your life in devotion. Serve. Pray.

Prayer
Lord Jesus,
I do not want to become
the monster I have seen in those
who made the world unhappy
because they could not enjoy what they could not run.
So scrub my ego hour by hour,
lest I lose joy by trading it for power.
Amen.

Are You Able?

Mark 10:38–40a

But Jesus said to them, "You do not know what you are asking for. Are you able to drink the cup that I drink, or to be baptized with the baptism with which I am baptized?" And they said to Him, "We are able." And Jesus said to them, "The cup that I drink you shall drink; and you shall be baptized with the baptism with which I am baptized. But to sit on My right or on My left, this is not Mine to give."

Are you able? This is not just the question I had for the sons of Zebedee. It is my question for the entire church. It is my question for all who would like someday to share in my glory. Christians often become an army of speak-easy recruiters. "Come to Jesus! Will you come? Won't you come? You've everything to gain and nothing to lose" is the evangelistic cry of all who want to build the kingdom. "Yes, come to Jesus! He's here with the goodies. Now you will see how much Santa and the Savior are alike. Here you go! Here's what's in his sack for you: peace, prosperity, human goodness, popularity, rest, loads of good times, and freedom from acne if you truly believe."

James and John weren't the real "grace bargain-shoppers," as some of today's eager converts are. They believed that I had so much more love for them than anyone else that they could just apply for top positions at special reduction prices. So they did. "Lord," they said when they had caught me a little away from the group (there was no use letting anybody and everybody in on their little secret), "How about it? We know you think just a little more of us than you do these other people. We were wondering, well . . . if . . . well, to be perfectly honest . . . we hate to just come out and say it like this, but you know . . . those special places, your right hand and your left hand, . . . we'd like those, OK?"

I met them with that choice question, "Are you able? Let's not talk about the good deal you feel you have the right to expect. Let's talk about the price you're willing to pay. Maybe we should talk about something even more basic. There's a lot at stake here, boys. Can you do it? Are you able? Have you ever seen a cross? Have you seen how the condemned die screaming by the roadside until their cracked voices are gone?"

Many come to me seeking privilege. They wonder if they will be faith's "Nominee of the Year." They are continually asking me for some reward, some milestone or achievement that matches their struggle. Oh, how they need to count the cost. They need to watch an execution, to visit a crucifixion. They need to answer one question: "Are you able?"

Prayer
Lord Jesus,
I ask you not for position.
I ask you rather
to give me the lowest position and
to enable me to be faithful.
Give me no elevated ruling place,
just one that's close enough to see your face.
Amen.

Light to Follow

Mark 10:46–52

And they came to Jericho. And as He was going out from Jericho with His disciples and a great multitude, a blind beggar named Bartimaeus, the son of Timaeus, was sitting by the road. And when he heard that it was Jesus the Nazarene, he began to cry out and say, "Jesus, Son of David, have mercy on me!" And many were sternly telling him to be quiet, but he kept crying out all the more, "Son of David, have mercy on me!"

And Jesus stopped and said, "Call him here." And they called the blind man, saying to him, "Take courage, arise! He is calling for you." And casting aside his cloak, he jumped up, and came to Jesus. And answering him, Jesus said, "What do you want Me to do for you?" And the blind man said to Him, "Rabboni, I want to regain my sight!"

And Jesus said to him, "Go your way; your faith has made you well." And immediately he regained his sight and began following Him on the road.

There is only one reason anyone receives a special gift from God: to enable him to serve me. Bartimaeus received his sight for that reason. No sooner did he receive light but that he followed me in the way.

Many have received God's special light and never followed me. Remember the ten lepers who were healed? Only one of them esteemed the healing enough to return to me and thank me. But you do not have to go back a long way in time to find a list of the calloused ungrateful. Look around. Are there many who would claim that they have received spiritual sight, but continue to live as blind?

There is an obligation in light.

Here is the epilogue to the story. Bartimaeus saw his new sight as a stewardship. To be free to see is to cherish those values we should want to see. He knew that it was good to continue to be blind to some things. What did he look at, and for how long? He felt the obligation to use his new vision to liberate those still in darkness. He did not use his new vision to take up needlepoint, making "God loves you and so do I" plaques for all his friends. Nor was his marvelous new vision only for novel reading.

His epilogue is missing from the gospel, so let's talk about your epilogue. You once were lost but now are found. You once were blind and you were given sight. You once groped in sin and were given the spiritual light to find your way to your eternal home. Do you use your new vision to see all those still lost in sin? When you see them, do you sense obligation? Bartimaeus got his light and followed me in the way. Now that you can see, who will you follow?

> *Prayer*
> *Lord Jesus,*
> *Once I was blind and now I can see.*
> *What I see mostly*
>   *is more who are blind.*
> *I want to bring the sightless unto thee.*
> *Please do for them all that you did for me.*
> *Amen.*

On Treeing Publicans

Luke 19:1–9

And He entered and was passing through Jericho. And behold, there was a man called by the name of Zaccheus; and he was a chief tax-gatherer, and he was rich. And he was trying to see who Jesus was, and he was unable because of the crowd, . . . he ran on ahead and climbed up into a sycamore tree in order to see Him, . . . when Jesus came to the place, He looked up and said to him, "Zacchaeus, hurry and come down, . . ."

And Zacchaeus stopped and said to the Lord, "Behold, Lord, half of my possessions I will give to the poor, . . ." And Jesus said to him, "Today salvation has come to this house."

I love to remember the day I treed a publican in Jericho. It was never easy to get publicans up a tree. In fact, publicans had a reputation for treeing just about everyone else. Those who heard a publican knocking at their front door beat a hasty retreat out the back. But now I had him. He was there and he was spiritually needy.

Zacchaeus wanted me both in his life and in his home. But being up a tree is sometimes good for us. It forces us out of that reluctance we find for claiming what we really want most. We are forced to answer while in the spotlight. There, amid the leaves and branches, Zacchaeus was forced to make up his mind. Could I come to his house or not? The issue wasn't really his house. The issue was his heart. Once he welcomed me into his heart, his house would be all mine, complete with a room and a bath.

"Yes . . . yes . . . yes!" his whole soul cried. None there but me could hear his inner reply. It came as an inward, awkward reaching out to me. He had a desire to become all that I was. "Yes," he stammered, sliding down the sycamore.

"Lord, if I have defrauded anyone . . ." He knew well he had.

" . . . I will repay them four times."

A confessing tax-gatherer was so rare that all the traffic stopped. He was converted. There was no question about it.

His heart made the transaction and I affirmed it: "Today salvation has come to this house!"

A party for the redeemed began. Everyone except the Pharisees rejoiced. They should have been converted, but it's always much harder to get Pharisees up trees. It's their long robes mostly. It not only keeps them out of trees, it also keeps me out of their hearts.

Prayer
  Lord Jesus,
  I want to be so sensitive
    to all of those who don't know you
    that I listen to your Spirit
    and feel those heart hungers
    that they are reluctant to speak aloud.
  The hunger after God needs no sure chart.
  It whispers "yes" within the human heart.
  Amen.

The Imperative of Risk

Luke 19:11–24

And while they were listening to these things, He went on to tell a parable, because He was near Jerusalem, and they supposed that the kingdom of God was going to appear immediately. He said therefore, "A certain nobleman went to a distant country to receive a kingdom for himself, and then return. And he called ten of his slaves, and gave them ten minas, and said to them, 'Do business with this till I come back.' But his citizens hated him, and sent a delegation after him, saying, 'We do not want this man to reign over us.'

"And it came about that when he returned, after receiving the kingdom, he ordered that these slaves, to whom he had given the money, be called to him in order that he might know what business they had done. And the first appeared, saying, 'Master, your mina has made ten minas more.' And he said to him, 'Well done, good slave, . . .'

"And the second came, saying, 'Your mina, master, has made five minas.'. . . And another came, saying, 'Master, behold your mina, which I kept put away in a handkerchief; for I was afraid of you, because you are an exacting man; . . .'

"He said to him, 'By your own words I will judge you, you worthless slave. . . .' And he said to the bystanders, 'Take the mina away from him, and give it to the one who has the ten minas.'

Discipleship has never been a religion of playing it safe.

In this parable, the sin committed is that of being overly cautious. Being too cautious is rarely called a sin. But when asked to take a teaching position in the church, you may have said, "Oh, I don't think I'd better try that."

My church has advanced or retreated totally on the basis of risk or the lack of it.

Paul the apostle said to Caesar, "Yes, I believe in Jesus."

"Are you sure?" thundered the magistrate, "You know what this will cost?"

"I know whom I have believed," said the witness.

"What? What did you say? Speak up! You better be careful of your answer. You will either deny Christ and live, or you will confess him and die! Speak up!"

"I know whom I believe. And I am sure that he is able to keep that which I've believed until the day I die" (2 Tim. 1:12) said the apostle loudly enough not to be mistaken.

"Are you sure?" bellowed Caesar.

"I am sure; for to me to live is Christ" (Phil. 1:21).

So answered all the martyrs. They invested their mina . . . took the risk. They were Christians. Christians have no choice but to invest their all.

Prayer
Lord Jesus,
I want to speak to those who need to know you,
but I am often so afraid.
Help me to realize that being afraid is not a sin,
only failing to act.
I will invest my all, though fearfully,
and face my final audit joyfully.
Amen.

Mary's Gift

John 12:2–5

So they made Him a supper there, and Martha was serving; but Lazarus was one of those reclining at the table with Him. Mary therefore took a pound of very costly perfume of pure nard, and anointed the feet of Jesus, and wiped His feet with her hair; and the house was filled with the fragrance of the perfume. But Judas Iscariot, one of His disciples, who was intending to betray Him, said, "Why was this perfume not sold for three hundred denarii, and given to poor people?"

There is a madness in loving that cannot be controlled by propriety. Mary loved me. Faith had claimed her life, and she found a way to say it so that the world would never forget it. Judas watched even as the costly perfume ran down across my feet. He saw no offering of devotion. He beheld only financial waste.

The New Testament rarely justifies lavish waste, but in the case of Mary's gift it was a classic example of extravagant love finding a suitable expression.

Lazarus's death and resurrection was still in the forefront of everybody's mind. In this atmosphere of death and near death, the argument over the cost of the perfume seemed odd. It was like people arguing over the cost of a funeral in front of someone who is about to die. Lazarus was confidently back from death. In light of this, Mary's extravagance seemed a rich and most appropriate offering of love.

In a way it was as if God himself was pouring out his lavish love upon all of us. God is not stingy in his dispensing of grace. His riches are poured out freely on all. The word *grace* means "gift." And the size of his gifts are usually in proportion to the size of his love. He who loves much gives much. Mary's gift, like God's gift, was no larger than her love.

And what of the manner in which she gave it? Who can contain the wildness that ecstasy mandates? When the press of our emotions are upon us, furious love demands lavish exuberance. When worship becomes exuberant, we often act in ways that make us feel embarrassed later. We are like David dancing naked before the ark of the Lord. His foes pointed out to him that his behavior was inappropriate. But love rarely make mistakes, exuberant or not. It may wipe feet with hair or dance naked before the Lord. The very wildness of the passion of loving God certifies the deed.

I long for those who love me with such strength that they cannot contain their love within the practical or the customary. Love me with Mary's intensity, and send Judas with all his pragmatism out into the night. Critics always dull the passion that lovers can't contain.

Prayer
Lord Jesus,
Do I love you enough
to be exuberant among the placid?
So often church is so dull
because people only love you reasonably.
Give me Mary's warm extravagance,
or David's insane willingness to dance.
Amen.

Lazarus, the Argument
That Wouldn't Go Away

John 12:9–11
The great multitude therefore of the Jews learned that He was there; and they came, not for Jesus' sake only, but that they might also see Lazarus, whom He raised from the dead. But the chief priests took counsel that they might put Lazarus to death also; because on account of him many of the Jews were going away, and were believing in Jesus.

Jewish officials felt they had to get rid of me. The desire became even more driving after the resurrection of Lazarus. His well-publicized funeral preceded his well-publicized resurrection. Even if they somehow got me out of the way, they would have to reckon with how to get Lazarus out of the way. The living Lazarus was such a powerful evidence of my Messiahship that many were leaving traditional Judaism to turn to my new teachings.

Have you ever asked yourself if your conversion builds an automatic intrigue about me? Have others ever seen my impact on your life and been drawn to offer themselves to me? There is no call to Christianity stronger than the evidence of the power of the gospel in someone else's life. Think of all those whose conversions produced such overwhelming changes in their lives that hundreds or thousands, indeed whole cultures, were drawn to me. While Lazarus in most ways was not historically notable, his resurrection was an incontrovertible evidence that I was the Son of God.

The key to winning others is the testimony of a living dead man. It doesn't have to be any special or notable person. It can be any living dead man. But the best example is the living dead man who stays spiritually alive once he comes physically alive. Lazarus stayed alive for years, and all the years that he stayed alive he remained "Exhibit A" for the power of the gospel.

As it was with Lazarus, so I pray it is with you.

During those last critical weeks of my earthly life, Lazarus certified that not everybody was coming out of Jerusalem to see me. They were coming out to see Lazarus. In him they found an intrigue that could not be shouted down.

May each new believer be an exhibit of my reality. May all who are dead in sin come so much alive in me that none would ever doubt that they have collided with saving grace. May your aliveness always speak of mine!

Prayer
Lord Jesus,
I want to be so alive
that all who know me
know instantly the reason for my overcoming life.
I want my life to be consumed
by him who summons dead men from their tombs.
Amen.

God's Specific Donkey

Matthew 21:1–3

And when they had approached Jerusalem and had come to Bethphage, to the Mount of Olives, then Jesus sent two disciples, saying to them, "Go into the village opposite you, and immediately you will find a donkey tied there and a colt with her; untie them, and bring them to Me. And if anyone says something to you, you shall say, 'The Lord has need of them,' and immediately he will send them."

I was about to fulfill the metaphor of the ancient prophets. There were actually two images in Judaism concerning how the Messiah should behave. The first image had to do with King David. David was Israel's greatest king—the warrior king. This image of the Davidic Messiah was of a powerful man astride a white stallion, leading a huge army. This political messiah would disembowel the Roman government and set up a literal kingdom of God on earth.

The other image was that given by Isaiah in his concept of the Suffering Servant Messiah. This Messiah would pay for the sins of his people and establish his control, not by killing and war, but by serving and dying. He would be "pierced for your transgressions and . . . crushed for your iniquities" (Isa. 53:5). Instead of killing to gain a kingdom, he would die to gain it. By choosing to enter Jerusalem on a donkey, I was fulfilling Isaiah's prophecy of the Messiah.

It was thus that I traded the white stallion to enter Jerusalem as a person of peace. I would act to fulfill the prophecy of Zechariah 9:9–10:

> "Rejoice greatly, O Daughter of Zion!
>   Shout! Daughter of Jerusalem!
> See, your king comes to you,
>   righteous and having salvation,
> gentle and riding on a donkey,
>   on a colt, the foal of a donkey. . . .
> He will proclaim peace to the nations.
>   His rule will extend from sea to sea
>   and from the river to the ends of the earth."

So the humble donkey would say what the neigh of a steed could not.

The sign was conclusive. God was going to save in a specific way. My Kingdom would claim peace, not by cutting the world up, but by allowing the Father to love it into redemption. My peace is the province of the heart and not the sword.

In your interrelationships and career vision for yourself, have you chosen a steed or a donkey? Come, let us take the path of humility that leads to the heart of God.

Prayer
Lord Jesus,
I realize that the donkey you chose
was a message of your utter submission to God.
I therefore choose to serve in deference
and live my life through sweet obedience.
Amen.

The Gentle Jesus

Matthew 21:4–5

Now this took place that what was spoken through the prophet might be fulfilled, saying,
"SAY TO THE DAUGHTER OF ZION,
'BEHOLD YOUR KING IS COMING TO YOU,
GENTLE, AND MOUNTED ON A DONKEY,
EVEN ON A COLT, THE FOAL OF A BEAST OF BURDEN'" [Zech. 9:9].

My coming in flesh was a statement: "God is mighty indeed, but there is no need to be afraid of him." I am Jesus the gentle. But do not see me as Jesus the weak. Gentleness and weakness are much different. Weakness is not being able to frighten your enemies, but gentleness is not being willing to. In terms of my triumphal entry, it could have been done on a splendid steed. There were of course white chargers stabled here and there throughout the city. But gentleness is not choosing a stallion just to make thunderous impressions. Weakness is not having any options but a donkey; gentleness is preferring one. Weakness is having no strength to stand against one's crucifiers; gentleness is yielding to one's crucifiers.

The day is coming when the wrath of God will be revealed from heaven against all ungodliness (Rom. 1:18). There will come the time when the sternness of God will at last answer all of those who spurned his gentleness. But God in my life is openly pleading and begging for you to believe. He now invites you to mercy, and you do not need to be afraid.

So it was for Jerusalem that day. I rode in on the foal of a donkey. I was vulnerable. It was quite possible to reject me. Indeed, I could be killed; and only five days later I would be. But Jerusalem and every nation will one day come to reckoning, when the season of the gentleness is passed and the season of God's requiring has come.

Then all of those who saw me as weak and at their disposal will see me emerge as a King, mighty and formidable. Then my Father will no longer plead for you to come to his enfolding love. Then all must give account of themselves before God (Rom. 14:12). Then at last I will come out of heaven on that great white horse (Rev. 19:11), in thunder and in judgment. But for now, I am a King lowly and gentle. God is in ordinary flesh, and grace comes softly. Come to my gentle grace and let me enfold you in my love.

Prayer
Lord Jesus,
You entered my heart as you once entered Jerusalem,
*   lowly and gentle and tender.*
I am glad you did not make me afraid of you,
*   or else I might never have believed.*
I receive you unafraid as any child.
I love you, gentle Jesus, meek and mild.
Amen.

The Blessed King

Luke 19:35–38

And they brought it to Jesus, and they threw their garments on the colt, and put Jesus on it. And as He was going, they were spreading their garments in the road. And as He was now approaching, near the descent of the Mount of Olives, the whole multitude of the disciples began to praise God joyfully with a loud voice for all the miracles which they had seen, saying, "BLESSED IS THE KING WHO COMES IN THE NAME OF THE LORD [Ps. 118:26]; Peace in heaven and glory in the highest!"

Never did a coronation spring more spontaneously from grateful people. These were my subjects and even more my brothers and sisters. I had healed their diseases, and they had seen my miracles. Their songs erupted spontaneously from their throats. No conquering general, from Alexander to any of the Caesar's, ever met with more sincere adulation. These were the ragtag army of the grateful. Old lepers sang now with flesh as clean and unblemished as that of children. Old cripples now needed no crutches to run before me shouting, "Blessed, blessed, blessed . . ." All of the forgiven were also in the streets: harlots, tax collectors. The demoniacs, in sensible joy, joined in the singing too.

There is a glory in heaven that is born on earth in the small centers of human gratitude. Here on Palm Sunday, as later generations would refer to it, the army of the simple woke the angels to brighter anthems. All of this hubbub was an evidence that there are none despised in heaven. God is more honored by the beggar who knows his name than the scientist who doesn't.

Of course, one class offered me no praise that day. The doubters were not there: the Pharisees, the Saducees, and their friends. While the simple people praised me, most of the power players could only think of the challenge my Lordship would bring to their control of these simple people. They hung back in the shadows, evaluating and conniving, figuring on the best place to bring against me their calculated entrapments.

These official frowners were the unmentioned sinners of Palm Sunday. In the roar of God's glorious kingship, to grumble is to miss the high elation of my soaring presence. Sinners? Yes, for it is always a sin to sit frowning in an ocean of joy.

Prayer
Lord Jesus,
Wash me from that ugly negativity
that grumbles when it ought to worship.
I would be so free of waving palm branches
to my own arrogant lordship
of my own too-central affairs
that I may at last cry, "Blessed is the King!"
Here is my palm branch and my will to sing.
Blessed is my Lord, who comes as King.
Amen.

Imperative Praise

Luke 19:39–40

And some of the Pharisees in the multitude said to Him, "Teacher, rebuke Your disciples."

And He answered and said, "I tell you, if these become silent, the stones will cry out!"

There are times when praise is imperative. The Pharisees rebuked me for not rebuking my disciples. Yet my rebuke of those multitudes jammed into the joyous plaster canyons of Jerusalem would have accomplished nothing. There are times when the Son of Man must be praised.

Do not see praise as something that God needs. Indeed, God needs nothing from human beings. Rather, praise is an offering that he rather receives in the process of his enjoyment of humankind. Remember the teachings of the older catechisms: "It is the duty of all mankind to praise God and enjoy him forever"? It is through praise that people learn to enjoy God.

But beyond this enjoyment, praise has for its most worthy goal the liberation of those who offer it. That day in Jerusalem, those who offered up their glad hosannas were not just pleasing God; they were setting themselves free as well.

Praise most often comes from those who are spiritually needy. It is not easy for those who have great material wealth to find an impoverished heart with which to look up toward God. But the "rabble in the streets" (as the religious elite might refer to them) were needy, and the praise they offered that Palm Sunday raised their focus above their own problems and fastened it to the sufficiency of God. Thus in praising God, the weight of all they carried wafted upward by the sheer lift of their celebrative hosannas.

How unreasonable the Pharisees were for asking me to stop the praise by which the city's needy were set free. I told them that. But I reminded them that since godly praise is the chief business of all people, God would liked to have received the Pharisees' hosannas too.

The psalmist said that all of nature is praising God. The very "heavens declare the glory of God" (Ps. 19:1). If all of nature offers praise, why should human beings ever withhold it? Indeed, they cannot. The stones, dumb and inert, have proceeded from the handiwork of God. If earth finds none to celebrate me, then those rocks will join the stars to declare my glory. But I will have praise.

Offer me your adoration in unceasing praise. It will honor me, and it will set you free of a killing focus on yourself.

Prayer
Lord Jesus,
I bless myself by blessing you.
I offer you the whole of all my praise,
    for there is none like you.
You have redeemed; you have called;
    you have given me a reason—my only reason—
    to bless each sunrise.
And so I sing to you in glorious shout
    lest to praise you, the very stones cry out.
Amen.

The Praise of Children

Matthew 21:15–16

But when the chief priests and the scribes saw the wonderful things that He had done, and the children who were crying out in the temple and saying, "Hosanna to the Son of David," they became indignant, and said to Him, "Do You hear what these are saying?"

And Jesus said to them, "Yes; have you never read, 'OUT OF THE MOUTH OF INFANTS AND NURSING BABES THOU HAST PREPARED PRAISE FOR THYSELF'?"

Out of the mouths of children God sometimes receives his greatest praise. This is not because children sing out of educated minds but out of trusting hearts. Children sing with a singular focus. They are too honest in their joy, too innocent to doubt.

Too honest in their joy, too innocent to doubt: these are two aspects of authentic praise. Look around you in church sometime and ask yourself if you are seeing honesty in joy. The stern expressions of the godly sometimes have a hard fixation about them. Sometimes the smiles you do see seem rehearsed.

For a look at honest joy, you may have to go to a party on Friday night or a sporting event on Sunday afternoon. There you will see that backslapping hilarity and camaraderie that is so honest it whoops, cheers, and perhaps belly-laughs. Still, the very best place to find authentic joy may be in church, while the children are singing "Jesus Loves Me."

Seek my reality in the fervor of children. See them: they weep, laugh, and reflect. If their worship seems excessive, you at least cannot doubt its exuberance. Children prove that no one can actually touch God and not feel something.

Next to being *too honest in joy*, the other quality I most desire is *too innocent to doubt*. Innocence and naiveté are not the same things. Innocence is what you had before you were capable of doubt, and naiveté is what you have because you've been protected from examining the nature of truth. Children are in the former category. They have been taught the Bible by those they believe are credible adults. So they believe. They cannot imagine being lied to about something so important by people they so much trust. Their consciences are utterly clear.

Remember how you loved me back when you thought everybody did. Sing "Jesus Loves Me" the way you sang it then. It may be harder for you now. For now you have been conditioned by doubt and skepticism. But let the child you used to be praise me, and the adult you have become will be refreshed.

Prayer
Lord Jesus,
The necessity of my praising you
must be tempered by the way I do it.
Give me the time, that I may not hurry my praise.
Give me the love that I may not be insincere.
I want to offer you my praise in style
like that which might be offered by a child.
Amen.

The Empty Promise of Israel

Mark 11:12–14, 19–22

And on the next day, when they had departed from Bethany, He became hungry. And seeing at a distance a fig tree in leaf, He went to see if perhaps He would find anything on it; and when He came to it, He found nothing but leaves, for it was not the season for figs. And He answered and said to it, "May no one ever eat fruit from you again!" And his disciples were listening. . . .

And whenever evening came, they would go out of the city. And as they were passing by in the morning, they saw the fig tree withered from the roots up. And being reminded, Peter said to Him, "Rabbi, behold, the fig tree which You cursed has withered." And Jesus answered saying to them, "Have faith in God."

I knew that the Passover season was not the season for figs. But the fig tree in Old Testament prophecy was often a symbol of Israel (Jer. 8:13, 29:17; Hos. 9:10, 16; Joel 1:7; Mic. 7:1–6). I knew that my disciples would see the symbolism of a nation that looked prosperous, like this green and leafy fig tree. But for all its appearances, Israel held no fruit of hope for the nations as God had intended. She was beautiful, but only at a distance. Close up, she was barren and fruitless.

Remember this: When the appearance of any truth is more beautiful than its content, it cannot be pleasing to God. The steeple of the church has been called "the finger that points to God." This noble idea is often eclipsed by those inside the church whose busy activities and empty souls invite the finger of God's judgment.

A certain kind of robe or collar may say of the wearer: here is a person full of the wisdom of God. Yet when you come to know that person, he seems secular and empty. His appearance suggested that you might go to him for hope. But when you approach him looking for God, you find only that dusty emptiness of soul that always disappoints you.

Israel wanted to be a nation under God. They had a rich religious heritage. They had the Holy Scriptures and the temple, where they believed that God himself occupied the mercy seat above the ark of the covenant. But whenever any Gentiles came to Israel looking for the one true God, those Gentiles were told that the God *of* Israel was the God *for* Israel. The nation talked about being a "light for the Gentiles"; but in truth, no Gentile felt warmed by that light.

So I cursed the fig tree for seeming to offer more than it did. May Christians in every age be all that they appear.

Prayer
> *Lord Jesus,*
> *I want to be just what I appear to be,*
> *nothing less, nothing more.*
> *This will be enough for me.*
> *May all that I appear to be today*
> *roar so loudly none hear the things I say.*
> *Amen.*

A Gentile Inquiry Signals the Hour of Glorification

John 12:20–23

Now there were certain Greeks among those who were going up to worship at the feast; these therefore came to Philip, who was from Bethsaida of Galilee, and began to ask him, saying, "Sir, we wish to see Jesus." Philip came and told Andrew; Andrew and Philip came, and they told Jesus. And Jesus answered them, saying, "The hour has come for the Son of Man to be glorified."

Heaven loves the seeker after truth. These Greeks came hungry of heart. They craved a more meaningful way to my Father. But the real glory lay in what was not said. The official Jews at that Passover were skeptical of my Messiahship. But here were some who ethnically had no claim to glory, but inwardly their hunger of heart marked them as instant candidates for the Kingdom.

These Greeks illustrate one other thing: The world is far more ready to hear what Christians know of me than Christians are to tell them.

The Greeks came to Philip, and Philip took them to Andrew. Have you ever wondered why he took them to Andrew? It was Andrew who was most interested in helping the spiritually needy find me. Indeed, the Scriptures most often speak of Andrew when he was bringing someone to me.

The Kingdom of God thrives on the hunger of the seeker. What a blessed hunger this is. Consider two pictures. There is a certain rich man who has always been rich. Since childhood, he has never known anything other than the joy of sitting down to a table filled with food. So he has become dull to the wonder of a full table gorgeously appointed.

Now consider a starving child from a needy nation, who by some act of glorious providence is ushered into the rich man's full table for the first time. What the rich man considers mundane the poor child considers a glorious wonder.

This is the difference between that Christian who has long drunk of grace and one who has just become a new believer. The old Christian gorges on the good things of God until they are no longer seen. But the seekers? Overwhelmed with hunger, they come to me to be filled.

Be like Andrew. Help me find the hungry. Then because of you they will one day know heaven, and because of your concern their eagerness will bless both them and you.

Prayer
Lord Jesus,
There are so many so hungry to hear.
I confess the sin of my blindness.
I have so often gutted at your table
that I no longer see those who have never eaten.
I want to help the starving as I should,
to direct them to a table rich with food.
Amen.

Life and Wheat

John 12:24–25

"Truly, truly, I say to you, unless a grain of wheat falls into the earth and dies, it remains by itself alone; but if it dies, it bears much fruit. He who loves his life loses it; and he who hates his life in this world shall keep it to life eternal."

Every grain of wheat contains the principle of reproduction. Still, it must die if it would live. Does that grain of wheat selfishly say, "I don't want to quit being what I am that I might be something better"? Of course not!

Still, the grain knows that germination is the end of everything explainable. If it surrenders its old familiar form, something new will result. The reluctant seed is like a baby about to be born. If the baby could frame words, he might say, "I like it here in the womb. It's warm, and I'm fed automatically. I don't have to eat or breathe on my own. My existence is somewhat confining, but it's cozy. No thank you, being born is not for me." Then comes birth: the next state. Real life! Ultimately there is sunshine and the freedom to go anywhere on earth the child pleases. Never again would that baby go back in even if he could.

Here is the principle of the Kingdom. Do not hesitate to give up your old life. Let it go, and like a piece of grain you will become the inheritor of a wonderful new kind of life. Out of your deadness will come the imperishable. Out of your dry, hard-crusted reluctance, your old shell of dead ego will achieve new life. The green, the beautiful, the living will replace that deadness that you have cherished too long. Unless you die to self, you cannot be born into life eternal.

Now let us see what it is that frames your reluctance.

Are you attached to a way of life, a church, a lifestyle, or elegant living? What would you have to give up to say good-bye to your old way of life? Remember one thing: "Things are always better further on and deeper into God." Therefore, leave your reluctance and die to yourself. You will discover that your voluntary death is the only way to enter into life.

Prayer

Lord Jesus,
Why I ever struggle to retain the worst parts
of what I am, I do not know.
I realize that if I would bury parts of me
or the whole of myself,
I would find such dying isn't dying at all.
I will find new life by turning from the night
and leaving dead reluctance for the light.
Amen.

Shall I Say Save Me, or Glorify Thy Name?

John 12:27–28

"Now My soul has become troubled; and what shall I say, 'Father, save Me from this hour'? But for this purpose I came to this hour. Father, glorify Thy name." There came therefore a voice out of heaven: "I have both glorified it, and will glorify it again."

In any crisis where you wish to measure your own faithfulness, ask yourself one question: Would you rather glorify your name or mine? Gethsemane is the place to bury all the pennants and photos of Palm Sunday. You hang on to those celebrative moments for as long as you can. Was the press there on Palm Sunday? Of course. Were there exhilarating circumstances, wonderful meals, and the rich applause of the whole world celebrating? Yes, that's the nature of Palm Sunday. But applause is like drinking sea water. The more you taste it, the more you will require it.

On that awful night of horror, I reaffirmed that which I had never doubted. I was not born to celebrate my public reputation. I came to redeem the world. In Gethsemane I knew it was time to get on with my purpose in life. All I had left to say was, "Father, glorify thyself."

In the midst of awful circumstances you may say, "God, I am going through an unbearable Calvary of suffering. I beg you, therefore, save me from this hour!" But do not pray this prayer too rapidly.

There is an old fable of two mothers whose children were both afflicted with the same deadly contagion. Both of them prayed for their children to be saved. One of those prayers was not answered according to the mother's satisfaction. The baby died. The second mother then prayed all the more earnestly, "God, please don't let my own baby die. I don't care about your will. I want my baby to live." The child got well. The mother exulted! But when he was grown, she had to watch him hanged on the gallows for a capital crime. It is never right in any Gethsemane of pain to demand from God the answers you might prefer. Rather, let your trial instruct your need.

Can you imagine the world that would have resulted if my human desire to avoid the cross had been granted? I would have escaped the horror of dying, but all of humankind would have perished eternally with never a hope. Find out why you were born, and then submit your life to me. Pray, "Father, glorify yourself!" It is the only phrase that delights the angels.

Prayer
Lord Jesus,
Here is the offer of myself:
  Knowing fully that I was made to serve you,
  I do not ask you to spare me any Gethsemane
  by which I might find some reason to magnify your name,
  even if it be only through my pain.
There is but one sweet phrase on my soul's shelf.
It's this: Oh, Father, glorify yourself.
Amen.

The Intimidated Confession

John 12:36b–42

These things Jesus spoke, and He departed and hid Himself from them. But though He had performed so many signs before them, yet they were not believing in Him; that the word of Isaiah the prophet might be fulfilled, which he spoke, "LORD, WHO HAS BELIEVED OUR REPORT? AND TO WHOM HAS THE ARM OF THE LORD BEEN REVEALED?" [Isa. 53:1].

For this cause they could not believe, for Isaiah said again, "HE HAS BLINDED THEIR EYES, AND HE HARDENED THEIR HEARTS; LEST THEY SEE WITH THEIR EYES, AND PERCEIVE WITH THEIR HEART, AND BE CONVERTED, AND I HEAL THEM" [Isa. 6:10].

These things Isaiah said, because he saw His glory, and he spoke of Him. Nevertheless many even of the rulers believed in Him, but because of the Pharisees they were not confessing Him, lest they should be put out of the synagogue.

A sick faith will not openly confess. The rulers of the Jews were afraid of the Pharisees, so they refused to confess. They had only half a faith, which is no faith at all. Confession is an agreement, a covenant between lovers, a refusal to be intimidated, a total unwillingness to be ashamed.

What loving husband would be ashamed to introduce his wife? What general of worth would be unwilling to sing his own national anthem? What Christian who has tasted of grace would not own up to loving me? Such stuff is the meat of martyrs and the soul of the dispossessed. Certain of these rulers wanted to believe in me but found their confessions shut down by grumbling Pharisees.

This is why I said, "Whoever acknowledges me before men, I will also acknowledge him before my Father in heaven" (Matt. 10:32). Do you not see that shame and confession are incompatible? If you are ashamed, you may be sure you lack the fervor of noble lovers. True lovers cannot be made so ashamed that they will let anyone speak ill of the ones they love. So confession is the marriage troth of those in love with a Lord they will not deny.

The word *Lord* can be a fearsome word. It is a word that may put your very life in jeopardy. Yet it is the word of honesty, the word of ownership, the word with which your Christian experience begins. Of course, it is a hard word to say. Yet without this word, there is no Christian experience. Never let any intimidation remove this beautiful word from the center of your open adoration and commitment. Find a way to use the word *Lord* every day so that all who know you may know at once your loyalty to me.

Prayer
Lord Jesus,
I want to be sure
*   that I never fail to own up to you*
*   or celebrate you so openly*
*   that everyone will know where I stand.*
Make our openness such a grand obsession
*   that all my life becomes a grand confession.*
Amen.

The Fine Art of Mountain Moving

Mark 11:23–24

"Truly I say to you, whoever says to this mountain, 'Be taken up and cast into the sea,' and does not doubt in his heart, but believes that what he says is going to happen, it shall be granted him. Therefore I say to you, all things for which you pray and ask, believe that you have received them, and they shall be granted you."

Is there some Everest or Fuji inconveniently located in your life experience? Some mountain that stands between you and God's purpose for you?

Mountains have always seemed formidable barriers. Mountains were special challenges when people laid the first railroads. Those who moved the mountains would sometimes dig a burrow back into the center of the mountain and pack it with blasting powder. Then they would lay a long wick to the center, tamping the tunnel full of rocks and debris. Moving far away from the blasting area, they would light the wick. A tiny flash of fire, small and barely alive, traveled the wick to the explosive heart of the mountain. Once it found the center of the mountain, the earth shook. The mountain fell. The way was laid for progress.

It will work the same way for you. The specific name of your mountain is Mt. Barrier-to-the-Will-of-God. The wick is called prayer and the flash of fire is called faith. The blasting powder at the center of the mountain is the power of God. Pray and trust. Then light the fire. Ignite the power of God. All that you thought was so indestructible will be brought down. Faith still moves mountains.

Gladys Aylward wondered how God would ever use her, a tiny little woman with dark eyes and coal black hair. Frankly, she wondered how she would get over the mountain of her own low self-esteem to do the will of God on the foreign mission field. As a young girl, she always lamented that she had not been born more Nordic. She inwardly wished for those wonderful Scandinavian genes that create tall, blonde, beautiful women.

When her missionary training was over, she went to China. She felt inadequate— too short, not at all commanding. In her own eyes she was neither blonde nor beautiful. But the moment she landed in China, she suddenly realized she was just right for the beautiful people of China. They were all short and dark-eyed with coal black hair. The mountain of her low self-esteem had been moved by faith, and she was ready at last to do the whole will of God.

So you see, it takes but a little faith to move the most formidable mountain. Locate your own barrier to God's fullest service. Pray and trust. Now, where was that mountain? Your faith has removed it and buried it in the deepest part of the sea.

Prayer
Lord Jesus,
I know quite well what mountain
lies within my path.
Its steep ascents even now prevent me
from following after you.
So take it all away, far, far from me
and plunge this barricade into the sea.
Amen.

Authority

Mark 11:27–33

And they came again to Jerusalem. And as He was walking in the temple, the chief priests, and scribes, and elders came to Him, and began saying to Him, "By what authority are You doing these things, or who gave You this authority to do these things?"

And Jesus said to them, "I will ask you one question, and you answer Me, and then I will tell you by what authority I do these things. Was the baptism of John from heaven, or from men? Answer me."

And they began reasoning among themselves, saying, "If we say, 'From heaven,' He will say, 'Then why did you not believe him?' But shall we say, 'From men'?"—they were afraid of the multitude, for all considered John to have been a prophet indeed. And answering Jesus, they said, "We do not know." And Jesus said to them, "Neither will I tell you by what authority I do these things."

No miracles were ever possible to the Pharisees, for they could not see me through the eyes of faith. Skeptics can be brilliant. They often wow audiences with a cynicism that is both clever and intellectual. But skeptics are more capable of pointing out error than pointing out meaning.

The Pharisees were full of argument and negative logic. They knew the Bible well. They were educated. They could build impeccable structures of argument.

But arguments—even those that are won—are not the stuff of personal peace and meaning. The Pharisees could tell you much about the doctrine of God, but nothing of the mystery of incarnation.

So it was that day that the Pharisees were really asking me, "Who do you think you are, anyway?" I knew well who I was and what I'd come to do. But rather than let them trap me in an argument, I asked them a further question that forced them into silence. For they did not want to be discovered as mere men of cold logic who despised the warm teachings of John the Baptist.

Could I ask you a question? Who are you, anyway? Would you define yourself as a bright denominationalist who knows a great deal? Or would you define yourself as a needy soul still hungering for the things of God you've not yet tasted? Have you long desired my elusive fullness and the delicious mystery of godliness? Well, then, come with me. Enter the way of the pilgrim.

Prayer
Lord Jesus,
I have studied for years
and yet, the things I know
seem only to whet my appetite
for what I do not know.
I want to follow you as you approve
and glory in your mystery of love.
Amen.

What Will the Vineyard Owner Do?

Mark 12:1–9

And He began to speak to them in parables: "A man PLANTED A VINEYARD, AND PUT A WALL AROUND IT, AND DUG A VAT UNDER THE WINE PRESS, AND BUILT A TOWER [Isa. 5:2], and rented it out to vine-growers and went on a journey. And at the harvest time he sent a slave to the vine-growers, in order to receive some of the produce of the vineyard from the vine-growers. And they took him, and beat him, and sent him away empty-handed. And again he sent them another slave, and they wounded him in the head, and treated him shamefully. And he sent another, and that one they killed; and so with many others, beating some, and killing others.

"He had one more to send, a beloved son; he sent him last of all to them, saying, 'They will respect my son.' But those vine-growers said one to another, 'This is the heir; come, let us kill him, and the inheritance will be ours!' And they took him, and killed him, and threw him out of the vineyard. What will the owner of the vineyard do? He will come and destroy the vine-growers, and will give the vineyard to others."

Mercy and justice, these are the two sides of God. If you repent the sin of unbelief on the front side of death, you will meet God in grace in this life. Consequently, you will never have to know his justice. But if you meet him beyond this life, never having known his grace, his justice will be all that is left for you. The question I posed to my disciples was, "What will the vineyard owner do?"

For all of those years the slaves had come to collect the rent, the vineyard owner was tolerant. But at the death of his son, a requirement fell upon the vine-growers. They must repent or perish. The day I died, a divine dilemma ripped the heart of God. Now this great crime against heaven must find resolve in human confession.

The sin that most breaks the heart of God is committed by those who feel no need to apologize for Good Friday. Each time you take the wafer or sip the wine of Communion, think on this: the bread and wine are there to call you to remember the price. They are there to remind you that, of all your sins, the most grievous is walking past Calvary without remorse.

In the final reckoning there is one fair question that even kings and emperors must answer: "What will the Lord of the Vineyard do?" Can you let a day go by without remembering the cost? You were not cheaply redeemed. 'For you know that it was not with perishable things such as silver or gold that you were redeemed from the empty way of life handed down to you from your forefathers, but with the precious blood of Christ, a lamb without blemish or defect'" (1 Peter 1:18–19).

Prayer
> *Lord Jesus,*
> *Help me never to forget the price of my redemption.*
> *Help me tell all that the day of God's most requiring question*
>   *is ahead.*
> *Here is the question reckoned unto you:*
>   *"What will the owner of the vineyard do?"*
> *Amen.*

The Cornerstone

Luke 20:16–19

"He will come and destroy these vine-growers and will give the vineyard to others." And when they heard it, they said, "May it never be!" But He looked at them and said, "What then is this that is written, 'THE STONE WHICH THE BUILDERS REJECTED, THIS BECAME THE CHIEF CORNER stone'? [Ps. 118:22]. Everyone who falls on that stone will be broken to pieces; but on whomever it falls, it will scatter him like dust."

And the scribes and the chief priests tried to lay hands on Him that very hour, and they feared the people; for they understood that He spoke this parable against them.

The Kingdom of God has one cornerstone. What an apt metaphor this is. The cornerstone is that stone which, placed low and near the foundation, held the structure of the building in place. Without that stone, the whole building would not long stand.

Why was it the Pharisees rejected me as the Cornerstone of God? Why did they not accept me as the Messiah, when Israel had been expecting me for centuries? The answer has to do with preconceptions. Their years of study had produced a definite mental picture of that Messiah. They had served these mental images for so long that they were now entirely captive to them.

These pictures were largely militaristic and politically revolutionary. Since the days when the Maccabees had thrown off the yoke of their Greek captors by guerrilla warfare, Israel's whole view of the kingdom had become oriented around power. If the Maccabees had successfully led Israel into war, surely the Messiah would do it too. In their minds, therefore, I should have been like David.

Among my own disciples there were the Zealots. David was their Messiah too. They were all eager to go and fight. The Pharisees and the Zealots both equally hated Roman oppression. Neither Zealots nor Pharisees had room for a Messiah whose peaceable kingdom was of the heart.

Have you any preconceptions of how I am to come again? Do you have firmly set ideas about how I want to minister through your life? Be careful that these mental pictures of yours do not force me into a spiritual box that leaves you no room for a wider definition. The Pharisees would never know the joy of Christianity because they could not permit me to exist in ways other than how they imagined me.

I am the Cornerstone of the church universal. Grant me the authority to be all that I am. For I will either be for you the chief Cornerstone or, I will be the stone that the builders rejected.

Prayer
Lord Jesus,
Be the chief cornerstone
in the architecture of my life.
Help me to study and to learn of you,
but never to make you small enough to be contained either
within the small confining space of my mind
or the little lexicon of my small definitions.
Be mightier than I can ever define,
too big to rule within my tiny mind.
Amen.

Those Who Were Invited Were Not Worthy

Matthew 22:1–8

And Jesus answered and spoke to them again in parables, saying, "The kingdom of heaven may be compared to a king, who gave a wedding feast for his son. And he sent out his slaves to call those who had been invited to the wedding feast, and they were unwilling to come. Again he sent out other slaves, saying, 'Tell those who have been invited, "Behold, I have prepared my dinner; my oxen and my fattened livestock are all butchered and everything is ready; come to the wedding feast."' But they paid no attention and . . . the king was enraged and sent his armies, and destroyed those murderers, and set their city on fire. Then he said to his slaves, 'The wedding is ready, but those who were invited were not worthy.'"

Why is it that those who were invited to the feast were unworthy? They were inhospitable toward God. In Revelation 3:20 is the strong message for the church at Laodicea: "Here I am! I stand at the door and knock. If anyone hears my voice and opens the door, I will come in and eat with him, and he with me." In a larger sense, I stand at the door of human experience and knock.

Let us take the image to the simplest unit of human experience, the believer. Here at the door of every life is the God of all time. In me, this God knocks. I want into every life. In some cases I knock for years without response. I knock while those, at whose heart's door I stand, live lives of empty routine. I knock while they hurry on, oblivious of God's great requirement for their lives. I knock because I want one thing—in!

All of those who did not come to the king's feast in my parable committed this great sin of inhospitality. Naturally, they fall under judgment. But consider those whose invitations brought delight. See this army of rogues and vagabonds who are now included as partakers of the banquet.

Is not grace a lovely inclusion? Is it not altogether wonderful that you who might never have known hope now are mine? How did it all happen? You did nothing very special. You heard the knock. You opened. Now you dine with the king forevermore. But beware! You are in the fellowship of grace and obligation. Obligation? Yes, for there are others in whose hearts the King still knocks. Go then. Tell them that the feast is ready. Go and beg them to lay aside their sins and say to the King, "Come in!"

Prayer
Lord Jesus,
I remember that wonderful night
I fell upon your grace.
Nothing I had done bade me enter this great banquet hall.
Yet there I was face to face
with the once condemned, now made the friends of God.
I laid aside reluctance and was free.
I do repent of inhospitality.
Amen.

Dressing in the Garments of Grace

Matthew 22:9–14

"'Go therefore to the main highways, and as many as you find there, invite to the wedding feast.' And those slaves went out into the streets, and gathered together all they found, both evil and good; and the wedding hall was filled with dinner guests. But when the king came in to look over the dinner guests, he saw there a man not dressed in wedding clothes, and he said to him, 'Friend, how did you come in here without wedding clothes?' And he was speechless. Then the king said to the servants, 'Bind him hand and foot, and cast him into the outer darkness; in that place there shall be weeping and gnashing of teeth.' For many are called, but few are chosen."

The dress code into heaven is the garments of grace. No other mode of dress will admit you to the celebration of the saved. Do not suppose that church awards or attendance pins will serve as passports to the marriage supper of the Lamb.

Bring me no list of all the wonderful things you did in my name. Do not come saying, "Lord! Lord!" Remember this: "Not everyone who says to me, 'Lord, Lord' will enter the kingdom of heaven, but only he who does the will of my Father who is in heaven. Many will say to me on that day, 'Lord, Lord, did we not prophesy in your name, and in your name drive out demons and perform many miracles?' Then I will tell them plainly, 'I never knew you. Away from me, you evildoers!'" (Matt. 7:21–23).

Grace is a wealth conferred from the treasury of heaven. God makes his children rich with foreverness. Many have trouble understanding this. You are forever possessed by a human idea that nothing is free. People assure you, "There is no free lunch!" These ideas have been so drummed into you that when you run into grace, you can barely accept it.

But here at last is the greatest truth that can impact the human heart: *there is a free lunch.* In fact, there is a lunch that is impossible to pay for. There is a lunch so resplendent, so nourishing, and so absolutely free that it alone is admission to eternity with me. Your self-righteous acts can never be anything more than a shabby garment. These will not admit you to the great feast. You need the pure clean garment of grace. You cannot buy this garment, for I have already paid for it. You cannot make it clean by yourself, for God has already washed it in the blood of the Lamb. You cannot labor to earn it; it is not for sale. You can but wear it; and join the countless millions who will come into God's presence wrapped in that acceptability that I purchased at the cross.

Prayer
Lord Jesus,
I cannot dress in any acceptable
resplendency except that which is conferred by you.
And so I reach up to accept
all of that which I can only have by receiving and never earning.
Give me heaven's glory, crown, and mace
by clothing me in iridescent grace.
Amen.

The Christian as Citizen

Mark 12:14–17a

And they came and said to Him, "Teacher, we know that You are truthful, and defer to no one; for You are not partial to any, but teach the way of God in truth. Is it lawful to pay a poll-tax to Caesar, or not? Shall we pay, or shall we not pay?"

But He, knowing their hypocrisy, said to them, "Why are you testing Me? Bring Me a denarius to look at." And they brought one. And He said to them, "Whose likeness and inscription is this?" And they said to Him, "Caesar's." And Jesus said to them, "Render to Caesar the things that are Caesar's, and to God the things that are God's."

For the past two thousand years you have had many brothers and sisters who lived and died in other civilizations that preceded yours. They, like you, were citizens of countries with differing flags and national symbols. Like you they were expected to render taxes to those governments. Those early nations have now fallen to others in a never-ceasing stream of countries with a never-ceasing stream of rulers. They made their own stamps, minted their own coins, and demanded their own kind of allegiance. Now they are all gone. Someday your own country will be replaced by the civilization that follows closely behind it. From millennia to millennia, nations come and go. Only the Kingdom of God remains.

You, like these nameless brothers and sisters from previous ages, are also a citizen of two kingdoms, the one that mints your money and the one that endures forever.

Whichever kingdom gets the best of your time, talent, and stewardship will tell you which kingdom rates highest. Your tax form and your church giving statement laid side by side will tell you which kingdom is uppermost in your conscious thought. It is perhaps fitting that a coin was used because the coin not only bore the image and inscription of Caesar, it also demonstrated the central symbol of the conflict in this matter of the two kingdoms. If the coin is spent or saved to promote or relate to our national citizenship, it demonstrates a "this worldliness." If the same coin is spent in an offering to God, it demonstrates the Christian's allegiance to the Kingdom of God.

The denarius is out of fashion now. It is a museum piece, dead coinage. But many of those who once spent those coins as offering unto God are quite alive and will be forevermore. They are waiting for you to join them in their foreverness. Will you be with them in this flawless eternity? Take a coin from your pocket. Study the image and inscription. Where will you spend that coin, and for what kind of merchandise?

Prayer
Lord Jesus,
Paying taxes is proper,
for I live in a great country and must
help others provide for the common necessities.
Giving you tithes and offerings of all I possess is also proper,
for you paid so much to buy my soul,
and my citizenship in heaven is eternal.
But help me not forget that I may spend
poor transient coins whose value never ends.
Amen.

One Bride for Seven Brothers, or, The Folly of Trying to Look Smart by Asking Foolish Questions

Luke 20:27–33

Now there came to Him some of the Sadducees (who say that there is no resurrection), and they questioned Him, saying, "Teacher, Moses wrote for us that IF A MAN'S BROTHER DIES, having a wife, AND HE IS CHILDLESS, HIS BROTHER SHOULD TAKE THE WIFE AND RAISE UP OFFSPRING TO HIS BROTHER [Deut. 25:56]. Now there were seven brothers; and the first took a wife, and died childless; and the second and the third took her; and in the same way all seven died, leaving no children. Finally the woman died also. In the resurrection therefore, which one's wife will she be? For all seven had her as wife."

From century to century, even the notable ones have tried to make themselves look smart by asking foolish questions. They often bring the full force of their swaggering atheism against faith. They try to harangue the unanswerable mysteries of God to make believers look stupid or naive.

It was in this spirit that the Sadducees asked this question about the resurrection. They did not believe in the resurrection and were asking their question to make me stammer out, "I have no idea." I countered their tomfoolery with a solid answer from the Bible (which is the best place to look for answers, even for those who don't believe it). Moses, when accosted by God at the burning bush, did not say, "Lord, you *were* the God of Abraham, Isaac, and Jacob." He said, "You *are* the God of Abraham, Isaac, and Jacob."

But consider the Sadducees' question of "one bride for seven brothers." This kind of question was an attempt to destroy my credibility.

Do not fear such arrogant folly. It will come to you in far-out questions designed to make you look at your feet and shuffle in embarrassed ignorance. But what are these great intellectual questions that skeptics lay against your frail intellect? The list is more predictable than the cynics suspect. "Where did Cain get his wife? Did Adam, being created by God, have a navel? Why did Joshua, in a heliocentric universe, ever say, 'Sun, stand Thou still'? Why do Jesus' lineages in both Matthew and Luke go to Joseph when he had nothing to do with fathering Jesus? Will thrice married widows be polygamous in heaven?" Greet all such questions as one great Christian in times past answered. When someone once asked him what God was doing all those years before he created the world, this scholar wisely replied, "Making switches to switch people who would later ask foolish questions." It is a good reply.

Prayer
Lord Jesus,
Help me to sift the questions
that come to me
so that I may struggle with the honest ones
and dismiss the rest.
Help me attend those questions of the heart,
not those designed to tear my faith apart.
Amen.

The Mark of a Christian

Mark 12:28–31

And one of the scribes came and heard them arguing, and recognizing that He had answered them well, asked Him, "What commandment is the foremost of all?"

Jesus answered, "The foremost is, 'HEAR, O ISRAEL! THE LORD OUR GOD IS ONE LORD; AND YOU SHALL LOVE THE LORD YOUR GOD WITH ALL YOUR HEART, AND WITH ALL YOUR SOUL, AND WITH ALL YOUR MIND, AND WITH ALL YOUR STRENGTH' [Deut. 6:4–5]. The second is this, 'YOU SHALL LOVE YOUR NEIGHBOR AS YOURSELF' [Lev. 19:18]. There is no other commandment greater than these."

The history of Christianity seems overlong because it has been the history of hate and struggle. From the contention of Christians in Acts 6 to the struggle of the church over missions in Acts 15–16, the history of the church is oddly the same: dissension and quarreling. The war of official Christians against dissent has been a tale of torture and inquisition, creating seas of the martyrs' blood.

Congregations have split and formed new congregations over such simple issues as where the pulpit flowers should be set or what color the new drapes should be. Churches have split over millennial views, differing over when I was coming back or what the nature of those circumstances would be when I did. People in these quarrelsome communities have become so incensed that they would not speak to each other for years. Called to be models of love and reconciliation, such churches often portray only dissension.

John offers us the best insight on love as the mark of the Christian: "A new command I give you: Love one another. As I have loved you, so you must love one another. By this all men will know that you are my disciples, if you love one another" (John 13:34–35). This verse should lead you to see that I did not love you because you were altogether lovely. In this same way, you must love those who are not always to your liking.

I do not love only the clean or the deserving. Even so must you love. I do not love only those whose friendship flatters my self-importance. Love likewise.

I did not only love those who could give me something in return; nor did I love those whose love would be politically useful to me in the corporate structure. I did not only love those who constantly flattered me. In all of these ways you must love others.

Grace may be defined as the love of the unlovely. So if there are those in the church or in the company who are hard to like, start loving them; and you will be giving others the very semblance of that love I freely gave to you.

Prayer
Lord Jesus,
Your greatest commandment
is my greatest challenge.
I want to love others
because I want to be like you.
If I hate even one it must be true
that I can never love my world like you.
Amen.

The Snare of Show-off Religion

Matthew 23:1–7
Then Jesus spoke to the multitudes and to His disciples, saying, "The scribes and the Pharisees have seated themselves in the chair of Moses; therefore all that they tell you, do and observe, but do not do according to their deeds; for they say things, and do not do them. And they tie up heavy loads, and lay them on men's shoulders; but they themselves are unwilling to move them with so much as a finger. But they do all their deeds to be noticed by men; for they broaden their phylacteries, and lengthen the tassels of their garments. And they love the place of honor at banquets, and the chief seats in the synagogues, and respectful greetings in the market places, and being called by men, Rabbi."

Many are into religion for fun and profit. They never mind putting God in the spotlight as long as a little of the light spills over on them. The twentieth century has produced an odd synthesis of servanthood and show-biz. Scarcely a day goes by when some "Christian personality" does not prove to be more personality than Christian. James said, "Do not merely listen to the word, and so deceive yourselves. Do what it says" (James 1:22). He was pointing out that how we live tells us who we are.

But the show-biz seduction of my kingdom begins not as that full-blown ego extravaganza in which it ends up. It usually begins in your heavy need to be idolized when you ought to be worshiping God. Preachers who start out sincerely wanting to preach people into the kingdom can end up preaching merely for compliments. Concert artists who start out singing to glorify God can end up singing mostly for applause. The worst liability of being either a preacher or an artist is that either of them may slide so gently into egoistic states that they never really know how it happened.

I castigated the Pharisees, and not unfairly.

People admired the Pharisees' phylacteries, those little Scripture pouches that marked them as "men of God." Since people admired their *little* phylacteries, they made them bigger. Their phylacteries grew with the compliments. Their religious tassels also got longer as popular esteem grew. They loved being called "Doctor" and "Rabbi" in the marketplace. And pretty soon, their love for God had been replaced by a pitiable and smaller need for human praise.

When you hear a compliment, remember who you are. When someone says that you teach the Bible well, thank them for the compliment. Then place it beneath my wounded feet. That is the only safe place to keep all your compliments. For if you listen to flatterers overmuch, your phylacteries will billow with your ego. Soon your usableness may be squandered in gathering the little ego goodies you once despised.

Prayer
  Lord Jesus,
  The warm church has for its best asset
    its greatest threat.
  Its compliments and warmth make me love it and you,
    but I realize I might be tempted to that narcotic addiction
    that at last loves only myself.
  I want to turn the spotlight full on you
    till in the darkness I am lost to view.
  Amen.

On Filching the Poor for the Kingdom

Matthew 23:14

"Woe to you, scribes and Pharisees, hypocrites, because you devour widows' houses, even while for a pretense you make long prayers; therefore you shall receive greater condemnation."

The children of my kingdom are often divided into two classes: the poor and the rich. Rich Christians are often divided into two classes as well: the compassionate rich and the rich who keep getting richer by profiteering off their poorer, often less educated, brothers and sisters. The Pharisees were among those who feathered their own nests with the thin resources of the poor.

The church has sometimes been incompassionate in her demands. The builders of the cathedrals often exacted terrible taxes that destroyed the poor and stole the widows' livings. So it was with the Pharisees.

Consider the plight of the widow, the unprotected woman. In times past, this woman whom disease or accident had robbed her of her man was virtually unprotected in the world. To see her struggle to feed her family or to care for her little ones is rending to the decent heart.

What shall I say?

Is such a woman to be punished merely for her gender? Will none look upon her and ask by what right she is to be held down or excluded from meaningful community? The church was born to exalt the dispossessed. In Christ, said Paul, there is neither bond nor free, Jew nor Gentile, male nor female (Gal. 3:28). The gospel is good news indeed for all. Yet even in my church, women who are in need are not given a place of compassion. Why after all these centuries do segments of my church not care about those gallant women who have suffered all kinds of socioeconomic grief and have paid a heavy price in life—merely because they were women?

Read again the gospels. See how often I stopped for women, exalted them to their proper place in my Kingdom. Notice how they followed me in my travels or were first at my tomb on the resurrection morning. They too are my disciples; and in addition to carrying on so much work of the Kingdom, they have born the storms of time. Let us stop this sin. Let us call again "anathema" on those who devour widow's houses. The Kingdom must be made of better stuff.

Prayer
Lord Jesus,
I want to be sure I do not take advantage
of those whom life has brutalized merely
to build my own fortune.
Make me a servant who cares for the oppressed,
who lifts the fallen, who loves the dispossessed.
Amen.

The Converts of Monsters

Matthew 23:15

"Woe to you, scribes and Pharisees, hypocrites, because you travel about on sea and land to make one proselyte; and when he becomes one, you make him twice as much a son of hell as yourselves."

God makes all people in a worthy image. But often when Christians make converts to my Kingdom, they make them in their own image.

Some have an odd neurosis at the heart of their personal faith. They may call it having a "burden for the lost." But this "burden for the lost" sometimes hides a private agenda. These would-be evangelists have little peace because many around *are not saved.* But they also have little peace about those who *are saved.* Why? Because it is so hard to get people to believe just the right kind of doctrine. Each personal evangelist wants people to be saved "his way"—holding similar conversion values and seeing conversion in roughly the same way. Since everyone who comes to Christ is an individual with individual ways of seeing the world, it is hard for the personal evangelist to make converts who are "just right" in their "walk with the Lord." It is neurotic work trying to get all converts to the right level of "saved."

The Pharisees had the same problem. Some were often most evangelistic in making proselytes. But it was not enough to simply make Gentiles into Jews. They only felt good if their converts had their own acceptable kind of religious hang-ups. Thus they brought people to Judaism only after they had scrubbed them up with a kind of doctrine that came close to brainwashing. They didn't want to bring people to just any old God, but a God who particularly liked the Pharisees' doctrine. So they never created free thinkers as servants of God. They only created the same kind of legalistic monsters that they themselves were.

My Kingdom can only live if you go into all the world and lead many into the faith. Teach them after you win them. But while you teach them, set them free of the necessity of seeing things your way. Assume that the Holy Spirit, who came to live inside them at their conversion, will himself be their finest teacher. Give him the free reign to lead them into all truth (John 16:13). Above all, in your zeal to make them my disciples, do not make them yours.

Prayer
Lord Jesus,
I want to lead the world to you.
But after I have done this,
I want each one of them to be like you
and never like me.
Help me disciple them with all that's true,
that all they come to be resembles you.
Amen.

Gnat Straining

Matthew 23:23–24

"Woe to you, scribes and Pharisees, hypocrites! For you tithe mint and dill and cummin, and have neglected the weightier provisions of the law: justice and mercy and faithfulness; but these are the things you should have done without neglecting the others. You blind guides, who strain out a gnat and swallow a camel!"

Lamentably, gnat straining and camel swallowing often go together. But nothing is more disappointing to God than saving people to do great things and seeing them spend the rest of their lives nitpicking. Legalists do little important work. Legalists package God's greatness in small human boxes.

All of our lives we have a love-hate affair with doctrine. Doctrinal sermons often seem boring. They sometimes seem to be nagging. The Pharisees were legalists: the champions of little truths. Judaism is a system of great truths. The great truths of Judaism liberated slaves and rattled tyrannical kingdoms. But by the New Testament era the Pharisees spent a lot of their time calculating their tithes. These legalists had tithe computation down to a science. They even had delicate balances that weighed out the various spices they grew in their herb gardens.

All around the city where they practiced their "microfaith," there were the starving and the lonely, the widowed and the needy. But when you are measuring the weight of your dill seed down to the very gram, you don't have all the time you need to be compassionate. The Pharisees were especially careful on fast days not to drink in a careless gnat that might have landed unseen on the surface of their wine. If you're going to fast, you shouldn't have meat, and while a gnat is not very meaty, it seemed a camel to these legalists. The Pharisees wouldn't want to be guilty of eating even one scrawny gnat while deliberately trying to please God.

I would like to tell you that all such meticulous nonsense was left back in the first century. Regrettably, it has not been. A great many in the churches spend their lives taking care of the little things. They have at various seasons taught that women should not wear makeup or jewelry. They have taught that men should not play various sports on Sunday. Even mixed swimming, movies, and the ballet have often appeared on the spiritual censure list.

I will not ask you to violate your little convictions if they are important to you. But never give them disproportionate time in an age when an entire culture is perishing for want of the gospel. Do great things for God. Leave gnat straining for those content to live insignificantly.

Prayer
Lord Jesus,
In a troubled, world
   rolling pointlessly around the sun
   in a spiraling path toward its own destruction,
I want to see these days I live as latter
   and give myself to things that really matter.
Amen.

On Dishes and Tombs

Matthew 23:25–28

"Woe to you, scribes and Pharisees, hypocrites! For you clean the outside of the cup and of the dish, but inside they are full of robbery and self-indulgence. You blind Pharisee, first clean the inside of the cup and of the dish, so that the outside of it may become clean also.

"Woe to you, scribes and Pharisees, hypocrites! For you are like whitewashed tombs which on the outside appear beautiful, but inside they are full of dead men's bones and all uncleanness. Even so you too outwardly appear righteous to men, but inwardly you are full of hypocrisy and lawlessness."

Have you ever drunk half a cup of something only to discover something unwashed and unclean on the bottom. Then you know the treachery of religious hypocrisy that feeds on its appearance of holiness.

Hypocrisy is a dirty cup. The problem with the Christian church is that some use dirty cups to give the water of life to the lost. Most of the lost really are thirsty, and they will admit it. But they are not so thirsty as to desire living water from unclean vessels.

There is a kind of death in keeping up sanctimonious appearances. Judas was the first to appear as my friend while remaining my deadliest enemy. Since that time, more harm has been done to Christianity by my apparent friends than my proclaimed enemies.

How can you be sure you are taking the strongest possible stands against hypocrisy in your own life? Ask yourself each morning and evening these three questions: Do I mean exactly what I say and leave no other impression when I speak? Am I just what I appear to be, or does my life connote something other than I intend? And here is the most important question of all: When people look at me, is what they are seeing on the outside really what I contain on the inside?

The worst hypocrisy comes from being "double-minded" (James 1:8). The double-minded man is unstable in all his ways. Double-minded souls are guilty of "doublethink." Doublethink is the process of holding two completely contradictory ideas in the mind at one time and accepting them both. Hypocrisy begins when we have two souls, one of which goes to church and loves God, and the other of which still enjoys a carnal attachment to values that the "church soul" rejects. The Pharisees offer us their own poor example of how we ought not to live.

First clean the inside of the cup. Then fill it with the water of life. The thirsty world will readily reach for the cup.

Prayer
Lord Jesus,
When what I am and what I seem to be are one,
*   I know my witness will become welded to your Spirit*
*   with such power, the world will come to me*
*   for a drink of life.*
So come and purge that I may come to be
*   a clean, free cup without hypocrisy.*
Amen.

How a Hen Gathers Her Chicks

Matthew 23:37–39

"O Jerusalem, Jerusalem, who kills the prophets and stones those who are sent to her! How often I wanted to gather your children together, the way a hen gathers her chicks under her wings, and you were unwilling. Behold, your house is being left to you desolate! For I say to you, from now on you shall not see Me until you say, 'BLESSED IS HE WHO COMES IN THE NAME OF THE LORD'!" [Psalm 118:26].

Watch a hen with her chicks. She will strut above them proudly; and if the slightest danger arises, she will cluck her little ones beneath her protection. Should her own life be endangered, the hen will draw her little ones to her to protect them with her dying warmth. If you kill the hen, in her dying she will spread her wings and her chicks will run in under her down-soft body to await her dying. She will die content to be giving her little ones her last bit of warmth. In dying, she will get them as far toward maturity as she can—to warm them for as long as she can in a cruel world.

Do not think this symbol grotesque. It is a splendid metaphor for describing the strength of my own passion as I lamented over the city. I was soon to die. As I saw this city filled with my countrymen, whom I loved, I longed to draw them to me. I wanted them to draw from me the last bit of my saving warmth. I wanted them to know that my blood would take the chill off their pointless, meaningless world. But when I called, they did not come. When I died, they turned heartlessly away. They died with no hope because they had rejected my hope.

Calvary is ever the hope. In but a few days those icy winds of hell that blasted Golgotha would become the warm, sweet gales of Pentecost. Then, bit by bit, the warm winds would bring the refreshing rains of grace. At Pentecost, while grace fell in storms of renewal, the poor and disconsolate redeemed would be washed in imperishable joy. There the fire would burn—Pentecostal tongues of flame—driven by the gales of a new age. And all of those who believed in me would leave the cold city and march into the world in a resurrection advance.

And Jerusalem, that hardhearted capital of legal, cold officialdom, would know the joy of dancing and singing. Thousands would be born into the kingdom of heaven. Then at last the love of God, like an hen, would gather together all confessing rebels who would bless my name. They would receive my life. They would cry with the sweeping armies of light, "Blessed . . . blessed . . . blessed . . . is he who comes in the name of the Lord!"

Prayer
Lord Jesus,
I want to receive you in this joy
*   by which you cried over an unfeeling city.*
I want your warmth to take the chill
*   off my foolish, icy views.*
I want to touch you and be healed of all my bogus ideas,
*   forgiven all my hypocrisies.*
I want to shout the glory of Isaiah's word:
*   Blessed is the name of heaven's Lord.*
Amen.

The Mite Magnificent

Mark 12:41–44

And He sat down opposite the treasury, and began observing how the multitude were putting money into the treasury; and many rich people were putting in large sums. And a poor widow came and put in two small copper coins, which amount to a cent. And calling His disciples to Him, He said to them, "Truly I say to you, this poor widow put in more than all the contributors to the treasury; for they all put in out of their surplus, but she, out of her poverty, put in all she owned, all she had to live on."

There are at least three levels in church giving: the shame level, the game level, and the fame level. At the fame level, a strange bout with pride begins. It is easy at this level to be proud and ostentatious. This was the level at which the Pharisees gave and made a great show of their devotion. When they gave, they held the coins high and dropped them with a brazen ring into the temple coffers.

At the game level, the giver tries to figure out what is the most blessing he can buy with the least down payment. Such givers try to figure out how to give a little bit in such flamboyant ways that they purchase a generous reputation with their well-publicized pittances. Game givers try to figure out what would "be reasonable" in comparison to what others are giving. They compare their offerings with the average and then give just a little bit more.

The shame level is the level of those who can never give enough. These givers always look at the price I paid on Calvary. Even when they give all, they wish it were more. They even feel a little ashamed that it is so little.

Consider the woman in the temple. She gave all that she had, and I complimented her. But see her as she slinks her way up to the coffers. She skulks like one who must give or die. She sees the large gifts of the partial givers and fails to see the worth of her own two copper coins. She thinks of all that God has done for her, and she feels only shame that she has given so little in return. She leaves the temple compound feeling frustrated and defeated.

She never knew that she walked into biblical history with her sacrifice. Even now when anyone gives all, wishing it could be more, his gift is called "the widow's mite."

This is the lesson of the widow: Give with the greatness of God in mind. Then your giving will be free of pride. Let a humble widow be your instructor on how to give.

Prayer
Lord Jesus,
I have been at pretense long enough.
I have given in pride
as though it were enough.
I rebuke all false motives;
remove my generous masquerade.
I give, remembering your holy cross.
All that I've counted gain I count as loss.
Amen.

The Habit of Sunrise

Matthew 24:1–3

And Jesus came out from the temple and was going away when His disciples came up to point out the temple buildings to Him. And He answered and said to them, "Do you not see all these things? Truly I say unto you, not one stone here shall be left upon another, which will not be torn down." And as He was sitting on the Mount of Olives, the disciples came to Him privately, saying, "Tell us, when will these things be, and what will be the sign of Your coming, and of the end of the age?"

All things are transient. The world has ever been in a state of passing away. To my disciples, the temple of Herod the Great seemed indestructible and eternal. So I tried to get them to see that the day was coming when the temple, made of magnificently quarried stones, would not exist. In their minds they believed that such an edifice would exist till there was no more time. In short, time and the temple were one. So it was natural for them to think that I was talking about the end of the world when I was talking only about the end of the temple.

They wanted to know when the end of the world would be. For most people, the end of the world is pretty much a calendar date. Somebody is always setting the date specifically to be on June 12 or October 3 or February 19. But the calendar of the end of the world is not nearly as important as our preparedness for it. The second coming is not synonymous with the end of the world, but the ideas are so related that it is difficult to separate them in the New Testament.

Let us turn our consideration to the disciple's question: When will I come again? The greatest enemy to the whole idea of the second coming is the habit of sunrise. The world is a predictable place, and God made it that way to make you feel secure. But the problem suggested by the habit of sunrise is that sunrise has always been there. Knowing it has always been there can lead us to the presumption that it will always be there! Thus we begin to take the calendar for granted.

Is there any way to know for sure that today is not more final than you suppose? Is there any real doubt that Armageddon and my imperative, imminent return are to come? This is not the dark mood I want my followers to serve, but it is the certain confidence I want them to know. Do not be terrified over what may come; I am the Lord of history. Read the signs of the times, but never despair. I have transcended history. In believing in me, you, too, have transcended history. Of course, the world is coming to an end. But never despair! You can get along without it.

Prayer
Lord Jesus,
Nothing is eternal except
    those things related to you and your kingdom.
The temple where you once taught is gone now.
So indeed will be the entire temple of
    western civilization.
And yet by faith I see that golden shore
    where I shall live when sunrise is no more.
Amen.

Masquerade Messiahs

Matthew 24:4–5

And Jesus answered and said to them, "See to it that no one misleads you. For many will come in My name, saying, 'I am the Christ,' and will mislead many."

It is common to hear men proclaiming themselves to be God. It is such an obvious lie. You would think people would find it more reasonable to choose some other masquerade. But still the nonsense persists from generation to generation. Godhood is a role ordinary men and women do not wear well. Nero and others were always championing their own divinity. One emperor promoted his steed to proconsul, and another proclaimed his horse a god. In various mental institutions there have always been those who were convinced they were me.

In my own day Jewish Zealots, some of whom were my disciples, had the stars of revolution in their eyes. They all wanted a Christ who could serve up political deliverance from Rome. Bar Kochba, or "Son of a Star," was another Messiah pretender near my time. Barabbas, who was set free when I was crucified, held the claim in the very meaning of his name, "Son of the Father." My age was thronged with people saying, "Lo, I am the Christ; follow me."

But make no mistake; your current time is heaviest of all with messiahs. There are cults without number vying for attention and acceptance. At the head of each of these is some guru, some self-ordained messiah. Most of them say, "My way is exclusive. It is the only way to salvation." They offer acupuncture or meditation or homotherapy or theosophy or spiritualism as a technique to discover the riches of their doctrine.

However, even in such a day you can learn to distinguish the true Messiah from the false. There is one certain way. Civil authorities are trained to ferret out counterfeit money not by learning the inconsistent graphics of that which is false. Such a method would be too diverse, for there are many ways to build the bogus, but only one way to make the real. Rather, these authorities have studied the real thing so thoroughly that the false is instantly suspect.

If you would spot cults and false religions for what they are, learn of me. Stand all pretenders to godhood beside me. Force them to measure up to what is real, and they will instantly be discovered false. Ask every pretender, "Who is like our Lord? Who is like our God?"

Prayer
Lord Jesus,
When I consider all the foolish ways
that people seek to give themselves to
false religions, I am grieved at heart.
For your true being stands apart, alone,
and orders false pretenders from their thrones.
Amen.

Armageddon

Matthew 24:6–7

"And you will be hearing of wars and rumors of wars; see that you are not frightened, for those things must take place, but that is not yet the end. For nation will rise against nation, and kingdom against kingdom, and in various places there will be famine and earthquakes."

Who could ever chart the bloody ways of human beings? They murder and kill and stab the earth with wounds from generation to generation. Before my second coming, war will be an ultimate issue. The continents of the globe will become continual killing fields. Armageddon will rise like a war dragon and march with bloody boots between scarlet oceans, killing and gloating in the blood.

These wars that precede my second coming will mark the time of my coming just as they have marked other ages. My own nation was wiped from the face of the earth only a few short decades after my ascension. My race then lived in dispersion, until these recent years when once again Israel was reborn.

Between the twelfth century and the nineteenth the English were at war for 419 years and the French for 373. Since there has been any recorded history, human beings have turned on their own kind. During any hundred years they have killed 19 million people. One historian has reckoned that the death of these 19 million every century would supply a blood-fountain running 200 gallons an hour since the beginning of history.

Such horrible statistics of war make it clear that humans are not *Homo sapiens*, "man the knowing," but *Homo ferox*, "man the savage." John wrote, "The angel swung his sickle on the earth, gathered its grapes and threw them into the great winepress of God's wrath. They were trampled in the winepress outside the city, and blood flowed out of the press, rising as high as the horses' bridles for a distance of 1,600 stadia" (Rev. 14:19–20). And the arch-horror of such blood will be Armageddon, the final battlefield of all time. "Then they gathered the kings together to the place that in Hebrew is called Armageddon" (Rev. 16:16).

There will be wars, many of them. But when I have come in the clouds, humanity's age of killing will give way to the age of life.

Prayer
  Lord Jesus,
  If ever I am to avoid killing in your name,
    I must first learn not to hate in your name.
  Help me to learn that you are in love with every person,
    even those who have been considered by some
    to be your enemies.
  I want to learn that grace is turning
    thumbs up on all your friends,
    O Christ.
  I want to turn the cheek and grace employ,
    seeking to build and never to destroy.
  Amen.

First Grace, Then the End

Mark 13:10

"And the gospel must first be preached to all the nations."

I uttered this prophecy during my final week of life. It expresses the heart of all that God is. God is in love with his world. He desires that every person hear of grace before the end comes. But consider how that which began as fledgling Christianity, with only twelve people, has in the last nineteen centuries circled the globe. Daily more and more believe, in sweeping world revivals that are turning the world to me. In fact, the West, which was once the center of world Christianity, is now slipping further and further into a slower missionary pace that is wildfire in third- and fourth-world countries.

We are quickly reaching that place where my gospel is literally being preached around the world. When I preached that I would only come after the gospel had been preached to all nations, there was still no general agreement that the world was even round. But now we know that my gospel is circling the globe.

It is right that you be especially watchful, for I am coming soon, now that all nations have had the chance to hear. Is the prospect of this world revival not thrilling? Do you not sample even now the thrilling call of grace to the discouraged and downtrodden of this planet? Can you not see that my Father so adores his children that he is not willing to let a single person perish unnecessarily? (2 Peter 3:9).

Mark the glorious, fastidious patience of my Father. So many for so long have been in need of grace. Those who will be most glad to see me are they who have had the least reason for wanting to remain here. Those drowning in wine and cream tortes will not be as glad to see me as their poorer brothers and sisters who have lived in the hovels of refugee camps. Most of those who eagerly await me are those who starve or freeze and die without hope. It is these for which my second coming has never been an academic argument. Nor are the poor of the world trying to wrench the secret of my coming out of the vaults of heaven. Rich and bored Christians in the West may try to figure it out, but not the world's destitute. These who have nothing are so looking forward to my coming again that they rise every morning and breathe those final words of Revelation: "Amen. Come, Lord Jesus" (22:20).

If you are a well-fed Western Christian, bless your needy brothers and sisters in every land. Love them as they wait for my return. Their pending salvation is heaven's passion.

> *Prayer*
> *Lord Jesus,*
> *Break me out of my little Western ghetto*
>   *of too much.*
> *Help me to find ways to care about my brothers*
>   *who live and die around the world,*
>   *claiming my same Lord,*
>   *believing my same Bible,*
>   *dying for my same Christ.*
> *I bless in other lands for which you came*
>   *my foreign family who loves your name.*
> *Amen.*

Keeping Your Christ-Love Alive

Matthew 24:11–13

"And many false prophets will arise, and will mislead many. And because lawlessness is increased, most people's love will grow cold. But the one who endures to the end, he shall be saved."

Faith has two qualities, truth and passion—or, what you believe and how you feel about what you believe. What we believe is dogma, and dogma is that part of faith that can be taught. Doctrine may seem sometimes to be unnecessarily boring, but never neglect its importance. Doctrine is that skeleton on which you hang such things as joy and relationship. I desire that you learn all the truth you can. Study the Bible as history. Study the Bible as doctrine. Study the Bible as literature. Study the Bible as the manual of disciplines for your faith and practice.

But love me with passion.

A man may know much about a woman. He may know her size, her convictions, her knowledge of mathematics, and her political affiliations. But if they are married, the woman will not consider such knowledge of great worth unless the man has expressed his love for her in ways that are passionate and caring. There are many who study me without loving me. Heaven is not given as a reward of scholarship. Heaven is awarded on the basis of love alone. Those who are content to know only *about* me are not candidates for union in Christ.

But I warn you of this: Passion is a fire that must be constantly rekindled. Do not neglect this flame. When the fire burns dim, rekindle it. When the fuel tank is low, refill it. When your ardor flags, restore its stamina. Love is made bright by discipline. It dies only from neglect. The way to avoid neglect is to major on the disciplines. Lovers keep their love alive by pursuing their loves and spending time with each other. Lovers who neglect seeing each other will in time cease to love each other. Divorce courts are filled with those lovers whose initial ardor was at last so cold that they forsook each other.

The same may be said of Christians who cease loving me. So meet with me in the pages of my Word. I will be waiting for you in the lonely places, and we shall keep our date with prayer.

Never lose your love for me through sheer neglect. Did I not caution the church at Ephesus that they had forsaken me, their first love (Rev. 2:4)? Did I not say to the Laodiceans, "I know your deeds, that you are neither cold nor hot. I wish you were either one or the other! So because you are lukewarm—neither hot nor cold—I am about to spit you out of my mouth" (Rev. 3:15–16).

Prayer
Lord Jesus,
I love you,
*   and yet I would not presume*
*   against that love one single day.*
Let me not pass an hour without saying it again.
I love you.
Let me embrace you through the night and day
*   lest ugly negligence steal faith away.*
Amen.

Keeping Our Altars Unprofaned

Matthew 24:15–18

"Therefore when you see the ABOMINATION OF DESOLATION [Daniel 9:27; 11:31; 12:11] which was spoken of through Daniel the prophet, standing in the holy place (let the reader understand), then let those who are in Judea flee to the mountains; let him who is on the housetop not go down to get the things out that are in his house; and let him who is in the field not turn back to get his cloak."

The Abomination of Desolation was a moment of Israel's ugliest history. It refers to that time when foreign marauders had vanquished Israel. These conquering Greeks sacrificed a pig on the altar of God. This treachery shattered the holiness of God. First of all, the Greeks had no right to be in the holy place, which was the sole province of the high priest in his work of atonement and blessing. But more than that, pigs were taboo in Jewish life. To slaughter one in defiance of Jehovah is still called the Abomination of Desolation.

Before my second coming, such spiritual treachery will recur.

But consider the meaning of the altar of worship in your own life. The altar is that place where you meet with God. The altar is where you reckon with God. The altar is that place where God may, if he so desires, reduce you to rubble or exalt you to usefulness. But at any time you meet God there, rejoice in the meeting. For bending at an altar means that you have not taken God for granted. Altars are always evidence that you are not willing to proceed in life without God. Altars are places of spiritual neediness.

A certain man whose son was far away from him longed daily for his son to come and see him. Day after day the selfish boy ignored the love of his longing father. The years went by and they both grew older. Finally the old man died, and his faithless son received notice of his funeral. He went to lay his father away in his grave. Then, following his funeral, the man sorted through his father's belongings. There he found an old diary, whose daily, single-line entries ran on for a thousand pages: . . . "Day lost! My boy never called . . . Day lost! My boy never called! . . . Day lost! My boy never called. . . ."

Do you think that leaving a lover waiting at the altar is not still an Abomination of Desolation? Do you think that the love my Father bears you should not at last bring judgment on his faithless lovers? Do you think that spiritual apathy is not the curse of empty worship? Kneel again and beg forgiveness. Restore your broken altar.

Prayer
Lord Jesus,
Cleanse my apathy.
Help me to see that not caring enough
about my relationship with you
is the sin unto physical death.
I beg forgiveness when my life and prayers
are coldly saying, God, I just don't care.
Amen.

Tribulation

Matthew 24:19–22

"But woe to those who are with child and to those who nurse babes in those days! But pray that your flight may not be in the winter, or on a Sabbath; for then there will be a great tribulation, such as has not occurred since the beginning of the world until now, nor ever shall. And unless those days had been cut short, no life would have been saved; but for the sake of the elect those days shall be cut short."

Tribulation is unendurable trial. The pain of the final times is a pain drawn in extremes. But do not quail in holy terror. You must remember this: I will never leave you nor forsake you (Heb. 13:5). In any time there are but two words you need to remember to claim my promise: "never alone!" For I will be with you; I am the Lord your God!

Even that final tribulation before my return is not something you will have to face alone. I taught all of my people a spirit of rejoicing when any fiery trials should come. Those trials, successfully navigated and conquered, with the victory given to me, lay up for you treasures in heaven. Remember I have said, "Blessed are you when people insult you, persecute you and falsely say all kinds of evil against you because of me. Rejoice and be glad, because great is your reward in heaven" (Matt. 5:11–12).

You are also given trials that their endurance may make you mature. "Consider it pure joy, my brothers, whenever you face trials of many kinds, because you know that the testing of your faith develops perseverance. Perseverance must finish its work so that you may be mature and complete, not lacking anything" (James 1:2–4). Do you doubt either the beauty or the reason, therefore, of those "fiery trials" (for that is what James's word *peirasmos* truly means).

With each test that comes your way, you are going through a wonderful period of training for absolute dependence on my sufficiency. Paul said, "Therefore I will boast all the more gladly about my weaknesses, so that Christ's power may rest upon me" (2 Cor. 12:9b). Those who are never tested rarely need anything that they cannot dredge from their own resources. But those who have known utter trial are earth's sweet vendors of my all-sufficiency.

Pray to be like them, but be careful. They only gained inner light as they struggled from time to time over trials they feared would shred their souls. And then as they squarely faced the demons, they were made to see the clear course of victory. Be like them. Receive your trials and call on me. I will be there. I will not take the trials away, but I will walk with you through them. The trial will be hard, but the walk will be sweet.

Prayer
Lord Jesus,
I am in need today.
I have another problem I cannot solve
* by myself.*
I bless this as an opportunity
* to meet you once again and find you*
* all-sufficient.*
You come amidst my trials and faith flows free,
* as you declare, "This thing has come from me."*
Amen.

The Vultures

Matthew 24:23–28

"Then if anyone says to you, 'Behold, here is the Christ,' or 'There He is,' do not believe him. For false Christs and false prophets will arise and will show great signs and wonders, so as to mislead, if possible, even the elect. Behold, I have told you in advance. If therefore they say to you, 'Behold, He is in the wilderness,' do not go forth, or 'Behold, He is in the inner rooms,' do not believe them. For just as the lightning comes from the east, and flashes even to the west, so shall the coming of the Son of Man be. Wherever the corpse is, there the vultures will gather."

I don't want you to become preoccupied trying to wrest from God the hour of my coming. When it happens, it will be as obvious as lightning in a thunderhead or vultures circling in the sky above the carrion below.

Have you not already imagined it a thousand times? It may not happen exactly like your imagining. In fact, I can tell you with great certainty that it will be much better than you could possibly imagine. But savor it in your mind. Can you not see the trembling heavens? Can you not see a jagged sky and hear the eagles scream? Do you not imagine what it will be like when I walk the stratosphere as surely as I walked on Galilee? Can you not in your imagination feel heaven's wounded hand clasp your own and draw you skyward? What deliciousness awaits you. Watch for it. Never stop desiring it.

But at the same time, do not be anxious about it. Do not fret that you do not understand prophecy. Do not struggle in your study of Scripture as though, when you know enough, you can wrench from my Father's grip heaven's most tightly guarded secret.

You cannot. I will come when he shall split the cosmos with divine love. I will not come one moment before that nor one second after.

So use your days well. Serve your world by looking down on human pain and not by looking up to try and catch the first glimpse of wide, dissolving skies. It is better to use your hands wrapping bandages for Earth's injured than to thumb the pages of someone's commentary of doom. There is much work to do. Preach, pray, and serve while you await this delicious moment of my coming. Serve rather than paint "The world is coming to an end" posters.

The vultures will come. There will be plenty of time to paint your poster then. But even then it might be better—even as the vultures circle—to preach my gospel and heal Earth's sick. I would prefer to have you ministering when I come rather than trying to be the first on your block to announce it.

> *Prayer*
> *Lord Jesus,*
> *I must confess*
>   *I daily savor that cosmic, splendid moment*
>   *when the clouds will give way*
>   *and I see you and know your glory*
>   *face to face.*
> *Until such time as you march through the skies,*
>   *help me to watch to see the vultures fly.*
> *Amen.*

The Trumpet of the Elect

Matthew 24:29–31

"But immediately after the tribulation of those days THE SUN WILL BE DARKENED, AND THE MOON WILL NOT GIVE ITS LIGHT, AND THE STARS WILL FALL from the sky, and the powers of the heavens will be shaken, and then the sign of the Son of Man will appear in the sky, and then all the tribes of the earth will mourn, and they will see the SON OF MAN COMING ON THE CLOUDS OF THE SKY with power and great glory. And He will send forth His angels with A GREAT TRUMPET and THEY WILL GATHER TOGETHER His elect from the four winds, from one end of the sky to the other."

In the middle of all the wonderful cosmic disturbance, you will hear a great trumpet. This trumpet is summons to all of those who have ever been redeemed. Can you imagine how you will feel at such a summons? At once you will be united with all who from any age have ever believed. This is the summons of the centuries.

"I declare to you, brothers, that flesh and blood cannot inherit the kingdom of God, nor does the perishable inherit the imperishable. Listen, I tell you a mystery: We will not all sleep, but we will all be changed—in a flash, in the twinkling of an eye, at the last trumpet. For the trumpet will sound, the dead will be raised imperishable, and we will be changed. For the perishable must clothe itself with the imperishable, and the mortal with immortality. When the perishable have been clothed with the imperishable, and the mortal with immortality, then the saying that is written will come true: 'Death has been swallowed up in victory'"(1 Cor. 15:50–54).

Can you not sense what a glorious trumpet blast this will be? In this one fanfare, the dead will come out of their graves and the living will join them in the air. This is the consummation of the ages. The trumpet will sound and my children will be gathered.

Now do you understand the meaning of the word *saved?* It is the strongest word in the Bible. It suggests that in God, nothing is ever lost. Do not be made disconsolate by those who overgrieve the loss of a loved one, if that loved one is a Christian. If you hear anyone say, "She was a wonderful Christian, a great believer in Christ, but, alas, we lost her last year," know the truth! No one who is saved will ever be lost. She is merely waiting the trumpet.

The ages gather around a silver horn. The trumpet wakes those who were faithful in every generation: brothers and sisters who were thrown to the lions and killed for my name's sake—bootblacks, carpenters, seamstresses, native chieftains, and sea pilots, from centuries seven, ten, and fourteen. The trumpet comes; then come the great reformers and wonderful saints from a dozen centuries. As Paul promised, none of these will be strangers unto you. You will know them even as they know you (1 Cor. 13:12).

There is a grand party on the way. Get ready for it. Listen for the trumpet!

Prayer
Lord Jesus,
How noble is the promise
that we shall not all sleep,
but that we shall all be changed.
Help me never to forget what I best know,
that every age waits for the horn to blow.
Amen.

Morality on the Edge of Time

Matthew 24:36–39

"But of that day and hour no one knows, not even the angels of heaven, nor the Son, but the Father alone. For the coming of the Son of Man will be just like the days of Noah. For as in those days which were before the flood they were eating and drinking, they were marrying and giving in marriage, until the day that Noah entered the ark, and they did not understand until the flood came and took them all away; so shall the coming of the Son of Man be."

This historical finale befuddles human imagination. On the edge of every holocaust, immorality prevails. You would not think it would be so. You would think that when the world is in dire straits, people would behave themselves. Alas, it is not so. Indeed, they do not yield to the signs of the time. Historical ultimatums do not call forth morality.

In Noah's day, in Sodom's judgment, in the sumptuous kingdom of Ahab and Jezebel, there was eating and surfeiting until the city was ablaze with apocalyptic fire. Do you remember the wickedness of Belshazzar's court? He profaned even the sacred vessels that he had taken from the temple in Jerusalem. He drank wine from the vessels of Yahweh and profaned the God of Israel. Then the hour of cultural judgment came. Into this drunken, immoral society came the scrawling fingers of a man's hand. The five fingers wrote, *Mene, Mene, Tekel, Parsin* on the wall. When this heavy judgment came, the drunken king was at a loss to interpret the cryptic saying. But God shortly gave him the interpretation. Daniel interpreted God's message of judgment for Belshazzar's moral license:

"But you his son, O Belshazzar, have not humbled yourself, though you knew all this. Instead, you have set yourself up against the Lord of heaven . . . you did not honor the God who holds in his hand your life and all your ways. Therefore he sent the hand that wrote the inscription. This is the inscription that was written: MENE, MENE TEKEL, PARSIN. This is what these words mean: *Mene:* God has numbered the days of your reign and brought it to an end. *Tekel:* You have been weighed on the scales and found wanting. *Peres:* Your kingdom is divided and given to the Medes and Persians . . . That very night Belshazzar, king of the Babylonians, was slain, and Darius the Mede took over the kingdom, at the age of sixty-two" (Dan. 5:22–30).

Are not such days as Noah knew come again? Are the clouds of storm and judgment not already gathering? Can you not see the moral license of a people who do not heed the signs of the times? Hurry into the ark. Hurry through a society that is drunken and self-seeking. Hurry through an abusive generation that mistreats her children, murders old men in parks, laughs at decency, and mocks chastity and morality. The ark is there. Its doors are open. Call out the requirements of God. Dare to stand in such a day as this. There is handwriting even now on the walls of culture.

Prayer
Lord Jesus,
Help me to read the writing on the wall
to all who cannot see the lateness of the hour.
I want to stand in time's immensity
and point all to the Lord of history.
Amen.

The Great Divorce

Matthew 24:40–42

"Then there shall be two men in the field; one will be taken, and one will be left. Two women will be grinding at the mill; one will be taken, and one will be left. Therefore be on the alert, for you do not know which day your Lord is coming."

The secrecy of my coming is preface to the great divorce. Do not presume that tomorrow you will get ready, for I may come at midnight. All the covenants of God are urgent. When he called Abraham, he did not give him decades to consider the importance of his call. What he demanded of Moses was instant commitment, though Moses would have liked to postpone the issue. When I called my disciples, saying, "Follow me!" I began walking away right that instant. They needed to follow me right then.

When I come again, the trumpet will sound in one moment. There will be no time at that historical blink of the eye to change the mind. It will have been done or not as of that moment. Then this great division will occur. Those who have believed will be instantly joined to the redeemed of all ages. Those who have not will wonder what has happened. The world will be confused; the heavens will be confident. It all depends upon which side of the great divorce you find yourself.

Let this tale of divided field hands and mill workers remind you that my coming will be swift. The only moment you have to make a sure decision is this present moment. Tomorrow's clock will have no hands. So be immediate in your decision.

Do not see this decision as a threat. In every moment of saying yes to God is sweet concurrence. Revel in the way your simple "Yes, Lord" brings heaven near.

The walk across history's finish line will be exactly like the walk up to it—accompanied. There will be grand drama at the end of time, but I will be both the producer and the star of that display. It will be as though you are attending a premier performance as a special guest of the producer. You will have both the front-row seats and a backstage pass at history's finale. You've nothing to fear. The drama will include you. The spectacle need not frighten you.

But when the great divorce occurs, remember those who were left. It is thrilling to be the one of the two field hands who was taken. But have you never wondered if the one who was left had worked for years beside the one who was taken? Did the one who was taken ever tell the one who was left? Are you in constant contact with someone whom you have never told about the coming great divorce? Why not?

Prayer
Lord Jesus,
When you shall come again,
will I be taken from the midst
of some that I have worked among
for years and never spoken of your Father's love?
Oh, let none feel that ultimate remorse
whom I've not told about the great divorce.
Amen.

The Thief in the Night

Matthew 24:43–46

"But be sure of this, that if the head of the house had known at what time of the night the thief was coming, he would have been on the alert and would not have allowed his house to be broken into. For this reason you be ready too; for the Son of Man is coming at an hour when you do not think He will. Who then is the faithful and sensible slave whom his master put in charge of his household to give them their food at the proper time? Blessed is that slave whom his master finds so doing when he comes."

Watching and serving are the double activities of the Kingdom. The servant who doesn't watch does not live in loving anticipation of our reunion. The servant who doesn't serve will have nothing to offer me when I do arrive. So watch while you serve me, and serve me while you watch.

Both activities belong to those disciples who want to be ready for the day of the Lord. The day of the Lord is an idea common to both Testaments, a time of rejoicing and a time of reckoning. It will come to all, but it will not have the same effect upon all. As Amos the prophet pointed out, there are some looking forward to it who shouldn't be: "Woe to you who long for the day of the LORD! Why do you long for the day of the LORD? That day will be darkness, not light. It will be as though a man fled from a lion only to meet a bear, as though he entered his house and rested his hand on the wall only to have a snake bite him. Will not the day of the LORD be darkness, not light—pitch-dark, without a ray of brightness?" (Amos 5:18–20). Many who do not know God's requirements are expecting the day to be glorious. Alas, their rejection of my Lordship can only leave them in outer darkness with no hope.

Can you see this fearful metaphor as it is? I come as a thief in the night. Night thieves prey upon that comfortable sense of security that tells the owner of the house nothing is wrong. Then in the middle of the night the house is plundered. All that the owner had of value is gone. Now the owner must weep, for the family has been dispossessed.

Long ago Peter wrote of the folly of their desolation: "But the day of the Lord will come like a thief. The heavens will disappear with a roar; the elements will be destroyed by fire, and the earth and everything in it will be laid bare. Since everything will be destroyed in this way, what kind of people ought you to be? You ought to live holy and godly lives" (2 Pet. 3:10–11).

Peter's question is fair: What kind of people ought you to be? Are you watching? Are you serving? Behold, I come quickly.

Prayer
Lord Jesus,
Since I know you will come quickly,
*   may I serve you earnestly*
*   and watch unceasingly.*
Prepare me for the everlasting light
*   by causing me to think of thieves at night.*
Amen.

Getting Ready—Staying Ready

Matthew 25:1–13

"Then the kingdom of heaven will be comparable to ten virgins, who took their lamps, and went out to meet the bridegroom. And five of them were foolish, and five were prudent. For when the foolish took their lamps, they took no oil with them, but the prudent took oil in flasks along with their lamps. Now while the bridegroom was delaying, they all got drowsy and began to sleep. But at midnight there was a shout, 'Behold the bridegroom! Come out to meet him!' Then all those virgins rose, and trimmed their lamps. And the foolish said to the prudent, 'Give us some of your oil, for our lamps are going out.' But the prudent answered, saying, 'No, there will not be enough for us and you too; go instead to the dealers and buy some for yourselves.' And while they were going away to make the purchase, the bridegroom came, and those who were ready went in with him to the wedding feast; and the door was shut.

"And later the other virgins also came, saying, 'Lord, Lord, open up for us.' But he answered and said, 'Truly I say to you, I do not know you.'

"Be on the alert then, for you do not know the day nor the hour."

Getting ready for my second coming is less important than staying ready. The foolish virgins were not foolish because they had not gotten prepared for the coming of the bridegroom, but because they didn't stay prepared. Spiritual preparedness is not something you do once and then put it out of mind and fall asleep. The prudent virgins were not prudent because they had extra oil for that *one* occasion. They always kept extra oil, to be ready whenever the bridegroom came.

Spirituality is not some garment we put on on Sundays so we can keep up appearances. It is a way of life. We ought always to pray. We ought always to read the Word of God. We ought always to minister. The kingdom of God suffers from spasmodic spirituality. Be like those desert fathers who lit their lamps long before daybreak every day. They rose to weep about their responsibilities to their heavenly Father. And long before they permitted themselves a crust of bread at first light, they had already dined on that wonderful meat that the world knew not of (John 4:32). This early feast of the Spirit prepared them to live the day as God purposed. They didn't do this so that others would perceive them to be men of God, but so they might actually be men of God.

Someday I will require of you an accounting of your stewardship. Your accounting must be of the instant. Do not think you can get ready in some hurried moment. Live ready. For those who meet the bridegroom and enjoy his presence are those who never have to try to buy their oil after midnight.

Prayer
Lord Jesus,
Preparation for heaven
is earthly vigilance.
I want to be one who never falls asleep
in Gethsemane.
I want to watch with oil in good supply,
alert at praise when comes your midnight cry.
Amen.

Our Ministry to the Hungry, the Wounded, the Lonely, the Sick, the Imprisoned

Matthew 25:32–36

"And all the nations will be gathered before Him; and He will separate them from one another, as the shepherd separates the sheep from the goats; and He will put the sheep on his right, and the goats on the left.

"Then the King will say to those on His right, 'Come, you who are blessed of My Father, inherit the kingdom prepared for you from the foundation of the world. For I was hungry, and you gave Me something to eat; I was thirsty, and you gave Me drink; I was a stranger, and you invited Me in; naked, and you clothed Me; I was sick, and you visited Me; I was in prison, and you came to Me.'"

The final reckoning is coming. It will do you no good to be interested only in "saving souls" while you care nothing about the squalid social conditions of the world around you. Remember, those who are terribly hungry will better listen to your sermons after they have been fed. The thirsty will show more interest in the gospel after they have been given a drink.

Do not speak your warm evangel while the cold are shivering against the winter. Give them a coat first, then tell them how to be saved. If you give them only the saving word, your crass insensitivity to their condition will be all they remember about you. Did you hear James's advice? "What good is it, my brothers, if a man claims to have faith but has no deeds? Can such faith save him? Suppose a brother or sister is without clothes and daily food. If one of you says to him, 'Go, I wish you well; keep warm and well fed,' but does nothing about his physical needs, what good is it? In the same way, faith by itself, if it is not accompanied by action, is dead" (James 2:14–17).

It is the coat for the naked man, the food for the hungry man, the visit to the sick, that make the good news believable. So give them a coat—yours, if necessary. Then after they are warmed, tell them of grace.

The sheep at the final judgment are those on the right. The goats are those on the left. The goats never saw the need of ministry. The sheep saw little else. But the sheep knew that when they tended the hurting, they had ministered unto me. If they ignored the hurting, they ignored me. See me huddled in the cold and give me your coat. See me starving by the wayside, and share your food. Can you see me? I am fevered. I need a cup of water . . . now.

Prayer

Lord Jesus,
I see you thirsty, naked, alone, cold, and imprisoned.
Here, then, is my coat, my lunch, my cup, my deed.
For I see you in every human need.
Amen.

The Sellout

Matthew 26:14–16

Then one of the twelve, named Judas Iscariot, went to the chief priests, and said, "What are you willing to give me to deliver Him up to you?" And they weighed out to him thirty pieces of silver. And from then on he began looking for a good opportunity to betray Him.

Can you be bought? Is your commitment to me up for sale to the highest bidder?

Of course, you will instantly say no! But do not be too hasty in your answer, for you may already have betrayed me for a smaller price than Judas.

Judas sought for opportunities to betray me. But it was not a hard search, for every day provided him many opportunities for betrayal. In fact, most of the time those opportunities seek you. How quickly they find you.

Did you listen to some off-color story, whose content was titillating to your mind but unworthy of your heart? Did you use my name in ways that you would not want anyone who respects you or me to know about? Did you allow yourself an office flirtation, a little leeway on your 1040 form, a tiny lie that made your boss think more of you than he would have if you had not told it?

If so, stop to consider a moment what betrayal really is. It is a breach in the holy wall of friendship. It is an injury made by the concealment of something sinister. It is a lie that looks like the truth. Betrayal is the hidden cobra in the offering of grain. It is the lowest wound to the deepest part of the unsuspecting heart.

And if you have never betrayed me, beware Peter's vain promise, "I am ready to go with you to prison and to death" (Luke 22:33) just before he denied me. Such loyalty oaths are for the crowd. They get you the reputation for standing true, but they are too loud, too shallow, too merely human to matter much. Beware of all loyalty oaths that have not been purchased from the purse of deep prayer and weeping. Such evil coinage buys sinister discipleship. Such silver purchases potter's fields. They are the coins of offense—of betrayal.

"But," you protest to me, "Lord, I have never done this to you!"

Do not speak too quickly. Silver buys all kinds of betrayal.

I felt it nonetheless. Not in your intentional desire to hurt me, for you would never do that. But I can feel it in your unwillingness to be open about our friendship. There have actually been times I felt you were ashamed to admit openly that we even have a friendship. Remember, you do not truly love me if you will not show your love.

Dig down in your purse. What is there? Is it silver to finance your discipleship at bargain prices?

Prayer
Lord Jesus,
I know that loyalty oaths from fickle disciples
are odious to you, for you cannot count on them.
They are the very paving stones of the Via Dolorosa.
They are the cheap deals made with convenience
and comfort at midnight.
I need to spend my nights 'neath olive trees
preparing to stand tall while on my knees.
Amen.

The Water-Carrying Man

Mark 14:12–16

And on the first day of Unleavened Bread, when the Passover lamb was being sacrificed, His disciples said to Him, "Where do You want us to go and prepare for You to eat the Passover?"

And He sent two of His disciples, and said to them, "Go into the city, and a man will meet you carrying a pitcher of water; follow him; and wherever he enters, say to the owner of the house, 'The Teacher says, "Where is My guest room in which I may eat the Passover with My disciples?"' And he himself will show you a large upper room furnished and ready; and prepare for us there." And the disciples went out, and came to the city, and found it just as He had told them; and they prepared the Passover.

Here is the sign for the Passover meal: a man carrying a pitcher of water. Such a man would not be hard to spot, for men generally left the water-bearing to women. So when a man was seen doing this kind of woman's work, he would stand out by sheer contrast.

Why would a man carry a water pitcher anyway? Would he not seem to be doing something menial and unmasculine? One messagehe would be that the chief virtue of the kingdom is service. By this small action he would deliver some woman of the burden of carrying heavy water in heavy pots. The man carrying water was an icon of the new Kingdom. The old ways were about to perish. Servanthood would own the day. No one can be more exalted than those who perform deeds seen as acts of self-abasement.

But the man carried water for an even more significant reason. My twelve friends were not meeting to celebrate the Passover. They were meeting, rather, to celebrate a new ritual. It would have some of the elements of the Seder, but it would shuck its ethnic, religious character to wear a broader definition. At this sacrificial meal, it would be customary for the proud to carry water and wash feet.

This new meal would focus on a simple tin cup and a stack of flat loaves that would symbolize the grandest thing that could be symbolized: the cross. At the cross all pretense must be laid aside: the vestments of special class or privilege would have to be laid by. Such a special communion would say to either men or women, "There is no role which relegates you to second class. Compared to him whose excellence redeems us all, we are all second class. For at this splendid ritual of bread and wine, there can be 'neither Jew nor Greek, slave nor free, male nor female, for [we] are all one in Christ Jesus'" (Gal. 3:28).

Do not pity a man who carries water. Do not lament his social station. Do not begrudge anyone the glory of the Kingdom ministry on the basis of their gender. Then find yourself a water pot—any old water pot will do—and serve me.

Prayer
Lord Jesus,
The Passover was made full
by what began in that furnished upper room.
Help me to realize that carrying water
may be a grand assignment
for all who would want to model your life.
I willingly serve tasks that make me less,
that I may lead the needy to confess.
Amen.

Letting the Servant Serve

John 13:5–9

Then He poured water into the basin, and began to wash the disciples' feet, and to wipe them with the towel with which He was girded. And so he came to Simon Peter. He said to Him, "Lord, do You wash my feet?" Jesus answered and said to him, "What I do you do not realize now, but you shall understand hereafter."

Peter said to Him, "Never shall You wash my feet!" Jesus answered him, "If I do not wash you, you have no part with Me." Simon Peter said to Him, "Lord, not my feet only, but also my hands and my head."

If you would be saved, you must let me serve you. I have served you a thousand times each day, making life easier for you. The kind of service I am talking about is the kind of strategic service I gave you on Good Friday. Throughout my Incarnation—that wonderful saving experience of my leaving heaven and becoming a man—I served you. I served you by remaining sinless so that my sinless sacrifice could redeem you. I served you by dying and by coming back to life.

But I also served you by providing a slave's image for you to live up to. The night I washed my disciples' feet, the slave who usually did that kind of service had been dismissed. So I washed feet. And as I did, so you must do. It was not degrading for me. It will not be degrading for you. When you confessed me as Lord, nothing would ever again be beneath your dignity.

But from babyhood on you are constantly being taught to take care of yourself, so that by the time you are a young child you are often heard to say, "Please-I'd-rather-do-it-myself." Self-sufficiency becomes the foundation of pride. Pride turns away from doing the base and menial. So that night in the upper room when I was washing feet, Peter drew his feet up into his robe and said rather loudly, "No thanks."

I told him that if I didn't wash them, he could have no part in me. He—as he often did—rather flamboyantly agreed. But what I was really saying to him was, "Unless you learn to receive, the whole Christ-life will be impossible to you."

Peter's problem had nothing to do with his feet. His problem was with his head. Once he learned to bow that, his feet were as good a place as any to meet God. So will it be with your life. Surrender not your pride, and the gold of heaven cannot be yours. Look, even now, I kneel at your feet. The basin is full of water. May I?

Prayer
Lord Jesus,
I have moved through too many days
carried by my pride and
unwilling to receive lest
I look incompetent or dependent.
But I now beg you,
bring the towel and basin. Where they meet
you'll find this needy soul with dusty feet.
Amen.

The Slave Is Not Greater

John 13:12–17

And so when He had washed their feet, and taken His garments, and reclined at the table again, He said to them, "Do you know what I have done to you? You call Me Teacher and Lord; and you are right, for so I am. If I then, the Lord and the Teacher, washed your feet, you also ought to wash one another's feet. For I gave you an example that you also should do as I did to you. Truly, truly, I say to you, a slave is not greater than his master; neither is one who is sent greater than the one who sent him. If you know these things, you are blessed if you do them."

There is one lesson to be learned in foot washing: Nothing that I ask of you is unreasonable. Slaves, who were owned by someone else, usually did the foot washing. Slaves had no right to their reputations, their bodies, their destiny, or their daily schedules. They often had no names except those given them by their overlords. They could be bought or sold at their owners' whims. If they got sick and could no longer serve, they could be killed rather than become a financial burden. If they were sold, they could actually be given a new name. Whatever they were asked to do, they did without question. Their survival depended upon their obedience.

"A slave is not greater than his master" is not just a clever proverb, but the basic truth on which the social structure of that day depended. Here, then, was my lesson to the church: If I had assumed a slave's role, and I was the church's Lord, then what is the church's role in the world to be? The answer to this is, of course, "Whatever I say."

Do not come to me for some crown of office. There is only one crown in the church. I wear it. Only I sit at the right hand of my Father. When you come to me asking for a crown, you will get only what everyone gets—a towel and a basin. Then you can start off in the world. Lift the needy from their sinful entrapments. Bury lepers. Visit those with the horrible stench of dying on their breath. Rebuke politicians for their selfish scams. Help the needy. Wash feet.

I once told my disciples, "You know that those who are regarded as rulers of the Gentiles lord it over them, and their high officials exercise authority over them. Not so with you. Instead, whoever wants to become great among you must be your servant, and whoever wants to be first must be slave of all. For even the Son of Man did not come to be served, but to serve, and to give his life as a ransom for many" (Mark 10:42–45).

Will you agree to become great? Wonderful! Here is your basin and towel. Today's assignment: dirty feet. Tomorrow's assignment: what you did yesterday.

> *Prayer*
> *Lord Jesus,*
> *I am your slave.*
> *Buy me, never sell me.*
> *Keep me and use me up,*
> *   all up,*
> *   any way you like.*
> *Give me whatever name you like,*
> *   for when I became your slave I lost identity.*
> *I take your towel, embrace humility.*
> *Amen.*

Table Betrayals

Mark 14:18–21

And as they were reclining at the table and eating, Jesus said, "Truly I say to you that one of you will betray Me—one who is eating with Me." They began to be grieved and to say to Him one by one, "Surely not I?" And He said to them, "It is one of the twelve, one who dips with Me in the bowl. For the Son of Man is to go, just as it is written of Him; but woe to that man by whom the Son of Man is betrayed! It would have been good for that man if he had not been born."

It is always difficult to believe that our best friends have not in every case proven themselves worthy. Which human being has not from time to time suffered some *betrayal*? Which human being from time to time has not been a *betrayer*? There are often terrible dreams that haunt you. They are somewhat the same for all. In this dream you are alone in a valley of twisted trees and being pursued by a night stalker. You hurry through the shadowy forest. Close behind you, you can feel the hot breath of your demon assailant. On you flee. The home of your best friend lies only a little way ahead; you can already see the lights through the rain-slick forest. Harder you run. Now you are out of the trees and the house is just ahead. You quickly approach the house and frantically knock. No one comes to the door. You knock again; now the stalker is close and almost there. You knock one last time. Your best friend in all the world—the one who might have saved you—is not at home. Now there is no recourse. None can help, and the monster is upon you. All alone you turn to face him. Lo! It is the fanged face of the very friend to whose house you have fled for hope.

Treachery surprises us at moments of need. I would have been arrested and crucified anyway. All the Jewish officials were angry with me, and many wanted to put me to death. But it was uncanny that Judas would be their servant. Even as we enjoyed the temporary warmth in the last frigid moments of Maundy Thursday, it was Judas who would betray me. I loved him. I ate with him. I had shared his company, his table, and his pilgrimage for three years.

Here was my night of need. I would be dying tomorrow, and I needed my friends. Alas, when I turned to these twelve who should have been there to save me and protect me, it was Judas's face that I could see was fanged. He whom I loved and called to special service was the kissing killer of Gethsemane.

Judas! Who would want to be like him? Promise me you will never dip your hand in my dish and later kiss me in Gethsemane.

Prayer

Lord Jesus,
I am yours, but then so was Judas.
I am known by all my friends to be your friend,
*   but then so was Judas.*
I have usually done my Christian duty well,
*   but then so did Judas.*
Help me to live in utter honesty,
*   lest I prove false in my Gethsemanes.*
Amen.

A Morsel for a Plea

John 13:23–26

There was reclining on Jesus' breast one of His disciples, whom Jesus loved. Simon Peter therefore gestured to him, and said to him, "Tell us who it is of whom He is speaking." He, leaning back thus on Jesus' breast, said to Him, "Lord, who is it?" Jesus therefore answered, "That is the one for whom I shall dip the morsel and give it to him." So when He had dipped the morsel, He took and gave it to Judas, the son of Simon Iscariot.

In our custom, the first morsel of the meal was the sign of utter friendship. The first morsel to be given pointed out the guest of distinction. But in my case, this first morsel was even more than that; it was a plea to Judas not to do it. It was my final attempt to throw a roadblock of love in the path of tyranny.

How many times will love beg for loyalty? It is the nature of grace never to stop. It is in a sense the most godlike of all human qualities. Have you never known a father who, having six sons who were disciplined and achieving, yet would die to save the seventh son who was a rebel? Why? Because it is in his father's heart to pursue each son till all are fully reclaimed.

I had eleven apostles who were all gallant. What they achieved is nothing short of miraculous. All but one of them died as martyrs defending my name. Three of them wrote gospels, and all of them scattered to the far corners of the world to preach and tell what they knew of me. Only one was a traitor. He was destined to carry out his evil role from the beginning of time. But if you see me as knowing this and making him pay for his sin, you misunderstand my office. Nor did I hand him the sop to point him out so that the others could mob him and prevent him from carrying out his betrayal. What he did was in some mysterious way a part of world redemption. Oh, that he had nobly owned a great purpose in his own mind. But Judas was in business for Judas only. He was on a purely selfish mission of gain. I pitied him because I loved him. If you tell me that I should not have loved him, I would tell you, "Then I should not be Savior to any, for there is something of Judas in every human being."

I handed him the sop. He knew what it meant. He felt his faithless treachery even as he received it. But if I had not loved him, the world itself would have been in trouble.

So now I give the sop to you. Here it is! You may go into the world and sell me cheap, or you may go into the world, saying as the Samaritan woman said, "I am loved by grace incomprehensible. Come see a man who told me all the things ever I did!"

Prayer
Lord Jesus,
I have been the outcast traitor
to so much of what you stood for.
Yet you reached across the crowd of my astonished peers
and handed me the sop.
Thus proclaimed as best of friends by grace,
I take the morsel and receive the mace.
Amen.

Night

John 13:27–30

And after the morsel, Satan then entered into him. Jesus therefore said to him, "What you do, do quickly." Now no one of those reclining at the table knew for what purpose He had said this to him. For some were supposing, because Judas had the money box, that Jesus was saying to him, "Buy the things we have need of for the feast"; or else, that he should give something to the poor. And so after receiving the morsel he went out immediately; and it was night.

There seem to be some nights that Satan owns. Nights do not belong to him. They are as good a time for measuring the immensity of God as days. But on this Thursday night the man with the purse hurried out into the darkness. My disciples all thought he was on a shopping trip to buy something for our entourage. Had they suspected what he was really about, they would never have let him leave the room.

Night closed in around Judas. It seeped into his soul and darkened his lust to earn money by playing the double agent. Shadows crept from alleyway to alleyway as he hurried through the streets. Darkness reached its tentacles around him and pulled him toward the last bastions of betrayal. The darkness seemed his friend, for it completely matched his motives.

How different he had once been. He once had loved the light. He once had anticipated the Kingdom. Still, he was in most ways a pitiable and odd man. He always seemed to fight and struggle with his own agenda. He could never decide whether he really wanted the kind of Kingdom I espoused. He wanted God's full reign over the earth, but he still liked the more political concepts of the kingdom of God. He wrestled with Satan, ever giving him more ground. He wrestled with evil mostly at night.

He yielded to evil at night too.

Once he had received the morsel, he left to complete history's bloodiest crime. His mission that Thursday represented an evil deed that could never be called back. The Kingdom plunged into confusion around the cross. This was a confusion from which only the Resurrection could ever fully make sense. Judas himself entered into the closing moments of his final struggle.

It was night, and by the next night his own faithless body would swing underneath the creaking timbers of his suicide. His life was over. Day should have been his destiny, but he sold his soul to night. Be careful of the night, lest the serpent beguile the daylight from your soul. Love the light, lest the darkness outside you may at last possess you.

Prayer
Lord Jesus,
I want to walk in the light
as you are in the light.
I want to be sure that I so esteem the day
that I make no deals with darkness.
I will not yield to night which death controls,
lest in the dark I cheaply sell my soul.
Amen.

The Prosaic Arguments of the Kingdom

Luke 22:24–26

And there arose also a dispute among them as to which one of them was regarded to be greatest. And He said to them, "The kings of the Gentiles lord it over them; and those who have authority over them are called 'Benefactors.' But not so with you, but let him who is greatest among you become as the youngest, and the leader as the servant."

A quarrel over greatness on the icy decks of the *Titanic* would be foolish. Yet that is what my disciples did on my final night of earthly existence. In a matter of hours I would be hanging by my hands, and Judas Iscariot was already on the way to complete his dark bargain. When I was all but crucified, once more my disciples fell to quarreling over who should be the greatest.

Part of me would have preferred not to have the gospel writers report their lunacy. Remember Paul's counsel: "Whatever happens, conduct yourselves in a manner worthy of the gospel of Christ. Then, whether I come and see you or only hear about you in my absence, I will know that you stand firm in one spirit, contending as one man for the faith of the gospel" (Phil. 1:27).

Heaven longs for all believers to think it obscene to argue over personal greatness in front of a lost world. Yet, while the world watches, Christian denominations have played king of the mountain. God weeps for such trivial partisanship in the Kingdom.

The day may be late. I am at the threshold of history. I may, at any moment, instantly break in upon these quarrelsome factions. The suddenness of my return calls for all to abandon the nonsense of arguing who is greatest. The universe is approaching a state of meltdown. "Since everything will be destroyed in this way, what kind of people ought you to be? You ought to live holy and godly lives as you look forward to the day of God and speed its coming. That day will bring about the destruction of the heavens by fire, and the elements will melt in the heat. . . . So then, dear friends, since you are looking forward to this, make every effort to be found spotless, blameless and at peace with him" (2 Pet. 3:11–14).

If you are in a church in which everybody wants to run the machine and no one wants to evangelize, you may want to remind them that on the *Titanic* it is pointless to worry about being properly rewarded for your years of service. It is better to know how to lower the lifeboats.

Prayer
Lord Jesus,
I used to want to sit at your right hand.
But nearly everybody does!
Just give me back-row seats
    and teach me there is grace abounding
    for all who want to serve and see you
    from afar.
For in the back are all of those who worshiped you
    but felt too non-executive to be well loved of God.
I'm happy here behind the vanguard crowd,
    humble, rearward, distant from the proud.
Amen.

The Gold of Heaven

Luke 22:28–30a

"And you are those who have stood by Me in My trials; and just as My Father has granted Me a kingdom, I grant you that you may eat and drink at My table in My kingdom."

Heaven is too often seen to be a place of "just" rewards. Most people speak of it as if it were the probation of the family will. They want to get what's coming to them. I will not deal with the arrogance of such presumptions. I want rather to speak to you of the true nature of heaven. It is true that it has streets of gold, but the paving is not the treasure of heaven. It is true that it has a glassy sea and a great white, translucent throne. It is true that its glory is borrowed from my radiance. But it is not heaven's radiance that is to be cherished.

All that John said of it is true: "I saw the Holy City, the new Jerusalem, coming down out of heaven from God, prepared as a bride beautifully dressed for her husband. . . . The wall of the city had twelve foundations, and on them were the names of the twelve apostles of the Lamb. . . . The foundations of the city walls were decorated with every kind of precious stone. The first foundation was jasper, the second sapphire, the third chalcedony, the fourth emerald, the fifth sardonyx, the sixth carnelian, the seventh chrysolite, the eighth beryl, the ninth topaz, the tenth chrysoprase, the eleventh jacinth, and the twelfth amethyst. The twelve gates were twelve pearls, each gate made of a single pearl. The great street of the city was of pure gold, like transparent glass" (Rev. 21:2, 14, 19–21).

Heaven will be a haven. A harbor. A well-deserved rest for those whose dying moments were given to the lions of Nero or the flaming stakes of Diocletian. Those who paid their dues in final hymns sung before jeering scoffers will be home at last. Do not suppose they have the slightest interest in gold or pearls. For them I was the only gold they ever found worthy in the tinsel world where they lived. I was the pearl of great price. I was the treasure hidden in the field, and they sold all their earthly enterprises to purchase our relationship. I am what makes heaven heaven, after all.

Are you eager to own a mansion? Are you desirous of golden streets? Or are you homesick with a yearning that can only be filled by my eternal presence? If so, bless your hunger. Come heavenward. Heaven is as anxious for your arrival as you are to get there.

Prayer
Lord Jesus,
Heaven is the goal of hearts
  who are hungry for the right things.
I need to know that all has been prepared for me.
And so
  I come to you! Thou art the gold of state!
  The gold that paves the streets will have to wait.
Amen.

The Hardest Commandment of All

John 13:34–35

"A new commandment I give to you, that you love one another, even as I have loved you, that you also love one another. By this all men will know that you are My disciples, if you have love for one another."

This new commandment is the hardest. Why? Because so much of its keeping is the responsibility of our discipline. Loving everybody is a labor some have called the cruel work of the Kingdom. Other people are always coming between us and the most direct path to our goals. The idea of loving the unlovely freezes our will.

Most of my followers all want to be Christians with their own will intact—loving those they choose to love. Leave the work of loving the unlovely to God. Everyone supposes that loving the unlovely must be easy for God. "Poor God!" they lament, "he's the only one in the universe who doesn't get to pick his friends." God has to love everybody who shows up.

But most Christians find it easier to love those they select. They adore their friends and criticize the rest of the world. In picking and choosing whom they will love and whom they will hate, Christians introduce an odd conflict into their lives. They are quite desirous to go to heaven. But even there they want to pick and choose their friends. They imagine that when they get to heaven, their obnoxious Christian acquaintances will all have been sanded down and revarnished to fit their acceptable standards.

Beware such foolishness. One mark of a Christian is love. In my lifetime I issued very few commandments, but this was one of them: Love one another. By this shall all people know you are my disciples.

Are you having a hard time loving your enemies? Repent that even you have enemies. Remember, your enemies are not mine; I have no enemies. Remember, you cannot hate others while you wear the mark of a Christian. Come to the foot of the cross; gaze up into my dying face; and remember what you see there. The anguish is for all. If you hate anyone I have died for—and I have died for everyone—you have despised the reason for my existence. Follow me by remembering your obligation to love. By this shall all people know you are my disciples. Even more than that, *you* will know you are my disciple. And that knowledge will set you free.

Prayer
Lord Jesus,
There's enough hate between believers.
I do not have to add my own.
I do repent for failing to esteem
*   all those for whom you died and thus redeemed.*
Amen.

The Prayers of Christ

Luke 22:31–34

"Simon, Simon, behold, Satan has demanded permission to sift you like wheat; but I have prayed for you, that your faith may not fail; and you, when once you have turned again, strengthen your brothers." And he said to Him, "Lord, with You I am ready to go to prison and to death!" And He said, "I say to you, Peter, the cock will not crow today until you have denied three times that you know Me."

I knew that day that Peter's swaggering promises would not hold. How much we promise, and always with grand words. I pray that you will avoid the world of grand promises about all you intend to do. I would rather that you learn to keep a quiet concord with me. Learn to pray that your faith fail not. All that you intend to do for me is at the mercies of your frailties. Strengthen those weaknesses with prayer.

The courtyard that Peter knew that night comes to all of us. What a temptation it is to go to the courtyard certain you will not deny me! Then you become broken because your resolve wilts. You discover that you were too weak to keep those rash promises. It is better to live aware of your weakness. Then you will depend on my strength.

I am your great high priest. Let the wisdom of Hebrews remind you that the might of my priesthood is available to you: "And it was not without an oath! Others became priests without any oaths, but he became a priest with an oath when God said to him: 'The Lord has sworn and will not change his mind: "You are a priest forever."' Because of this oath, Jesus has become the guarantee of a better covenant. Now there have been many of those priests, since death prevented them from continuing in office; but because Jesus lives forever, he has a permanent priesthood. Therefore he is able to save completely those who come to God through him, because he always lives to intercede for them" (Heb. 7:20–25).

My promise to you is exactly as it was to Peter: I am praying for you. I am making intercession as your special priest that your faith fail not. Night and day I am on my face before my Father on your behalf. But it is not only I who am praying: "In the same way, the Spirit helps us in our weakness. We do not know what we ought to pray for, but the Spirit himself intercedes for us with groans that words cannot express" (Rom 8:26).

Every cock's crow brings some humiliated disciple to tears. Trust me. I am praying for you that your faith fail not.

Prayer
Lord Jesus,
High Priest and Intercessor,
I meet with you in your high and holy office
and hear you praying for my own steadfastness.
Thank you for all those prayers that I should plead,
I beg you, Spirit, always intercede.
Amen.

The Wine and Loaf

Mark 14:22–24

And while they were eating, He took some bread, and after a blessing He broke it; and gave it to them, and said, "Take it; this is My body." And when He had taken a cup, and given thanks, He gave it to them; and they all drank from it. And He said to them, "This is My blood of the covenant, which is poured out for many."

I took the food symbols that belonged to the Seder and christened them with new meaning. My people had always used unleavened bread to stand for the haste with which Israel had to leave Egypt. Now this same unleavened bread would stand at the center of Christianity. In Judaism it celebrated the Exodus in which God had delivered the Jewish people. In Christianity it celebrated my sinless life which would redeem all people.

New meaning flowed into old truth. But no symbol was violated that night. Both the Jewish Seder and Christian Communion stood for a God who loved and redeemed his people. Such rituals were given to two great world faiths as a reinforcement of remembrance. The bread and wine would call out to each of the five senses. The eye would see the redness of the wine and think of the blood I shed to make redemption possible. The hand would touch the cup and think of the chalice the disciples used that night. The tongue would taste the texture of the loaf and remember the chafing wood. The ear would hear the breaking bread that symbolizes my brokenness.

The greatest realities are those that transcend all of the senses. But in such rituals as the Seder or Communion, the sensory meets the spiritual. And where they meet, the Red Sea and Calvary live again.

Can the loaf and cup symbolize redemption?

Wrangle with the symbol. Bless the cup and loaf, as the church has done throughout the centuries. Taste the bread; but see me, the sacrificed Christ. Sip the wine, and understand the cost of grace.

That's what Communion does—it brings the spiritual to the sensory. We experience by touch an affair with the Spirit who cannot be touched. And in this glory the invisible is seen. The inaudible is heard. The intangible is touched. What could never be savored is tasted.

Communion is a little photograph, taken by the camera of grace. At the celebration of the Lord's Supper you take the little photograph out and look at it in remembrance of me. And as you stare at this ancient picture, I will walk into your life. When the bread and wine is present, I am beside you, recalling the price love once paid in the theater of hate.

Prayer
Lord Jesus,
I want to break bread and drink wine,
    savoring often the price of my salvation.
With simple loaves of bread and ruddy wine
    I call to memory the love that's mine.
Amen.

The Final Drink before Foreverness

Mark 14:25
"Truly I say to you, I shall never again drink of the fruit of the vine until that day when I drink it new in the kingdom of God."

On that night when the Lord's Supper was initiated, I set the cup down and said, in effect, "No more wine till the Kingdom comes!" My dying was yet to come, but close upon it, by a mere matter of weeks, would come the era of the new Kingdom, born in fire and wind. Those who had drunk the wine of the new covenant with me would be accused of keeping late hours with lots of wine on the day of Pentecost. Wine would, in time, become the symbol of my saving life.

On that night I instituted the Lord's Supper. They who reclined with me could never guess the cosmic nature of my redemption. Nor could they really understand it when I said, "I will drink no more of the fruit of the vine until that day I drink it new in the kingdom of God." But a battle was in progress—the final battle of cosmic forces that would resolve itself only when I closed my eyes in death. See the great chasm that was bridged? When I died, I surrendered all control to my Father. I knew I would rise again, yet have you ever noticed how the New Testament never phrases it that way? The New Testament rather says, "I was raised." In all such passages my coming alive again was the work of my Father. If he had not raised me, I would be there yet. When I closed my eyes in death, I was totally aware that I would not live again unless God shook the earth with Easter.

So I drank a final glass of wine. I would never have another on this earth. I would thirst on the cross, and they would pass up to me a sponge filled with vinegar and gall. But the wine would be my last real drink. Beyond the wine was the work of Calvary. And beyond Calvary was Pentecost. And beyond Pentecost was the age of the church. Then the whole church would drink the wine and remember.

Communion is my gift to you. You hold the ordinance now. You drink the wine. Shortly I will come again, and the necessity of loaves and wine will be gone in the age to come. Till then Communion is a constant reminder that the time is coming when you will see me face to face. Taste the wine and watch the skies. Drink and believe.

Prayer
Lord Jesus,
A final drink of wine,
and all the prophets knew
had come gloriously to pass.
And all the prophets prophesied
was confirmed in the looming
shadows of the long cross,
falling across a brand-new age,
the age of the church.
You drank the wine; the world came of age.
I drink it now and wait the final page.
Amen.

Untroubled in Temporary Separation

John 14:1–3

"Let not your heart be troubled; believe in God, believe also in Me. In My Father's house are many dwelling places; if it were not so, I would have told you; for I go to prepare a place for you. And if I go and prepare a place for you, I will come again, and receive you to Myself; that where I am, there you may be also."

The conversation in the upper room had become heavy.

I was going to die and rise again and go to my Father. In the process, I would be paving the way for them to make the same journey. I repeated for them what the writer of Hebrews would later say of me: "Therefore, since we are surrounded by such a great cloud of witnesses, let us throw off everything that hinders and the sin that so easily entangles, and let us run with perseverance the race marked out for us. Let us fix our eyes on Jesus, the author and perfecter of our faith, who for the joy set before him endured the cross, scorning its shame, and sat down at the right hand of the throne of God" (Heb. 12:1–2). The word for *author* in these verses is the Greek word *archegos,* which really means "first-goer."

I was the first to make that fearsome journey through the night and into eternal day. I was the glorious *first-goer.* I told the disciples that I would go to prepare a place for them. I assured them that where I had gone, they too could go. My victory was to be their victory.

Here was my final preparation for the ordeal of Calvary. My ugly dying would appear terminal to them. The wood, the ghastly suffocation, the lacerating wounds, the ashen flesh, the initial stages of gangrene: all these crucifixion symptoms would make them wonder if my promises of a new kingdom had been only talk. But when they saw that even that kind of death could be defeated, they would quickly change their minds. Gloom would erupt in joy, and the word *archegos,* the first-goer, would come alive as one who had completed the rough passage between worlds.

Have you lost a loved one? Are you ill yourself? Have you faced the idea that your final moments are on the way? Do not despair, I have made the passage safe. I have prepared the way. I have paved the drive from the grave to glory. Still afraid? Then in the cold of dying, when the dark comes, hold out your hand. I'll help you across. Believe me, since that long-ago day in spring, I know the way.

Prayer
  Lord Jesus,
  I want my prayer to be that wonderful old hymn:
    I know I will never have to cross Jordan alone.
  You have died all my sins to atone.
  When the darkness I see,
    you'll be waiting for me.
  I won't have to cross Jordan alone.
  I celebrate that fearsome trek you made,
    which conquered death and left me unafraid.
  Amen.

One Door and Only One

John 14:4–6

"And you know the way where I am going." Thomas said to Him, "Lord, we do not know where You are going, how do we know the way?" Jesus said to him, "I am the way, and the truth, and the life; no one comes to the Father, but through Me."

"I am *the* way" is one of my most troublesome teachings. In our current "all religions are about the same" world, it stirs people to hostility. "Be fair," they cry! It is bigoted to say that only Jesus saves. Give place to other world faiths!"

Here is the most controversial and the most hopeful of all truths. I am the way to heaven. If you would go there, you must come through the door.

"But," reason the broadminded and the politically correct, "are there not many roads that lead to London?"

Indeed there are. But there is only one road that leads to heaven; I am that road. I am that way, that truth, and that life.

"But what if we sincerely believe there are many other doors? Will sincerity not make an opening in the broad, cold heavens for those who sincerely believed they were right?"

Sincerity, however fervent, will not make a wall a door.

"But what about the ignorant heathen who have lived beyond Christian light all of their lives? There must be other doors for those who've never heard that Christ is the only door," the logician pleads.

There are no other doors. It is the church's responsibility to tell all those who have never heard the saving gospel that there is but one way into heaven. If people could be saved simply by never hearing of me, was it not cruel that I came to Earth in the first place? Would it have not been much better if I had never come so that no one would ever have heard or known the obligation of believing?

The apostles were right when they said: "Salvation is found in no one else, for there is no other name under heaven given to men by which we must be saved" (Acts 4:12). There is but one way, one truth, one life. There is but one way to heaven, one truth that saves, one life whose service saves. There is but one way out of hell, one truth that will spare believers, and one life by which anyone can dwell forever in the house of the Lord.

You may come in by the way or not. You may believe or not. You may have eternal life or not. But you are not free to rewrite Christian truth. You are not free to rechart the way, to rewrite the truth, or redefine the life everlasting. There are no alternatives, no easier heavens, no more congenial and comfortable roads that lead to eternity. Come to me. I am the door—the only door.

Prayer
Lord Jesus,
I will not presume
that there are alternate heavens
or other more effective messiahs
written up in other gospels.
I reach for heaven, certain ever more
that all eternity has but a single door.
Amen.

The Mirror Image of God

John 14:8–10

Philip said to Him, "Lord, show us the Father, and it is enough for us." Jesus said to him, "Have I been so long with you, and yet you have not come to know Me, Philip? He who has seen Me has seen the Father; how do you say, 'Show us the Father'? Do you not believe that I am in the Father, and the Father is in Me? The words that I say to you I do not speak on My own initiative, but the Father abiding in Me does His works."

I came as God into this fallen world. The only sure way to understand what God is like is to study the image in the mirror that I held up to heaven. The mystery of the ages has been answered in that mirror. I have ended the human puzzle as to what God is really like. For he who has seen me has seen the Father.

You can imagine my disappointment that here on the final night of my ministry, this major cloud still hung above my apostles. I had run out of time to live on earth. Regrettably, I was also out of time to teach them those major truths of the faith.

Children around the world continually ask one question. It is the desperate search behind every world religion. "Mommy, what is God like?" But it is more than a child's question. It is the longing cry of old people in rest homes and the strangling issue of cancer wards. It rises from the wounded on battlefields and threads its way through novels and cinemas. This desperate hungering and longing to know God is universal.

Philip was looking for an easy God, a touchable God, a God with skin on him. I was in effect saying, "Philip, I am the God of Abraham, Isaac, and Jacob. For the first time in his eternal history, God has skin on him. If you want to know what my Father looks like, then look at me."

God is a Spirit, and Spirit, while far more real than anything material, leaves human beings a little edgy. Most people feel uncomfortable with the idea that God the Spirit is quietly lurking around them. They want him to show up with enough skin on him to be touchable.

I came to show you how God looked when he became touchable. You have seen me. I am the invisible God, made seeable. I am the inaudible God, made hearable. I am the intangible God, made touchable. Tell others that you have touched me and, in so doing, you have seen and heard and touched the Father.

Prayer
Lord Jesus,
I have seen you.
It is enough for me.
God the Father is so splendidly
 revealed in you
 that I have no doubts whatever
 that God is just like you.
I have seen my Father clearly in his Son
 and cannot doubt that Christ and God are one.
Amen.

The Memory Helper

John 14:26
"But the Helper, the Holy Spirit, whom the Father will send in My name, He will teach you all things, and bring to your remembrance all that I said to you."

One of the blessed functions of the Holy Spirit is that he is committed to the work of helping people remember those places at which the glory of God touched their lives. God, the Holy Spirit, is the great memory jogger. Consider all of these places where God speaks of jogging your memory in the Bible. First of all, in Deuteronomy he used Moses to remind Israel to write the *Shema* on their houses and carry it in little pouches on their bodies. Why? He obviously did not want Israel to forget!

Moses said: "Hear, O Israel: The LORD our God, the LORD is one. Love the LORD your God with all your heart and with all your soul and with all your strength. These commandments that I give you today are to be upon your hearts. Impress them on your children. . . . *Be careful that you do not forget the LORD,* who brought you up out of Egypt, out of the land of slavery" (Deut. 6:4–9, 12, emphasis added).

Later when Israel crossed through the Jordan River, Joshua commanded twelve men of the tribes of Israel each to take up a stone and carry it out of the middle of the riverbed that God had dried up so they could cross. Joshua said: "Each of you is to take up a stone on his shoulder, according to the number of the tribes of the Israelites, to serve as a sign among you. In the future, when your children ask you, 'What do these stones mean?' tell them that the flow of the Jordan was cut off. . . . These stones are to be a *memorial* to the people of Israel forever" (Josh. 4:5b–7, emphasis added).

The *Seder* was to be such a memory jogger. When the son asked the father, concerning Passover, "How is this night different from all the rest?" the father would tell the family the old story of God's redemption so the land would never forget. Likewise, all Christians, through all ages, have been instructed to break the bread and drink the wine so that they would never forget my cross. On the night the meal was established, "This is my body given for you," I said, "do this *in remembrance of me*" (Luke 22:19, emphasis added).

Not only does God give us these rituals of remembrance, but his Spirit is there in each one of you to quicken your memory so that you never forget he is the Helper who will teach you all things *and bring to remembrance all that I have said.*

Prayer
Lord Jesus,
Lest I forget,
*   send your Helper to help me remember,*
*   I want to walk with you, Christ.*
You have forgiven and forgotten
*   all my sin.*
And I want to walk with you too, Holy Spirit.
Cause me to remember all of Christ's covenants
*   with me.*
I lift the cup, remembering I'm free,
*   and count it joy to own the memory.*
Amen.

The Nature of Peace

John 14:27
"Peace I leave with you; My peace I give to you; not as the world gives, do I give to you. Let not your heart be troubled, nor let it be fearful."

Peace soothes us with security. We cannot have peace while we are afraid. Fear steals peace as flood steals fire. If, for instance, you lie down tonight and sleep soundly, it will be because you believe that nothing will come upon you to destroy your security. If you feel that during the night your livelihood might be stolen by thieves, you will not sleep well. If your doctor has told you that you have a serious condition and that one night you will simply lie down never to wake again, you may stay awake all night just to make sure you don't die in your sleep.

Obviously these things that keep you awake all night fall under the category of future fear. It is those "not yet" anxieties that keep us from having present peace. I came to destroy this fear of the not-yet. When I saved you, I gave you a new kind and quality of life that is essentially unthreatenable. Nothing can happen to you to take you out of my hand (John 10:29). In fact, Paul reminds the church: "For I am convinced that neither death nor life, neither angels nor demons, neither the present nor the future, nor any powers, neither height nor depth, nor anything else in all creation, will be able to separate us from the love of God that is in Christ Jesus our Lord" (Rom. 8:38–39).

I have saved you with the guarantee that your future is indestructible. Nothing can hurt you terminally. Ultimately whatever goes wrong in the night is of no enduring consequence. No fiend can take your eternal life. No sudden stroke can slay you. You cannot suffer any evil that can ever threaten your peace. Not even death itself can separate us.

I have given you my peace. It became a part of your soul when I moved into your life. Nothing can take this peace from you, for there is nothing that can remove me from your life. I am the Prince of Peace. I am the eternal Indweller. I will never leave you nor forsake you (Heb. 13:5). You are as indestructible as God, and the peace you contain is as everlasting as myself.

Prayer
> *Lord Jesus,*
> *You have come and taken*
> *   up your very residence at the place*
> *   I feel fear first—*
> *   my heart.*
> *Live then within my insecurity,*
> *   make peace my meat and drink consistently.*
> *Amen.*

The Vine

John 15:1–5

"I am the true vine, and My Father is the vinedresser. Every branch in Me that does not bear fruit, He takes away; and every branch that bears fruit, He prunes it, that it may bear more fruit. You are already clean because of the word which I have spoken to you. Abide in me, and I in you. As the branch cannot bear fruit of itself, unless it abides in the vine, so neither can you, unless you abide in Me. I am the vine, you are the branches; he who abides in Me, and I in him, he bears much fruit; for apart from Me you can do nothing."

There are only two things grapevine branches must do to produce. First, they must yield last year's producing stems to the pruning knife. Second, they must abide in the vine. As long as the vine is alive and they will submit to the lopping off of their unproductive tendrils, they will know the joy of bearing fruit.

Pruning is mandatory. Those tendrils where last year's grapes hung, will never produce again. So they must be cut back to allow next year's vine to produce. Pruning is painful. But as the branch yields to that hurt, the possibility of fruit is born. It was for this reason that I said to my disciples, "You are already clean." Of course, I meant by this that they had already been pruned and were ready to bear fruit.

The pruning never stops. Those vines that are really productive bear fruit year after year. To be continually productive they must know the pain of being continually pruned. We shrink from the Father's knife. Old ideas, ungodly philosophies, new grudges, longings for power, the refusal to give up old platforms of honor gracefully: all of these things must be cut away. If we will not suffer them to die under the knife of God, then we will never know the joy that follows the pruning.

After the pruning, to be productive we must abide in the vine. The vine is the one vital link between the branch and the nutriments in the soil. Abiding implies your patient attachment to my life. The branches do not produce because they struggle trying to suck the elixir of life from the vine. Branches do not scheme or wrangle or beat the vine to get all the nutrients they might. These branches never sweat and strain in the struggle to produce. And when they have lived through an entire growing season of pruning, pain, and joy, the fruit always comes. What a blessed relationship belongs to all who settle into my sufficiency and know the joy of abiding.

Prayer
Lord Jesus,
I wait as branch to vine.
I abide, waiting for you to fill me
with all that makes it possible
for me to produce fruit
and return it to you as
an offering of love and trust.
What I produce I yield up not as mine.
What comes is born abiding in the vine.
Amen.

No Greater Love

John 15:13
"Greater love has no one than this, that one lay down his life for his friends."

Hear a tale of a mother and her son. The son in his fifteenth year could live no longer. His kidneys would no longer sustain his life. The dialysis machines were of no consequence. The boy was jaundiced and dying. His mother, in a last attempt to save his life, went to the hospital with him. On twin gurneys, mother and son lay side by side beneath bright floodlights. Two surgeons took knives and cut the unscarred bodies of both the mother and her son.

Both doctors exchanged the organs. Bit by bit the cadre of nurses began to breathe easier. The sleeping mother and son were breathing easily now. Both of their life signs were strong. The operation was proclaimed a success!

The interns and nurses broke into applause. A miracle had occurred. A mother, who loved her son too much to let him die, had risked dying herself that he might live. If you could see them both today at the beach that they love, they walk happily along in the sun and the surf, thrilled at the life they both enjoy. Who can say which of them is happier? The scars of their giving and receiving are both very obvious, running across both of their bodies.

The savior and the saved they are—the giver and the receiver of life. Did the mother love? Yes indeed. When the son wakes every morning, he calls my holy name in prayer. Then he thanks my Father for the scars I wear in my body that provided him eternal life. And then he thanks my Father for the scars his mother wears in her body for him, providing him temporal life. These double scars hold a spiritual fascination from which he never wishes to be set free.

I have scars that I now wear eternally for you. They are the rich emblems of my love. This love makes cynics yearn for such meaning.

On that day I took your sins, your clothes, your selfish lifestyle, all that was unlovely and uncommendable about you. I mounted the hill. I died for you. The scars of your redemption shall mark me through eternity. And someday we shall walk the shoals of the everlasting, crystal sea. We shall laugh over what I have given and what you have received. Then you will know that there is no greater gift than this, that a man lay down his life for his friend.

Prayer
Lord Jesus,
I know I've never been loved like this before.
I know that I never shall be again.
I pray that I will wake to praise your scars with every sunrise.
You gave the greatest gift to me that can be given.
I weep to think of all that it has cost
*   to buy my soul on such a rugged cross.*
Amen.

Friends

John 15:15

"No longer do I call you slaves, for the slave does not know what his master is doing; but I have called you friends, for all things that I have heard from My Father I have made known to you."

Friend is a noble word. It knows no condescension or triumph. Friends and peers are equals. One does not own the other. One will not coerce the other. Each sets the other free. Each respects the other. Each is on the same footing. Neither resents the age, the income, or the intelligence of the other. They are simply friends.

My disciples could not grasp the grandeur of the word *friend* on the evening of my glorification. After my resurrection, when there was no longer any doubt at all that I was the Son of God, the notion was so exalted as to be nearly overwhelming for them. But the day I first called my disciples friends, I pointed out to them the difference between a slave and a friend. Slaves are not conversation mates with their owners. Slaves never know what their masters are doing. Masters never feel a need to tell the slaves their business, for masters never see slaves as people with a right to know their business. If the notion of our friendship overwhelmed them, it was because they were so one-sided in their consideration of some condescension on my part. They knew they wanted to be friends with me, but couldn't fathom that I wanted to be friends with them. But this friendship was the longing of my heart too.

I want to be your Friend too. Do you sense the glory of it? I have made you a partner in all the business I have on this earth. I have given you a calling, and I have let you know what I want with you. I will go on doing this for the rest of your life. We can sit and talk anytime you want. In fact, the more often we talk, the better for me and the better for you.

Further, any master would resent it if his slave went around telling people that his master and owner was secretly his friend. Please, I beg you, publicize our friendship in the streets. Wake the town and tell the people! Tell them how close we are. Tell them how I long for you to come into my closet of prayer. Tell them that I ache with joy when we are together and I feel your love for me. Tell them that you love me so much that I am your very best Friend and there is absolutely nothing I wouldn't do for you.

We're friends. Friends forever. There's nothing you can't ask of me. Is there anything I can't ask of you?

Prayer
Lord Jesus,
All I wanted was to serve you,
*   but you have bought me*
*   to set me free*
*   to make me your friend.*
We shall be friends as friends should live and be—
*   forever friends, through all eternity.*
Amen.

The Helper

John 16:7
> *"But I tell you the truth, it is to your advantage that I go away; for if I do not go away, the Helper shall not come to you; but if I go, I will send Him to you."*

When I was on Earth, the Holy Spirit within me was localized to that specific geographical location where I was. If I was with believers in Capernaum, I could not, at the same time, be with those in Jerusalem. But once I had bodily left Earth and my Spirit had returned without me, I could then be with believers everywhere around the world and all at once. So it was necessary that I end my earthly existence and return to heaven to allow the omnipresent Spirit to come back.

Do not believe that because I have returned to heaven, there has been a shortage of those miracles of power that the Spirit performs. It is not so. The miracles I performed were many, but not as many as all the glorious things the Spirit has accomplished in my disciples throughout the world. The coming of the Spirit was a wonderful fulfillment of all I had promised.

The disciples had done many wonderful things while I walked physically with them. They healed and cast out demons (Luke 10). But to see what yieldedness could really do, you have to look at all they achieved when the Spirit moved upon the church in the Book of Acts. In the wake of the Spirit's power, the church came alive with signs and wonders.

Until I return, behold all that the Helper is doing. It was necessary that I go away and that the Helper come. Even now, he surrounds the globe with wind and fire. The emphasis of the Spirit is that the Kingdom will always grow until I come again to claim my church. This is an advance whose global scope those early Christians never imagined. They never dreamed that their witness and miracles would in time give rise to a world where there are literally thousands of Christian universities and seminaries. Even though they saw more than three thousand saved at the first visitation of the Spirit, they could not conceive that the current church would be making thousands of converts every day.

The Helper is here—my Spirit doing my work!

Prayer
> *Lord Jesus,*
> *The old hymn speaks my adoration:*
> *I want the Holy Spirit to "breathe on me,"*
>   *to "fill me with life anew,*
>   *that I may love what thou wouldst love,*
>   *and do what Thou wouldst do."*
> *For I must turn, dear Helper, unto you*
>   *to daily know what I must do.*
> *Amen.*

The Role of the Spirit

John 16:13–15

"But when He, the Spirit of truth, comes, He will guide you into all the truth; for He will not speak on His own initiative, but whatever He hears, He will speak; and He will disclose to you what is to come. He shall glorify Me; for he shall take of Mine, and shall disclose it to you. All things that the Father has are Mine; therefore I said, that He takes of Mine, and will disclose it to you."

What is the role of the Holy Spirit? It is summed up in these four words: "He shall glorify me!" Have you ever heard someone say, "I just had this wonderful revelation from the Holy Spirit, and I feel all bubbly inside. I was slain in grace just after I talked in the unknown tongue. I hope I get filled again and again because it feels so wonderful"? Receive all such messages in joy, but remember that the Holy Spirit exists primarily to glorify me. Not every emotional experience in church has come from the Spirit. Many these days are prone to view the blessed Spirit as little more than the Mr. Fun-and-Tears person of the Trinity.

There is certainly nothing wrong with emotion in religion. In fact, an emotionless religion is one that has not touched God. The Spirit's fullness should bring you to that altar of obedient joy that compels you to emote. But the Spirit was not given to supply emotion for the church. He came to glorify me, not to change your "Hallelujahs!" into "Wows!" All who drive merely for some ecstatic and oozy emotion in the name of the Spirit blaspheme his noble purpose.

Emotion is only valid in the Christian's life when it is the by-product of some overwhelming *insight* or *encounter*. Discovering new truth produces laughter, tears, or even rapture. Once Augustine heard a child's voice saying in imperative Latin *tole, lege*, "take up and read." And so he did. Placing his finger at random in the Book of Romans he read: "Let us behave decently, as in the daytime, not in orgies and drunkenness, not in sexual immorality and debauchery, not in dissension and jealousy. Rather, clothe yourselves with the Lord Jesus Christ, and do not think about how to gratify the desires of the sinful nature" (Rom. 13:13–14). With this insight, Augustine's emotion welled up and spilled over the brim of his soul to the profit of my church.

The Spirit drives the emotion of the soul. If in your insight I have been glorified, the experience is from the Spirit. Seek out the Spirit, the fountain of real joy. Under his transport, glorify me.

Prayer
Lord Jesus,
Send your Spirit upon me,
  for I want to glorify your name
  with such power
  that heaven and earth agree:
The Holy Spirit is that fluid fire
  that crowns believers with a Christ-desire.
Amen.

Asking the Extravagant

John 16:23–24

"And in that day you will ask Me no question. Truly, truly, I say to you, if you shall ask the Father for anything, He will give it to you in My name. Until now you have asked for nothing in My name; ask, and you will receive, that your joy may be made full."

The angels are amazed that heaven is a vault of promises that Christians rarely draw upon. God is rich beyond measure. He can afford so much more than Christians ask for. But herein lies a conundrum. Either Christians ask for too little with too little faith, or they ask for so much that, if it were given to them, they would no longer need God. How, then, should you ask?

It would seem that most Christians really do not believe in asking for anything more than they can provide for themselves. Christians pray in these kinds of words: "Lord, I pray that you will make Aunt Mary well." However, they only pray this if she has no really serious ailment. If she *is very sick* they pray, "Make Aunt Mary well, *if it is your will,* O God!" This is their faithless generosity that gives God a chance to save his dignity when Aunt Mary dies, as they secretly expect her to.

Most Christians never use the phrase "If it is your will" unless they are pretty sure they are not about to get the prayer answered the way they would really like. "If it is your will" is a nice way to get God off the hook when real prayer has been abandoned as futile.

Please, never pray "If it is your will" just to protect God. He really doesn't need you to cover for him. Just ask him for what you want in my name. If it is not good for you, you will not get it. If it is, you will.

God is not as concerned about granting your indulgences as you are in being indulged. Do you see why the "name-it-and-claim-it" prayer movement is so odious to me? These prayers rarely see God as a responsible Father. Fathers do not allow their children to "claim" all they "name." Good fathers know this is the way to build egocentric children whose swaggering arrogance will ultimately destroy them.

He answers those prayers which express the desires of the heart. The psalmist has well said, "Trust in the LORD and do good; . . . Delight yourself in the LORD and he will give you the desires of your heart" (Ps. 37:3–4). It is true. But ask God extravagantly for whatever you want. If you want only material things you will baffle the angels, who will wonder why you are only asking for "stuff" when you ought to be desiring God himself.

Prayer
Lord Jesus,
I want more of you.
Guard my heart against wanting
  all those things that would stand between us
  and hide you from my need.
Lord, will you give me anything I say?
  Good! Hide yourself within my heart today.
Amen.

Facing Loneliness

John 16:32–33

"Behold, an hour is coming, and has already come, for you to be scattered, each to his own home, and to leave Me alone; and yet I am not alone, because the Father is with Me. These things I have spoken to you, that in Me you may have peace. In the world you have tribulation, but take courage; I have overcome the world."

Shall I tell you what is one of the heaviest pains that can be borne? It is friendlessness. When you must endure life with no counsel, you have taken up the heaviest work there is. I told my disciples the night before it happened that they would flee to their own homes and abandon me to the mob and the executioners. I wanted them to know that they would do it, so that afterward they would not overincriminate themselves. I wanted them to see their betrayals as something that I expected. Then following my death, I could call them together without their being driven away from me by the guilt of their unconfessed abandonment.

So from Gethsemane on, my only companion was often my Father. On the *Via Dolorosa* it looked like I was alone, but I was not. Betrayed by all, I never ceased to feel his unforsaking faithfulness. He was there. When they cut my back to ribbons, my Father stood there, looking on and weeping. When they put a reed in my hand and mocked me and cuffed me, heaven shuddered. When they drove the nails in white, hot pain through my wrist, my steadfast Father stooped unseen to kiss the wounds. And when the rain began, it was his tears that cooled the fiery pain in my sagging, suffocating form.

There is a saying that given a good friend, a man can put up with a world of hate. Given a weeping and loving Father, I withstood everything. All through that long day of dying, I kept hearing my Father say, "This is my beloved Son, in whom I am well pleased."

Do you know him? Are you walking through pain even as you read this? Have you turned and looked for him through your dark circumstances? Look! He is there. His hand even now dresses your wounds. He is there absorbing your fear. Is there no friend with you? Breathe the word *Father*, and you may be sure that even though he is unseen, you are standing in the very middle of his embrace.

> *Prayer*
> Lord Jesus,
> Sometimes I wish the eyes of my heart
>   were fitted with such spectacles
>   that they could see for ten seconds the invisible.
> I know what they would see.
> They would see my Father God,
>   standing, reaching in the lonely night,
>   embracing me with arms of holy light.
> Amen.

They Have Kept Thy Word

John 17:4–6

"I glorified Thee on the earth, having accomplished the work which Thou hast given Me to do. And now, glorify Thou Me together with Thyself, Father, with the glory which I had with Thee before the world was. I manifested Thy name to the men whom Thou gavest Me out of the world; Thine they were, and Thou gavest them to Me, and they have kept Thy word."

This was my pleasurable word about my disciples at the hour of my death: they had kept my word. At the hour of one's death, nothing can be said that is more important than the issue of integrity. I loved my twelve men. Except for Judas, they had kept my word.

Why was this important? Because the future leadership and instruction of the church would be founded upon their integrity. All that later generations would need to see as the central repository of truth, my disciples kept. To be sure, the disciples were not as stalwart in the face of fear as I had hoped they might be. In fact, they all turned and fled in my hour of greatest need. But as for the truth that I had spent three years teaching them—that was unshakably secure.

As we basked in the camaraderie of our good times, it was often hard to tell if they were getting the message. When you hike both lonely trails and heavy trafficked roads for three years, you talk about many things. I sensed that they missed their families and hometown friends. There were the pressures of public scrutiny that came on the whole group when I fell under excessive criticisms. There were many private agendas that some of the disciples had—take Simon the Zealot, for instance. Matthew was also criticized by the Pharisees for trying to appear to be a religious man when "he was nothing but a Roman employee—a tax agent!" Those kinds of criticism took special understanding. And when there was a shortfall in the group purse, which the recluse Judas kept, we talked about the fiscal needs of our itinerant evangelism. All in all, I wondered if any of my teaching was sinking in. Where would their faith be when I was back in heaven? Would they retain it all when I left them in charge of the church? They must remain faithful.

But the necessity of their faithfulness was really no different from what the church would have to own in every age. Every generation of the church has been only one generation away from extinction. Unless my first disciples remained faithful about what they knew, the faith would not have survived the first century. But unless you are now faithful about what you know, it will not survive the twenty-first.

> *Prayer*
> *Lord Jesus,*
> *I know you only because*
>   *those disciples of yours passed down the truth*
>   *to my generation.*
> *Help me to see my own place in this*
>   *unfolding chain of witnesses.*
> *Make me for heaven's truth a grand trustee,*
>   *to pass along what others gave to me.*
> *Amen.*

Oneness: The Longing in the Heart of the Father

John 17:20–22

"I do not ask in behalf of these alone, but for those also who believe in Me through their word; that they may all be one; even as Thou, Father, art in Me, and I in Thee, that they also may be in Us; that the world may believe that Thou didst send Me. And the glory which Thou hast given Me I have given to them; that they may be one, just as We are one."

There is a longing in the heart of God that all my followers know the same kind of unity that he and I experience. A certain father had two sons who had not gotten along together in years. They quarreled often. Each resented the other for the most petty reasons. They were each jealous of any affection their father showed to the other. Every family reunion erupted in dissension. On one occasion they both asked, "Dad, we love you. We want to give you a gift. What would you like?"

"Ah," said the old man as tears brimmed up in his eyes, "My sons, there is one gift that if you could give me, would delight me as nothing else ever has!"

"Yes, yes," they eagerly answered. "Yes, Father, what is it?"

"I want you two boys to love each other!"

My Father has really one supreme gift he earnestly desires for his church: he wants churches and church members to love each other. He wants them to quit comparing their budgets and competing with their rate of church growth. Believers struggle over the most carnal of competitions. Certain churches brag on having the biggest church. Others boast they have the biggest budget. Still others believe they have the best organ or the biggest choir.

My Father doesn't want liturgists to feel superior because they think structured worship is more holy than casual worship. He doesn't want those who baptize in one way to feel they are doctrinally superior to those who baptize in some other way. He doesn't want rich churches to snub poor churches or poor churches to convince themselves that their poverty makes them more godly.

Can you hear heaven crying? All eternity is longing for God's church to be one. Yield to those tears.

Prayer
Lord Jesus,
I want to love you and obey you.
I want to please you.
I will not pretend to have done either
while I reserve a little walled cloister of prejudice
toward those who love you and obey you
in ways that are different from my own.
I pledge myself to seek for one accord
and name as friend all those who call you Lord.
Amen.

You Can Count on Me . . . Sorta

Mark 14:27–31

And Jesus said to them, "You will all fall away, because it is written, 'I WILL STRIKE DOWN THE SHEPHERD, AND THE SHEEP SHALL BE SCATTERED' [Zech. 13:7]. But after I have been raised, I will go before you to Galilee." But Peter said to Him, "Even though all may fall away, yet I will not." And Jesus said to him, "Truly I say to you, that you yourself this very night, before a cock crows twice, shall three times deny Me." But Peter kept saying insistently, "Even if I have to die with You, I will not deny You!" And they all were saying the same thing, too.

Peter was a man who never bridged very well between his intentions and his capabilities. What about you and your promises? I want you to be able to express to me in prayer the kind of life you'd like to live for me. Write on the tablets of your heart all you would like to do for me. Now think through those times you were not able to carry out your commitments. Think of how frequently you have promised me things and not been able to deliver. Did you, at such moments, hear the crowing of a cock? You must know something of Peter's dilemma.

I encourage you to a life of honest insecurity rather than insecure honesty. I have wanted my disciples in every century to be tentative in this matter of overstating their capabilities. I'd much rather my disciples be afraid they can't hold out than to make grandiose promises they break.

Such joy comes from hearing a cock crow in the full knowledge that they were true to what they feared they never could accomplish. There is nothing more pleasant than to realize that you did better than you thought you could. God is often able, through honest weakness, to do more than the weak can imagine. And once they achieve their promises, their step is a little more brisk. Their pace is a little more confident. Their smiles are a little brighter.

But best of all, they remain a little wiser. They know that promises can't be made in big chunks. They have to be done with manageable bits of bravado. Great stands are usually achieved in small spurts of courage. Be fearful as you promise. Then when the cock crows, you will celebrate our love.

Prayer
Lord Jesus,
I want to stay with you
    to prison and to death.
But would it be okay if I promise "to prison"
    on Thursday
    and "to death" on Friday?
That way I'll stand a better chance
    of doing them both within the same week.
If it comes down to it,
    before I die for you so unrehearsed,
    I'd better try just living for you first.
Amen.

The Cup

Matthew 26:36–39

Then Jesus came with them to a place called Gethsemane, and said to His disciples, "Sit here while I go over there and pray." And He took with Him Peter and the two sons of Zebedee, and began to be grieved and distressed. Then He said to them, " My soul is deeply grieved, to the point of death; remain here and keep watch with Me." And He went a little beyond them, and fell on His face and prayed, saying, "My Father, if it is possible, let this cup pass from Me; yet not as I will, but as Thou wilt."

I knew even as I knelt to pray for strength that Judas was on the way to the garden with the soldiers. The ordeal was, at long last, at hand. I had no intention of backing out, but my humanity shrank before all that was about to transpire. Thus I pled with God for another set of alternatives: "If there is any other way than the way of the cross, Father, I would like to go that way."

My heart was troubled even unto death.

But there was such longing in my question: "If it be possible . . ." Gethsemane was a meeting of longings. I reached up to my Father in utter need, and he reached down to me in utter assurance. I would not bear the pain alone.

The same cleavage of soul was Abraham's when he was asked by God to give his son as a sacrifice on Mt. Moriah. Can you see the old man and his son? They start off with the wood toward the mountain. The old patriarch and his son come at last to the place of the offering. Abraham took the wood for the burnt offering and placed it on his son Isaac. He himself carried the fire and the knife. As the two of them went on together, Isaac spoke up and said to the old one, "Father?"

"Yes, my son?" Abraham replied.

"The fire and wood are here, but where is the lamb for the burnt offering?"

Abraham answered, "God Himself will provide the lamb" (from Gen. 22:6–8).

In this wonderful story, when the dying time came, there was a ram caught in the thicket. Thus the son did not have to die.

In my mind I pled, "Let there be a ram in the thicket . . . please, Father."

But my Father only drew close. We wept. Isaac's life had been spared. Mine would be spent. There was no ram trapped in the thickets of Gethsemane. The cross loomed large and dark. Its shadow of horror fell over the olive trees. Heaven wept and earth agreed.

Prayer
   Lord Jesus,
     What you gave up for me
      in that dark garden
      gave me the right to live.
   I glorify your name.
     For never shall I understand the cup
      that emptied you to fill my future up.
   Amen.

One Hour

Matthew 26:40–46

And He came to the disciples and found them sleeping, and said to Peter, "So, you men could not keep watch with Me for one hour? Keep watching and praying, that you may not enter into temptation; the spirit is willing, but the flesh is weak." He went away again a second time and prayed, saying, "My Father, if this cannot pass away unless I drink it, Thy will be done." And again He came and found them sleeping, for their eyes were heavy. And he left them again, and went away and prayed a third time, saying the same thing once more. Then He came to the disciples, and said to them, "Are you still sleeping and taking your rest? Behold, the hour is at hand and the Son of Man is being betrayed into the hands of sinners. Arise, let us be going; behold, the one who betrays Me is at hand!"

My need in Gethsemane was companionship. My friends slept while I agonized. Please keep in mind that God never ceases to care about his hurting world. I learned in Gethsemane what you may also have observed: it is sometimes hard to stay awake when other people are hurting. Even as you read this, God is reaching to those of his children who are starving around the world. Even now there is a mother in tears for the child she cannot save.

It is sometimes hard to stay awake through other people's agony. Isn't it glorious that my Father never sleeps while anyone hurts? He has been in touch with human agony through every second of the whole of human history. I beg you to remember that God has never left Gethsemane since Adam left the garden. Night after night he watches over Earth's hurting children. They are not his children in the same sense that I am his Son. Still, not one of them has ever died without his reaching toward them. "Are not two sparrows sold for a penny? Yet not one of them will fall to the ground apart from the will of your Father. And even the very hairs of your head are all numbered. So don't be afraid; you are worth more than many sparrows" (Matt. 10:29–31). Each human being receives his worth of soul in being made and loved by God.

Will you not watch one hour with him? Will you not enter into prayer with God about the needs of a dying planet? Just as I died in pain that Friday long ago, millions more die every day. They are grieved. They are frightened. Many die praying, "God, let this cup pass from me if it be possible." There are fields of new brokenness and grief with every sunrise.

God weeps. Will you tell these sufferers you pass that they have a Father? Will you become a nightly watcher in Gethsemane? Will you watch one hour with me?

Prayer
Lord Jesus,
So many are called and so few are chosen,
Gethsemane knows no geography;
it is worldwide.
Someone dies nightly,
never knowing how to say "Father."
Make me a wakeful witness to that plea—
a nightly watcher in Gethsemane.
Amen.

The Kiss

Mark 14:44–45

Now he who was betraying Him had given them a signal, saying, "Whomever I shall kiss, He is the one; seize Him, and lead Him away under guard." And after coming, he immediately went to Him, saying "Rabbi!" and kissed Him.

If you would hide some treachery, hide it in a sign of peace. Such a sign was the kiss of Judas.

During those three years that I traveled with my disciples, there were countless instances of parting and reunion. Sometimes the men would go home to see their families for a few days and then come back. We kissed, always glad to see each other. Sometimes they only left me to go into town and buy groceries, and when they came back we acknowledged each other with a kiss. Sometimes there were weddings or funerals or reunions to which they went: in all these cases our manner of parting and greeting was the same as it was between all close friends in those days. The kiss was the way people greeted. A kiss was what the handshake became in later ages.

But Judas hid hate in his sign of love. There was a cobra in his bouquet, a needle in his balm, a dagger in his embrace. What sin resides in treachery! It devours the loaf of love like canker worms. It leaves the outside clean, the inside vile. It is like a whitewashed tomb, outwardly beautiful and garnished with flowers and inwardly full of corruption.

Never face a needy friend with pretense in your love. Do not kiss your way into Gethsemanes if it is your intent to kill. For there is no more priceless gift than love. To sin against it marks you as unlike God.

What does Gethsemane look like in the theater of our relationships?

A father who brings his child a scolding when he should have offered a caress has given a Gethsemane. A boss who vents his frustration upon an undeserving employee is delivering Gethsemane. A wife whose bruised needs are met by an unfeeling husband understands betrayal. Gethsemane is the province of bitter and betraying kisses.

If betrayal has happened to you, hang on to the sensation—not so you can rehearse your bitterness, but so you will never forget the sting of treachery. I will never forget the warm, moist fire in Judas's kiss. It burned like a hot iron; it seared my soul. Tears shattered my consciousness. That kiss was like the fang marks of a snake hidden deep within his soul. It burned my cheek, and the burning continued through the night. Its searing betrayal still tingled while I stood before Pilate and Antipas. When the ripping flog fell on my back, I felt again the hot, dead, bitter, killing kiss of Judas. Ask my Father to let you live in such a way that what you are and what you appear to be are the same thing.

Prayer
Lord Jesus,
I want to be the actual friend
of all of those who call me friend.
I want to meet with love
all those who need my love.
I want to live in such simplicity
that what I am is what I seem to be.
Amen.

An Ear in the Way of Evil

Luke 22:48–51

But Jesus said to him, "Judas, are you betraying the Son of Man with a kiss?" And when those who were around Him saw what was going to happen, they said, "Lord, shall we strike with the sword?" And a certain one of them struck the slave of the high priest and cut off his right ear. But Jesus answered and said, "Stop! No more of this!" And He touched his ear and healed him.

The healed ear was but a tiny miracle in the path of cosmic wrong. Still, a man was healed. The tiny miracle did not stop the machinery of crucifixion, but it marked the presence of good in evil circumstances. On that particular Thursday hate was rolling, and it takes a great deal of love to stop its march. Naturally my disciples wanted to defend me. But their bizarre attempt to stop the marauding host by ear chopping had to be corrected.

But Malchus, the man who lost his ear, clearly exhibited God's power. To see him hopping around Gethsemane on one foot, holding the bloody side of his head, was both touching and amusing. After I replaced his ear, he was amazed. So were the soldiers. You would have thought they would back off and go away, completely awed over the miracle. But nothing was to stop the political machinery that evening.

Can you imagine the bizarre story Malchus told his friends and acquaintances for the next few years? Nobody could bring up the story of my judgment without Malchus feeling the side of his head and wondering at this special story—that little bit of grace—tucked into a night of horror and a day of dying.

But in a way, is Malchus any different from you? What were you doing when the night came for you to receive Christ? Did you not get a sense that your small necessity of grace was little in comparison to the magnificence of redemption? Never feel that your hour of need was so plain as not to cause any stir in heaven. The truth is that every act of grace sets heaven to rejoicing. And Malchus made his small entrance into Scripture to let the world know that healing and salvation is available to all at the moment of their need, regardless of surrounding circumstance.

There were mighty things happening in the world that night. Satan and his demons gathered at my trial in hellish laughter. They left Pilate's judgment hall only to reassemble at my cross. But consider Malchus. In the middle of redemption's grand pageant, he met the power of God in a very special way. Earless in Gethsemane, Malchus found the cosmic God personal enough to care.

Prayer
Lord Jesus,
There is in my small testimony
nothing very universal.
Nor can I say that my experience of grace
would hold the world in thrall.
But my significance must cheer
the dying God who saved a servant's ear.
Amen.

Naked Indecision

Mark 14:48–52

And Jesus answered and said to them, "Have you come out with swords and clubs to arrest Me, as against a robber? Every day I was with you in the temple teaching, and you did not seize Me; but this has happened that the Scriptures might be fulfilled." And they all left Him and fled. And a certain young man was following Him, wearing nothing but a linen sheet over his naked body; and they seized him. But he left the linen sheet behind, and escaped naked.

Even without Judas, there were twelve in the garden that night. John Mark was the extra man. He was reluctant to name himself in his own gospel, going home naked as he did. John Mark always tried to be a little braver than he really was. He was a very idealistic teenager. Steadfast commitment is a little harder to come by when you are young. You may remember that Paul later became discouraged with Mark because Mark left him and Barnabas on their first missionary journey (Acts 13:13). Mark, even then, was still not quite mature enough to handle the difficulties of missionary work.

That night in Gethsemane he was determined to take a stand on my behalf. If it had not been for the utter gravity of the evening, his stand might have appeared a little comical. He was from a better known Jewish family with a house large enough to have an upper room where we could have the Last Supper. He was definitely "upper crust." He had his image to think about. But he knew the danger I was exposed to. There was an edgy nervousness about the evening that he must have read even before he decided to go all the way to Gethsemane with us. He was lightly dressed and when the soldiers came, they made one grab at him as he hurried into the darkness. When they grabbed at him, all they got was his toga. Slipping out of that sheet, he quickly melted into the shadows and escaped naked.

Mark was not the first to take a stand and back down from it. But his nakedness is not just literal. It is, rather, symbolic. Most indecision has a way of making you feel as if you're undressed at a moment when you wish you were in full armor.

The worst part of his evening was likely when he arrived home. The explaining he must have had to do! Sheets were neither plentiful nor cheap in that day. All cloth was a high cost item. But even if his mother didn't mind the loss, she must have probed to discover what he was doing wandering naked in the streets.

The danger of backing down from a strong and open witness is always an embarrassment. Once we have marched off to die, to show back up alive makes us wish we were dead. Keep your commitments to yourself until you're reasonably sure that you can follow through with them. Be careful of those Gethsemanes you swore you'd commit to. Wear more than a sheet. Take stands that you can live out.

Prayer
Lord Jesus,
Help me to pick from among a wide list of causes
some that really make a difference.
I want to be sure
I do not want to run cowardly
from some abandoned Gethsemane.
Amen.

Self-Disappointment

Luke 22:55–62

And after they had kindled a fire in the middle of the courtyard and had sat down together, Peter was sitting among them. And a certain servant-girl, seeing him as he sat in the firelight, and looking intently at him, said, "This man was with Him too." But he denied it, saying, "Woman, I do not know Him." And a little later, another saw him and said, "You are one of them too!" But Peter said, "Man, I am not!" And after about an hour had passed, another man began to insist, saying, "Certainly this man also was with Him, for he is a Galilean too."

But Peter said, "Man, I do not know what you are talking about." And immediately, while he was still speaking, a cock crowed. And the Lord turned and looked at Peter. And Peter remembered the word of the Lord, how He had told him, "Before a cock crows today, you will deny Me three times." And he went out and wept bitterly.

Broken resolve is the most disappointing of virtues. Therefore, Peter wept bitterly. The sense of failure never left Peter. Years later Peter more honestly recounted his third denial: "After a little while, those standing near said to Peter, 'Surely you are one of them, for you are a Galilean.' He began to call down curses on himself, and he swore to them, 'I don't know this man you're talking about'" (Mark 14:70–71).

The white-hot profanity of his denial remained vivid in his broken remembrance some twenty-odd years later. Why was he so broken? Because he considered me the finest friend he had ever had.

He was disappointed in himself. He wept. He dreamed himself so much more courageous than he turned out to be. How it hurts to fall short of long-held plans we thought were so unimpeachable. The apostle Paul spoke of this self-disappointment in Romans: "I do not understand what I do. For what I want to do I do not do, but what I hate I do. And if I do what I do not want to do, I agree that the law is good. As it is, it is no longer I myself who do it, but it is sin living in me" (Rom. 7:15–17).

Truly it was sin in Peter that led him to do what he had promised he would never do. What sin? The sin of presumption. He had presumed he would not betray me. Holy fear is a sweeter virtue than arrogant presumption. Fear can be a good counselor, teaching us to weld our needy selves to the Father's sufficiency. When we feel we cannot achieve, God gets ready to surprise us with victory. It is better to live in fear and seek God's power than to walk in presumption, losing everything.

Prayer
Lord Jesus,
I'm afraid to promise you what terrifies my soul.
To promise you anything
   will demand that I must face
    the fact that I have never accomplished
   many of my own fickle intentions.
Here is your servant weak in all his ways.
Enable him to stand on shaky days.
Amen.

Are You the Christ?

Luke 22:66–71

And when it was day, the Council of elders of the people assembled, both chief priests and scribes, and they led Him away to their council chamber, saying, "If You are the Christ, tell us." But He said to them, "If I tell you, you will not believe; and if I ask a question, you will not answer. But from now on THE SON OF MAN WILL BE SEATED AT THE RIGHT HAND *[Ps. 110:1] of the power of God."*

And they all said, "Are You the Son of God, then?" And He said to them, "Yes, I am." And they said, "What further need do we have of testimony? For we have heard it ourselves from His own mouth."

There is but one critical question in all of this world. Are you the Christ? My accusers had the critical question, but not the critical answer. They answered, "See, Jesus, from your own mouth you convince us that you are a lunatic!"

Honesty must drive the answer clearly to one of these two poles. You cannot say to me, "Jesus, I believe you are partly lunatic and partly Savior. You are sorta the Son of God."

Does it strike you as odd that those who wanted to crucify me had no trouble arriving at the firm decision that I was not the Son of God? But nowadays the scholars who want to convince others that they believe speak of me only as "sorta" saving. These scholars would probably say candidly that they believe I am the Son of God, but they have not the slightest confidence that I was born of a virgin or risen from the dead. Further, they say that my disciples loved me so much that when they "wrote me up" in the Gospels, they accorded to me a lot of miracles that I never really did.

Most of these so-called scholars would say that it is good to believe in Jesus because faith is good. But what is good about a faith in an uncertain Savior whose origin and destiny are uncertain? What is good about a Savior whose deluded disciples said he did more than he actually did? To most of these scholars I remain a "sorta" Savior.

Give me either open enemies or firm friends. I want those who say, "Yes, I believe." But spare me those who dissect the miracles in some bogus attempt to tell which miracles are more likely to have happened and which are less.

Those in the first century who said I was a lunatic were declarative enemies. Anyone can respect their reluctance to choose whoever they want for a messiah. But those who cut the heart out of faith and then order it to continue beating are false. The cross that I endured is raised anew in every doubting decade of the human story.

Prayer
Lord Jesus,
Help those who cry that you are Christ
but qualify your majesty with doubt and unbelief
to understand they injure and destroy.
For those who need you need to know that you're
that certain Lord who makes the doubting sure.
Amen.

Things You Can't Take Back

Matthew 27:3–10

Then when Judas, who had betrayed Him, saw that He had been condemned, he felt remorse and returned the thirty pieces of silver to the chief priests and elders, saying, "I have sinned by betraying innocent blood." But they said, "What is that to us? See to that yourself!" And he threw the pieces of silver into the sanctuary and departed; and he went away and hanged himself.

And the chief priests took the pieces of silver and said, "It is not lawful to put them into the temple treasury, since it is the price of blood." And they counseled together and with the money bought the Potter's Field as a burial place for strangers. For this reason that field has been called the Field of Blood to this day. Then that which was spoken through Jeremiah the prophet was fulfilled, saying, "AND THEY TOOK THE THIRTY PIECES OF SILVER, THE PRICE OF THE ONE WHOSE PRICE HAD BEEN SET by the sons of Israel; AND THEY GAVE THEM FOR THE POTTER'S FIELD, AS THE LORD DIRECTED ME."

Remorse and repentance are two different things. Repentance is sorrow toward God. But remorse is sorrow for the self. Judas readily admitted that he had sinned in betraying me. He even took back the money, trying to "undo" the deal. But it was of no use. You can't fall down before your own self-pity and undo much of the harm that you do in life. Wrong never gets itself righted until the sinner sees that all sin is inevitably against God.

David had to learn what many people never seem to learn. Remorse may only be our attempt to pay for our own sins by feeling badly about them. Remorse may be only a kind of homemade atonement. Many people think that if they feel badly enough, long enough, about some sin, they will in some way pay for that sin without the ugly necessity of coming clean before God.

> Have mercy on me, O God, according to your unfailing love;
> according to your great compassion
>   blot out my transgressions.
> Wash away all my iniquity
>   and cleanse me from my sin. (Ps. 51:1–2)

Judas hanged himself because he felt bad for all the weaknesses he found within himself. Would it not have been wonderful if Judas had been able to focus on what he had done to me? If he had been able to say to God, "Against you and you only have I sinned" (Ps. 51:4), he would have been captured by the Almighty love that would have washed betrayal from his life by a tidal flood of grace. Alas, he only felt guilt. And guilt alone always stops short of grace.

Prayer
Lord Jesus,
Help me to learn that feeling bad
*   is never a substitute for godly brokenness.*
I need your tidal washing to be cleansed.
Against you and you only have I sinned.
Amen.

Modeling a Life Purpose

John 18:36–37

Jesus answered, "My kingdom is not of this world. If My kingdom were of this world, then My servants would be fighting, that I might not be delivered up to the Jews; but as it is, My kingdom is not of this realm." Pilate therefore said to Him, "So You are a king?" Jesus answered, "You say correctly that I am a king. For this I have been born, and for this I have come into the world, to bear witness to the truth. Everyone who is of the truth hears My voice."

There is a frequent cry in the counseling room that cannot be ignored. One of the first major life questions after "Who am I?" is "Why was I ever born?" Those who know the answer to the first question usually know the answer to the second. At my trial, it was clear that I knew the answer to both.

I spoke in certainty to Pilate that night. I knew who I was and why I had been born. It was unnerving for him to see me standing arraigned and on trial, yet far more confident than he himself was. In my humanity I shrank from Friday's duty, but I had no doubt about what I was about to do or why I was doing it.

Next to salvation, it is my Father's clear purpose to give to every person a firm knowledge of who he is and why he has been born. Every Christian who seeks me will feel this sense of compulsion. Paul, the apostle, believed that God had called him to preach the gospel. He phrased his compulsion in this way: "Yet when I preach the gospel, I cannot boast, for I am compelled to preach. Woe to me if I do not preach the gospel!" (1 Cor. 9:16).

Indeed, this "woe point" that Paul felt, every Christian may feel. Do you know why you were born and what God has called you to do? Do you know what your "woe point" is? Here is how you may discover it. Sit down and write out these words: "Woe be unto me if I do not _____."

This short phrase will tell you what your calling is.

Paul also listed in his letters (in Rom. 12; 1 Cor. 12; Eph. 4) the gifts of the Spirit. In these lists are many things the Holy Spirit leads those who follow me to do. In these ministry lists are all of those things the church must do to serve its world.

My security before Pilate can be yours. Do you know why you were born? Do you know what you came to do? I will not keep you in ignorance: I love you too much not to tell you why you are on the planet and what you have been called to do. Seek me with all you heart. Enter into my presence and dwell there. All of your "whys?" will find a radiant "because!" in my love.

Prayer
Lord Jesus,
I know that I never knew fully who I was
till I found you.
I never knew why I had come to be
till I found you.
Now bring to full completion within me
everything that I was born to be.
Amen.

Redemptive Innocence

John 18:38

Pilate said to Him, "What is truth?" And when he had said this, he went out again to the Jews, and said to them, "I find no guilt in Him."

The heart of sanctity is innocence. All the sins of human history were met on Good Friday by the most powerful force in the world—innocence. All of hell cannot deal with the pure, clean force of holiness. There is but one substance powerful enough to redeem the world: my sinlessness.

And why is this so everlastingly important? Because all through human history people have reached up to whatever gods they worshiped. What caused them to reach up? They longed to touch someone who was morally superior to them. They found their sins so burdensome that they cried out to any supreme being whose touch would make them better. But it never happened. Only in one tradition—the Hebrew-Christian tradition—did God make people in his image. In all other world religions human artists made gods in their images. These gods were always ideal in their appearance. The gods of the classic religions were tall, muscular, and strident. Physically they were beautiful. But morally they behaved pretty much like their makers.

What came of the Greeks and Romans making their gods in their own image? Did they achieve moral purity? Hardly. They made Olympus into a brothel of sexual liaisons. Their gods were as jealous and petty and conniving as their sculptors. They cheated, stole, fought, and killed. They were in constant power ploys trying to line up mortals on the various sides of their grievances and struggles. They were far too human to offer much virtue or any salvation.

But my own sinlessness was powerful in its redeeming. I was as moral as Romans and Greeks had wanted their philandering deities to be. I lived without sin. I became the one person to whom all human beings could point and say, "That's what I want to be like." I was God's perfect sacrifice for sin. There was no fault in me.

At the cross the power of sin was destroyed with holy innocence. Death was shattered by the sheer force of life as it was meant to be lived.

Prayer
Lord Jesus,
Your sinless sacrifice
has cleansed me.
Your powerful resurrection
has loosed me from the grasp of death.
I sing with all the ransomed of eternity.
"I'm clean and death has lost its hold on me."
Amen.

"Miracle Your Way Out of This Mess, Jesus!" —Herod

Luke 23:6–8

But when Pilate heard it, he asked whether the man was a Galilean. And when he learned that He belonged to Herod's jurisdiction, he sent Him to Herod, who himself also was in Jerusalem at that time. Now Herod was very glad when he saw Jesus; for he had wanted to see Him for a long time, because he had been hearing about Him and was hoping to see some sign performed by Him.

The king who had taken John's head was intrigued by what these rustic people hoped to find in a king. I think he was fascinated with trying to discover how different a king of God's choosing would be from the kings of his own bloody dynasty. But it's difficult to look at a naked, beaten man and see anything kingly about him. How odd that in the fullness of time, Herod would be remembered a tyrant. The naked, beaten man he studied would rule the hearts of millions.

Herod hadn't changed since the day he had taken John's life. He wanted the show that he thought should accompany messiahs. He wanted me to walk on the water or change it to wine. He wanted me to change stones to loaves or multiply them. He wanted something showy to be at the heart of simple Christianity.

There is too much Herod in all of humankind. The need for glitzy miracles can possess you so that you are more impressed with the "Wow!" than the "How?" of my salvation. Evangelists often create an urge to "see" what religion can do. I want more preachers who are less impressed with signs. I want to teach the pure of heart to avoid the miracle-lust of Herod.

One major fault of religious showmanship is that it indicates that God always works in big ways before big crowds. This leaves the impression that the inner life, which is less showy, is not very important. I want my church to learn that showy miracles cannot sustain the soul for long. Only the indwelling Christ can do that.

The miracles that Herod sought are the work of yesteryear. Do not misunderstand me; I work many miracles in these days too. But these current miracles, like those long ago, will perish with those who receive them.

But the miracle of my relationship with you will outlast the stars themselves. So do not give honor to the Herod that lives in you, tempting you toward vaudeville faith. Rather, give place to the Spirit who enters into the quiet place and is nourished by the praying heart.

Prayer
   Lord Jesus,
   I have needs so deep that spiritual fireworks
      will never touch.
   I want you.
   I wake up with hunger,
      I sleep with this thirst.
   Give me no sign you are God's holy Son.
   Give me yourself, and all of heaven's won.
   Amen.

The Freedom of Barabbas

Matthew 27:15–21

Now at the feast the governor was accustomed to release for the multitude any one prisoner whom they wanted. And they were holding at that time a notorious prisoner, called Barabbas. When therefore they were gathered together, Pilate said to them, "Whom do you want me to release for you? Barabbas, or Jesus who is called Christ?" For he knew that because of envy they had delivered Him up. And while he was sitting on the judgment seat, his wife sent to him, saying, "Have nothing to do with that righteous Man; for last night I suffered greatly in a dream because of Him." But the chief priests and the elders persuaded the multitudes to ask for Barabbas, and to put Jesus to death. But the governor answered and said to them, "Which of the two do you want me to release for you?" And they said, "Barabbas."

Barabbas's name literally means "son of the father." Which of us do you judge to be the true son of his father? Barabbas was an insurrectionist. I died literally in his place.

But isn't that true of you as well? Was it not my dying that gave you life? Did the crowd not cry, "Release _____"? (Yes, this space is blank. Is it long enough to fit your name in?) For you were set free by the price I paid for your atonement.

Is it possible that Barabbas went out into the night, never acknowledging he had been set free only because I had taken his place? Would he be so ungrateful? Would you?

Barabbas was not just free; he was just apathetic. He was free without the slightest concern for my suffering.

Calvary may be spurned. Indeed, there are two ways to lose its saving power. The first is done by those who look, measure the cost, and walk away, having seen the provision and rejected it.

But the second kind of rejection is more to be pitied. The apathetic reject the cross with no consideration of the consequence. These are the sons and daughters of Barabbas, who see the cross, but only from the corner of their eyes. They only glance at suffering and then live as though it isn't there. They hear what I have done for them, but pass my cross as nothing.

Are you grateful in your daily prayers for my gift to you? Do you glory in the price I paid, or are you apathetic? Be a partner in my suffering. Come to me in glorious confession and speak to me of your gratitude. Bless my name and speak of my sacrifice in joy.

Prayer
Lord Jesus,
I want to celebrate your love.
I thank you for the price you paid.
I am Barabbas; will you hear my plea?
I know you died that I might be free.
Amen.

The Issue of Power

John 19:10–11

Pilate therefore said to Him, "You do not speak to me? Do You not know that I have authority to release You, and I have authority to crucify You?" Jesus answered, "You would have no authority over Me, unless it had been given you from above; for this reason he who delivered Me up to you has the greater sin."

The night of my trial, I had to remind Pilate of the addictive dangers of power. It was a good reminder, for he had never stopped to tremble over what he could do to others or, even worse, what power would do to him.

Power is the ugly killer that breeds addiction to its own necessity. Bullies, knowing they can hurt others, cannot long live without the pleasure they feel when they do it. "You could have no power except that which is given from above" was my cry to Pilate.

"Might is right" was a customary idea among ancients. Those who had the power were right, and anyone who inferred they were wrong had to suffer their abuse. But later I came and gave to humankind a more noble idea: not *might is right* but *might for right*.

It was this righteous power that would characterize my kingdom. Paul the apostle wrote, "I am not ashamed of the gospel, because it is the power of God for the salvation of everyone who believes: first for the Jew, then for the Gentile" (Rom. 1:16). I, creator of the cosmos, had a kind of power that Pilate and the Romans could never understand. I stood that Thursday evening, appearing weak before the governor, who appeared to be my judge. I stood before the throne of Pilate, who could not imagine himself one day standing before my throne.

Pilate exemplified the divine comedy among worldly rulers. He saw me as naked and alone, a dispossessed pariah about to be crushed in the huge political machine of Rome. But at that trial the world caught its breath. When that weekend was over, the whole issue of power would be forever redefined. God would be God. People would be saved. And Rome would bow its marble head to the fearless dying of the author of real power: the Son of God.

Learn the true doctrine of power, which I labored in vain to teach a Roman: Power yielded to me is power gained with God. Give up your right to control, and control shall be yours. Yield to acquire.

Prayer
Lord Jesus,
Reign over despots.
It's the world's only chance to live.
I need you, Jesus, every waking hour,
*   for I am weak; and you alone are power.*
Amen.

The Murder in Mockery

Matthew 27:27–30

Then the soldiers of the governor took Jesus into the Praetorium and gathered the whole Roman cohort around Him. And they stripped Him, and put a scarlet robe on Him. And after weaving a crown of thorns, they put it on His head, and a reed in His right hand; and they kneeled down before Him and mocked Him, saying, "Hail, King of the Jews!" And they spat on Him, and took the reed and began to beat Him on the head.

Human beings are never less like God than when they dehumanize their peers. At my trial they stripped my clothes from me. In that same horrible exposure in which I would die, I felt the sting of that reproof that cannot be answered while we must stand naked before our accusers. To be naked is to be weak. Those who wear the clothes contain the power.

God himself was naked and in the hands of a lynch mob. Yet here is the hallmark of grace: that the God who had the cosmic power to squelch political power would permit his own abuse. But God, who is longsuffering in his tolerance of human abuse, waited through the mockery. I held to a single theme: redemption. When the cross came, my father would defeat his old enemy forever. Satan, who is the father of man's inhumanity, would go down. The cross endured the mockery that it might destroy it forever.

My jurors handed me a reed, a cattail. They blindfolded me. They beat me, then told me to prophesy who had struck me. There was no use replying. Yet I had the urge to remind them that I was granting them the very power they used in their abuse of me. I gave them the very breath by which they mocked me.

Mockery further isolates and humiliates. My friendlessness now reached its zenith. Still I knew that on the way was the grand heartache: my Father's time to look away from me was coming. I felt ahead of time the pain of his forsaking. I thought of Psalm 22:1: "My God, my God, why have you forsaken me?" But for this needy moment, his accompaniment was all around as I stood before the rabble. He was there, reminding me that my redeeming work would not be accomplished while I stood all alone.

Somewhere beyond the rim of angry eyes were my once valiant men, skittering like frightened rabbits. They were afraid to own up to any connection with me. At the same time they were afraid not to.

Prayer
Lord Jesus,
I am ashamed
*   that on your lonely*
*   persecution*
*   fell my sin*
*   full weight.*
I need your cross to purge my doubt and sin
*   and all your mockeries to make me clean within.*
Amen.

Simon's Grace

Mark 15:21

And they pressed into service a passer-by coming from the country, Simon of Cyrene (the father of Alexander and Rufus), to bear His cross.

I started down the *Via Dolorosa* carrying my own cross (John 19:17). But weak from sleeplessness and mob brutality, I could not carry it far. Someone pressed upon Simon of Cyrene, a hapless passerby, to carry my cross. It was grace to him to have this privilege, which he did not at first see as privilege.

The service he rendered pleased all of heaven. The angels broke into applause when the heavy beams fell full upon him. It is a noble thing to carry anybody's cross. He carried mine and earned a place in history. His two sons, Alexander and Rufus, later became notable Christians in the Roman church (Rom. 16:13). In the course of time, Simon would be celebrated as the servant to the condemned Savior. Therefore see his life in metaphor: when fathers serve me carrying my cross, their children often rise up and call me blessed.

Further on in time, much further, I called a certain woman to serve me who had two sons. The woman herself came so late to faith that her adolescent sons were unimpressed. I made such an impact on the woman's life that she could barely hear my name without breaking into tears. Her sons would see her weeping when at prayer and considered their mother quite affected.

The boys would have abandoned her to her quaint madness had she not contracted cancer. The disease came so furiously upon her that it soon filled her body with ever-growing death. She was in terrible pain, yet she rarely complained. She faced the specter of her approaching death with an almost pleasant spirit. She loved listening to hymns and delighted in reading the Bible. "Boys," she would say to her sons, "this cross I carry is far too heavy for me to bear for long. I must die and go to the Savior. Promise me you will someday love him too."

Her sons were two of her pallbearers and the oddest mood stole over them as they carried their mother's body toward her grave. Now they were weeping as their mother had done. Only now a maturity was conferred upon them by their tears. They no longer considered weeping to be foolish.

Now their mother is with me. And the boys? Well, whenever they hear my name they too weep and give their tears as gratitude. Their mother bore a cross, and they have come to bless my name. Their names are not Rufus and Alexander, but they might have been.

Prayer
Lord Jesus,
I want to see you on the cross
and remember him who bore the
timbers to your dying place.
I want to bless the man who helped
you to the dying that you gave to me.
I want to praise you for the love supreme
and bless the name of Simon of Cyrene.
Amen.

Weep for the Thing that Makes God Cry: The Human Predicament

Luke 23:27–31

And there were following Him a great multitude of the people, and of women who were mourning and lamenting Him. But Jesus turning to them said, "Daughters of Jerusalem, stop weeping for Me, but weep for yourselves and for your children. For behold, the days are coming when they will say, 'Blessed are the barren, and the wombs that never bore, and the breasts that never nursed.' Then they will begin TO SAY TO THE MOUNTAINS, 'FALL ON US,' AND TO THE HILLS, 'COVER US' [Hos. 10:8]. For if they do these things in the green tree, what will happen in the dry?"

On the way to Golgatha I was touched by the women who followed me to the cross. I reminded them of those days of ultimate finality when the entire world would weep. My words en route to Calvary should serve as a double reminder to the world that God hurts when humanity aches.

Those who see God as some universal apathetic supervisor of history have not seen my Father at all. Wherever people die—at Auschwitz, the killing fields of Cambodia, or Burundi—God weeps.

I don't want to give anyone the impression that God only wept once in history— the day I died. My death was special to God, and it was horrible. But so were others, such as the children separated from their mothers at the horrible burning of Lidice, Czechoslovakia. A Jewess screamed out of a trench to Adolph Eichman, "Please take my baby," and was forced to hear the crack of rifle fire that destroyed her little one, then the shot that folded them both into the mass graves of Poland.

During the famine in Somalia, a young woman carried her skeletal and starving son for many miles to try to get him to the U.N. food compound before he died. She did at last get him to the wonderful oasis of survival. The wheat trucks brought the grain for their survival. It looked as though they might live. But she herself was so emaciated and worn from the long trip that she died. Her son was compelled by love to try and dig her grave. After he had finished digging and had placed his mother in the grave, he found himself too weak to crawl out of the hole. He and his mother were both buried in the same grave.

If you think God only cried in Jerusalem on the day I died, I can tell you he has cried in Somalia and Poland as well. The daughters of Jerusalem wept for me as God weeps for all. Will you join my Father in caring for all of those who suffer. Let my love motivate your caring.

Prayer
Lord Jesus,
You bought my soul
by walking up a hill where
women cried for you.
Help me to cry for those whom no one grieves.
I give myself to touch all those who cry
and lift to life all those about to die.
Amen.

Forgiving Those Who Hurt You

Luke 23:34a

But Jesus was saying, "Father, forgive them; for they do not know what they are doing."

Had my crucifiers known what they were doing and to whom they were doing it, the cross would not have happened. "Father, forgive their ignorance" was my cry. They stood before me with bloody hammers and a curious wash of self-excusing innocence.

The cross provides the lesson in knowing how far you should go to forgive. Have you been hurt? So was I. Deliberately? I also. Did those who hurt you enjoy the protection of society or your community of friends? Mine likewise!

I encourage you to forgive them for two reasons. First of all, if you do not, the grudge at the center of your own soul may devour your heart with bitterness.

Second, I encourage you to forgive them so you can be like me. Christlikeness is the first requirement for my disciples. But, you may be prone to argue, it hurts so very much. You're right, of course. But if you want to be like me, endure the pain. Forgive. Upon my cross I could hardly say, "Father, forgive." My tongue was so swollen. My mouth was so dry. But I said the words, and my followers learned how important those words are and how dearly they are sometimes bought.

Once in a distant kingdom, some rude boys decided they would beat up the king's young son who was traveling through the forest alone. They grabbed the young man, cuffing him with their fists and kicking him severely with their boots. Finally, when the young man lay hurt and bleeding, they left him for dead. The leader of this ruffian group was named Jacques; it was he who had done the most harm and brought the most blood.

An old man happening through the forest found the wounded boy and took him to his hut. After he had nursed him back to health, the prince returned to his father and asked for a horse and twenty knights to begin a search for the ruffian who had caused him such pain. Word went out of the kingdom in every direction, and Jacques fled, fearing for his life. He moved so fast and was so often in hiding that he rarely shaved or bathed. He traveled dense trails, always by night.

It was inevitable that the prince and his knights would at last close in upon him. Alone and defenseless, Jacques came out of the caves and knelt before the prince. He bowed his head and bared his neck for the decapitation he was sure would come.

But the prince drew him to his feet and kissed him. "My friend," he cried, "at last I have found you. I wanted to find you so that I may forgive you. So," said the prince, "you must now forgive all your enemies, and they will become as dear to you as you are now to me."

Prayer
Lord Jesus,
I long to meet old enemies
*　to tell them we may yet be one in Christ.*
I want to bless all those who hung me on some cross
*　of their own choosing.*
Go in grace, forgiving older pain,
*　that older foes may be my friends again.*
Amen.

The Divine Alternative

Mark 15:29–32

And those passing by were hurling abuse at Him, wagging their heads, and saying, "Ha! You who are going to destroy the temple and rebuild it in three days, save Yourself, and come down from the cross!" In the same way the chief priests also, along with the scribes, were mocking Him among themselves and saying, "He saved others; He cannot save Himself. Let this Christ, the King of Israel, now come down from the cross, so that we may see and believe!" And those who were crucified with Him were casting the same insult at Him.

"He saved others," they mocked, "himself he cannot save." There is wisdom in this insult.

See this glorious dilemma by which you have been redeemed. God at Calvary reached out to save in two directions. He loved me and he loved you. He wanted to take me from the cross, but he did not want you to die with no hope of eternity. So he made the choice we had agreed upon before time began. I died. You live. But in God's choice, the heaviness of obligation fell on you. Now you must choose as God did.

Once I closed my eyes in cooling, calming, sweet death, there was only one way that your debt could ever be erased. You had to say, "Father, forgive me!"

There is little use arguing that you are not responsible. You cannot blame my death on those who lived in another century. The crime is yours too. This was not the crime of a particular age-locked people. Calvary belongs to every age.

Once a young man struggling with the necessity of being saved dreamed a strange dream. He was at my trial. He saw the man who flogged me, shredding the flesh of my back with a whip. He was so incensed at the brutality that he ran up and stopped the beating by grabbing the man's hand. When the man with the flog turned around to protest the interruption, he was stunned. The man who had stopped the beating was aghast to see that the face of the man who held the flog was his own.

So you see, the heart of God was torn at Calvary. He was like that poor mother whom the Gestapo once tortured. They asked her which of her two sons she would like to have shot. If she did not make a choice, they would shoot both. So she had to choose, but the choice was one of immeasurable pain. She ran in madness from one of her children to the other crying, "This one . . . no this one!"

I died so you could live. Repent of the obligation that your salvation forced upon my Father. And know this: You were saved only at the expense of utter love that would not abandon either me or you.

Prayer
Lord Jesus,
I praise you for
the price you paid for me.
I cannot fathom love that paid this price
or bought my soul at such a sacrifice.
Amen.

Two Desperate Viewpoints

Luke 23:39–43

And one of the criminals who were hanged there was hurling abuse at Him, saying, "Are You not the Christ? Save Yourself and us!" But the other answered, and rebuking him said, "Do you not even fear God, since you are under the same sentence of condemnation? And we indeed justly, for we are receiving what we deserve for our deeds; but this man has done nothing wrong." And he was saying, "Jesus, remember me when You come in Your kingdom!" And He said to him, "Truly I say to you, today you shall be with Me in Paradise."

The three of us were dying together. We all knew the agony of rough wood and metal spikes. We all felt the horror of strangling in our own saliva and the torture of trying to raise our weary bodies away from that hellish vertical beam enough to catch our breath. Pain makes instant brothers of those who suffer. Yet those criminals who died with me were not of one mind. One of the thieves—in spite of his ordeal—seemed to join the cynicism of the crowd who had called for my crucifixion. The other reached out to me, as though in his dying, he needed to believe.

How did I reckon with the feelings of two such opposite souls?

People die pretty much as they have lived. The doubting thief did not doubt any more at his dying than he had during his lifetime. The believing thief, all of his life, was more prone to believe. This is not to say that in the last moments of life, people cannot change camps. But these dying thieves illustrate that the best time to deal with our doubts is while we live. When you are dying, you often have neither the time nor will to think through the issues of eternity.

Many think that throughout their lives they will live with one attitude toward the living God, and reverse themselves at the last moment. But it is not common for libertines or agnostics to come down to the zero hour of life saying, "How foolish I have been. God, I do repent my folly. I come to you, completely free of all my former foolishness." Those who make fun of the living God in life will likely die scoffing.

Dying beside me was a foolish thief and a wise thief. The wise thief cried the music of his longing soul. "Lord, remember me!" You may be sure I did not forget him.

I entered my Father's presence arm in arm with this bloody criminal. It's the nature of the Kingdom. Thieves and priests are all one company with my loving Father. That thief is still in heaven. He always will be, for he was a careful steward of his last few minutes of life. Grace will not quit while anyone responds.

Prayer
Lord Jesus,
Time is a gift.
It is the gift you never quit giving until our pulse is still
*   and our breath is gone.*
Help me to love this thief who accompanied you into heaven.
He knew that grace never quits while one soul anguishes,
*   refusing to abandon hope.*
Give me that wisdom that precedes belief.
Make me as wise as was a dying thief.
Amen.

Entering the Family of Faith

John 19:26–27

When Jesus therefore saw His mother, and the disciple whom He loved standing nearby, He said to His mother, "Woman, behold, your son!" Then He said to the disciple, "Behold, your mother!" And from that hour the disciple took her into his household.

Mothers never quit being mothers. They never quit caring and loving their children. However old their children are when they are forced to undergo any trial, mothers cannot escape the pain their children must endure.

Here at last an old man's prophecy to my mother was fulfilled: "And a sword will pierce your own soul too" (Luke 2:35). My mother suffered even as old Simeon had predicted she would some thirty-three years earlier. Besides the thorns and nails, I felt that inner pain of seeing her suffer. To see me dying naked on the cross had reduced her heart to shuddering grief. But sons suffer too. When I saw her agony, I felt her suffering added to the pain of my crucifixion.

I studied her torn soul that Friday. Oh, how I longed to embrace her broken form and dissolve her tears in my embrace. Alas, I could not even move my hand to touch her. Nor could I cover myself to hide the naked shame I felt.

Here upon my cross, I knew, was the proper place to teach her the nature of the Kingdom. So in our common broken states, I offered my mother a final lesson of grace. There beside her was my disciple John. How loyal John had proved himself when I was dying. He came to the cross when others fled. I managed the suffocating pain of speaking in very short sentences: "Mother, here is your son John. John, this is your mother."

Mary turned her eyes from me and looked directly at my disciple. I then looked directly into John's eyes and said in inner words I had not the breath to speak: "Yes, John, my mother is your mother. This is the nature of the Kingdom. Those who believe take care of each other in such desperate hours as these."

If there can be sweetness at crucifixions, I saw it there. The young and grieving disciple put his arm around my mother. "Let's go home!" he said.

My mother made her way home supported on the shoulder of my young friend. When the stone rolled away three days later, the Kingdom's motto could have been, "Watch out, world!" If a young disciple and a grieving mother could care this much for each other, then a new age was truly being born in a Kingdom whose hurting subjects helped each other.

Linger near my cross. Put your arm around those whose grief runs deep, and say to them, "I love you. You shall not face this hurt alone."

Prayer
*Lord Jesus,
By definition, the cross is not where
    we meet you to deal only with ourselves.
At a crucifixion, all kinds of hurting people gather.
Who can transcend his pain and look around
    to see how he may give solace in the dying name of Jesus?
Make me the martyr who adores your cross
    enough to see some other's pain and loss.
Amen.*

The Utter Loneliness of the Cross

Matthew 27:45–46

Now from the sixth hour darkness fell upon all the land until the ninth hour. And about the ninth hour Jesus cried out with a loud voice, saying, "ELI, ELI, LAMA SABACHTHANI?" that is, "MY GOD, MY GOD, WHY HAST THOU FORSAKEN ME?"

Redeeming humankind was lonely work. There was one supreme prize that I had treasured all through my earthly ministry: my relationship with my Father. It is not possible for mortals to know the splendor of such love. I had known this unbroken love since the beginning of time. When chaos swirled in empty space longing to become the first vast field of stars, this love was mine. Before time erupted in sunlight, or shadows were born, this love was mine. Before my Father and I sat down and discussed the redemption of his unformed universe, this love was ours.

But after I was baptized by John, there never dawned a morning when I did not meet with my Father. In the grass, the sea, the sky, the canyons of Trans-Jordan, my Father came to me as all-embracing love. I saw my Father's love as easily in the leathery faces of the old scholars as I saw him in the innocent eyes of the children I touched and blessed.

In Gethsemane I felt his love again. My task was horrible to meditate upon; but I agreed that as he loved me, I would perform all that he asked. I knew that in spite of his love, there would come an awful moment of separating horror. This would be the weight of his requirement. I knew that when I fully bore the sin of the world, his holiness would require him to look the other way. In the excruciating pain of the cross I could only cry out the words of the psalmist: "My God, my God, why . . . ?" (Ps. 22:1).

Now the blackness fell full weight upon me. My eternal lover would not . . . no, *could not* look upon me. His holiness and my burden of the world's sin had estranged us. I carried too much. He could not stand to look upon the degradation that had brought me to the cross. Now he who readily met me in flowery fields of Galilee was not there. He who walked with me through Gethsemane itself demanded that I face this ugly, dying moment alone.

Oh, how I anguished!

This estrangement was the only way to pay the price to redeem for your sins. I wonder if that which cost me so much has reached the center of your love. May the pale Friday sun of Golgotha shine once again upon my wounded face. Come to me, abide with me, adore me.

Prayer
Lord Jesus,
I love you for one particular moment
  when, in all of history,
    you and your Father were estranged on my behalf.
I bless such love.
The nails were mine, and yet
  the nails that split your hands that painful day
    bought pain far less than when God turned away.
Amen.

The Last Thing You Will Ever Say

Luke 23:46

And Jesus, crying out with a loud voice, said, "FATHER, INTO THY HANDS I COMMIT MY SPIRIT" [Ps. 31:5]. And having said this, He breathed His last.

My last earthly words were a quotation from the Bible. What will be yours?

Some say that anyone's final words reflect what most occupied the thoughts during life. We say at last what we thought about the most.

Notice that my last words were a celebration of my relationship with my Father.

An old woman once faced death all alone. When her pastor arrived, she was quite candid: "Pastor," she said, "I do not want to be alone when I die. Will you be here at my moment of crossing?"

The pastor, believing her death to be imminent, agreed that he would. But it surprised him that, while she was not expected to live through the night, she was still alive the next day. The pastor had stayed with her, holding her hand, through the long night. He rarely left her bedside for the next two days. By the end of the week, her doctor informed both the woman and the pastor that her condition was so improved that she would not die.

The principle of healing that delivered her was the same principle that had caused her to seek him out in the first place. Relationship is the benediction of the dying. Those who die alone die amputated in spirit from the world where they have lived. But to have someone there at the moment of dying is a treasure immeasurable.

"Be there when I die." These are the final hopes of all who must cross the chasm of death.

"Father," I said on the cross, "we are here together at the moment of dying as we were ever together during our lives. My Spirit has always been in your hands. Now receive my Spirit, as we enter and celebrate our oneness, forever."

> *Prayer*
> *Lord Jesus,*
> *Help me to love you with such singleness of mind*
>   *that my dying confidence could not possibly be any different*
>   *than the living confidence I felt in you all the way along.*
> *Help your confident last words to be my confident last words.*
> *"Father,*
>   *May these, my dying words, be grand:*
>   *'I now commend my spirit to your hands.'"*
> *Amen.*

The End of the Dividing Wall

Mark 15:38
And the veil of the temple was torn in two from top to bottom.

The significance of the tearing of the temple veil is rooted deep in the hidden holiness of God. There was a time when all Jewish people believed that the fullest presence of God resided on the mercy seat of the ark of the covenant. The ark and God's presence always resided in the Holy of holies. This Holy of holies was sometimes called the inner sanctum. This inner sanctum was divided from the holy place by the veil of the temple—a rich, heavy tapestry several inches thick. While priests could go into the holy place, only the high priest could enter the Holy of holies, and then only once a year.

But when I died, the temple veil was split in two and thrown back. The era of God's aloofness was symbolically over. Now anyone could enter the Holy of holies. God had ended his hidden seclusion. I cried, "It is finished," and the veil was torn in two, right down the middle. In the finality of my death I had brought God and humankind together. Paul wrote that this tearing of the curtain was the end of the "middle wall of separation." He wrote: "For he himself is our peace, who has made the two one and has destroyed the barrier, the dividing wall of hostility, by abolishing in his flesh the law. . . . " (Eph. 2:14–15a).

The wall is down. You can enter freely into the presence of my Father. Think of the glory of this; you are but a human being. Yet you can go to my Father in utter freedom as often as you like. Glory in your free access to God. No one has to be your priest. You can enter the Holy of holies and lay your hands on the very mercy seat of the ark of the covenant. There you may ask what you will.

The temple veil has been split. Lay down your life with longing so that those who are hurting and in need may find this same access that you enjoy. For most still live, never suspecting that this open way to God even exists. Be for them the good news. Demonstrate the joy of being able to enter freely into his courts with thanksgiving and praise.

Prayer
Lord Jesus,
I treasure those moments when I freely
enter your Holy of holies.
I thank you for my free access through your blood
to kneel before you as a priest,
invoking your own all-glorious forgiveness.
Dear Christ, your cross gave oneness to my heart.
The veil that kept us two is torn apart.
Amen.

Not a Bone Shall Be Broken

John 19:31–34

The Jews therefore, because it was the day of preparation, so that the bodies should not remain on the cross on the Sabbath (for that Sabbath was a high day), asked Pilate that their legs might be broken, and that they might be taken away. The soldiers therefore came, and broke the legs of the first man, and of the other man who was crucified with Him; but coming to Jesus, when they saw that He was already dead, they did not break His legs; but one of the soldiers pierced His side with a spear, and immediately there came out blood and water.

The thieves who died with me were not quite dead when the high holiday arrived. It was a custom to break the legs of the crucified to hasten death. When the legs were broken, the condemned could no longer straighten their bodies against the upright beam. Suffocation resulted instantly. But when the soldiers came to break my legs, I was already dead. All further indignity was spared my lifeless body.

The spear was thrust into my body and fluid gushed from the wound. Blood and water! Some beg a medical explanation and say my heart had ruptured, spilling out the clot and sera, or blood and water. But see the symbol. In the water is the cleansing of all sin that the cross achieved. In the blood is the sacrifice beyond which none is greater. When we have given our lives, there is no secondary offering to be made.

The symbols of water and blood are two of the greatest in the Christian faith. Water symbolizes that cleansing of repentance by which our hearts are made ready for redemption. Not far from where that spearhead did its brutal work, the Spirit came in wind and fire on the day of Pentecost. John wrote of the power of these symbols: "For there are three that testify: the Spirit, the water and the blood; and the three are in agreement" (1 John 5:7). It is this trio of symbols that bears witness to my earthly life.

In these symbols is my saving office. My cleansing, my sacrifice, and my indwelling Spirit are those indispensable elements of grace. Glory in this trinity of symbols. Serve this trinity in joy, even as I did. As you give the water, the world will be cleansed. As you offer the blood, the world will be saved by my sacrifice. And as you offer them the gospel, the Holy Spirit will come to indwell their lives.

Come, we will celebrate this trio of symbols. Count on my cleansing. Depend on my sacrifice. Be filled with my Spirit.

Prayer
Lord Jesus,
Blood and water,
redemption and cleansing:
I am thankful for the cross and for the washing
of the Spirit.
Teach me to wake every morning with two anthems on my lips.
The first should be the anthem of the blood,
the second of the cleansing.
The spear drew blood and water in its stream.
Praise be to God who cleanses and redeems.
Amen.

The True Disciple and the Risk of Identity

Mark 15:42–43

And when evening had already come, because it was the preparation day, that is, the day before the Sabbath, Joseph of Arimathea came, a prominent member of the Council, who himself was waiting for the kingdom of God; and he gathered up courage and went in before Pilate, and asked for the body of Jesus.

Joseph of Arimathea "gathered up courage" and admitted that he knew me. It was no little thing he did, for he was a prominent member of the Council. To admit that you are the friend of a despised and executed criminal is an act of courage.

Joseph of Arimathea expressed his courage in this way: "Please, sir, may I have his body?" The question took all the courage he could muster. He knew that years later the elitists of Jerusalem would still be whispering and pointing at him as he passed them on the street.

In many ways the century in which you bear witness to me is like the first century. In the West, it is increasingly hard to find those with the courage to speak openly and frankly of their love for me. It is hard to believe openly and face being ridiculed by secular atheists.

There are many who still pay immense prices for their convictions. There are young men whose integrity is squarely in the way of corporate deals; some have lost their jobs or been forever prevented from moving into well-deserved positions of honor in their firm. There are civil leaders motivated by my love to make the world better, yet ever battling the more permissive and the indulgent. There are young women, passed by in life, because they refuse to compromise their moral ideals.

Perhaps you are living right now under the scrutiny of someone's judgment. Perhaps your income or your reputation is suffering because of the esteem in which you hold my name. Take heart. Remember Joseph of Arimathea. See him in his courageous bid for my body. See him laying his social standing on the line and begging those who hated me to give him my body.

Then you can see things as they really are. Pilate and Herod and all of the officials of that time are gone. Their names are unhallowed. But the world will long remember a man who laid his reputation on the line to preserve my own. Naturally my Father loves Joseph. Even so, he loves you each time you lay your honor on the line to safeguard mine.

Prayer
Lord Jesus,
Am I as brave as Joseph of Arimathea?
Do I openly acknowledge my friendship with you
　　in the center of hostile environments?
Where others hold you in shallow and philosophical contempt,
　　am I courageous enough to say,
　　"Him whom you have recently blasphemed
　　is my most significant friend"?
All honor comes to me as hope or shame.
My own importance pales beneath his name.
Amen.

Watching Rocks

Matthew 27:62–64

Now on the next day, which is the one after the preparation, the chief priests and the Pharisees gathered together with Pilate, and said, "Sir, we remember that when He was still alive that deceiver said, 'After three days I am to rise again.' Therefore, give orders for the grave to be made secure until the third day, lest the disciples come and steal Him away and say to the people, 'He has risen from the dead,' and the last deception will be worse than the first."

Life seems ever to boil down to two choices. Either we expect the exciting and unbelievable; or, like Pilate's garrison, we watch graves expecting nothing. These sentries expected nothing supernatural, so they sat up for three days and nights watching for grave robbers. Then when God blew the lid off the tomb, they were shocked into comas, silent as dead men. Those who never expected me to live again were shocked by the detonation of joy that makes all life possible.

In this life people will either trust and find themselves gaping over the unbelievable things that God brings their way, or they doubt and stumble over the acts of the unbelievable God. Those who doubt are forever confused that the great mysteries of God never blessed them but only stupefied them.

Unbelief sets guards over sealed tombs—guards who expect nothing.

These "rock-watchers" watched to make sure no one stole my body. They all claimed to love God and honor all of Judaism's promises of Messianism. Yet my Easter life surprised them. Can it be that men and women can love God with some passion and yet really be ignorant of the awesome possibilities in tombs? Yes! Religion sometimes wears a smug and practiced religiosity that is without vitality, expecting nothing. Most churchmen have long ago given up of ever seeing me, the living Christ. They have traded their lost expectations for the dull habit of guarding rocks.

Now let us come to Easter. Some rocks turn out to be worth watching. These rocks quaked and split. Then I, with certain tread, marched out as Victor. And this unsettling event left the soldiers at first quaking and later lying about what they saw.

But those doubtful, frightened followers of mine began a dance of joy that continues to the present. And the rocks will not live as long as that heraldic cry that split them open. "He is risen!" is an anthem that outlives both rocks and unbelieving people.

Prayer
Lord Jesus,
I want to give you my unbelieving nature.
I want to trust.
I want to stumble upon the shocking evidence
   of your glorious reality.
Surprise me with joy!
Validate my life with things so wonderful and unexpected
   that I walk through life
   looking for your delightful surprises.
There are those stony souls as dull as night.
Make me like those who shatter rocks with light.
Amen.

Grief Keeps the Vision Low

Matthew 28:5–6

And the angel answered and said to the women, "Do not be afraid; for I know that you are looking for Jesus who has been crucified. He is not here, for He has risen, just as He said. Come, see the place where He was lying."

The women were bringing spices for my burial. They were also weeping, the best evidence that they meant well. Tears come when the face is toward the ground. It's a pity too. For God can manage things born far above a downcast spirit. Bring me no burial spices. I am alive. I can manage your broken affairs. Look up! See me! I am at the right hand of my Father. I am alive forevermore. I have won joy, and I place this prize inside you.

"He is risen!" was the shout heard around the world.

Do not all people approach my tomb in the same way? Tenuous, afraid. They want to be Christians, and yet they fear that if it really is true, its very truth has every right to lay its claim on them. To believe that I am alive means that those who encounter me must lay by all claims to themselves and submit to me.

The weeping women met an angel. Then they heard the words that the mind cannot contain. And finding out that I was alive, they entered a glorious and befuddling state of grace. Who could tell of their delirium? They were mad with joy! What were they to do? Tell it, they must! They had to surrender their sanity and tell the world they have met an angel. Bit by bit the group insanity filters in from all quarters.

I am alive! Some have seen me here. Some have seen me there. Some don't want to talk about it. They are laughing, crying, whispering, and shouting. That's how it is when dead men come alive too suddenly. Yet in this marvelous and hysterical truth there is a new and powerful force loose. The joy can never be contained. If you see an angel, go ahead and tell your friends.

Let their hysteria rage. Who would want a Savior who is predictable and explainable? Joyous mayhem is better than secular emptiness.

I am risen!

Tell your friends. Some will doubt it and be condemned; others will come to the party of the mad and gain life eternal. Let them doubt your sanity but not your commitment. I am Lord. "'I am the Alpha and the Omega,' says the Lord God, 'who is, and who was, and who is to come, the Almighty'" (Rev. 1:8). "'I am the Living One; I was dead, and behold I am alive for ever and ever!'" (Rev. 1:18). Is this not the grandest, most glorious insanity the world has ever known?

Prayer
Lord Jesus,
I so often see my wounds and focus on my hurts.
Never yet in such a state, have I known your living presence.
When I weep my downcast way along the lanes of "poor-little-me-ism,"
send your angel to remind me it is gloriously futile
to seek the living among the dead.
Sear my fuzzy thoughts with light that lets me see
and fill my mind with rich insanity.
Amen.

The Panic Born in Unbelief

John 20:2
And so she ran and came to Simon Peter, and to the other disciple whom Jesus loved, and said to them, "They have taken away the Lord out of the tomb, and we do not know where they have laid Him."

Believe the unbelievable! Put away mere logical truth with the incredible actions of God. Believe the unbelievable and you will feel fear; you will doubt. Fear and doubt go together. The first person to discover the empty tomb both feared and doubted. In so doing she missed the meaning of the obvious miracle set before her.

Mary Magdalene ran in panic to tell what she could have walked in confidence to announce. I had risen, but not seeing the truth of the miracle, she spread only gloom. Joy would be her second opinion, but that would have to wait till her fears and doubts were past.

Bad news is often more readily accepted than good. The official word that first Easter reported that my body had been stolen. That was not the truth, but it was more logical than the truth. So most of Jerusalem preferred to see it that way.

How many times in the Bible does the whole issue of truth rest on a single soul who takes a lonely stand in the middle of a defiant culture? Elijah lamented that he was the only one who had not bowed the knee to Baal. On Maundy Thursday, I was the only one who was right when I stood before an immense sea of crucifiers. So when Mary told the apostles that my body had been stolen, she had all too quickly joined the vast majority of those who believed the erroneous story.

In your life you will face this same lie. It is old now. There are all kinds of theories and ideas that tell exactly how my "supposed" resurrection might have happened or might be explained. Think it over. Do not yield, there is more life in a thimble of Easter joy than a basket of secular logic. Stand! Rebuff the popular view! Never grow to love the sound of your own voice explaining things. In the irrational there is life.

Prayer
Lord Jesus,
So often I have come back from the empty tomb
forgetting you are alive.
So I spread what I am most full of—doubt.
Help me not to counsel the spiritually needy until
I have faced the miracle of life and seen it.
Then hope can be my gift to the world.
The crowd is always large but rarely right,
I'll name that "day" that others call the night.
Amen.

Clinging

John 20:15–17

Jesus said to her, "Woman, why are you weeping? Whom are you seeking?" Supposing Him to be the gardener, she said to Him, "Sir, if you have carried Him away, tell me where you have laid Him, and I will take Him away." Jesus said to her, "Mary!" She turned and said to him in Hebrew, "Rabboni!" (which means, Teacher). Jesus said to her, "Stop clinging to Me, for I have not yet ascended to the Father; but go to My brethren, and say to them, 'I ascend to My Father and your Father, and My God and your God.'"

Mary's clinging was a natural reaction to her uncertain faith. She could see I was alive. But her eyes could hardly believe, and so her fingers tested me. Mary's sin was Thomas's. Both of them wanted to touch the "impossible" to test their belief system.

Every person is both an innate believer and a skeptic. Mary wanted to believe with all her heart, but her mind was not as instantly generous as her heart. So she grabbed me to prove to her doubtful mind that I was real enough to be "clingable." Then she could tell herself and the world that I really had come back from the dead—arms, legs, torso, and all.

But I wanted her to reach out in a surer way of trust. Can trust be sure?

Indeed. All those sensory evidences fade the further you get from them. A month later, how would she have viewed her clinging to me? She would have questioned herself: "Just how solid was he? Could I, in the darkness, have embraced a tree trunk? Was I so sleepy I might have been deluded? Were my eyes too bleary with the sunrise and my fingers too numb with the cold to really test his existence?"

There can never be enough "proof" in testing miracles to satisfy the inquisitive heart. So I told her to quit testing reality with her fingers. Materiality is never the index to enduring values anyway. What is most real cannot be touched, tasted, or seen. What is most real gains all its everlasting substance by dwelling in those dimensions of reality untestable by the senses.

I am real, and I am at the right hand of the Father. Is my spiritual reality enough for you? Are you clinging? Trusting the mystery affords healing and hope.

Impatience picks the fruit too green. Be rather like those who see the folded napkin, as John did. With no other evidence than that, he believed (John 20:7–8). From Mary's scattered doubt came a skitterish discipleship. From John's unclinging faith came five New Testament books.

Prayer
Lord Jesus,
I release my death grip
on all that cannot be held for long.
I reach instead with a heart of trust.
I am willing to cling to true reality
and trust that the science of the heart is belief.
Your gifts to me are ever so immense.
My faith needs no other evidence.
Amen.

Buying Doubt with Bribes

Matthew 28:11–13

Now while they were on their way, behold, some of the guard came into the city and reported to the chief priests all that had happened. And when they had assembled with the elders and counseled together, they gave a large sum of money to the soldiers, and said, "You are to say, 'His disciples came by night and stole Him away while we were asleep.'"

There were two stories that circulated concerning my death: the true one which believers joyfully reported, and the "official" story put out by the authorities. The official story was financed by bribes. It was reported and quickly died. The faith report erupted in joy and has lived across the centuries.

The faith report, for all its inscrutable mysteries, was really easier to believe than the official story. Consider the loopholes in the elders' report. In the first place, the soldiers, knowing the penalty for falling asleep on a watch, were confessing to being very poor watchmen. Then too, just how logical was it that anyone could have come to move a dead body in the middle of the night? This eerie tale violates the Jewish taboo of touching corpses. Even if the Resurrection is to be explained on the basis of the body being stolen, how are we to answer the issue of where the body was moved? The officials would have relished having my remains as a way of proving my messianic claims were over. Such a corpse would have been a great coup for the Sadducees as the primary evidence that Christianity's founder was an impostor. The lie the officials concocted was simply too convoluted. The simple truth was easier to believe.

What really happened? I had been raised from the dead by my Father. At the very moment that the officials were trying to explain away this great miracle, I moved in and out of the startled lives of my followers. I appeared in sealed rooms and walked with them on the way to the country village of Emmaus. The Sadducees and Pharisees were dealing with a new kind of reality they wished they could bribe out of existence. But what the officials could not fathom became the disciples' source of joy.

So is it in your life. What puzzles you most about your own faith is the mystery of the resurrection. You cannot answer how a dead man could come back from the dead. Yet it is this mystery that makes Christianity the only reasonable motive for being a Christian. Who would want a Christ they could figure out, a God whom they could explain? Enter into my mystery, and let the power of the mystery call you to unshakable hope. Disbelief is the companion of heavy logic. Doubt always behaves like Pharisees bribing tomb guards. There is only one way to life. You have found the way. The treasure is the mystery. The mystery is yours.

Prayer
Lord Jesus,
In a world where it is hard to know the truth
and harder to tell the truth about what we know for sure,
make me a person of conscience.
There are so few people who tell the truth
when there is a threat on their place in their community.
Confession is the believers' bag of gold.
They hold to truth and love the truth they hold.
Amen.

Of Scars and Scripture

Luke 24:13, 28–32

And behold two of them were going that very day to a village named Emmaus, which was about seven miles from Jerusalem. . . . And they approached the village where they were going, and He acted as though He would go farther. And they urged Him, saying, "Stay with us, for it is getting toward evening, and the day is now nearly over." And He went in to stay with them. And it came about that when He had reclined at the table with them, He took the bread and blessed it, and breaking it, He began giving it to them. And their eyes were opened and they recognized Him; and He vanished from their sight. And they said to one another, "Were not our hearts burning within us while He was speaking to us on the road, while He was explaining the Scriptures to us?"

Two evidences undergird the undeniable proclamation of the church. The first is the *stigmata*, those scars that will mark my body throughout eternity. The other is the eternal Word of God. As I walked with the disciples that day, I explained to them the Word of God and helped them see that the Crucifixion and Resurrection were not patches on the plan God adopted once my popular acceptance didn't work out. The Scriptures all bore witness of a carefully executed plan by which I would redeem the world.

On the way to Emmaus, I reasoned with these two about how God's eternal plan was faithfully executed when I died. But their minds were so clouded with grief that they could not grasp the glorious truth.

When I broke bread with them they saw my hands. The stigmata convinced them that the Resurrection was more than rumor. Scars and the Word represent those two indispensable attributes of faith that never can stand separately. Doctrine is one arm of faith, and passion the other. Do not believe those who say, "I just love Jesus, but I have no use for doctrine." Emmaus is the evidence that they must be taken together.

On the Emmaus road we wrangled over the ancient teachings. In the Old Testament, there is much written of me. How important is this truth! Without it the New Testament would degenerate to an emotive, undefined, and vastly unconnected faith. The great anointed teachings of the Old Testament bore witness to my saving work. My scars say how far that love is willing to go to save.

What is the Emmaus lesson? First, read the Scriptures incessantly. Let their blessed teachings tell you how much I love you and define what my love means. But meditate at every communion service on my scars. See them every time you break the bread. Let them remind you how far my love went to rescue you.

Prayer
Lord Jesus,
I thank you for the Word of God,
by which I know the great dimensions
of your love.
I thank you too for the stigmata
which makes it impossible for me to misunderstand
the strength of your passion.
When I am prone to doubt why you were sent,
the scars and Scriptures both are testament.
Amen.

Eating Fish, Devouring Doubt

Luke 24:36–43

And while they were telling these things, He Himself stood in their midst. But they were startled and frightened and thought that they were seeing a spirit. And He said to them, "Why are you troubled, and why do doubts arise in your hearts? See My hands and My feet, that it is I Myself; touch Me and see, for a spirit does not have flesh and bones as you see that I have." [And when He had said this, He showed them His hands and His feet.] And while they still could not believe it for joy and were marveling, He said to them, "Have you anything here to eat?" And they gave Him a piece of a broiled fish; and He took it and ate it before them.

To prove to my disciples that I was not a ghost, I asked for fish. As I ate the meat, I devoured their doubt as well.

After my resurrection, I was always trying to get them to accept what they were seeing: a dead man can live again. But I really wanted them to see what all the church would later grasp: the resurrection was not difficult for God. The great miracle is not that I could live again but that God would become a man in the first place. Why should my Father care about living and dying for all those blasé civilizations, when he could stay comfortably at home in heaven?

Human beings were fascinated by the resurrection. I was more fascinated during my earthly existence by the kind of love that cared about humanity. But the disciples were puzzled about the reality and power of the resurrection. Later they would understand it and die to proclaim its liberating truth. In the meanwhile, I ate a little fish to help them over the hurdle of having to explain me away as some kind of apparition.

In time one notable thinker would write *Cur Deus Homo?* That's the real question. Why did God become a man? The real issue was not *Could I transcend death?* The real issue was, *Am I not the very definition of life—the life unstoppable—the life redemptive—the life everlasting?*

You are a believer, and the issue of Easter is settled for you. You readily confess the resurrection. You accept it easily. Don't lose the glory of what really happened. Confess my Incarnation and celebrate its glory. Doing so could make you an incarnation of my love! It will leave you overwhelmed with wonder.

> *Prayer*
> *Lord Jesus,*
> *The world's greatest sin lies not*
> *in doubting empty tombs,*
> *but in never honoring that Almighty love*
> *that came willingly to this planet to die*
> *for human ingratitude.*
> *Forgive me when I do not stop to celebrate*
> *such all-consuming love.*
> *I cannot shake this wonderment away:*
> *that God should wear a robe of human clay.*
> *Amen.*

The Holy Spirit

John 20:20b–24

The disciples therefore rejoiced when they saw the Lord. Jesus therefore said to them again, "Peace be with you; as the Father has sent Me, I also send you." And when He had said this, He breathed on them, and said to them, "Receive the Holy Spirit. If you forgive the sins of any, their sins have been forgiven them; if you retain the sins of any, they have been retained." But Thomas, one of the twelve, called Didymus, was not with them when Jesus came.

None of what I have called you to do can be done without the Holy Spirit. I breathed on my disciples to remind them that ministry done in my name needs my empowerment. Do not trust your own zeal to accomplish what can only be done with the breath of God. In the Scriptures there is a correlation between the words *wind, breath,* and *Spirit.* The *wind* is the *breath* of God, and the *breath* of God is the *Spirit* of God. In the first chapter of Genesis, the *Spirit* or creative *breath* of God hovers over the waters, and creation is born. In the second, God breathes into Adam the *breath* of life. In the fourteenth chapter of Exodus, God sent a redeeming *wind* to hold back the waters of the Red Sea. In the third chapter of John, Jesus said that the new birth was like *the blowing wind*; it was necessary to be born of the *Spirit* to have eternal life. When the church was fully assembled on the day of Pentecost in Acts 2, the *Spirit* came with the sound of *a mighty rushing wind.*

In this same empowering sense I breathed on the disciples. They needed to remember the principle of the *breath* of God. So do you. Do you sometimes feel that your faith consists of running to church? Could it be you are merely worshiping in a mad cycle of churchy activities? Are you doing the work of God? If so, in whose name are you doing it? Are you ministering in my power or out of your own spent fatigue?

I wish for you the filling of the wind. I want you to know the sheer thrill of doing the unbelievable in my name. I want you to stand back in wonder when it occurs to you that I am in you, making you more for the sake of this needy world than you could ever be on your own.

Are you ready for such an adventure? Then draw close to me. I am ready to breathe on you. Stand still. Receive.

Prayer
Lord Jesus,
I am yours, but not merely to belong to you.
I want to be your hands and feet
    to continue your work in the world.
I want to touch this planet with that elusive empowerment
    that wakes your church with wonder.
Save through me.
Heal through me.
Resurrect the dead and
    do the unbelievable, all through me.
I yield my life and enter into death
    to gain the power that lives in Jesus' breath.
Amen.

Stay Where the Evidence Is

John 20:26–28

And after eight days again His disciples were inside, and Thomas with them. Jesus came, the doors having been shut, and stood in their midst, and said, "Peace be with you." Then He said to Thomas, "Reach here your finger, and see My hands; and reach here your hand, and put it into My side; and be not unbelieving, but believing." Thomas answered and said to Him, "My Lord and my God!"

Consider the words "after eight days . . . Thomas was with them." Thomas had lived in agony a week longer than necessary because at my first resurrection appearance, he was not there. What had Thomas actually missed by not being with the other disciples when I appeared? Mere togetherness with the family of God? Some will tell you that Thomas's absence the first time I appeared is a rebuke to all those who do not attend public worship. The church ought always to be gathered together in expectancy, waiting for me to come. To miss public worship is to cheat yourself of the pleasure of being with the family of God when God shows up in power.

The church is a wonderful community, but the writer of the Book of Hebrews had something more than mere community in mind when he wrote that we ought not to "give up meeting together" (Heb. 10:25). He was in part instructing us. The number one gift of community is not togetherness. It is worship. And worship can supply God's people with supernatural evidences of his reality.

Thomas was an honest doubter. He doubted because it is human nature to doubt. But doubt steeped his wretched soul in agony. Few people doubt on Sunday in church. They see too much evidence around them that God exists and that I am Lord of all human circumstances. Believing is Sunday's business. On Sundays the sick are made well. On Sundays the lame walk. On Sundays the living God is glorified. But later in the week, it is easier to suffer from unholy amnesia. By Thursday, Christians can forget what they affirmed on the first day of the week. Doubt crowds into their lives. They are less sure of my reality.

Thomas's sin was more than doubt. Thomas's real sin was that of missing church on that very Sunday I came in living power. Come and meet me when the church is assembled. Worship me on the first day of the week, and I will never have to say to you as I did to Thomas, "Reach out your finger . . . reach out your hand." For you will already have cried in glorious worship, "My Lord and my God!"

Prayer
Lord Jesus,
Your church contains some people who are hard to like.
I may be that kind of person
*   to someone else in the congregation.*
But we are the needy redeemed.
We need to go each week and shout, "He lives!"
*   and celebrate the grace and peace you give.*
Amen.

Blessed Are Those Who Trust the Inner Evidence

John 20:29

Jesus said to him, "Because you have seen Me, have you believed? Blessed are they who did not see, and yet believed."

There is a simple glory that silences the angels. It is the confession, "Lord, I have seen; I believe!" But there's a hush at the throne itself when anyone cries the grand confession: "Having not seen, I believe." Catch Job's wonder:

> Oh, that my words were recorded,
>> that they were written on a scroll,
>> that they were inscribed with an iron tool on lead
>> or engraved in rock, forever!
>> I know that my Redeemer lives,
>> and that in the end he will stand upon the earth. (Job 19:23–25)

Job's is the confession of real faith.

Thomas believed as he stared down into those jagged wounds that marked my hands and side. But Job had a faith beyond seeing. Job could see only by lifting up the inner eyes of faith. Trial had given Job the gift of sight. Losing everything had washed his inner vision with the clarity of unwavering faith.

You must believe with Job's faith and not Thomas's. You must with your inner vision arrive at the logic of the apostle Paul: "And if Christ has not been raised, your faith is futile; you are still in your sins. Then those also who have fallen asleep in Christ are lost. If only for this life we have hope in Christ, we are to be pitied more than all men" (1 Corinthians 15:17–19).

About thirty or so are recorded as having seen me alive after that first Easter. Only these few would ever be able to see what Thomas saw. So it was important for me to say, "Thomas, you have required too much. Christianity will be a movement of thirty people only if all people make the same requirement of seeing me that you have made."

There is a better and a much stronger way to arrive at believing. My majesty within you is the evidence that I am alive and will be forevermore.

Prayer
Lord Jesus,
Help me to believe
as instantly as sunrise.
Help me to know that there is so much of you in my heart,
there could be nothing of you remaining in the tomb.
I know you are alive, for I can see
your wounded hands are daily holding me.
Amen.

Catching Nothing

John 21:1–3

After these things Jesus manifested Himself again to the disciples at the Sea of Tiberius, and He manifested Himself in this way. There were together Simon Peter, and Thomas called Didymus, and Nathanael of Cana in Galilee, and the sons of Zebedee, and two others of His disciples.

Simon Peter said to them, "I am going fishing." They said to him, "We will also come with you." They went out, and got into the boat; and that night they caught nothing.

Peter and the other disciples had fished all night and caught nothing. When I came upon them they had been throwing the nets off the left side of the boat. "Throw your net on the right side of the boat" (John 21:6) I called to them. It must have sounded as foolish as it sounded that night some years before when I had said the same thing. But they yielded to heaven's logic and hauled in 153 good-sized fish (John 21:11).

The bulging net full of fish was a miracle they celebrated for a few weeks, but it was a lesson that they remembered the rest of their lives. They had been alternately depressed and elated. They had lost continuity and forgotten their calling. They had even forgotten their new titles, *apostles*. The word means "missionaries." They had been called to spread the gospel, the good news that "God was reconciling the world to himself in Christ" (2 Cor. 5:19). But they had become depressed and returned to fishing.

It wasn't that their nets were empty after a long night of catching nothing. They were empty. But dark depression can turn on a coin when God gets involved. They let down their nets and suddenly their nets were full. Now they were leaping in the water like children. Suddenly they were hungry for more than breakfast. They wanted a newness that would fill their empty lives as my Father had filled their nets.

I love all those who come eagerly to me for the filling. And they did. It was one of the last times we would ever get together on this planet. We celebrated a breakfast banquet by the sea. They ate the hot fish and were filled, but they drank even more deeply of that which only I could supply. I gave them of myself.

Let me ask you this: Are you hungry? Have you fished all night and caught nothing? Have you hungered for that meal that can only be supplied as you open your life to the bread of heaven? Then cast in your nets on the other side of your productless life. And you will see there is fullness. When you face those sterile, empty, and productless times of your life, look for me. I am ever on the shoreline of your life. I will be calling to you, "Let down on the other side!" And you will find abundance, where once the sea was gray and empty.

Prayer
Lord Jesus,
Often I feel I am doing nothing important.
Often my product is so minimal
I feel like my life is wasted.
Are you there on the shore?
I need to know.
Tell me on which side of my empty life I may find your abundance.
I'm empty in my soul where you have been.
Bid me let down my nets. Fill me again.
Amen.

The Critical Question

John 21:15

So when they had finished breakfast, Jesus said to Simon Peter, "Simon, son of John, do you love Me more than these?" He said to Him, "Yes, Lord; You know that I love you." He said to him, "Tend My lambs."

There is one critical question for the servant: "Do you love me?" It's a nettling question you might prefer to answer tomorrow, when tonight's party is over . . . when you're free to withdraw from your current round of sin. That morning by the Sea of Tiberias, I forced Peter to answer the question.

Peter didn't need to answer it so I'd feel better knowing I was loved. I made him answer it so he could set himself free. There are only two answers to the question, yes or no. The no answer usually means, "No, thank you! I'm self-absorbed."

Most are not inclined to say no, for that is too blatantly honest. They would rather just keep busy. They simply do what Peter did that morning. The question has so much responsibility hidden in it that Peter preferred not to answer it at all. He flippantly shot out an unfelt reply, "Yes, Lord, you know I love you . . . and by the way, that was great fish."

The third time I asked him, he broke into tears. He was stung with his three-fold betrayal some weeks before.

The question I have for you is this: How do you deny me? You are not an atheist, who would decry my existence. You would openly say that you believe in me. You own up to our friendship each time you recite the Apostle's Creed. But could your liturgical response really be saying, "Yes, Lord, I love you. Still, you can't expect me to cut back on my own agenda. I have to make a living, spend time with the children, and take care of my financial obligations. I'll get down to the actual demonstration of my love later."

I had something for Peter to do. I wanted him to feed my sheep. There is responsibility that goes with the question "Do you love me?" Peter answered quickly because he knew there was a requirement in love.

So it is with you. If my Father asks you to do anything, it will be hard. Indeed, it will require the spending of your soul. But remember this: "My yoke is easy and my burden is light" (Matt. 11:30). Nor will I ever ask you to do anything alone. Whatever the task, you have the promise of my presence. I'll be there under the yoke with you, guaranteeing the outcome, honoring your faithfulness.

Prayer
Lord Jesus,
I love you, (but I am) afraid of all you might ask
    when I have finished my confession.
But I know that there is no better way to live
    than to love you who loved me to the limits of Calvary.
Yes, I love you.
Show me how to love you and to trust,
    to let you carry all I know you must.
Amen.

Mind Your Own Business

John 21:18–22

"Truly, truly, I say to you, when you were younger, you used to gird yourself, and walk wherever you wished; but when you grow old, you will stretch out your hands, and someone else will gird you, and bring you where you do not wish to go." Now this He said, signifying by what kind of death he would glorify God. And when He had spoken this, He said to him, "Follow Me!" Peter, turning around, saw the disciple whom Jesus loved following them; the one who also had leaned back on His breast at the supper, and said, "Lord, who is the one who betrays You?" Peter therefore seeing him said to Jesus, "Lord, and what about this man?" Jesus said to him, "If I want him to remain until I come, what is that to you? You follow Me!"

There is a natural tendency among people to worry why they have it so hard when others have it so easy. Peter could tell from my prophecy that he was not going to have it easy. He knew how I died. So when I told Peter he would be a martyr, he naturally wanted to know what kind of deal John was going to get. I told him that John might never taste of martyrdom or death. At least, it could be so if I willed it.

Have you ever felt that life is requiring from you so much more than you can deliver? Have you, in such moments, looked across from you and seen someone who appeared to be having it easier, resenting them for getting the good deals of life? Have you asked that most useless of all questions, "Lord, what shall this man or woman do?"

Remember, I will not lay upon you more than you are able to bear. I simply want you to live your life faithfully, doing what I have asked. It would have been so typical of all that is human if in Gethsemane or on the cross, I had complained to God that I was, after all, his Son. While I wanted to redeem humankind, surely he could think up some easier way for me to get it done.

Do you remember what I wrote through the angel to the church at Smyrna? "Do not be afraid of what you are about to suffer. I tell you, the devil will put some of you in prison to test you, and you will suffer persecution for ten days. Be faithful, even to the point of death, and I will give you the crown of life" (Rev. 2:10).

Peter was martyred, and John died in old age and in exile. But the question for either was the same: "Did you finish what I specifically gave you to do? Were you faithful?" These are the only questions appropriate for you as well. "Are you doing what I specifically asked of you?" If so, your obedience is our common joy.

Prayer
Lord Jesus,
My only question to you is not
"What shall this person do?"
* but*
"What am I to do?"
And, oh yes, there is one other question:
* "Will you be with me?"*
If so,
* just give me all you are and I'll ask then*
* not why you gave, but only how and when.*
Amen.

The Indefinable, Uncontainable Life of Christ

John 21:24–25

This is the disciple who bears witness of these things, and wrote these things; and we know that his witness is true. And there are also many other things which Jesus did, which if they were written in detail, I suppose that even the world itself would not contain the books which were written.

John was but a fisherman whose simple life collided with my Godhood. When he finished writing his wonderful Gospel, he reached this glorious conclusion: My life was bigger than his Gospel.

John was right: the world itself could not contain the books that could be written were my whole life to be recorded. There is a greatness in my Father's love that forbids the telling of it all. So in these meager Gospels there is not all the truth that might be told of me—only enough truth to save you.

The Gospels are sufficient to whet the earthly appetite to know me. In the Gospels you have seen but the tip of truth, but it is a resplendent tip that causes you to know there is a deeply submerged body of glorious truth. The great hymns often focus on this truth. You can't have the whole story. It is too immense for even a large book. Therefore, you will never have the fullness of your longing satisfied. My life and the awesome glory of my Incarnation transcend the short and simple Gospels.

All you may know of my earthly existence comes from four biographies, Matthew, Mark, Luke, and John. But John admits his small goose quill dipped in berry juice was too little to write the full story of the everlasting God. That would take a cosmic pen and parchment that circled the earth. But read what he wrote, and glory that he told you enough to be saved.

Then get ready. For I will come in a moment, in the twinkling of an eye, and the glory of the full story will at once be magnified. My story is bigger than you are. It is bigger than John was. But then, who would want a Savior who could be measured in even an extended biography? Lose yourself beyond the pages of these small Gospels, but only after you have found yourself within them.

Prayer
Lord Jesus,
I hunger to know
what now is hidden.
I want to see you in all your glory—
I want to behold the whole truth
which now transcends the glory that has saved my soul.
You are much more than mortal eye can see,
a book in time for all eternity.
Amen.

The Promise of Authority

Matthew 28:16–20a

But the eleven disciples proceeded to Galilee, to the mountain which Jesus had designated. And when they saw Him, they worshiped Him; but some were doubtful. And Jesus came up and spoke to them, saying, "All authority has been given to Me in heaven and on earth. Go therefore and make disciples of all the nations, baptizing them in the name of the Father and the Son and the Holy Spirit, teaching them to observe all that I commanded you."

This noble passage is best read "since you're going into all the world anyway, make disciples as you go." My church has been left weak by a huge misunderstanding of this verse. Most see the Great Commission as a call to a few special people to leave their home country and go to some continent far away. Since most don't feel this international call, they ignore this verse altogether. A double view then comes to exist: some are called to give their money, and others are called to die for me in a foreign land.

Tell all you meet, "Do not brush off your obligation to this verse merely because you were born in some particular country and plan to die there. The idea central in this Great Commission is that everybody is to go somewhere, even if it is only across the street. And since you're going anyway, preach the gospel where you do go."

There was a man who lived in a certain city who felt called to be a foreign missionary. He gave his life to me and started studying so that someday when his studies were done, he could be commissioned by a mission board, fly to Africa, and *poof* suddenly become a missionary!

He went weekly to an African-American restaurant to eat. He took his clothes to a Chinese-American laundry. These wonderful Buddhist people needed to know my saving grace. Yet he never told them about my love. He knew an old Laotian man in his apartment building. The old man worshiped only his ancestors. Yet this student never once mentioned me to him.

He did at last graduate and went to Africa as a missionary. A simple ocean crossing changed nothing. He could not instantly become in Africa what he had steadfastly refused to be at home.

Are you currently walking by someone who does not know me? Who is in your carpool or office? Since you're going into all the world anyway, be faithful where you are. The needy in your own neighborhood would be foreign to a missionary from some other continent. Save them the trouble of crossing the ocean to tell what you only have to cross the street to announce.

Prayer
Help me to open up my eyes
    and see what need unfolds itself.
The lost are not somewhere else.
They are here, waiting, seeking, needing
    who I know.
    not what I know.
The gospel-needy world is not out there,
    it's here, it's there, it's now, it's everywhere.
Amen.

The Promise of Power

Acts 1:3–5

To these He also presented Himself alive, after His suffering, by many convincing proofs, appearing to them over a period of forty days, and speaking of the things concerning the kingdom of God. And gathering them together, He commanded them not to leave Jerusalem, but to wait for what the Father had promised, "Which," He said, "you heard of from Me; for John baptized with water, but you shall be baptized with the Holy Spirit not many days from now."

In the last few earthly moments of my resurrected glory, I chose to remind my disciples that I would not leave the redemption of the world in their hands. I would make them more than human beings. I would fill them with myself, and all that they would be asked to accomplish in my name they would be enabled to do with my power.

Have you discovered this power? Liken my empowering Spirit to a hand that fills a glove. You may lay a glove on the table and shout your commands down at it. "Glove! Hear me! I command you, pick up this book. Write with that pencil." All of your shouting will not make the glove obey you.

But slip your hand into the glove, and you will be amazed what can be done. The weak, inanimate glove now can grasp, write, lift, and move in splendor because of the inner power that fills it.

Now you are but a powerless glove awaiting the infilling hand of God. What you could never achieve on your own is now made possible. You can heal, raise the dead, preach the all-persuasive gospel. Everything is possible when the power comes.

In this final promise to my church I contrasted two baptisms. The baptism of water was a baptism in which human beings choose to confess their faith. This baptism is their declaration that they are with me in the Kingdom enterprise.

But the baptism of the Spirit in tongues of flame is not from human intention. I alone am the giver of Pentecost. I freely empower my church to prove that the fullness of your potential cannot be accomplished by what you choose to give God. The fullest human potential comes in a baptism of fire. There the weak human glove knows the powerful filling of God's hand.

When was the last time you knew the thrill of that power dwelling in you? When was the last time you knew the joy of tackling something too big for you and had to depend on God? If you have only been going to church and helping out "as best you can," stand back and prepare yourself. The fire is burning. The wind is blowing. With an honest confession and a willing openness, the difficult is easy, the impossible is immediate.

Prayer
Lord Jesus,
Baptize me in your holy fire
so that my plain life
may at last be measured
by the remarkable.
I come to you cold ashes of desire
in search of your incendiary fire.
Amen.

The Promise of the Future

Acts 1:9–12

And after He had said these things, He was lifted up while they were looking on, and a cloud received Him out of their sight. And as they were gazing intently into the sky while He was departing, behold, two men in white clothing stood beside them; and they also said, "Men of Galilee, why do you stand looking into the sky? This Jesus, who has been taken up from you into heaven, will come in just the same way as you have watched Him go into heaven." Then they returned to Jerusalem from the mount called Olivet, which is near Jerusalem, a Sabbath day's journey away.

My final earthly appearance ended in my ascension a week and a half before the day of Pentecost. The apostles had imagined neither the force of Pentecost nor the power of the Spirit. It was easy on the mountain to see the disconsolation of my disciples.

My post-Resurrection appearances had left them edgy. My dropping in and out of sealed rooms and my sudden arrivals and eerie disappearances wore on their nerves. It was even more nerve-racking for them to try to figure out how all of these unscheduled appearances would finally end. I had told them how important it was that I go away, for if I didn't go away the Comforter—my blessed Holy Spirit—could not come.

But my Father took special action to help them past the pain of my leaving. At my ascension two angels stood beside me. These angels remained on the mount even as I began rising into the sky. They turned their heads upward and said, "This same Jesus, who has been taken from you into heaven, will come back in the same way you have seen him go into heaven" (Acts 1:11).

Here is the promise that separates the Christianity of theological study from Christianity as an event. The real witness of these angels is that Christianity was not over with the Ascension. The best of all had not happened yet. The Gospels tell only part of my story, the story of Christianity down to Ascension Sunday. I've yet one wonderful thing I must do upon the earth.

Are you prone to lament, "I wish I could have been alive in Jesus' day to personally see all that he did"? Rejoice! The best part of my life may still be yours to behold. It is possible that you will be alive when I come again. You may be on the extreme end of history—across all of Christian time—that will have the privilege of seeing what those on Mt. Olivet could only dream about. You may see the grand event, history's conclusion, my second coming. This sky-splitting finale may be yours to behold. Watch! This hour—in all its glory—could belong to you!

Prayer
Lord Jesus,
I wait as one in eagerness
to see what the apostles
only dreamed about.
Come, holy Lord, and quickly redeem
and bless that hour we daily do esteem.
Amen.

To Tell the Truth

Luke 1:1–4

Inasmuch as many have undertaken to compile an account of the things accomplished among us, just as those who from the beginning were eyewitnesses and servants of the word have handed them down to us, it seemed fitting for me as well, having investigated everything carefully from the beginning, to write it out for you in consecutive order, most excellent Theophilus; so that you might know the exact truth about the things you have been taught.

I came to the earth to redeem it. The faith I established on earth is built upon this glorious tension. Everyone must seek an utterly interior affair with me,.but should have an open affair with truth. The dynamic power of Christianity has always come from a holy introversion that supplies power to the believer. But the missionary force of faith comes from an equally holy extroversion that tells all the truth it knows about my love.

Luke knew of this interior seeking and exterior telling. It was not mankind to whom he wrote. In fact, he had no idea that his Gospel would still be the spiritual bread of billions after two thousand years. He was writing his Gospel for his friend Theophilus. He wanted to write this friend to tell him all of the truth he knew about me. In being open to all he knew about me, he told this truth to more people than he ever dreamed.

Theophilus had met in Luke a man of inner hunger and outer boldness. Yet by his own admission, Luke was only telling others what he had learned from those who had actually seen me. These eyewitnesses told what they had seen, and those they told told others yet. And so Luke's truth moved down across recorded time. In this telling-and-retelling principle, you yourself are debtor to Luke.

Now you are the latest link in this unbroken chain of truth between my lifetime and your own. This begins the season when all the world finds people getting ready to celebrate my coming to Earth. See yourself a new way this season. Take seriously what Luke took seriously. Who is your Theophilus? Who is alone? Who is needy? Whose family is in a radical and dissolving state of dysfunction? Who is that person you simply must tell about our very special friendship? What a way to honor my coming! Tell someone so that the season will wake a cosmic chord in the life of someone who needs to hear. Then your own life will be marked by a glorious new vitality.

Prayer
Lord Jesus,
I remember and celebrate
that special day I first heard
about your love.
I thank you for including me
in the circle
of your Kingdom.
And I thank those who told
me of your claim
upon my life.
Except for those who brought your Word to me,
I never would have known this liberty.
Amen.

In the Beginning for the Now

John 1:1–3

In the beginning was the Word, and the Word was with God, and the Word was God. He was in the beginning with God. All things came into being by Him, and apart from Him nothing came into being that has come into being.

In the beginning is such mortal terminology. Time is a human category devised by those who have so little of it. When seventy years is all you may live, you must measure and cherish time. You must divide it into seconds, minutes, and years. You have to speak often of endings and beginnings.

But I am here millennia before you were born. I was ahead of you in time, loving you and counting every thousand years as but a day (2 Pet. 3:8). Even the stars that light your night are too young to measure my being. I was here before your world ever found a galaxy in which to rest.

So many mortals are fascinated with the beginning, the origins of all that is. But my Father was there then, and he always will be the God of the *now*. He does not live through time measuring its passage from past to future. He stands above time, knowing what you call the *past* and the *future* as the *now*.

If you would come to know my Father, you must meet him in the *now*. Come in the *now* to love him. Come now to adore him. Come now, there is no other time.

But this God of the *now* longs to let you know all about him. He reveals himself, he discloses all he is. This is the meaning of *the Word*. We use words to instruct, enlighten, and inform, to communicate and form relationships. God is all of these things. He is not *a* word but *the* Word. He is exalted in the heavens, needing nothing from any human being. Yet he has voluntarily revealed himself, striking up a conversation that human beings could never have done. No one can ever force God to declare himself. None has the lever to pry heaven from the shadows nor the force to make God talk.

God first revealed himself as a word to the prophets. But then God sent me to the planet. Now I am the Word. All that I have said is his Word. I am his last, best voice. I speak, and you hear him. I touch you, and you feel him. And I am eager to reveal myself to you. I came to earth for the sole purpose of getting to know you. Are you eager to get to know me? From eternity past you have been in my mind. Receive the Word. Receive me. I am the source of your being. I am the God of the *now*, and now is where I long to meet you.

Prayer
Lord Jesus,
I know you stood before
the great celestial clockwork
ever clicked the
hurried seconds
of eternity.
The beginning was too long ago to seem quite true
and too far distant to be of use to you.
Remove the future. Put the past away.
But give me every moment of today.
Amen.

The Boundary of Servanthood

John 1:4–5
In Him was life, and the life was the light of men. And the light shines in the darkness, and the darkness did not comprehend it.

At the edge of every dark chasm there is but one true friend, the light. We cannot walk the quaking precipice of time without it. It was John, my kinsman, who first began to preach this joyous truth. I must tell you how I loved him and why. John was most popular, yet it was not a popularity he made into a god. How rare was his commitment to the truth. So many who become loved for telling the truth end up loving not the truth but loving only to be loved.

Not John.

He knew that life without God was a chasm. He knew I was the true light and that only with me at the heart's center could human beings traverse the slippery ledges of existence. People loved John's sermons and offered him the reputation of a lesser god.

He would not have it. It was enough for him to say, "There is a light, I am not it."

In John the love of my Father took root in the sanctity of human spirit. Those who know they are not god and say so are blessed indeed. Such lives can distinctly point to the one who is God. In such integrity is hope born. It all depends upon what you do with mere human compliments.

Do you seize them? Taste and savor them? Hold their sweetness in your mouth? Beware the deceptive sweetness of public acclaim. It can lock you up in the narrow framework of fame. Like John, bear witness to the light that is greater than you are. Quickly call God *God*, for if you hesitate, the enemy may tempt you to wear the heavy word yourself.

Be a light at the edge of the darkness. Recognize that, like John, you can point out the dangers of self-sufficiency to those who have never sought my sufficiency. Then you will find such joy in helping me save others that you will not see yourself as central in your life. John and I were partners in a great plan. You and I can be too. I died to save those who might not notice me unless you point to me and say, "See, there he is . . . the light of the world!" Will you enter into this partnership? Are you willing to let me save while you serve as the trumpet that announces my approach to all those hearts that will admit me? Carry a trumpet. I will save.

Prayer
Lord Jesus,
In the beginning was
the Word and light in
such sufficiency to make it known.
Make me like John the Baptist,
who would not let the world crown him a king.
I want to point to Christ and then say, "See,
here is the light of God's resplendency."
Amen.

Find Royalty Somewhere beyond Yourself

John 1:6–8

There came a man, sent from God, whose name was John. He came for a witness, that he might bear witness of the light, that all might believe through him. He was not the light, but came that he might bear witness of the light.

Consider my servant John the Baptist. He never wrote a book, nor did he change the social system of his day. He did not count himself to be Caesar or start his own religion. He did one simple thing: he pointed at me and said, "Behold, the Lamb of God." He was the first person to say my name aloud and call me the Messiah.

It was no little thing.

To stand in an uncaring world and say "See, here is the Christ" is an act of raw courage. It is such fearsome work that few ever manage to do it. Yet those who, like John, bear witness to me never do it because they take a vow to be courageous. They often are frightened and feel afraid. Why, then, do they do it? Because they have committed themselves to integrity. They have taken a vow to be honest. John the Baptist knew that the Kingdom of God could only come to be if those who sought its rule in human hearts would talk openly about their king. He knew that this is a world where everybody wants to be a king or queen of some sort. He knew that to press the issue of my all-demanding Kingdom was risky business. But he would not compromise.

I cannot be anyone's king unless I am given a heart-sized throne in the center of that person's life. John knew that I never save multitudes of believers at once. I save one heart at a time.

John never saw himself as brave, only honest. He was the first person to try to get others to call me King. He was the first to tell the truth about my Kingdom. Naturally, I love him.

To see that there are billions of Christians who have called me as Lord may blur the one grand idea that John never forgot. One by one is how the millions have come. The light may be seen by multitudes at once, but multitudes are not saved as multitudes.

So imitating John's declaration may be much simpler than you imagine. My Father does not hold you responsible for mass oratory. Just be faithful in your corner of the world. Look what John accomplished in the remote jungles of the Jordan River.

"I am not that light," he said. No matter. When he got through preaching the light, his world was well lit.

Prayer
Lord Jesus,
My single greatest problem
is that I remain central
in my view of things.
I wish that I could step
aside and let
the King pass by.
Forgive me, Lord, when I strut all around—
a small, lost ego in a paper crown.
Amen.

The Glory and the Grace

John 1:14

And the Word became flesh, and dwelt among us, and we beheld His glory, glory as of the only begotten from the Father, full of grace and truth.

Do not doubt my Father's existence or his love. It was for you he gathered up his vast reality and reduced me to redeeming proportions. Once here I was called Jesus. Then, God in flesh, I looked longingly back into the skies and obeyed his passionate desire to save. Yet "I and the Father are one" (John 10:30); no one can divide that glorious indivisibility that is ours. Why is my love for him so overwhelming? He heard the universal groanings of human beings, so his cosmic love came to earth as an infant and the great Word became flesh.

This Incarnation was my Father going as far as he could go to say, "I love you." There was no other step divinity could take. I am the God become man. I am fully human. So you see, I understand you. Are you tired? I too have known bone-weary fatigue. Are you in tears? I too have wept. Hungry? I fasted forty days once. Are you lonely? I agonized in friendlessness. Are you oppressed by cold social structures? I stood alone before a condemning government.

Look to me if you would understand how the Word became flesh. And when you look to me, bow your head to say, "I believe, Lord." Then you will behold my glory as the only begotten of the Father, full of grace and truth. Integrity and grace were born the day I left heaven and touched down on the planet.

Grace and *truth:* these words speak of the mercy and justice of my Father.

Grace means something given. It can never be earned. If gifts could be earned, they would no longer be gifts. Grace is mercy and love wrapped together, offered to the destitute of hope. Grace furnishes the spiritually penniless with wealth.

Truth is the stem and root of integrity. It says that all God says may be trusted to be, even as God has spoken it. I am the truth. Count on my words. I am grace. Receive freely what cannot be bought.

Prayer
Lord Jesus,
I look upon the
Word made flesh and see
that at the center of
the grandeur is a rich
simplicity.
Grace is undiluted when all
we see within it
is the empathy of love.
I glory in your true humanity—
your Word made flesh for such a one as me.
Amen.

God's Family

Matthew 1:5–6a

And to Salmon was born Boaz by Rahab; and to Boaz was born Obed by Ruth; and to Obed, Jesse; and to Jesse was born David the king.

On the list of my countless grandmothers were a harlot and an Arab girl. Grace being what it is, none should ever gloat overlong about their chosenness. Chosen was not a status conferred by God so those who received the word could be haughty about racial superiority or purity. To be chosen is to be selected for the privilege of ministry—to carry the special burden of serving my will.

There are some who like being smug about their genealogies. But consider those whom God selected for my lineage. He chose Rahab, a prostitute, whose sin may seem too vile to allow her to be enrolled among my forebears. Not so. It is not righteousness that fits people into the plan of God but a willingness to be used. My nation has not seen many offerings of peace given to Arabs, yet two Arabs are among my grandparents' grandparents.

Do you see how all encompassing my grace is? To be a Christian has never been a matter of social position or ethnic superiority. To be a Christian is to find that you are loved for yourself. No race is too inferior for grace: Ruth was an Arab. No sin can stand against my saving love: Rahab was a prostitute.

God, my Father, is ever confounding all human ideas of propriety. Just when you are prone to brag about how much you are like God or how special you are, you will be able to hear Him say, "The world is not redeemed by people who thought well of themselves, but by those who confessed their neediness to an all-sufficient Savior. Once grace has scrubbed the soul, anyone may take their place in the lineage of the Son of God."

So if Gentiles can be found in Jewish family trees, then you must admit that my Father is out to love everyone. None is so ethnically impure as to be excluded from my Father's plan. Ask Ruth. None are so sinfully perverse as to be unusable. Ask Rahab the prostitute. There is room for you too. God can use you, whoever you are, whatever your past. Isn't that wonderful?

> *Prayer*
> *Lord Jesus,*
> *In the long unfolding*
> *plan of God*
> *Rahab appears—a Gentile woman*
> *whose character*
> *seems unbefitting your own royalty.*
> *I like her, for she, like me,*
> *makes grace believable.*
> *If Rahab brought forth those of Jesse's rod,*
> *then grace must be another name for God.*
> *Amen.*

The God of Hopeless Souls

Luke 1:13

But the angel said to him, "Do not be afraid, Zacharias, for your petition has been heard, and your wife Elizabeth will bear you a son, and you will give him the name John."

My Father delights in seeing old men dream. There is an odd vacuum of hopelessness that often camps in the souls of the elderly. Perhaps they have been made disconsolate by being often disappointed with humankind's insatiable greed and cruel inhumanity. Joel the prophet prophesied that one sign of the Spirit's coming would be the wonderful sign of elderly souls effused with youthful visions.

Zacharias was an old man. Both he and Elizabeth were childless, with no one to survive their final, empty, dreamless years. Then into the hopeless humdrum of their days comes an angel with a message: "You will have a son, Zacharias—a preacher son—who will turn Israel back to God."

Visions have never been frequent, but they can be quite spectacular. Still, visions fade with time, as Zacharias found out. For the old man, it was better when the angel was gone and the sun came up! Then the old man waited while his wife's thin old frame grew thick with child. Well beyond her years she carried a son, and the son's name was hope.

Can you tell such old ones whose vacant eyes have seen little of their own significance, "God's not finished with you yet. Are your legs stiff, old one? Get them ready for dancing. Are your eyes glazed? Wash them out and fill them with God's finished vision of your life." It is a sin to quit believing too early that God is finished with us—that we have lived beyond our usefulness to him. Not so! God is the keeper of our vision. Age has nothing to do with God's call. He gives the best lessons of the future to those who are most thrilled by the privilege of serving him.

So when morning dawns and the task of getting out of bed seems a kind of sacrifice you can't afford, bless God. Are your legs too slow? Bless their pace and surrender your legs to him. Are your eyes unwashed by tears? Give them to your Father anyway. Do not cry out to see better; cry only to see God.

Prayer
Lord Jesus,
Aaron's rod, long dead,
budded at the greening touch
of God.
Barrenness is more
than childlessness.
It is that
emptiness of soul that
begs the greening touch of God.
When nothing that is living stirs in me,
my sterile life must find vitality.
Amen.

You Are Not Alone

Luke 1:28-30

And coming in, he said to her, "Hail, favored one! The Lord is with you." But she was greatly troubled at this statement, and kept pondering what kind of salutation this might be. And the angel said to her, "Do not be afraid, Mary; for you have found favor with God."

Behind Gabriel's salutation is the grand requirement. Whenever any messenger of God says, "The Lord is with thee," the person addressed should understand that God is about to ask for the spending of the soul. Mary was afraid. There was a good reason for her fear. Those who have no fear of God have never gotten very close to him. Pay small attention to those who, in a chatty and casual manner, tell you they have met God. Such braggart spirituality should talk less and tremble more. Such easy saints have rarely quaked before the all-demanding, threatening Spirit.

When you hear the phrase "The Lord is with you," you are about to be asked to do something so nearly impossible that only the direct enabling of God will make it possible. Still, there are two things of which you may be sure. If God asks you to do it, it can be done. And second, if God asks you to do it, he will supply the enabling.

My Father is the great affirmer. He compliments the feeble into great achievement. He first addressed Gideon as a "mighty warrior" (Judg. 6:12). A ripple of giggles must have passed through all the host of angels at God's compliment. Gideon, the trembling self-excuser, a mighty man of valor? Yet whatever God names soon fulfills its title. Sure enough, Gideon—yellow of spine and green of experience—trembled his way into historical greatness.

So did Mary!

But behind the angel's "The Lord is with thee" came Mary's trial. The trial required her to try to explain her miraculous pregnancy to unbelieving villagers. Behind "The Lord is with thee" came the pain of trying to convince her fiancé of her chastity. But God's glory lies in the pain of all that God asks. His love lies in his allurement. His glory is our utter spiritual dependency. In the burden of God's requirement is himself. And in himself is the treasure eternal.

So if you meet an angel, he will likely greet your quaking with a "Fear not!" It will be good for you to serve a God whose very nearness makes you tremble. But even as you tremble, adore him. Then you will learn that a God who is big enough to make you afraid is powerful enough to accomplish in your life all he is about to ask you to do.

Prayer
Lord Jesus,
Help me to remember
  you have not promised I would win
  every battle
  or gloat upon my everyday success.
But you have promised me
  your unforsaking presence.
This is the greatest promise that I own:
  I never face a single trial alone.
Amen.

The Name

Luke 1:31–33

"And behold, you will conceive in your womb, and bear a son, and you shall name Him Jesus. He will be great, and will be called the Son of the Most High; and the Lord God will give Him the throne of His father David; and He will reign over the house of Jacob forever; and His kingdom will have no end."

Gabriel instructed my mother to give me two names. Mark both names, for when you speak of me to others, you will need them both. Consider the second name I was given: I was to be called "the Son of the Most High." This name emphasizes my separation from the ordinary human experience. It is a regal and aloof name. It is an austere name that fits the unapproachable reign of my utter power over all nations and souls.

The first name Gabriel gave Mary is a more friendly name: Jesus. Of course, it literally means "Jehovah saves." But it was a common name that many mothers named their sons. Its basic connotation was less grand than its intimate value. My name "Jesus" is still seen in that way. People in your day rarely call me "Jesus" unless they are emphasizing the personal relationship. They will call me "Christ" in public ceremonies or liturgies. It is usually when they want to speak of the heart of our relationship that they call me Jesus. Believers never sing "What a Friend We Have in the Son of the Most High," but rather "What a Friend We Have in Jesus."

This is the glorious paradox of faith. I want to be both names to you. I want to be the powerful King who can speak to every mountain in your path and level it to make your pilgrimage more easy. I want to work miracles in your life to bring you joy. I want to rebuke the storms and calm the waves for you. I want to enable you to do the glorious and impossible things that will cause you to glorify my Father.

But I want to be Jesus to you too. I want to be your most intimate friend. I want to come to you when your heart is breaking. I want to sit with you when all have abandoned you. I want to share your lonely dungeons and help you face your fears in the valley of death. I want to stay so close you that when you sing "Jesus, What a Friend for Sinners," your face will light up with an honest confession that all can see.

Prayer
Lord Jesus,
There's power in your name.
When our hearts are crushed
and life is all despair,
we've but to speak
two syllables, Jesus,
and all our storms fold up their
thunderbolts and leave.
One name heals hurt and bandages our pain,
turns boiling turbulence to peace again.
Amen.

Yes, Lord

Luke 1:34–35

And Mary said to the angel, "How can this be, since I am a virgin?" And the angel answered and said to her, "The Holy Spirit will come upon you, and the power of the Most High will overshadow you; and for that reason the holy offspring shall be called the Son of God."

The only real way you can reply to the demand of God is to say, "Yes, Lord." But "Yes, Lord" is usually not the kind of reply you can speak quickly. When Gabriel explained to Mary her role in history, she was overwhelmed with her inadequacy. But she did not say, "No, Lord, get somebody else!" She understood that "No, Lord" was contradictory. Mary was like most others who have to deal with the heavy requirement of God. Their own self-doubt keeps them from saying a hasty "Yes, Lord."

Mary used a common alternative to "No, Lord." She said, "How can this be?" My Father never minds the question and is eager to explain how his impossible requirement is to be done, as much as God's deeds can be explained. Mary was young and still had to learn that my Father's *difficult* requirements are usually done quickly; his *impossible* requirements take a little longer . . . and they often take a little explanation.

"This will be easy, Mary," said the angel. "The Holy Spirit will overshadow you." While Mary demonstrates true yieldedness, she still doesn't really know how God is going to do the impossible. But she trusts that God will do all he says, and that, after all, is what really matters.

If human beings could understand God's "hows," then human beings would be gods themselves. "*Hows*" are usually the questions raised by skeptics. Mary has some right to skepticism, humanly speaking. Here the angel has just abridged all of natural law by telling her she is going to become a mother having never known a man. But Mary's yieldedness would ultimately focus on the questions of *why* and *when*.

When the angel told her "how," it really wasn't very helpful. At least it was not the kind of procedure she could explain in Nazareth. So Mary submitted to the truth of the mystery: God's how's are never very rational.

And I, of course, became her son in time, but more than that—her Lord and Savior. God might have picked another mother for his Son. But Mary served the world by offering herself. Keep in mind that all God asks you to do, he might have asked of anyone. Yieldedness places his blessings fully in your lap. Bless him for the asking. Serve him for the privilege.

Prayer
Lord Jesus,
Help me remember
that all my prayers,
if they be heard,
must be laid on the
low, low altar
of my full consent.
So use me up any way you would.
Your smallest request exceeds my finest good.
Amen.

Nothing Is Impossible with God

Luke 1:37–38

"For nothing will be impossible with God." And Mary said, "Behold, the bondslave of the Lord; be it done to me according to your word." And the angel departed from her.

The reason you fight against the will of God for your life is that it is always difficult. Anytime you think you have an opportunity for ministry but it appears easy, you may be sure God has not required it. When God asks you to do anything, it requires the spending of your soul. The angel asked Mary to be the mother of the Son of God. The very weight of glory seemed impossible for any human being to bear. To conceive a child with no human father stretched Mary's faith to the very limits of credulity.

While she tried to wrangle some sense out of the heavy idea, the angel said, "Nothing is impossible with God."

The statement is true as far as God is concerned, but it is wonderful as far as people are concerned. God can do anything, but his every act is a point of wonder for those people whom he calls to participate in it. When he acts through humanity to accomplish his will, the flow of his power through doubting servants astounds them beyond belief.

When Mary said, "Behold the handmaid of the Lord" (Luke 1:38), she used an Old Testament idea. A handmaid was a woman consigned to surrogate motherhood. Handmaids were called into the service of a barren couple to provide the possibility of children they could not manage on their own. The handmaid had a child she knew could never be her own. Directly after the child was weaned, the baby was taken from her, and its care and upbringing were totally in the hands of the adoptive parents. Only a mother can really understand how much it means to surrender a child. So Mary served selflessly in that clear manner that yielded up her very right to the word *mother*. All of this Mary understood. Her baby would never be *her* baby. He would belong to God and his needy world. Ahead of all her months of waiting she gave away her right to natural motherhood as she surrendered to the supernatural plan of God.

My Father is constantly seeking the obedient heart. He is perhaps even now stating his agenda as he calls you to take your position in his world plan. He is forever speaking your name and waiting to hear you offer him Mary's reply: "Behold, here I am." Is he asking you to take up the mantle of some great area of service? Mary yielded and gave the world a Savior. Only God knows what your own surrender might mean.

> *Prayer*
> *Lord Jesus,*
> *So often when you ask*
> *something of me*
> *I look at it as though*
> *it was my task alone.*
> *Tell me that someday*
> *I'll begin to face the tasks you give*
> *with a cheerier outlook.*
> *Give me the confidence in all I do*
> *to know that he who strengthens me is you.*
> *Amen.*

Blessed Are You

Luke 1:41–42
And it came about that when Elizabeth heard Mary's greeting, the baby leaped in her womb; and Elizabeth was filled with the Holy Spirit. And she cried out with a loud voice, and said, "Blessed among women are you, and blessed is the fruit of your womb!"

Imbedded in Elizabeth's greeting is the most wonderful gift one human being may give another: affirmation. What a gift!

See these women as they were. Elizabeth, an old woman well beyond the reach of years, is blessed with pregnancy. Hers was the difficult prospect of trying to help her skeptical community understand that God can bestow the miracle of motherhood on whom he will.

Mary too has special needs. Her pregnancy cannot be hidden. Nazarene women pass her at the well and mentally indict her for her swelling form. As it becomes increasingly clear that she is pregnant, the gossip becomes caustic. Mary knew the Mosaic law even provided that such women could be stoned in public execution. While Roman overlords generally prevented that from happening, they could not always do so. Mary had to face the ugly small-town society of Nazareth and decide the best course of action for her and her unborn child.

Mary fled to the hill country to see Elizabeth.

The hurting women met. Never was there a more joyous reunion. How each reached to the other's need! They had both been broken by community isolation and were bound by the sheer joy of bearing their very special children. They longed for touch and human understanding. Mary greeted Elizabeth, who cried, "Blessed are you!" Oh how the words washed Mary's soul with bright affirmation. Suddenly she felt a sense of worth once more. No longer was she the cursed libertine of her small community; she was the blessed of God. Could it really matter now what the community gossips of Nazareth think of her? God gave her a friend to bear a welcome word.

Would you know the heart of God? Then seek to be like Elizabeth. Find those who carry some heavy plan of God, and bless them for their yieldedness. Be like Elizabeth, that special messenger of grace. Bless those who cry out for kindness. Lift up the crushed and remind them of their special status before God. Teach the broken of the special pleasure available beyond their lonely pain.

Prayer
Lord Jesus,
I know
we bless the world
in all that we affirm.
It is the work of God
to bless the
lonely and oppressed.
I gladly take this task
upon myself.
How much I need to bless all those in pain,
conferring dignity on someone else's shame.
Amen.

The End of Pride

Luke 1:46–49

And Mary said: "My soul exalts the Lord, And my spirit has rejoiced in God my Savior. For He has had regard for the humble state of His bondslave; For behold, from this time on all generations will count me blessed. For the Mighty One has done great things for me; And holy is His name."

Mary learned that there is really only one way to deal with spiritual or psychological depression. It is a way open only to those who are willing to give to God his right to ask anything of us that he will. Such persons know that God will never ask of us anything that is unreasonable. So when he asks of us something that is difficult and soul splintering, we must accept the burden of it. Such burdens will at times steal everything except the pleasure of your obedience. But if the task is hard enough, joy will sometimes abandon you. Joy, not God. Still, when your joy is absent, your gloom may degenerate to spiritual depression.

Do not see this as a suffering that has come only to you. Read the Scriptures and you will see that nearly all of God's servants have suffered from depressions. Men and women throughout history have felt its ugly talons sink deeply into their souls. But spiritual depression is rarely shaken off by the intention alone. Nor can you summon enough sheer willpower to free you of its bondage. But there is a way to beat it. Give yourself to the art of praise.

Consider how Mary's tender soul dealt with the death-blow of all she must have felt. She praised the Lord. When you hurt beyond all imagined repair, praise God. Praise heals hurt, even immense hurt. So sing even when you don't feel like it, for singing begets singing. When your spirit is abased, pay no mind to gloom. To fail to sing is to give darkness a place in your soul—to wallow in the defeat you are trying to escape.

Rather, sing and exalt the Lord. Magnify his utter greatness. As you lift his name in praise, your own pedestrian heart will learn to fly. Hear a peasant girl singing and try to master her praise. Ask yourself three questions the next time you are immersed in gloom.

First, does your soul magnify the Lord? Second, does your spirit rejoice in Christ your Savior? Third, has the Mighty One done great things for you? If so, sit down right where you are and make a list of all the Mighty One has done. Now, do you feel relief? You don't? Then start all over again with the same three questions, and this time don't merely recite them; sing them to God. Once you are singing your questions, your praise will kill the gloom and drive depression from your life. Ask Mary. Her answer to trouble was a song. It was a powerful song. Hell is still reeling before its melody.

Prayer
Lord Jesus,
I know my pride is
often so exaggerated that it leaves me
free to worship
none but myself.
Help me to lift you up with lofty praise
so gloom will leave as joy takes its place.
Amen.

The Furnace of Intention

Luke 1:51–52

"He has done mighty deeds with His arm; He has scattered those who were proud in the thoughts of their heart. He has brought down rulers from their thrones, And has exalted those who were humble."

Mary, simple hill girl that she was, understood that "high and mighty" people are rarely used of God. The "mighty" are usually "too high" to be used at those lower altitudes where God has so much to do. They are usually "too mighty" to seek the strengthening of God, so most of the work of God gets done by people with less reputation.

Most rulers are brought down from their thrones eventually, and they discover that their thrones were not as lofty as they supposed. Still, human beings are fascinated by the pretty, the proud, the popular, and the powerful. Ask children what they want to be when they grow up. None will ever say, "I want to be humble and abased." But later they are broken by the circumstances they sought to conquer. Their circumstances really conquered them. With shattered dreams in hand they seek counselors and ministers, asking, "Is this all there is?"

Mary, in her youthful motherhood, sought only the way of God. He who scatters the proud took her life as a lump of yielded clay, fired it in the furnace of his intention, and built of her singular commitment a monument to his own glory. Three hundred years before her rural and simplistic life came Alexander the Great. The Great? Not really all that great. This mewling child-man once wept that he was so globally victorious that there were no more worlds left to conquer. He died at thirty-three years of age, my age exactly when I met my cross. And at my hour of naked dying, my mother came and watched. Her heart was broken to see me dying there.

Long before my cross she sang the overcoming truth. My mother's song has now resounded throughout the world. My Father does bring down the self-impressed and exalts the humble. The swaggering warlords of the Roman Empire martyred my disciples by the thousands. They supposed themselves mighty. But now the martyrs are exalted, and those of high degree have been eternally abased.

What does this mean in terms of your life? Perhaps you should seek humility and save yourself a worthy place within my Father's high, exalted plan. Do not complain when the world is slow to exalt you. Learn from a maid in Nazareth. Wait on Mary's wisdom. There's a throne awaiting you that the Caesars would have envied.

Prayer
Lord Jesus,
You temper steel in fire
to make it strong.
Teach me to love the
forge whereon
I take those blows
that toughen me for service.
Help me to treasure you with strong desire
and cherish always your refining fire.
Amen.

Potential

Luke 1:76–79

"And you, child, will be called the prophet of the Most High; For you will go on
BEFORE THE LORD TO PREPARE HIS WAYS; *To give to His people the knowledge of salvation,*
By the forgiveness of their sins, Because of the tender mercy of our God, With which the
Sunrise from on high shall visit us, TO SHINE UPON THOSE WHO SIT IN DARKNESS AND THE
SHADOW OF DEATH, *To guide our feet into the way of peace."*

There was a day in the era of the Caesars when an old man and woman held a baby,
and that baby held the world. Most parents hold their children too tightly. They hold
them only to release them for such goals as they have in mind. They hold rich destinies
for their children—destinies that will flatter them. They want their children to
outperform them, to succeed where they have failed, to have power where they held only
weakness. They say to their children, "Honor us! Run where we have only walked. Leap
where we have only stumbled. Dance where our poor feet were mired in self-pity." Such
parents often lay upon their children burdens too heavy to be borne.

Zacharias and Elizabeth would not inflame their son with high-minded human
dreams so that his success would inflate their egos at family gatherings for years to come.
They were old when he was born and knew that they would never live to see his
achievements.

He was not their child; he was God's. That was what they would teach him as they
nourished him in God's own special wisdom. After that he was God's alone. In this small
way they set themselves free of their need for John to succeed, and they set John free to
serve whatever use God might make of him.

John could freely receive the promise of his full potential: "You, child, will be called
the prophet of the Most High God." It was wonderful beyond his parents' old
imagination. This child would ring down the curtain of the ages with heaven's
hallelujahs. They could not know how gloriously the centuries would celebrate their son.
Yet through this son God wrote their own unselfish names in time.

Here is Zacharias's and Elizabeth's lesson. Your children are not your own. When
you became my disciple, you gave me everything. That surrender included your family.
So give your children cheerfully to me. With each sunrise, hold them up as praise and lay
them on the high altar of your best sacrifice. Then your children will be mine as I
intended. Then I will make of your family a holy family.

Prayer
Lord Jesus,
Each infant is a life
made special
by the fact that its service
lies decades out ahead.
Each baby always comes as certainty
that you still intend to use humanity.
Amen.

The Desert

Luke 1:80

And the child continued to grow, and to become strong in spirit, and he lived in the deserts until the day of his public appearance to Israel.

Deserts are places of introspection. Other people are the mirrors we use to find out who we are. But in the desert there are no other people and no mirrors. In the desert we must face ourselves and wrangle with the issues of our own identity and calling.

John grew "up" in the desert; but he also grew "inward." In the desert where rain is so infrequent that all growth is threatened, the very aridity causes those who live there to treasure every drop of water. As the aridity causes the body to cherish water, so the formidable loneliness causes the soul to cherish company. John lived where loneliness rose like heat waves from the burning sands.

He cried to God, "What will you have me do?" And so until the day of his appearing John listened, and listened, and listened. The jackals howled, the sirocco winds moaned, and God whispered, "The Kingdom is at hand. Preach repentance, and wash all those who repent in the waters of baptism. Warn the wicked to flee like fearful snakes before the prairie fires of divine wrath."

John did all that God commanded. After years of solitude, never speaking to any person, he was ready to speak to all people. In the lonely desert he had learned the Spirit's mightiest truths. Most of all he had learned that you cannot speak to the world if you are content to live in it.

Are you alone? Do not despise your loneliness. Thank God for it. Are you in some social wilderness, bewildered by huge doubts and lacking good counsel? Are you stalked by predators of jealousy, corporate envy, or financial need? Then you have but to listen and you will hear a voice of splendor calling you. Listen! The voice will ready your soul for the calling God intended for you all along. Therefore, never despise your loneliness. Use it to know God. That's why he gave you the desert. He hoped you might live without the crowds long enough that you might, at last, serve the crowds.

Prayer
Lord Jesus,
There's not enough planned aloneness
in the cityscapes where we must live.
I know you want me
to find those lonely places
that leave us time for friendship.
The still and lonely deserts know no crowd.
But in their silence Jesus speaks out loud.
Amen.

The Unconventional

Matthew 1:18–19

Now the birth of Jesus Christ was as follows. When His mother Mary had been betrothed to Joseph, before they came together she was found to be with child by the Holy Spirit. And Joseph her husband, being a righteous man, and not wanting to disgrace her, desired to put her away secretly.

When others think well of you, they will hear you when you stand to speak. Those who trust you will hear you and say, "Ah, let us gather before this fine man, this exceptional woman. His moral strength, her exemplary wisdom, will not fail us." A good reputation is the cutting edge of power both in the secular world and in the Kingdom.

Joseph was just a carpenter who did things right. If he sawed a board to an exact length, it varied not a centimeter from how it should have been cut. He was ethical to a fault. He measured his morality with exactitude. He was engaged to Mary—indeed, betrothed. His engagement was official and binding in Jewish law. The Jewish betrothal was the exact equivalent of marriage, awaiting only sexual consummation.

Then into this fragile shell of propriety came God with an unconventional miracle. Mary was pregnant. Joseph's blood scorched his face with shame. His godly reputation had been smudged. He could not tolerate Mary's sin, as he saw it. He would divorce Mary. On the grounds of infidelity in Jewish law he could do this before two witnesses if she consented. If she did not consent, then he would be forced to shame her publicly.

Men of reputation have for their worst fault an unspeakable pride. This pride can blind them to one blatant truth: God rarely acts within convention. The holy virgin birth is hard on those who want to cling to natural and explainable things. Moses was surprised to find water in the rock. It was not conventional. When Elijah called down fire from heaven, it was unconventionally fatal for Baal's prophets.

The hardest things my Father will ever ask you to do may seem so bizarre you'd rather not obey. But always obey, for when he bids you to do the bizarre, there will be manna on the rocks. Water will stand in walls. Axeheads will float. You may walk on water.

Mary's chastity was the point at which I began to deal with Joseph's pride. It would take an angel to explain it to him; but once he understood, he made a wonderful step-father to the Son of God.

Prayer
Lord Jesus,
You never act in ways
*   we think you will.*
It's not what you want us to do
*   that makes us so afraid*
*   but the way you choose to do it.*
We're frightened when we face your godly chores.
We've never seen it done that way before.
Amen.

The Savior

Matthew 1:20–21

But when he had considered this, behold, an angel of the Lord appeared to him in a dream, saying, "Joseph, son of David, do not be afraid to take Mary as your wife; for that which has been conceived in her is of the Holy Spirit. And she will bear a Son; and you shall call His name Jesus, for it is He who will save His people from their sins."

Against Joseph's pride there comes an angel. He is a special angel called to stand against almighty egotism.

Joseph was good. The problem with being good is that you soon may feel that's why you were born. Good is nice, but nobody was born to be morally ornamental. Good should be only the by-product of the way we live because we are faithful to a purpose. Serving such a purpose, we develop character.

Goodness is not a goal. Obedience is the goal. Goodness is the mystique. Goodness is the glove that wraps the fingers of faithfulness. But when people praise us for being good, insidious pride can develop. Then with only a little practice we can become proud of just being good. After that we can become protective about our reputations.

Joseph was so good that Mary's pregnancy caught him off guard. He pondered a quiet divorce and met an angel.

"Divorcing Mary so you can keep your reputation, eh, Joseph?" asked the angel. "Rather, you should marry her so she can keep hers. Don't be so interested in your reputation that you sacrifice Mary to become the gossip fodder of the Nazarenes. Marry Mary, and give her your fine and spotless name. Her child is conceived by God's Spirit. Call him Jesus the Rescuer, for he shall rescue people from their sins."

Angelic rebukes work wonders.

Now the proud carpenter ceased caring about what was proper and began to care about what was right. Pride was replaced by obedience. Humility took charge of his soul. "Yes, God," said Joseph, "I will name your Son Jesus for a world that is desperate. May he grow in sweet Mary's womb, and I will grow childlike till I can say to all, 'God is never found when we worry how we appear, but only when we tremble in fear lest we drop the cup of his requirement.'"

Prayer
Lord Jesus,
You came to save us
from eternity without you,
but more than that,
you came to save us from
our small agendas
and empty meaninglessness.
Our desperation looks across the waves
and stills the tempest, crying, "Jesus saves!"
Amen.

Immanuel

Matthew 1:22–23

*Now all this took place that what was spoken by the Lord through the prophet might be fulfilled, saying, "*BEHOLD, THE VIRGIN SHALL BE WITH CHILD, AND SHALL BEAR A SON, AND THEY SHALL CALL HIS NAME IMMANUEL," *which translated means, "*GOD WITH US.*"*

"God with us" is the most glorious truth there is. It is the only redeeming truth there is. Here are the four great syllables of human glory—Immanuel. The word is a tribute to the worth of humankind in the eyes of my Father. And what does this word really mean? It means that God so loved the world that he was not content to stay in heaven, raining blessings down upon the distant faithful. Nor did he enjoy the fiendish pleasure of hurling thunderbolts to correct the wicked and remote.

Immanuel is God looking out across the universal barricades of space and grieving that humankind was trapped in lives that held no reason and deaths that dumped their swift decay in shallow graves. It is not distance that forms the barricades of God. It is materiality. My Father exists everywhere. He has always been *among* persons; but in the blessed Immanuel event, he *became* a person. It has been well said that many men throughout the centuries tried to become a god, but only once did God try to become a man. Try? No. God does not try. He does. In the Incarnation, Immanuel became a man to prove that there was a raging love affair at the center of the universe. God Immanuel? Was there ever love like this?

Who can measure the glorious and biological impossibility of the virgin birth? A virgin conceives while the Spirit overshadows her. The virgin birth is as real as it is incongruous. God acted in a tiny womb of time to include himself in time. Let none doubt either my virgin birth or resurrection. The virgin birth landed me in time, and the Resurrection-Ascension took me out of it again. These two miracles are the bookends of my time within time, thirty-three years of God in human flesh, sandwiched in-between vast, immeasurable eternities. Destroy the Resurrection and my decaying form is still in some lone Syrian grave. Destroy the virgin birth and God, my Father, still lives far away from human desperation. God became a person for the sake of persons, and the glory of it is greater than your song. It is a song whose melody aimed at your redemption and whose lyrics included your name.

Prayer
Lord Jesus,
You volunteered to be
what we would sometimes like to escape,
to be a human being.
It's hard for us to try to understand
the kind of love that transforms God to man.
Amen.

The Hospitality of Grace

Luke 2:1–7

Now it came about in those days that a decree went out from Caesar Augustus, that a census be taken of all the inhabited earth. This was the first census taken while Quirinius was governor of Syria. And all were proceeding to register for the census, everyone to his own city. And Joseph also went up from Galilee, from the city of Nazareth, to Judea, to the city of David, which is called Bethlehem, because he was of the house and family of David, in order to register, along with Mary, who was engaged to him, and was with child. And it came about that while they were there, the days were completed for her to give birth. And she gave birth to her first-born son; and she wrapped Him in cloths, and laid Him in a manger, because there was no room for them in the inn.

I was born in a stable because the world was full of people who had all settled in for a night of rest. Had anyone in Bethlehem guessed that I was about to be born and that history would record the selfish actions of local innkeepers, they would have treated my weary parents with more respect. But Bethlehem is ever symbolic of the work of God. He often arrives incognito and embarrasses the selfish with the blessings of abundance that they have denied him.

There's so little room for God in the human scene. God ever comes to humanity having to elbow his way into his own holidays. And so it goes in Bethlehem and Boston, in Bosrah and Bangladesh, in Baltimore and Bangkok and Bonn. Now, of course, in the clear light of history, perspective looks back and says, "We should have given Jesus space. Others should have taken the stable—not him."

In the clear light of history, a church has been built—not where the rude inn was located, but where the crude cave gave me a little straw. "The Church of the Nativity" is its name.

"Such a travesty," you say, "that needy human beings could brusquely refuse God space." Do you remember last week, when I wanted in your life, and you said to me, "Try down the block; my schedule is full." Do not call the inns of Bethlehem unfriendly while you keep forcing me from your own privatized agenda. Do not crowd me from your life, even if you later plan to build a shrine of repentance above your nice refusals. It will never really be Christmas till I am born with your full permission in all the busy affairs of your life. I do not want to be adored on the back lot of your business, but squarely in the middle of all your involvements.

Prayer
   Lord Jesus,
   The greatest words of mercy
      may be the simple invitation,
      "Come in."
   One who is outside
      without shelter always waits and hopes
      for those inside
      to really care.
   Lord, there must be room inside of me
      to grant you grace and hospitality.
   Amen.

The Terror of His Presence

Luke 2:8–11

And in the same region there were some shepherds staying out in the fields, and keeping watch over their flock by night. And an angel of the Lord suddenly stood before them, and the glory of the Lord shone around them; and they were terribly frightened. And the angel said to them, "Do not be afraid; for behold, I bring you good news of a great joy which shall be for all the people; for today in the city of David there has been born for you a Savior, who is Christ the Lord."

All are frightened by the unbridled joy of angels whose praise gets out of control. Its no good telling terrified shepherds "Fear not" after you've burst upon them with a loud sky anthem that has them pinned to the ground in terror. But then real joy is never a quiet assignment. You can't whisper an anthem that's designed to set the world sideways. The quaking shepherds, like most who have ever dealt with angels, found their side of the conversation lacking. After all, what do you say to an angel? It is far easier to listen to them than to try and work the small chitchat of your daily life into their grand conversations.

So into the stammering bewilderment of befuddled herdsmen, the angel announced that the focus of the midnight fireworks was a baby. If you were a shepherd, you would likely have asked, "Well, then, why terrify us? Couldn't you have just sent us a birth announcement?"

No, my quaking friends, this baby is too special to announce in ordinary ways. Get into town and fall on your knees. Your homage will begin the reign of God in human form. Leave your sheep and teach the world that all things can wait when God himself comes wrapped in coarse cloth.

Can you see the miracle, you modern shepherds? Divinity has come to town and is so content to be humanity that he whimpers till he's full of human milk. And to think, he did all this so shepherds could have a Shepherd.

The angels are through singing. It's all on greeting cards now. Still, you must rejoice. God is in town. How long will he stay? Long enough to know exactly how it feels to be a human being.

> *Prayer*
> *Lord Jesus,*
> *The fear of the Lord*
>   *is the beginning of wisdom.*
> *Give me fear.*
> *Make me wise.*
> *Your nearness is the joy of all I seek.*
> *I thrill at it, and yet it leaves me weak.*
> *Amen.*

Gloria in Excelsis

Luke 2:14–15

"Glory to God in the highest, And on earth peace among men with whom He is pleased." And it came about when the angels had gone away from them into heaven, that the shepherds began saying to one another, "Let us go straight to Bethlehem then, and see this thing that has happened which the Lord has made known to us."

It was Jerome who translated the first Bible. It was Jerome who recorded that these angels sang in Latin, *Gloria in Excelsis Deo.* It does sound good in Christmas pageants, especially when performed in Gothic cathedrals. Still, the shepherds spoke Aramaic, so the angels sang to be understood. You can mark it down that God speaks only in those languages which we understand. You'll never hear his angels singing Spanish hymns to Mandarin congregations.

At the center of the angels' song is a message of peace to those of good will. The angels' song came in the fourteenth year of the emperor Augustus. The conquering, war-mongering Romans were enjoying as much of a time of peace as ever came to Rome. So universal was this time of peace that they called it the *Pax Augusti,* the Peace of Augustus.

But the angels knew that my peace was much greater than that. It was the *Pax Christi,* the peace of Christ. My peace was for men and women whose good will was extended to God, who wanted to move inside them with an inner peace not subject to war or turmoil. There is a peace, as the psalmist recalled, that cannot be threatened even when a table is prepared in the midst of your enemies. My peace is more than the song of angels; it is the song of martyrs. My peace is the prayer in the tempest, the stillness at the center of every human storm.

Gloria in Excelsis is still alive. My peace I still give. Let not your heart fear, neither let it be afraid. Rather, my peace marks you as a trusting disciple. Think what my coming means in your life. Does not the joy of this thought wake you at midnight with gratitude? Then let your *Gloria in Excelsis* rise at midnight if necessary. Let it bring the victory of my Incarnation to every doubting season of your year.

> *Prayer*
> *Lord Jesus,*
> *The voice of human*
> *praise sets all of us*
> *weak mortals free of the*
> *awful necessity of ourselves.*
> *Help us to praise as angels do*
> *that we at last*
> *may learn their constant joy.*
> *If more angelic glorias touch the sky,*
> *perhaps our praise may teach us too to fly.*
> *Amen.*

The Storehouse of the Heart

Luke 2:19–20

But Mary treasured up all these things, pondering them in her heart. And the shepherds went back, glorifying and praising God for all that they had heard and seen, just as had been told them.

In the wondrous night of boisterous angels and bewildered shepherds, the miracle of my birth did not shout its reality to any in Bethlehem. The great miracles do not always shout. Sometimes they whisper their reality. Mary found a quiet place to store these quiet holy truths—her heart. The heart is that small fleshly vault that holds treasures none can ever take away.

I met Mary where she pondered the miracles of that holy night. But every night is holy if the heart has need to celebrate. So often that celebration comes after the tearing turmoil of all that has preceded it. Remember all that had been going on in Mary's life in the months just prior to my birth? She had been castigated by her community and nearly "sent away" by her embarrassed fiancé. She had felt reprimanded and had made two desperate journeys during her pregnancy—one to the hill country, and the other to Bethlehem during her final month of waiting. Mary had been worn by asking to carry all anyone can carry. But after her baby came, the pain reverted to joy! She was healed in spirit. She was ecstatic over the blessings of God. She made a storeroom of souvenirs out of her heart.

Do you honor that quiet place in the center of your own soul? Do you keep, in the quiet center of your life, a still retreat where you may think of all the wondrous things we've shared? Most hearts are too noisy to understand that they are the filing cabinets of the soul.

Does your life hold many miracles? Do you remember where it was that first we met? Was the meeting special to you?

Would you be my special friend? Then retreat to the silent center and count the treasures you've laid up there. There are no great persons who do not daily rehearse the great moments in their pilgrimage with God. Rehearse God's love continually in your heart, and you will soon become what you rehearse. Celebrate my presence in your heart, and your heart will hold a love affair so rich that angels will envy you.

Prayer
Lord Jesus,
Help us learn Mary's art of meditation.
Maybe as we stir up
  yesterday's confidence in God,
  we make tomorrow possible.
I love remembering each day of grace.
I store them in a celebrative place.
Amen.

The Pigeons of Poverty

Luke 2:22–24

And when the days for their purification according to the law of Moses were completed, they brought Him up to Jerusalem to present Him to the Lord (as it is written in the Law of the Lord, "EVERY first-born MALE THAT OPENS THE WOMB SHALL BE CALLED HOLY TO THE LORD"), and to offer a sacrifice according to what was said in the Law of the Lord, "A PAIR OF TURTLEDOVES, OR TWO YOUNG PIGEONS."

You are more defined by what you give away than by what you keep. Mary and Joseph were poor, and at the temple ritual they offered only doves in sacrifice. Sacrifice for the wealthy might have been an ox or lamb, but for the poor it was only a pair of doves. Unto every level of means, so is the requirement of God.

But the point of your sacrifice is not how much you give; it is only the issue of surrender. In sacrifice you take something that means a great deal to you—that you could use for yourself—and you give it away. In the case of Jewish religion, Mary and Joseph gave the doves to the priests in the temple.

Can their sacrifice instruct you at this season? Is this a time for you to surrender your money to help someone else, or is this merely a season for you to enjoy your own abundance?

Mary and Joseph illustrate that sacrifice is not the habit of those who can afford it. Nor does it require us to commit ourselves to poverty. Rather, it frees us from loving too much the gifts that we surrender.

This is why God honors your sacrifice. It is better to give some of your living to him rather than keep it all for yourselves. For if you feel your gifts are too much for you to give away, you have already chained yourself to a very low altar of greed. If you keep all that you own, soon you will worship only your position and your goods. Resist such greed. Give freely, and God will loom large at every sunrise of your adoration.

Christmas is the season to test Mary and Joseph's viewpoint. Give something to God this season, and you will feel a kind of worship you did not feel just by giving gifts to your family or friends. Christmas celebrates the season God gave freely to you. Give to God and understand the season of his abundance.

Prayer
   Lord Jesus,
   Here at the
     season of your birth,
     help me to give
     my finest offering to you.
   If Mary's offering of grace is small,
     it still must be that she has offered all.
   Amen.

Nunc Dimittis

Luke 2:25–32

And behold, there was a man in Jerusalem whose name was Simeon; and this man was righteous and devout, looking for the consolation of Israel; and the Holy Spirit was upon him. And it had been revealed to him by the Holy Spirit that he would not see death before he had seen the Lord's Christ. And he came in the Spirit into the temple; and when the parents brought in the child Jesus, to carry out for Him the custom of the Law, then he took Him into his arms, and blessed God, and said, "Now Lord, Thou dost let Thy bond-servant depart / In peace, according to Thy word; / For my eyes have seen Thy salvation, / Which Thou hast prepared in the presence of all peoples, / A LIGHT OF REVELATION TO THE GENTILES, / And the glory of Thy people Israel."

It is a gift to have a single goal for living and to know exactly the moment you achieve that goal. Old Simeon's eye had wandered for years across a dream of unsatisfied longing. In some long-ago instance of his worship, it seemed he heard God within the echoes of his soul. The God of faith cried out to him, "You are selected; I have chosen you; you will not die until you see the Messiah with your own eyes."

The voice inside Simeon came and went with the seasons. The promise of God grew old as he grew old. At doubtful midnights he would ask himself again and again, "Was there a voice? Has God promised? When, if ever, in my never-ending stream of relationships, will the moment come?" Passover followed Passover as the years dragged on. Sometimes the promise seemed so dim, so very far away. His friends and family died away. Funeral by funeral he donned his prayer shawl, went to the synagogue, and prayed. Sometimes he rebuked God. Sometimes he reminded God that his life could go on only a little while more. His hearing diminished; his vision darkened. "Where, God? When, God?"

Then on a nameless day, when his bent old back could hardly hold him straight, on weary feet he shuffled off to the temple worship, and in the maddening throng saw a young Nazarene woman holding her baby. The scales fell from his eyes. He was mad with joy! He saw that the God of promise never fails. He greeted the woman and gently took her baby. He held her little one to the sun and in his scratchy old voice, breathed *"Nunc Dimittis.* Now let your servant depart, for my eyes have seen the salvation of God."

Let Simeon's passing years rebuke impatience. God always keeps his word—all that God says he will do. Trust and wait. Great is his faithfulness.

Prayer
Lord Jesus,
Help me to mark
the clear and studied purpose of my life.
I want to live my life so when it's through
I know exactly what I came to do.
Amen.

The Sword

Luke 2:35

". . . and a sword will pierce even your own soul—to the end that thoughts from many hearts may be revealed."

Mothers give birth only to discover that while their children can live outside their bodies, they can never move outside their hearts. A mother dies at every gallows where she must stand beside a dying son. Never is a child cut down in battle but that the mother feels the blade. Old Simeon told Mary that the price she would pay to bear the Son of God would at last result in the skewering of her soul. This sword, the *romphaia,* was not the short broad *machaira* of the Roman legionnaires. The *romphaia* was a long sword that more resembled an impaling stake.

Was old Simeon heartless to forecast so dire a threat? Could he force the mother of the Son of God to live through the next three decades waiting for the long and dreaded sword to arrive?

Six times the Scriptures speak of Mary as "blessed." Perhaps it is because she waited and kept faith with me. She celebrated every accolade that came to me, rejoicing when Palm Sunday made me king. Oh, but she anguished when the hammers fell, and the nails shot blue-white pain through the splintering of my wrists. She cried the day the sword came, but she remembered the long-ago words of an old man.

God's gift at Christmas is not the sentiment of the manger story. The gift was a tale written in blood. I wish that every Christmas service contained a communion. At the season of joy, intermingle the loaf and cup. Lift up the cup and cry, "Behold, the Lamb of God, which takes away the sin of the world!" In the time of birth, do not forget why I was born. It was not my birth that washed away your sins; it was my blood.

The sword that pierced Mary's soul through was the same sword that purchased your redemption. The will of God is never bargain stuff. The cross is costly. At Christmas when you celebrate my birth, do not sing your glad noels without thinking of all it means to subject yourself to the dying life. Purchase your *Glorias* by submitting your soul to the infant King. Sing "Joy to the World!" Now, follow up your Christmas joy with Easter obedience. Take up your cross and follow me.

Prayer
  Lord Jesus,
  There is no such thing
    as uninvolved crucifixion.
  To watch a martyr die
    and remain unchanged
    is a sin.
  To help another live as you might do
    requires the sword to pierce your our own soul through.
  Amen.

The Little Place

Matthew 2:1–6

Now after Jesus was born in Bethlehem of Judea in the days of Herod the king, behold, magi from the east arrived in Jerusalem, saying, "Where is He who has been born King of the Jews? For we saw His star in the east, and have come to worship Him." And when Herod the king heard it, he was troubled, and all Jerusalem with him. And gathering together all the chief priests and scribes of the people, he began to inquire of them where the Christ was to be born. And they said to him, "In Bethlehem of Judea, for so it has been written by the prophet, 'AND YOU, BETHLEHEM, LAND OF JUDAH, ARE BY NO MEANS LEAST AMONG THE LEADERS OF JUDAH; FOR OUT OF YOU SHALL COME FORTH A RULER, WHO WILL SHEPHERD MY PEOPLE ISRAEL.'"

The comedy of God is the never-ending laughter of divine surprise. God rarely speaks to the earth from her capitals of world power. It was not from crowded Thebes but from a lonely, fiery desert bush that he spoke to Moses. David only made Jerusalem his final home after he learned of God in the desolate rocks of Engedi. The timeless prophecies of Jeremiah came from the tiny town of Anathoth and those of Amos from Tekoa. Elijah lived in the wilderness and John the Baptist in the Jordan River jungles.

So Bethlehem amazed every metropolis of every age. David came from there. His poems still astound us, and many of them were written in and around this small, unknown town. His star marks Judaism still as the symbol of all that blesses giant cities and yet is born in tiny towns. Bethlehem was also my birthplace. There it was that God touched down in a few pounds of human flesh to cry out to the architectural empires of urban Rome, "Take note, for God is among you."

Why does my Father choose such unknown tiny places to declare himself? It is because he plots a rural way to make his presence known. In the quiet places, there is ample space to hear his voice and to declare his presence. To hear the laughter of God is to know the joy of simple people who wait upon him beyond the press of business. Here where farmers touch the warm earth and patriarchs need God, he will declare himself and lay his all-encompassing and global demands on every soul.

Yet for all my small-town roots, I came to claim the cities. For the cities are the dwelling places of the masses. Bethlehem is where I was born, but I died in the city; and when my spirit came at Pentecost, the urban era of the church was born. You live in the most urbane day the world has ever known. What are you to do in the city where you live? First of all, live in the city until the city begins to live in your heart. Then weep over it as I once wept over Jerusalem. Finally, go into it with my redeeming message. I am every city's only hope of joy.

Prayer
Lord Jesus,
You do the grandest things
in the smallest places.
My life is small;
do something big in me.
If Bethlehem could hold the infant God,
I must give my own neighborhood a nod.
Amen.

Insincere Worship

Matthew 2:8

And he sent them to Bethlehem, and said, "Go and make careful search for the Child; and when you have found Him, report to me, that I too may come and worship Him."

Nothing bars the way to worship more than insincere motives. Herod wanted to know my whereabouts, not to adore me, but to destroy me. Most who seek to worship me mean me no harm. Still, never more than at Christmas does the insincerity of public adoration manifest itself. In this season there are many who celebrate their own affluence and trifle with my dignity. They often celebrate my birth with abusive drunkenness. In honor of the Son of God, who had nowhere to lay his head, they give each other diamond necklaces and matching sports cars.

But it is not this greed that most abuses God's pure love. It is Herod's sin that most offends. Herod wanted to find the infant king and kill him to assure his own sons after him the right to hold his place. This is worship's awful sin, that in my presence people can become themselves what they refuse to worship in another—a king. Herod's sin still frequents churches where members seek to be a king rather than to have one.

Thus in the houses of Almighty God are those who come at Christmas—and sometimes only then—to be seen. They occupy the chief seats, promote their own importance, rule with their exalted godhood. Do not, therefore, ring down on Herod any criticism of false claims that he would worship me to do me harm. Others do me harm by using God's house to pick up business contracts or advance their social position—by making friends with those important members who guarantee them sales or community esteem. God's house is for worship, and worship is for God alone. God is a Spirit, and those who worship him must worship him in Spirit and in truth (John 4:24).

At this holy time of year, ask yourself—while on the way to church—exactly why you are going. Is there a longing that compels you to enter into adoration like the ancient kings? Are you coming, like the magi, to lose yourself in honest adoration? I want to meet you at the altar of my birth, and there I want to feel your honest love as I give you my own. I want to hear you sing "Oh Come All Ye Faithful," and not look at your watch while you do it. I need your love. You need my grace. Come. Worship me.

Prayer
Lord Jesus,
Forgive me for those
insincere times when I come
into your presence to worship you
with secret reasons of my own.
Forgive me, God, for entering in prayer
and leaving, not knowing you were there.
Amen.

The Gifts

Matthew 2:10–11

And when they saw the star, they rejoiced exceedingly with great joy. And they came into the house and saw the Child with Mary His mother; and they fell down and worshiped Him; and opening their treasures they presented to Him gifts of gold and frankincense and myrrh.

There were three gifts, perhaps three wise men. Their wisdom matters more than their number. They were wise enough to see the footprints of the infant Messiah in the stars. They were astrologers, wise men in pagan religions.

Why did they come at all? Perhaps their astrology caused them to see what the Roman poet Virgil had seen some decades before it ever came to pass. Virgil had foreseen the conjunction of Jupiter and Saturn in the constellation Pisces. These two stars, in conjunction, appeared a single star of great brightness. Such stars often signaled the birth of some new king. The colossal brightness of this conjoining produced an indomitable splendor in the heavens. It only happens every seven centuries or so. How did they read this astrological event? Jupiter was the king of all the Roman gods. Saturn was the god of time, notably the last days of time. Pisces was the constellation of Palestine. All of this information to these primitive astrologers could only mean that the *King of the Last Days had been born in Palestine*. It need not be assumed that this Jupiter-Saturn conjunct was the Star of Bethlehem. But the conjunct may well have furnished the wise men the astrological information they needed to find their way to Bethlehem.

So they came. Notice what they laid before the Son of God. Gold, enough to symbolize to Mary that God would provide ample income to take care of her and Joseph and their new little boy. They gave frankincense to symbolize the sweet odor that life assumes when God is put in charge.

But what of myrrh? Why was this strong narcotic made a gift? Myrrh was the gift of stern remembrance, often a burial spice. But more than that, it was a narcotic given to the dying to numb their pain. I was not quite two years old when myrrh was given to me as a gift. Thirty-one years later they mingled myrrh in the crucifixion wine (Mark 15:23) and put it on a sponge to lift it to my lips. This chilling omen reminded Mary of Simeon's prophecy, of what I would have to undergo to save humankind. The myrrh was there at either end of my thirty-three-year life. At the first, myrrh was a gift. At the last, it was a symbol of the price I paid. Celebrate the myrrh. Let its powers awaken you to the full joy of my incarnation.

Prayer
Lord Jesus,
If the wise men gave
*   those gifts that inspire us to*
*   give gifts ourselves,*
*   help us to remember that their*
*   finest gift to you was worship.*
In looking at the frankincense and myrrh,
*   we fail to see what their gifts really were.*
Amen.

Terror in the Joy

Matthew 2:13–18

Now when they had departed, behold, an angel of the Lord appeared to Joseph in a dream, saying, "Arise and take the Child and His mother, and flee to Egypt, and remain there until I tell you; for Herod is going to search for the Child to destroy Him." And he arose and took the Child and His mother by night, and departed for Egypt; and was there until the death of Herod, that what was spoken by the Lord through the prophet might be fulfilled, saying, "OUT OF EGYPT DID I CALL MY SON."

Then when Herod saw that he had been tricked by the magi, he became very enraged, and sent and slew all the male children who were in Bethlehem and in all its environs, from two years old and under, according to the time which he had ascertained from the magi. Then that which was spoken through Jeremiah the prophet was fulfilled, saying, "A VOICE WAS HEARD IN RAMAH, WEEPING AND GREAT MOURNING, RACHEL WEEPING FOR HER CHILDREN; AND SHE REFUSED TO BE COMFORTED, BECAUSE THEY WERE NO MORE."

Fear fell upon Joseph and Mary when Herod's henchmen came like bloody fiends to run their blades through every crib in Bethlehem. It was not a large town, but even so, scores of infants died. From the very infancy of my life, trouble erupted. The plan of God woke all the forces of hell, and it was first in Bethlehem that lives were massacred as mothers wept. Earth once again had proved herself a madhouse of hate and senseless death. How aptly had the prophet seen those stark, gaunt women of Bethlehem, "mourning and great weeping, Rachel weeping for her children and refusing to be comforted, because her children are no more" (Jer. 31:15).

But while the mothers sent their hopeless wails to heaven, Joseph and Mary took me and traveled down to Egypt.

When life seems senseless, where do you personally go? Where is your Egypt? Have you sought a flight into that solitude where you knew your fears and grief would find joy? Egypt is where Herod's murderous fiends cannot threaten. It isn't just Egypt either. It's the flight down empty roads in desert moonlight where you know God is waiting even in the shadows of your flight. When circumstances drive you beyond every hope of normalcy, there is some sweet, healing Egypt. In Egypt there is hope of peace. In Egypt my Father is calling you himself.

In Egypt, there is shelter from your enemies. In Egypt, God beckons you to his protective care. Does God care? Yes. "God is our refuge and strength, an ever-present help in trouble. Therefore we will not fear, though the earth give way and the mountains fall into the heart of the sea" (Ps. 46:1–2). Leave Bethlehem, where life foams mad. Let Egypt be your meeting place with God. There he will meet your needs. There He will shelter you in your day of calamity.

Prayer
Lord Jesus,
The Christmas season so often lulls us
into artificial peace.
Beyond those places
where the Christ child reigns,
death lives and suffering and pain.
Amen.

Home Again

Matthew 2:19–23

But when Herod was dead, behold, an angel of the Lord appeared in a dream to Joseph in Egypt, saying, "Arise and take the Child and His mother, and go into the land of Israel; for those who sought the Child's life are dead." And he arose and took the Child and His mother, and came into the land of Israel. But when he heard that Archelaus was reigning over Judea in place of his father Herod, he was afraid to go there. And being warned by God in a dream, he departed for the regions of Galilee, and came and resided in a city called Nazareth, that what was spoken through the prophets might be fulfilled, "He shall be called a Nazarene."

Home is the sweet word. Herod died, and I, the child Christ, could make my way to Nazareth again. There my mother and father, some years before, had met and become engaged. There my father had once been a carpenter, and there I would learn my father's trade.

Bethlehem is a noble town in Christian hymns and carols. But see the simple splendor of Nazareth. For three decades, it became the hometown of the incarnate Son of God. Nothing very glorious is to be said of hometowns. There you grow from birthday to birthday and learn those mundane rules of etiquette and politics. There you learn the letters of the alphabet and study with teachers who seem very much like yourselves.

In Nazareth I grew up, a noncitizen of an empire that hated our kind. I learned early the ugly pain of anti-Semitism and how Jews beneath the prejudice of Rome were never seen as real human beings. But from Mary and Joseph I early learned the role of love in a world filled with prejudice and hate. I knew, as God's Son, that hate is not permitted in a world that God has come to save. There would be many who would hate me, but I would have no enemies. For I loved all whom God loves, and God loves everyone.

Peace was the heart of Nazareth. Egypt had been a place of safety from Herod, but Egypt could never be home. We were not Egyptians. We were Jews. We needed a community where there would be people with our faith and values. We needed a place where I could grow up and learn the Torah. We needed Nazareth.

So there I grew up. There in Nazareth God provided me with the basic Jewish education I would need to prepare for my stormy ministry among Jews. And there I knew three decades of peace. For me, Nazareth was the bridge between heaven and earth. Nazareth was the path of the Incarnation.

Prayer
Lord Jesus,
Your first two years of life
moved you from
Bethlehem to Egypt and
back to Nazareth.
A wandering child loved
by your Father
teaches us to see
that Egypt yields to Nazareth in shame,
and you were born to free us from our pain.
Amen.

The Nazarene

Matthew 2:23

. . . and came and resided in a city called Nazareth, that what was spoken through the prophets might be fulfilled, "He shall be called a Nazarene."

I was called the Nazarene. I was the Son of God with a local address. As I might be located in the twentieth century, I was God with a zip code.

Only once in the unfolding ages of humanity could God be located by longitude and latitude. Nazareth was that place where my character and spirituality passed under human scrutiny. I could never cease being aware that I was God's Son, and in those future years when I stood and proclaimed my Messiahship, all those who had seen me grow up would remember my maturing years and never be able to remember one single discrepancy between my claims and my former behavior.

Consistency may be the greatest gift of Nazareth. In daily confronting propriety, you learn what's *proper*. *Proper* should never be a god, but *proper* is an instructor. *Proper* locates society and tells you where their values are. *Proper* gives you the norms, so even if the norms have to be discarded or violated, you know what you must do to confront the improper *proper*. But *proper* has hardly ever done anyone any good. *Proper* is critical. *Proper* is judgmental. *Proper* is aloof and unfeeling. So Nazareth, while filled with propriety, needed to become open and authentic. *Proper* is usually in the way of all things open and authentic.

But Nazareth was a place of community. It was a safe little town a long way from any big towns. So Nazareth was my hometown, away from the Decapolis and so far off the road that the Romans paid little attention to it. It was a place of both community scrutiny and peace. Where is your Nazareth? Wherever that city is, there your character was formed under scrutiny.

I am the Nazarene—thirty years I lived as a Nazarene. It means nothing except that my sinlessness became established among those who knew me. Some were content to believe me sinless, but most were anxious to catch me at some inconsistency that would set them free of the obligation of trusting in me.

Nazareth is the proving ground of all reputation. I never sinned.

Prayer
> *Lord Jesus,*
> *All those from Nazareth*
> *   called you a Nazarene.*
> *By such a word we locate*
> *   you in time.*
> *But Heaven was your real address.*
> *Help me to prize your Nazareth, then come*
> *   and offer thanks to you for where I'm from.*
> *Amen.*

Growing Grace

Luke 2:40, 52

And the Child continued to grow and become strong, increasing in wisdom; and the grace of God was upon Him. . . . And Jesus kept increasing in wisdom and stature, and in favor with God and men.

To mature is to grow in four ways: in wisdom, in stature, in favor with God, and in favor with people.

To grow wise is to understand the heart of God.

To grow in stature is to become big physically. Let your physical size suggest your spiritual size.

To grow in favor with God and not with man is to become other-worldly and be so heavenly-minded you might be of some earthly good.

To grow in favor with people and not with God is to become so secular in your walk with Christ that you will not seek God for direction in life. Growth in all four of these areas is balanced growth. Maturity is the plan of God for all who want to serve Him.

Let my life serve you as if to say, "Grow; get constantly bigger in each of these four areas." This is the evidence that great grace will be in every area of your maturity. Then your life will bear witness to me; for as you mature, you will win large respect. Growth in character testifies to the presence of God in the life.

Some parents have a child who for some physical reason never matures. Such parents love such children, but long for them those maturing qualities their child can never have. The child becomes their anguish. Years later the child still knows nothing, for he has not grown in wisdom. The child has not matured physically, he still crawls and cannot stand on his own. He has not grown in stature. This baby—always a baby— brings both pleasure and pain to the parents. His loving parents are not broken because this dependent child has not blessed them. They love their child desperately. But for all their care and love, there has been no growth.

God will love you whether or not you grow in spiritual understanding. But please be a positive witness to the grace of God. Get bigger! Grow and delight your loving Father with your maturity.

Prayer
Lord Jesus,
The Bible verse saying that you grew graciously
  reminds us how God would have
  each of us mature.
With those qualities that settle down on youth,
  we should learn to hate all lies and cherish truth.
Amen.

Lost and Found

Luke 2:41–44

And His parents used to go to Jerusalem every year at the Feast of the Passover. And when He became twelve, they went up there according to the custom of the Feast; and as they were returning, after spending the full number of days, the boy Jesus stayed behind in Jerusalem. And His parents were unaware of it, but supposed Him to be in the caravan, and went a day's journey; and they began looking for Him among their relatives and acquaintances.

It was a busy holiday, and they simply couldn't remember when they'd seen me last. I knew where I was, and I knew the way back home to Nazareth. It is the custom of older people to think of their missing children as lost. So my parents sought for me, believing me to be lost. I only thought of myself as not being where they were. But we were seriously separated.

When they first discovered I wasn't with them, they played that anguished game, "I'm sorry, dear; I thought he was with you." Then they became anxious. They began to look for me. They hurriedly walked back to Jerusalem, trying to remember exactly where they'd lost me. Then they remembered. It was in the temple that they had last seen me.

Lost! It became a word I would ultimately use a lot. Lost is what results when something of great value cannot be located. Lost things are not findable, not usable. They are worthless when they cannot be found because they cannot serve.

God, my Father, is unchanging and evermoving. But he is also everlonging in his desire to maintain his faith relationship with you. So if you don't feel close to God anymore, guess who moved?

Are you lost to the purposes of God?

If one day in your busy life you discover that you and I aren't together, I recommend you return to the place where you last remember seeing me. What were you doing? What "significant" event came between us? Did you leave me in the guilt of some desperate sin? Did you lose me between the sultry chapters of some common disobedience? Did you gossip me out of your prayer life? Did you refuse to help in the ministry of your church? Did you neglect to tell some hurting friend that I am the Great Physician?

Where did you lose me? Seek me as you once did—with all your heart. You will find that I am still about my Father's business.

Prayer
Lord Jesus,
When you sat among the Doctors of Theology,
did they really understand
you or your Father?
Were they able to start simple enough?
Was their sight too blurry
through the thick lenses?
Were they too impressed with
their academic self-importance?
How marvelous that youth can sometimes see
what's hidden in obscure theology.
Amen.

The Scholar's Gifts

Luke 2:45–47

And when they did not find Him, they returned to Jerusalem, looking for Him. And it came about that after three days they found Him in the temple, sitting in the midst of the teachers, both listening to them, and asking them questions. And all who heard Him were amazed at His understanding and His answers.

When Mary and Joseph found me, I was sitting in the midst of the doctors. I love the affection scholars have for the Word of God. Who can be released from the mesmerizing power of the Scriptures? Even at twelve years of age I was struck by the look of old eyes in leathery faces staring down at Hebrew letters, copied by hands which even then were lost in distant Jewish centuries. But the words they copied were not silent. The words were alive and spoke in power. That's how the Word of God is.

God has always used scholars. Do you thank God for them? Do they seem too ivy-towered? Too remote? Remember, it is these thinkers who do my Father the great service of translating ancient texts of languages no longer spoken and putting those powerful words in alphabets others understand. None should ever despise or look down on scholars. They give us the Word, faithfully translating the ink and alphabet of one century to make the ink and alphabet of the next century accessible.

Christians should celebrate those men and women who, across the ages, have studied the ancient books of God. They should always honor those whose straight and black-inked columns tell of all the wondrous acts of God. Yes, I asked them questions that day. I wanted to feel the movement of God as he shone through their old, wrinkled, and thin blue skin. How long had they known him? What could their love of ancient books tell us of the world God wanted to save? What did a thousand years of prophets and poets have to teach the world of God?

Even then the hunger of my heart was to please my Father. So long he had spoken through the holy books of old. But now his time of talking from goose quills and berry ink was all but gone. Now my Father would speak through my life. The Word that once was merely ink was now made flesh. Once the ancient prophets had spoken the Word of the Lord through Jeremiah or Isaiah. Now the Word of the Lord was alive and in the world. I was the only begotten Son of God, the Word made flesh.

Prayer
  Lord Jesus,
  Every time I pick up your Word
   I am reminded again
   that I am indebted to a great
   many scholars,
   who across the ages have
   labored over books and spent their lives
   in parchment and ink.
  Their generations and those that follow them
   have given millions access to God's printed Word.
  Thank you for those scholars who are bent
   on giving us your Word with one intent.
  Amen.

The Settled Calling

Luke 2:48–50

And when they saw Him, they were astonished; and His mother said to Him, "Son, why have You treated us this way? Behold, Your father and I have been anxiously looking for You." And He said to them, "Why is it that you were looking for Me? Did you not know that I had to be in My Father's house?" And they did not understand the statement which He had made to them.

It was the first time I ever declared it to them—it would not be the last. I had to be about my Father's business. My life constantly declared this single fact: I had no business of my own. All that I desired was to do my Father's business. It wonderfully clears the mind when we are dead to self and ambition.

My Father's business: I knew this would be my business. Indeed, I knew the world would have no other significant business. My Father is your Father. If his business was my business, it is your business. I know the conflict you feel in trying to make his business your business. Your earthly business is so all-requiring, isn't it? It sews you up in tiny little stitches of minute agendas. But then if you want to be a bigger person, get a bigger business. Stop giving so much attention to your frantic little business, and get busy doing my Father's business.

Do you really understand what Paul meant when he said, "Count yourselves dead to sin" (Rom. 6:11), or why he confessed, "I have been crucified with Christ and I no longer live, but Christ lives in me" (Gal. 2:20)? Paul meant that he had died to any agenda of his own. He wanted to do nothing more and nothing less than what God wanted him to do.

I cried with the writer of Hebrews, "Here I am, I have come to do your will" (Heb. 10:9). I was not one of those children who one week wanted to be a farmer and the next an architect. I woke every morning praying, "What, O righteous Father, will you have me do today?" I went to sleep each night seeking obedience. I lived in joy.

Consider the stretch you often feel in trying to decide if you would rather do God's will or pursue your own ambitions. You can use a lot of energy running between your own desires and his requirement for your life.

Find yourself some high Gethsemane. Ask God for the cup. Resolve to drink it all. And you will find that you drank of hope.

Prayer
Lord Jesus,
You knew everything.
You knew what God had called you
to be
and all that calling would require.
Let me also dare to persevere
until I understand why I am here.
Amen.

Defining for Others
God's Purpose with Our Lives

Luke 2:51

And He went down with them, and came to Nazareth; and He continued in subjection to them; and His mother treasured all these things in her heart.

I continued in subjection to my earthly parents all through my remaining maturing years in Nazareth. I honored my father and mother. The fifth commandment promised that all who did this would live long upon the earth (Exod. 20:12). For most, this principle is true. My life would be cut short, and my mother would be there at the moment of my dying. But even when that day required her grieving heart to break, there would be no shadow in my life against the fifth commandment. I would die cherishing every value that she and my earthly father had taught me.

My mother treasured all the things we had lived through—the pleasures and crises of our lives. She pondered them in her heart. Mothers are like that. They keep a running list of blessings. Most of them were on file in my heart too. Perhaps that's what it means to be a faithful son or daughter. A heart analysis of a good mother and a good child would have roughly the same contents. I loved my mother.

Some theologians have tried to suggest that what I said to her in the temple was impudence ("Why were you searching for me? . . . Didn't you know I had to be in my Father's house?" [Luke 2:49].) It was not impudence. I but reminded her of what the angel had told her before I was born. My whole life belonged neither to her nor to all whom I would later die to save. In point of fact, it did not even belong to me. It belonged to my Father in heaven.

Those men and angels who came to my mother in life often called her *blessed*. I loved her, and I also *blessed* her full obedience to God. So whatever she asked of me, I did. I submitted myself to her instruction. I learned the art of carpentry so I could care for her when my father no longer could. And my whole life was true to the fifth commandment.

If I, the Son of God, obeyed my parents, this must be everyone's commandment.

So, live long. Prosper. Exalt your parents. And when you have honored them with all your heart, you will have become like a child once raised in Nazareth to rule the universe.

Prayer
Lord Jesus,
Once we draw from our
    lack of surety
    our reason for being
    and then announce it to the world,
    we find a confidence we never
    could achieve
    when we were less certain.
Help me to emulate my parent's worth,
    that I may long endure upon the earth.
Amen.

EXPERIENCING GOD
every day of your life

EXPERIENCING GOD DAY-BY-DAY DEVOTIONAL
HENRY T. BLACKABY & RICHARD BLACKABY

Building on the remarkable success of previous *Experiencing God* books, this devotional includes a page for every day of the year, each with a Bible verse and meditation. The readings are rich and profound, filled with insights from Richard and Henry Blackaby's writing and ministry. An exceptional gift or family keepsake.   0-8054-1776-1

EXPERIENCING GOD
HENRY T. BLACKABY & CLAUDE KING

God reveals Himself to each of us in special and exceptional ways, so our perception of Him is unique. This remarkable book will help any believer renew and revitalize his love for the Lord by seeing His love for us. *Experiencing God* is designed to help each of us recognize our own personal relationship with God as He reveals His divine plan and guiding hand.   0-8054-0197-0

EXPERIENCING GOD DAY-BY-DAY DEVOTIONAL/
JOURNAL   HENRY T. BLACKABY & RICHARD BLACKABY

Written in the convenient one-page-per-day format and building on the acclaimed *Experiencing God* concepts, this exciting devotional/journal encourages regular journaling for tracking spiritual growth and teaches the reader how to draw closer to God.
0-8054-6298-8

available at fine bookstores everywhere